Pricing Decisions in the Euro Area

Pricing Decisions in the Euro Area

How Firms Set Prices and Why

Edited by
Silvia Fabiani
Claire Loupias
Fernando Martins
Roberto Sabbatini

UNIVERSITY PRESS
2007

Oxford University Press, Inc., publishes works that further
Oxford University's objective of excellence
in research, scholarship, and education.

Oxford New York
Auckland Cape Town Dar es Salaam Hong Kong Karachi
Kuala Lumpur Madrid Melbourne Mexico City Nairobi
New Delhi Shanghai Taipei Toronto

With offices in
Argentina Austria Brazil Chile Czech Republic France Greece
Guatemala Hungary Italy Japan Poland Portugal Singapore
South Korea Switzerland Thailand Turkey Ukraine Vietnam

Published by Oxford University Press, Inc.
198 Madison Avenue, New York, New York 10016

www.oup.com

Oxford is a registered trademark of Oxford University Press

Library of Congress Cataloging-in-Publication Data
Pricing decisions in the euro area : how firms set prices
and why / edited by Silvia Fabiani . . . [et al.].
p. cm.
Includes bibliographical references and index.
ISBN 978-0-19-530928-7
1. Pricing—European Union countries.
I. Fabiani, Silvia.
HF5416.5.P735 2007
338.6'041094—dc22

2006026534

9 8 7 6 5 4 3 2 1

Printed in the United States of America
on acid-free paper

To Alberto, Clotilde, Raquel, Olimpia

Foreword

This book presents the results of a major research program undertaken by the Eurosystem central banks on price setting decisions by firms in the euro area. The studies in the volume have one thing in common: they are based on answers to surveys, launched by the Eurosystem central banks, asking firms to explain how they set the price of their output (their pricing strategies) and why (the rationale of these strategies). The result is a rich picture of how pricing decisions are made in the euro area, drawn by the firms themselves. The book offers to economists, policy makers, and market analysts an unprecedented wealth of information, collected and analyzed using modern research methods and internationally comparable, on how the price system of the euro area functions.

Why are we interested in pricing decisions? First and foremost because they guide consumer choices and the allocation of productive resources, and hence ultimately determine the efficiency and the performance of the economy as a whole. Central bankers are interested in pricing decisions also because of their implications for the movements of aggregate inflation—the main variable they try to control—and because they affect the way monetary policy influences the economy—the so called transmission mechanism. Theory says that if prices move smoothly, in a rational forward-looking fashion, central banks are better able to keep inflation under control without generating undesired variability of output and employment. For this reason, the price formation mechanism is a constant object of research in central banks. After the launch of the euro, in 1999, the need to provide the newly created European Central Bank with updated analysis in this area became more urgent, and the list of questions longer. How do pricing decisions occur in the different countries that form the euro area? Do they generate rigidity, or persistence, in the inflation process? Are there significant differences across countries that may complicate the exercise of monetary policy and make its effects geographically uneven? If so, what policies should be adopted to improve the performance of the price system? Can the euro itself, with the greater transparency and competition it injects in the European economy, change such performance for the better? And many others.

The Eurosystem central banks decided to approach these questions by launching a research program along three lines. First, data on individual producer and consumer prices were analyzed, to enlighten the microeconomic mechanisms and factors behind pricing decisions. Second, inflation data were also studied, to understand the macroeconomic forces driving the dynamics of aggregate price indices. Third, surveys were conducted along similar lines in all countries, asking firms directly about their price setting strategies. Combining different sources of information is helpful: first, more reliable results can be obtained by cross-checking evidence from independent sources; second, asking agents directly about their behavior helps identify causal links that may remain hidden behind the statistical evidence. This book provides a complete account only of the third line of research, but extensive bibliographies and summary sections help the reader connect with the rest of the work and understand the general message of the whole research.

To conduct this work, researchers from all central banks of the euro area joined in a group, the Inflation Persistence Network (IPN). I had the privilege and the pleasure to serve as chairman and organizer of the IPN for three years, from its start in 2002 to my departure from the European Central Bank in 2005. It was a fascinating and rewarding experience in many ways: for the important results it provided; for the novel and successful format of the group, in which researchers from many countries and institutions shared knowledge and data, with enthusiasm and a sense of common purpose; for the opportunity we had to attract the interest of, and establish a dialogue with, the world academic community working in this field. I am grateful to the European Central Bank for providing an ideal environment for this work, and to all colleagues of the IPN, including the academic consultants whose names appear in the book, for sharing with me this experience and for teaching me many things along the way.

Ignazio Angeloni
Ministry of Economy and Finance, Italy
July 2006

Acknowledgments

This book is the result of a collective research effort conducted within the Eurosystem Inflation Persistence Network (IPN). We would like to thank all the authors of the chapters collected in this volume and the other IPN members, in particular Ignazio Angeloni (who acted as chairman of the network), Filippo Altissimo, Michael Ehrmann, and Jordi Galì (who was one of the academic consultants of the network). The launching of such a large scale project across the euro area would have not been possible without the support of the European Central Bank and of the national central banks of Austria, Belgium, Germany, France, Italy, Luxembourg, The Netherlands, Portugal, and Spain. We also benefited greatly from the comments received by the participants in various conferences and seminars where the material reported in the book was presented, in particular the National Bureau of Economic Research Summer School (Boston, July 2004), the conference organized by the European Central Bank (Frankfurt, December 2004), the meeting of the American Economic Association (Philadelphia, January 2005), the meeting of the European Economic Association (Amsterdam, August 2005). We would like to thank John Pelham from Access English for his excellent linguistic assistance.

The book presents the personal opinions of the editors and of the authors of the various chapters, and does not necessarily reflect the views of the Institutions they belong to.

Abbreviations

BCL	Banque centrale du Luxembourg
BCS	Business Cycle Survey
CB	Central de Balanços
CPI	Consumer Price Index
ECB	European Central Bank
EMU	European Monetary Union
GDP	Gross Domestic Product
GVA	Gross Value Added
IFO	Institute for Economic Research at the University of Munich
IPN	Inflation Persistence Network
NACE	Nomenclature of Economic Activities in the European Communities
NBB	National Bank of Belgium
NCB	National Central Bank
NSI	National Institute of Statistics
OeNB	Oesterreichische Nationalbank
PPI	Producer Price Index
QP	Quadros de Pessoal
WIFO	Austrian Institute of Economic Research

Country abbreviations:

AT	Austria
BE	Belgium
FR	France
GE	Germany
IT	Italy
LU	Luxembourg
NL	The Netherlands
PT	Portugal
SP	Spain

Contents

Contributors

Luis J. Álvarez is senior economist at Directorate General Economics, Statistics and Research of the Banco de España. He received his M.A. in Economics at Universidad Complutense de Madrid. His publications have appeared inter alia in the *Journal of the European Economic Association*, *Journal of Economic Perspectives*, *Econometric Theory*, *Journal of Policy Modelling*, and *Revista Española de Economía*.

Ignazio Angeloni is Director General for International Financial Affairs at the Economy and Finance Ministry of Italy. Previously he was Deputy Director General for Research at the ECB and Chairman of the Eurosystem Inflation Persistence Network. A graduate of Bocconi University and of the University of Pennsylvania (Ph.D. in Economics, 1985), he has published extensively in the fields of European integration, monetary policy, international economics, banking, and financial markets.

Luc Aucremanne is advisor at the Research Department of the National Bank of Belgium. His research interests include inflation measurement for monetary policy purposes, price rigidities, and inflation persistence.

Josef Baumgartner is economist at the Austrian Institute of Economic Research (WIFO) in Vienna, Austria. He was assistant professor at the Department of Economics at the Technical University Vienna and lecturer at the Department of Economics at University of Linz, Austria. His major research interests are macroeconomics, applied econometrics, business cycle and inflation analysis, and forecasting.

Stephen G. Cecchetti is the Rosenberg Professor of Global Finance at the International Business School, Brandies University, and a Research Associate of the National Bureau of Economic Research. From August 1997 to September 1999, he was Director of Research at the Federal Reserve Bank of New York. He has written extensively on a variety of topics, including banking, securities markets, and monetary policy. He is also a regular contributor to the *Financial Times*.

Emmanuel Dhyne is economist at the Research Department of the National Bank of Belgium, where he conducts research on firms' price setting behavior. He also teaches applied econometrics at the Université de Mons-Hainaut.

Martine Druant is assistant advisor at the Research Department of the National Bank of Belgium. Her main research interests are in pricing behavior of firms and labor costs.

Silvia Fabiani is senior economist at the Research Department of the Bank of Italy. She received a Ph.D. in Economics at the University of Cambridge (United Kingdom). She has written numerous papers on price dynamics and price setting in Italy and in the euro area.

Vítor Gaspar is Special Adviser at Banco de Portugal. He served as Director–General Research at the European Central Bank between 1998 and 2004. He has also been Director of Research at the Banco de Portugal and Director of Economic Studies at the Portuguese Ministry of Finance. He is the author of numerous research papers and books on central banking, monetary policy, general equilibrium modelling, and public finance.

Angela Gattulli is economist at the Research Department of the Bank of Italy. She has conducted research on price setting behavior and on inflation persistence.

Ignacio Hernando is senior economist at Directorate General Economics, Research and Statistics of the Banco de España. He received his B.A. in Economics at Universidad Complutense de Madrid, an M.A. in Monetary Economics at CEMFI, and a Ph.D. at UNED. His publications include articles in *European Financial Management*, *European Journal of Political Economy*, *Oxford Review of Economic Policy*, *Economics Letters*, *Investigaciones Económicas*, and *Moneda y Crédito*.

Marco Hoeberichts is researcher at the Economics and Research Division at de Nederlandsche Bank and at the University of Amsterdam. He has worked on monetary policy games and transparency and communication of central banks.

Claudia Kwapil holds two M.A. degrees in economics, one from the University of Vienna and the other from the London School of Economics and Political Science. Since 1999 she has been working as economist at the Economic Analysis Division of the Oesterreichische Nationalbank, where her main field of activity is related to monetary policy. In particular, her research interests are monetary policy rules, the monetary policy transmission mechanism, and inflation in general.

Hervé Le Bihan is senior economist at Banque de France. He has conducted research on macroeconomic modelling and forecasting (in particular on the estimation of the "New Phillips Curve") and microdata-based research on consumer price setting.

Andrew Levin is Chief of the Monetary Studies section at the Federal Reserve Board in Washington, DC, and is a International Research Fellow of the Centre for Economic Policy Research. During 2003–2005, he served as an external consultant to the European Central Bank and was actively involved in the Eurosystem Inflation Persistence Network. In recent years he has also been an adjunct professor of economics at Columbia University, Georgetown University, and Johns Hopkins University, and has published research papers in the *American Economic Review*, the *Journal of Monetary Economics*, and the *NBER Macroeconomics Annual*.

Claire Loupias graduated from Panthéon-Sorbonne University (Ph.D. in Economics, 1994, Paris). She was senior economist at Banque de France while writing this book. She is now Assistant Professor at EPEE, Université d'Evry (France).

Patrick Lünnemann is economist at the Monetary, Economic and Statistics Department of the Banque centrale du Luxembourg. He previously worked as an economist at the Securities Department of the Banque Générale du Luxembourg. His fields of interest include monetary economics and financial markets.

Fernando Martins is senior economist at the Research Department of the Banco de Portugal and Professor of Statistics and Data Analysis at the Universidade Lusíada of Lisbon. The implementation of monetary policy under uncertainty and the assessment of price stickiness on the basis of survey data have been his most recent topics of research.

Thomas Mathä holds an M.A. and a Ph.D. in Economics from the University of East Anglia (United Kingdom). After several consultancy appointments with the European Investment Bank, he joined the Monetary, Economic and Statistics Department of the Banque centrale du Luxembourg. His fields of interest include international and monetary economics.

Roland Ricart is head of euro area outlook division at the Banque de France. His activity covers short-term forecasts and economic analyses. He worked several years as head of business survey division at the Banque de France, where he was in charge of producing surveys.

Fabio Rumler is economist at the Economic Analysis Division of the Oesterreichische Nationalbank. He specializes in the fields of inflation and monetary policy. Additionally, he gives presentations at scientific seminars and conferences and holds a position as a lecturer at the Vienna University of Economics and Business Administration.

Roberto Sabbatini is senior economist at the Research Department of the Bank of Italy. His major research fields include inflation dynamics, core inflation, time series analysis, and short-term forecasting. He has published numerous articles on inflation developments and price setting in Italy as well as in the euro area.

Johann Scharler is economist at the Oesterreichische Nationalbank. In addition, he teaches macroeconomics and applied econometrics at the University of Vienna. He holds a Ph.D. from Simon Fraser University and his research interests include macroeconomics, monetary economics, and business cycle theory.

Frank Smets is Deputy Director General of the Directorate General Research of the European Central Bank. He is a research affiliate of the Centre for Economic Policy Research in London and a coeditor of the *International Journal of Central Banking*. He has written and published extensively on monetary, macroeconomic, financial, and international issues mostly related to central banking. Before joining the European Central Bank in 1998, he was a research economist at the Bank for International Settlements in Basel, Switzerland. He holds a Ph.D. in economics from Yale University.

Harald Stahl is economist at the Deutsche Bundesbank in the economics department. Before he joined the Bundesbank he worked at the Center for European Economic Research, Mannheim, in the department of industrial economics and international management (1992–1998).

Ad Stokman is researcher at the Economics and Research Division at de Nederlandsche Bank. He was involved in macroeconomic modeling and was a member of the Eurosystem's Working Group on Forecasting. Topics he has been working on in recent years are the role of FDI in international spillovers, price convergence in Europe, and nonlinear leading indicator models of growth.

Philip Vermeulen is senior economist at the European Central Bank. He has written numerous papers on the investment behavior of firms. He has investigated the effect of uncertainty, financing constraints and while member of the Monetary transmission network, he worked on the transmission of monetary policy through investment.

Giovanni Veronese is economist at the Research Department of the Bank of Italy. He has published articles on indicators of the business cycle and on core inflation. His major research fields include time series analysis, inflation forecasting, and business cycle.

Jouko Vilmunen is head of research at the monetary policy and research department of the Bank of Finland. He is also lecturer on modern theories of monetary policy at the Department of Economics, Helsinki University. His main research interests are optimal monetary policy, inflation dynamics, and intertemporal consumption behavior.

Pricing Decisions
in the Euro Area

Introduction

Silvia Fabiani, Claire Loupias, Fernando Martins,
& Roberto Sabbatini

MOTIVATION

Since the publication of Keynes's *General Theory* (1936), a recurrent theme in macroeconomics has been whether the adjustment of prices and wages is sufficiently rapid to allow an efficient allocation of resources. In recent decades, a substantial amount of theoretical research devoted to improving the microeconomic foundations of macroeconomic behavior has shown that the nature of nominal rigidities plays a key role in determining the effects of different shocks on the economy. This research has made clear that a thorough understanding of the extent and causes of the sluggish adjustment of nominal prices is crucial to the design and conduct of monetary policy. In this respect, empirical work aimed at an improved characterization of the price setting behavior of firms is of major interest for monetary policy making.

The objective of this book is to deepen our understanding of the behavioral mechanisms driving agents' pricing decisions, adopting a methodological approach—asking firms directly about how they set prices—that is particularly well suited for the purpose at hand.

This introduction provides first a concise description of the Eurosystem research project—the Inflation Persistence Network (IPN)—in which the empirical analysis reported in this book was carried out. It then discusses the advantages of firms' surveys as a method for understanding the rationale underlying price setting strategies, in particular as concerns the extent and the nature of price rigidities. Finally, after briefly describing the structure of the book, it summarizes the main empirical findings obtained in the context of the IPN on the basis of micro data, both qualitative and quantitative. Clearly, the IPN produced many other results (see Altissimo et al. 2006) some of which will be mentioned in the final chapter when exploring the related policy implications.

DESCRIPTION OF THE IPN

The survey results described in this book reflect a research effort conducted within the IPN, a team of Eurosystem economists who, for three years from the beginning of 2003 to the end of 2005, undertook a joint research on inflation persistence in the euro area and in its member countries. The main goal of the IPN was to understand the dynamic properties of inflation, notably the speed and pattern of inflation adjustment in response to shocks of different nature, and the role of the price setting process of firms and retailers in generating inflation persistence. This research combined theoretical and empirical analyses using three different data sources: individual consumer and producer prices; surveys of firms; and aggregate sectoral, national, and area-wide price indices.

The work was organized in various research groups. On the theoretical side, the research groups dealt both with methodological issues, such as the definition of the key questions to address regarding inflation persistence and the implications of aggregation (across goods, firms, sectors, countries) for inflation persistence, and with the implications of different degrees of persistence in the euro area for the common monetary policy. On the empirical side, a remarkable contribution to the assessment of price setting behavior at the micro level came from the investigation of firms pricing strategies through surveys. A considerable amount of research was also devoted to the analysis of individual micro data on consumer and producer prices, with the aim of assessing whether such data could support or reject certain types of price setting behavior. These firm-level databases provided a unique opportunity to establish and document a number of important facts about price setting in the euro area. They were also unprecedented by international standards, as their coverage goes well beyond the data available for other economies, including the United States. Other studies within the IPN investigated the statistical properties of inflation dynamics, based on both univariate and multivariate models at the sectoral and aggregate level, and estimated New Keynesian Phillip Curve (NKPC) models for the euro area countries and the area as a whole.

THE RATIONALE FOR FIRM SURVEYS

The use of surveys to explore the price setting behavior of firms was pioneered by the seminal work of Blinder (1991) and Blinder et al. (1998) for the United States, although a very early example of this kind of study can be found in R. Hall and Hitch (1939). Blinder's work has led to the conduct of similar surveys in other countries: Köhler (1996) in Germany, S. Hall et al. (1997; 2000) in the United Kingdom, Apel et al. (2005) in Sweden, Amirault et al. (2004) in Canada, and Nakagawa et al. (2000) in Japan.

Economists are often reluctant to use the interview method for two main reasons. First, respondents can be easily influenced by the precise wording of the questions, and second, they may have no incentive to respond truthfully or thoughtfully. However, the survey approach has the advantage of allowing interviewers to ask decision makers directly how they set and adjust their prices, and why they do not react more quickly in response to shocks, thus providing an important complement to more traditional tools.

Moreover, surveys allow researchers to investigate aspects of pricing behavior that cannot be assessed by analyzing quantitative data. It is, in fact, very difficult to test theories of price rigidities with econometric methods; indeed, these theories all predict that prices adjust less rapidly than some unmeasured benchmark and often rely on variables that cannot be measured themselves. Finally, by giving the price setters themselves the opportunity to explain and describe their own behavior, surveys can reveal whether rigidities arise at the first step of the adjustment process, in which firms evaluate whether their price needs to be changed, or at the second step, in which the price is actually changed.

The results reported in this volume are based on surveys carried out in nine countries—Austria, Belgium, France, Germany, Italy, Luxembourg, the Netherlands, Portugal, and Spain—covering 94% of the euro area GDP. Overall, more than 11,000 euro area firms were interviewed. The national surveys were designed by the central banks and submitted to firms on the basis of a decentralized approach. A high degree of harmonization of the national questionnaires was guaranteed by the coordination within the IPN. As shown in this book, many of the results arising from these surveys hold across countries, despite the differences in terms of sample coverage, actual strategies of submitting the questionnaires, precise wording of the questions, their order and the options available, and business cycle conditions. This robustness lessens substantially the potential significance of the drawbacks traditionally attached to the use of surveys.

PRICE RIGIDITY

Price rigidity—or price level stickiness—is defined as a low responsiveness of prices to fundamentals (Altissimo et al. 2006). It can arise, for instance, in the presence of impediments to an immediate adjustment of prices, such as costs of changing them, or of contracts stipulating the price of a product to be delivered. A low frequency of price changes does not mean necessarily that prices are rigid. Indeed, if there is no change in costs or demand, there is no reason to adjust prices. Nevertheless, price rigidity is often used as a shortcut for low frequency of price changes.

The surveys presented in this book address both nominal and real (or relative) price rigidities. The former occur if prices are not fully flexible and changes in nominal (but not real) demand have real effects (for instance, due to the existence of implicit and explicit contracts, menu costs, informational problems, unsynchronized price setting, or interaction between price and wage setting). An important distinction in this respect is between anticipated nominal changes, which affect only nominal prices but leave quantities unchanged, and unanticipated ones, which do not affect prices but have a real effect by impacting on output. Real rigidity arises, instead, when relative prices fail to adjust fully to a given change in real factors (for instance, due to inventory holdings, customer markets, kinked demand curves, or collusion among firms).

The presence of nominal rigidities is regarded as the cornerstone of New Keynesian models, cast in terms of imperfect competition, which are widely used for macroeconomic analysis. However, although imperfect competition is known to lead to inefficiency in production, it does not in itself cause nominal rigidity, and its implications for price adjustment are not straightforward (see Andersen 1994 for a description of these mechanisms). The adjustment of nominal prices to nominal changes for a single firm depends not only on the nominal scale variable but also on the pricing decisions of other firms. For instance, in the case of monopolistic competition, the higher the prices charged by other firms (the level of aggregate general prices), the higher the price set by each individual firm. There is, thus, a positive relationship between prices. This strategic complementarity turns out to be important for most explanations of sluggish price adjustment, but it does not lend support to the often made assertion that the larger the market power of firms (that is, the lower the elasticity of demand), the more rigid prices are. It is, once again, crucial to ask price setters directly how important is the price of their competitors for their own pricing strategies.

THE STRUCTURE OF THE BOOK

The book is structured as follows. Part I provides the theoretical background and some insights on the use of survey data to investigate price setting behavior (chapter 1), and a summary of the main results of the surveys carried out in nine euro area countries (Austria, Belgium, France, Germany, Italy, Luxembourg, the Netherlands, Portugal, and Spain) between 2003 and 2004 (chapter 2). Part II reports in detail the findings of the national surveys (chapters 3–11). Part III is devoted to comparative analysis. In chapter 12, the findings for the euro area are compared to those obtained by similar surveys conducted in other countries—Canada, Japan, Sweden, the United Kingdom, and the United States. Chapter 13 provides an empirical overview of the incidence of the degree of market competition on the price adjustment process. A comparison of the survey results with those obtained within the IPN on the basis of micro quantitative data on consumer and producer prices is reported in chapter 14. Part IV concludes by drawing the policy implications of the empirical evidence discussed in the book (chapter 15).

WHAT HAVE WE LEARNED FROM FIRM LEVEL DATA?

The scope of this section is to summarize the main results on price setting in the euro area based on the micro level empirical analyses conducted within the IPN. These results rely on the quantitative data collected by statistical institutes for the computation of producer and consumer price indices (presented in more detail in chapter 14) and on the qualitative information from the surveys of firms extensively described in this book (and summarized in chapter 2). The two sources complement each other, in the sense that the former documents facts about price changes, whereas the latter helps find explanations for those facts.

We can synthesize the main findings on price setting practices at the micro level in eight stylized facts.

Fact 1

Firms in the euro area change their prices infrequently, in particular when compared to the United States. This finding holds across all member countries for which evidence is available and is supported both by the quantitative evidence from consumer and producer prices and from survey data. In particular, whereas in the euro area the frequency of consumer price changes—the share of prices that are changed every month—is 0.15, in the United States the equivalent figure is 0.25 (Bils and Klenow, 2004). These frequencies imply an average duration of prices close to one year in the euro area and slightly above half a year in the United States.

Fact 2

The frequency of price changes varies systematically by sector. As regards consumer prices, the frequency is relatively high for energy products and unprocessed food and low in services and, to a lesser extent, in the nonenergy industrial sector. Similar evidence is found for producer prices, with energy and food products showing a higher frequency of price change than the other components. Survey results confirm that firms in the services sector adjust their prices less frequently than those in manufacturing.

Fact 3

Price changes are sizeable. The average size of consumer price changes is 8.2% in the case of price increases and 10% in the case of reductions. This evidence is consistent with what has been found for the United States, where the size of price decreases is also slightly higher than that of increases. Among the various components, energy prices are in general changed very often but by a limited amount.

Fact 4

There is limited evidence of downward price rigidity, except in the services sector. On average, reductions account for 40% of consumer price changes and 45% of producer price changes, in line with the figures obtained by Bils and Klenow (2004) for the United States. Looking at the sectoral breakdown for consumer prices, food and energy products are characterized by almost perfect symmetry between price increases and decreases. There is, however, significant asymmetry in services, where only two out of ten price changes are reductions.

Fact 5

Price reviews are more frequent than price changes. The surveys show that in most euro area countries the modal number of reviews lies in the range from one to three times a year, but most firms actually change their prices only once a year. In the services sector price reviews and changes are less frequent than in the other sectors.

Fact 6

Firms' price setting is characterized by elements of both time and state dependence. The surveys point to the adoption of mixed strategies by the majority of firms. According to the studies based on consumer prices, the latter respond rapidly to special events such as changes in indirect taxation or the euro cash changeover (see Aucremanne and Dhyne 2005; and Fougère et al. 2005).

Fact 7

Markup pricing over costs is the dominant approach to price setting. This rule is adopted by 54% of the firms interviewed in the surveys, while around one-third of them set their price on the basis of their competitors' strategies. This evidence supports the view that firms operate in an imperfectly competitive environment. Moreover, there is a systematic relationship between the frequency of price change and the degree of market competition (see chapter 13), as firms facing more intense competition review and change their prices more often and are less likely to adopt a markup pricing strategy.

Fact 8

According to the surveys, implicit and explicit contracts, cost-based pricing, and coordination failure are the most important reasons underlying price stickiness. In contrast, menu costs and costs in obtaining and processing information, which are the most explored in theoretical and empirical work based on macro data, are ranked very low. This evidence is relatively uniform across sectors, with the exception of retail trade, where, as one might expect, factors such as pricing thresholds rank higher than in other sectors.

REFERENCES

Altissimo, Filippo, Michael Ehrmann, and Frank Smets. 2006. Inflation persistence and price-setting behaviour in the euro area. A summary of the IPN evidence. European Central Bank Occasional Paper Series No. 46. Frankfurt am Main: European Central Bank.

Amirault, David, Carolyn Kwan, and Gordon Wilkinson. 2004. A survey of the price setting behaviour of Canadian firms. *Bank of Canada Review* Winter 2004–2005: 29–40.

Andersen, Torben M. 1994. *Price Rigidity: Causes and Macroeconomic Implications*. Oxford: Clarendon Press.

Apel, Mikael, Richard Friberg, and Kerstin Hallsten. 2005. Microfoundations of macroeconomic price adjustment: Survey evidence from Swedish firms. *Journal of Money Credit and Banking* 37: 313–338.

Aucremanne, Luc, and Emmanuel Dhyne. 2005. Time-dependent vs. state-dependent pricing: A panel data approach to the determinants of Belgian CPI. European

Central Bank Working Paper No. 462. Frankfurt am Main: European Central Bank.

Bils, Mark, and Peter J. Klenow. 2004. Some evidence on the importance of sticky prices. *Journal of Political Economy* 112: 947–985.

Blinder, Alan S. 1991. Why are prices sticky? Preliminary results from an interview study. *American Economic Review* 81: 89–100.

Blinder, Alan S., Elie R. D. Canetti, David E. Lebow, and Jeremy B. Rudd. 1998. *Asking about Prices: A New Approach to Understanding Price Stickiness*. New York: Russell Sage Foundation.

Fougère, Denis, Hervé Le Bihan, and Patrick Sevestre. 2005. Heterogeneity in consumer price stickiness: A microeconomic investigation. European Central Bank Working Paper No. 536. Frankfurt am Main: European Central Bank.

Hall, Robert L., and Charles J. Hitch. 1939. Price theory and business behaviour. *Oxford Economic Papers* 2: 12–45.

Hall, Simon, Mark Walsh, and Antony Yates. 1997. How do UK companies set prices? Bank of England Working Paper No. 67. London: Bank of England.

Hall, Simon, Mark Walsh, and Antony Yates. 2000. Are UK companies' prices sticky? *Oxford Economic Papers* 52: 425–46.

Keynes, John Maynard. 1936. *The General Theory of Employment, Interest, and Money*. London: Macmillan.

Köhler, Annette. 1996. Nominale Preisrigidität auf Gütermärkten: eine empirische Überprüfung neukeynesianischer Erklärungsansätze. CIRET-Studien No. 51. Munich: Centre for International Research on Economic Tendency Surveys.

Nakagawa, Shinobu, Hattori Ryota, and Izumi Tagagawa. 2000. Price setting behaviour of Japanese companies. Bank of Japan Research Paper. Tokyo: Bank of Japan.

Part I

Firms' Pricing Behavior in the Euro Area: An Overview

1

The Use of Survey Data to Investigate Price Setting

Theory and the Research Design for the Euro Area

Stephen G. Cecchetti, Fernando Martins,
Roberto Sabbatini, & Harald Stahl

This chapter first reviews the main theoretical aspects of firms' price setting behavior analyzed in the nine national surveys reported in the rest of the book, and whose main common results for the euro area are summarized in chapter 2. It focuses on the determinants of prices, on the characteristics of the price adjustment process, in particular the reasons underlying nominal stickiness, and on asymmetries in price changes.

The second section of the chapter deals with the pros and cons of the use of surveys to investigate price setting and with the main characteristics of the research design for the euro area; in this context, the section also reviews the structure of the national questionnaires and how they were conducted at the national level.

THE THEORETICAL BACKGROUND

The surveys provide information on numerous aspects of price setting practices. These are logically divided into four categories: determinants of prices, factors that lead nominal prices to be sticky, the differences between price changes and price reviews, and whether firms treat price increases and decreases symmetrically. We begin with a straightforward description of how prices are set. Given that prices are going to be changed, what factors are most important in the firms' calculations of the new nominal price? Do firms simply apply a fixed markup over costs? Or do they focus primarily on the price charged by competitors?

We then move to the discussion of theoretical explanations for why firms allow their prices to deviate from their optimal level. When asked, what reasons do firms give for nominal price rigidity in the face of changes in their operating environment? Is it that there is a fixed cost associated with price changes? Is it a consequence of explicit or implicit contracts with the firm's customers? Or is it that firms set prices as a markup over costs and the latter themselves change infrequently?

Although price changes can be studied, at least in principle, by examining the price data alone, there are times when firms review their prices but do not change them. A distinct advantage of surveys is that we have the ability to ask firms about both their price changes and price reviews. Since a change requires a review, we provide an extensive discussion of strategies associated with the timing of price reviews. In particular, we examine whether the timing of reviews is time dependent, occurring every so many days, weeks, or months regardless of changes in the market conditions, or whether the timing is state dependent, occurring when shifts of the environment within which the firm operates have been sufficiently large.

Since Keynes, macroeconomists have speculated that nominal prices are more likely to go up than down. The surveys allow us to examine whether price increases and decreases are precipitated by different sorts of events. For example, is it more likely that a cost increase will lead to a price increase than that a cost decrease will lead to a price cut? What about demand shifts? Do they lead to asymmetric responses?

In the remainder of this section, we survey the various theories that form the basis for the questions related to three of these aspects of firm pricing behavior: potential reasons for price stickiness, the timing associated with price reviews, and the asymmetries of adjustment in reaction to shocks.

Factors Leading to Price Stickiness

The list of factors that could cause nominal prices to be rigid is a long one. It includes fixed costs of price adjustment, costly information, cost-based pricing combined with sticky marginal cost, explicit contracts, implicit contracts, attractive price thresholds, the possibility that shocks are temporary, adjustment of other factors rather than prices, coordination failure, and the possibility that customers judge quality by price.

The list alone makes clear the difficulties researchers face in distinguishing among these various explanations. As Blinder (1991) points out, if all one has is the actual path of firms' prices, it is impossible to discern the relative importance of the factors that may be causing price stickiness. Surveys face no such obstacle. It is with this in mind that the national surveys all ask firm managers questions whose purpose is to elicit information that allows us to distinguish among these various theories.

It is useful to summarize the theories of price stickiness considered in the surveys.

Fixed Costs of Price Adjustment   Menu costs form the basis for the classic explanation for price stickiness. As discussed by Sheshinski and Weiss (1977), the physical act of changing prices—printing and distributing new price lists, or menus—is costly. Wishing to minimize these costs, firms will change prices infrequently, thus allowing actual prices to deviate from the optimal ones by small amounts. Profit maximization means balancing these fixed costs of adjustment with the lost profits that arise from the failure to adjust nominal prices, changing them only when the cost is less than the profit loss.

Costly Information   Ball and Mankiw (1994) suggest that "the most important costs of price adjustment are the time and attention required of managers to gather the relevant information and to make and implement decisions" (p. 142). That is, there is more to the costs of price adjustment than the costs of reprinting new menus. After all, someone has to spend time and energy collecting information to compute the proper price. Again, the novelty of the survey technique allows us to ask about the relative importance of information costs in pricing decisions.

Cost-Based Pricing   It is surely possible that firms do not change their prices because their costs do not change. That is, if firms set prices as a markup over costs, and costs are constant, prices will be, too. One reason for this is that there may be adjustment lags at various stages of the production process. As Blanchard (1987) shows, even small lags in adjustment of a single firm can lead to long lags in the reaction of the cost of goods at the final stage. Although a commodity input price shock could have an impact on the cost to supplier at the beginning of a production supply chain, it could take some time to reach the end seller of the product, thereby making marginal cost, and hence prices, to be very sticky.

Explicit Contracts   Firms could have contractual arrangements with their customers that guarantee the prices of specific products for fixed periods. There are a number of reasons that firms might find it advantageous to write explicit contracts. First, setting the price might require negotiation between the supplier and the customer. A contract minimizes the costs of this time-consuming activity. Second, the explicit contract could be for both a quantity and a fixed price, making orders more predictable, improving planning, and helping to lower production costs. Finally, explicit contracts are a way to build long-term relationships with customers who value the predictability of future prices they will have to pay, thus allowing them to reduce the shopping costs they would otherwise have to bear.

Implicit Contracts   Closely linked to the theory of explicit contracts is the theory of implicit contracts. The idea is that firms aim to win customer loyalty by using pricing policies that are perceived to be "fair." First proposed by Okun (1981), the theory notes that shoppers are always faced with a distribution of available prices. They could derive an optimal stopping rule and use it to search every time they go out to shop. But this is costly, and customers do not really want to do it. Instead, they prefer to stick with a given supplier unless disappointed by its pricing policy, thereby avoiding the costs of a search. Stable prices encourage customer loyalty.

More recently Rotemberg (2002, 2005) expanded on this idea by focusing on what he calls "consumer anger." Customers are disappointed by firms whose pricing policies they perceive to be unfair. As a result, when deciding whether or not to change their prices, firms must take into account the possibility of angering their customers. The result is price rigidity, with price changes occurring only infrequently.

Attractive Price Thresholds   Firms tend to charge prices that they find "attractive." Among the various types of attractive price thresholds, the theoretical literature has focused on "psychological prices," putting forward several explanations as to why they are so pervasive. First, the increase in sales might be greater when the price is lowered from €1.00 to €0.99 than when it is lowered from €0.99 to €0.98 (see Gabor and Granger 1961, 1966). Buyers may unconsciously undervalue the last digit, so that €0.99 seems like €0.90. This could be because they have a limited ability to recall information, so they ignore the last digit, which is the least significant in terms of amount spent (Holdershaw et al. 1997). Second, it has been argued that buyers perceive round numbers (€1.00, €2.00, etc.) as "fair prices"; a price just below that level (€0.99, €1.99, etc.) thus presumably leads consumers to feel that they are getting a bargain (Shindler 1991; Thaler 1985).

Attractive pricing strategies can cause price stickiness, because firms may postpone adjustments in the face of small shocks calling for small price changes until events justify a large price change to the next pricing threshold.

The Possibility that Shocks Are Temporary   If firms believe that a shock to demand or costs is temporary, they may decide to forego a price adjustment, not wishing to change prices again soon after. Two points are worth making about this reason for price rigidity. First, it relies on the existence of adjustment costs, without which the firm would not care about changing prices frequently. Second, it is the firm's perception that matters, not whether the shock is truly temporary.

The Possibility of Changing Non-price Factors   Firms can use more than just price to influence the cost of a product to a customer. As Carlton (1986) noted more than two decades ago, firms can keep prices fixed but vary delivery times. In general, a firm could adjust the level of service that comes with a product without adjusting its price. Related to this, Blinder (1982) points out that firms can modify their level of inventories used to buffer unexpected demand shifts, and again not change their price.

Coordination Failure   Competition creates strategic interactions that can lead to price rigidity. First introduced by Clower (1965) and Leijonhufvud (1968) in their analysis of the labor market, this theory was applied by Rotemberg and Saloner (1987) to repeated price setting. The basic idea is that firms assume that their price increases will not be met by increases of competitors' prices, so by increasing prices they will drive away customers. By contrast, competitors will match price decreases, thus leading to a loss of revenue. So although a firm might want to raise prices following a shock, it will only do it if it can be sure its competitors will follow. Without a coordinating mechanism that allows firms to move together, prices may remain unchanged.

Judging Quality by Price   The role played by non-price factors in inducing price stickiness is also at the core of the theory of asymmetric information between firms and customers. Under weak market conditions firms might be reluctant to decrease the price of their product because customers might wrongly interpret this as a reduction in the product quality. It is worth mentioning that this is only a potential explanation of downward nominal price rigidity, and it does not justify price stickiness when the conditions for increasing prices occur. Blinder et al. (1998) tests for this possibility by asking whether firms feel encouraged in raising prices because they think that at least some of their customers will regard it as indicative of a product quality improvement.

Price Reviews

Before changing prices, firms need to review whether an adjustment is appropriate. The long list of reasons for which prices might be sticky applies to reviews as well as to actual changes. As mentioned above, surveys are uniquely suited to determining the importance of price reviews; we are particularly interested in their timing. As we explain below, different timing patterns have different implications for macroeconomic fluctuations. Specifically, we care about whether reviews are time or state dependent.

Time-dependent reviews occur at times that are independent of the deviation of the firm's current (fixed) price from the profit maximizing optimal one that it would charge in the absence of the various costs listed above. Over the years, two models of time dependence have emerged, one deterministic and the other stochastic. In the first model (Taylor 1980), firms change prices at a preset calendar frequency. For example, a firm may decide to review its prices every six months and stick to that frequency regardless of what happens. As contracts are not synchronized, a fixed proportion of firms change their price in each period. It is for this reason that Taylor dubbed this practice "staggered contract." In the alternative approach, introduced by Calvo (1983), a fixed fraction of firms change their price each period, and whether a particular firm is in that group is completely random. An important aspect is that whether a firm is in the group changing prices in one period is completely independent of what happened before (technically, it is modeled as a draw from a Poisson distribution, which has no memory). The crucial difference is that in the Taylor model firms know with certainty the future dates on which they will change their prices, whereas in the Calvo model they do not.

Time-dependent models generate persistent real effects of nominal shocks—the Holy Grail of monetary economics. To see how, consider what happens after a shock hits the economy. Immediately after, no one has adjusted its price, so all firms' prices deviate from their optimal level. Now, some proportion of firms is given the opportunity to change their price, either because it is their scheduled date or because they are randomly chosen. They need to decide what price to set, knowing both that not all firms are adjusting and that they will not have an opportunity to adjust again for a while. Since firms care about relative prices, and the prices of competitors are not being changed, prices that are changed incorporate the "mistakes" of the firms that could not change. And when those other firms do get their turn, they will set prices relative to the ones that incorporated the earlier mistakes. This creates persistence.

State-dependent price reviewing rules are the other alternative. Firms following these rules review prices whenever there is a shock that induces a large enough discrepancy between the optimal and the actual price they are currently charging. In the works by Sheshinski and Weiss (1977), Caballero and Engel (1993), and Dotsey et al. (1999), fixed costs of price change are the basis for the discontinuous adjustment under state-dependent rules. State-dependent models assume that, in each period, firms decide to change their nominal prices only if the related gains outweigh the adjustment costs. Because firms want to be aware of shocks in order to react as quickly as possible, price reviews are potentially more frequent than price changes; this contrasts with time-dependent models, in which firms review and change their prices only on a periodic basis (although they do not need to change prices following every review). In general, whereas nominal shocks have real effects in models in which prices are state dependent, there is less persistence than in the case of time dependence.

Related to the timing of price reviews is the information used by firms to establish their prices. The models of price setting behavior have somewhat different implications for the relative importance of past price changes on current decisions. In the staggered-contract model of Taylor (1980), price setters look both backward and forward. The stochastic time-dependent model of Calvo (1983) has firms looking only to the future. Most monetary economists find the pure forward-looking formulation more appealing. Unfortunately, the empirical implementation of the New Keynesian macroeconomic models based on these various theories of price adjustment requires that price setters be partially forward looking and partially backward looking. Surveys allow us to ask whether they look ahead or back.

Asymmetries of Price Reactions

Some of the ten explanations for price stickiness described earlier in this section imply asymmetries in adjustment. For example, demand curves could be kinked. That is, customers' responses to price increases could be to reduce demand much more than they would increase it in response to an equally sized price decrease. The reason for this goes back to implicit contracts and fairness. Price increases are more likely to be viewed as unfair, sending previously loyal customers out shopping. A price cut is much less likely to elicit this response. This same logic can also explain asymmetric responses to changes in cost and demand. As Okun (1981) suggests, "price increases based on cost increases are generally accepted as fair, but many that might be based on demand increases are ruled out as unfair" (p. 170).

Ball and Mankiw (1994) argue that trend inflation is another reason for which we can expect to see asymmetry. The intuition is straightforward. In the presence of positive inflation, a firm knows that in the absence of any shocks its next price change will be upward. This makes it more likely that it will respond to a shock by raising prices than by cutting them.[1]

THE METHOD OF ANALYSIS

This section discusses how surveys can be used to explore price setting practices. This approach was pioneered by the seminal works for the United States by Blinder (1991) and Blinder et al. (1998). Below we discuss how this approach has been implemented by nine national central banks of the euro area in a manner that allows direct comparison.

Investigating Price Setting through Surveys

There exists a tradition of interviewing firms to assess their business confidence and the state of the business cycle. For instance, the European Commission coordinates harmonized monthly surveys, mainly of a qualitative nature, among firms and consumers of the European Union that provide important complementary information to official (quantitative) statistics.[2] Several central banks also conduct regular surveys that provide important inputs in their decision process.

The empirical literature confirms that regular surveys are indeed useful to anticipate, using econometric techniques, the evolution of quantitative indicators, such as industrial production, GDP, producer prices, and production costs (European Central Bank 2004). In some cases, surveys provide a unique piece of information on economic variables that are not collected by official statistics, such as the rate of capacity utilization. Responses provided by firms and consumers are also used to identify economic factors underlying short-term developments, thus complementing regular, quantitative statistics. This is particularly useful in the presence of exceptional events (for instance, after the terrorist attack of September 11) in order to assess the likely consequences of shocks for economic developments.

One of the main advantages of regular (monthly) surveys is that time-series techniques can be exploited for both filtering irregularities in the answers and assessing their informative content. Moreover, questions are generally quite simple and respondents get used to them over time, and that enhances the quality of the answers. Such advantages are much more limited in the case of occasional surveys aimed at investigating specific aspects of firms' behavior, such as price setting practices. The main drawback is that businessmen, when interviewed about their behavior, might not always be truthful. Although in principle this caveat also applies to regular (monthly) surveys, in the latter case the risk of getting false signals from surveys is likely to be much lower for two main reasons: first, the time-series dimension allows assessment of the informative content of qualitative data through the comparison over time with actual quantitative statistics; second, managers have to express their view on general aspects related to economic developments rather than answer detailed questions regarding a strategic variable such as their own prices.

Concerning specifically the investigation of price setting strategies, there might be further reasons underlying the possibility of collecting poor information through one-time surveys. First, the person who fills in the questionnaires might not always be aware of all aspects and steps involved in the process, since many senior managers could be engaged in pricing decisions, particularly in large firms, in a context in which such decisions are far more complex than the survey assumes.

Second, respondents might misunderstand the questions, particularly if the interview is conducted over the phone or the Internet. This problem relates to the objective difficulty of presenting economists' ideas in layman's language. In addition, the categorization of thought processes into boxes for providing answers might be misleading due to an imprecise knowledge of the behavioral process or through an attempt to oversimplify the answers. Face-to-face interviews could partly prevent these difficulties, but at the price of substantially higher costs of carrying out the survey.

Third, a firm's refusal to participate in the survey might depend on the firm's specific characteristics, thereby inducing a selection bias in the analysis of the results. For instance, the response rate might differ according to the size of the firm or to the economic sector to which it belongs.

Fourth, respondents might be tempted to provide answers that the interviewer would like to hear, not necessarily because they are genuine "liars" (a possibility that cannot be excluded when asking about things such as tax evasion, collusion, labor safety regulations, etc.) but, for instance, because they try to take the viewpoint of the researcher rather than that of the price setter.

In spite of these drawbacks, there is no doubt that crucial aspects of firms' pricing polices can only be investigated on the basis of the qualitative information obtained from direct interviews. For instance, it would be hard to discriminate among the various theories of price rigidity based on their prediction, since they all predict that prices are rigid. Recent empirical analysis based on quantitative consumer and producer micro prices[3] provides accurate descriptions, in particular, of the periodicity and magnitude of price changes in a number of economies. Nonetheless, it does not allow understanding of other key aspects of price setting, such as the relative importance of nominal versus real rigidities, the type of information used in the revision of prices, and whether responses to shocks differ depending on the nature (costs/demand) or the sign (positive/negative) of the disturbances. The bottom line is that surveys represent an important complementary source of knowledge to that provided by quantitative data. They shed light on crucial aspects of the price setting process and can be used for cross-checking the evidence obtained from quantitative information.

The work of Hall and Hitch (1939) represents a very early example of the use of surveys to explore firms' pricing behavior. Despite the rather limited number of firms interviewed (just fewer than forty British companies, mostly belonging to the manufacturing sector) and some other drawbacks in the way the analysis was carried out (for instance, the firms interviewed were not randomly chosen but selected on the basis of the authors' personal knowledge), the ideas developed in that work affected for quite a long time the debate on price setting practices. Further studies in this field, surveyed by Blinder et al. (1998), are Kaplan et al. (1958), Haynes (1962), and Lanzillotti

(1964) for the United States, Fog (1960) for Denmark, Nowotny and Walther (1978) for Austria, and Gordon (1981) for both Canada and the United States. During the 1980s other attempts at asking firms about aspects of their pricing practices were accomplished by Jobber and Hooley (1987) for the United Kingdom, and Smiley (1988). However, the first systematic and method-ologically solid work in this field was carried out by Blinder and coauthors at the beginning of the 1990s for the United States (Blinder 1991; Blinder et al. 1998). This work inspired similar research for other countries: Köhler (1996) for Germany, Hall et al. (1997, 2000) for the United Kingdom, Apel et al. (2005) for Sweden, Amirault et al. (2004) for Canada, and Nakagawa et al. (2000) for Japan (see chapter 12).

Research Design and the Advantages of a Coordinated Strategy

In the context of the Inflation Persistence Network (IPN), between 2003 and 2004, surveys of firms' pricing behavior were conducted in nine countries (Austria, Belgium, France, Germany, Italy, Luxembourg, the Netherlands, Portugal, and Spain), representing 94% of euro area GDP. They were desi-gned by each national central bank and submitted to firms on the basis of a decentralized approach. However, a high degree of harmonization of the national questionnaires was guaranteed by coordination within the IPN in order to allow a meaningful comparison of results across countries. The main differences in the actual structure of the national questionnaires are due to two factors. First, surveys were carried out in different periods and this allowed latecomers to benefit from the experience, which was extensively discussed within the research group, of those who had carried out the earlier surveys. Second, the national questionnaires were also aimed at analyzing specific issues particularly relevant for each economy.

Despite these differences, common results emerge across countries, which are described in chapter 2. This consistency of the empirical evidence—regardless of how the surveys were conducted; the number, order, and wording of the questions asked; and the business cycle conditions prevailing at the time of the survey—allows a generalization of the results to the euro area as a whole.

The Structure of the Questionnaires

All questionnaires have a standardized form, that is, the various questions are not tailored to the characteristics of the firm interviewed, such as its size or the economic sector to which it belongs.[4] The main risks of using a structured questionnaire are related to the possibility of a large number of unanswered questions, potentially leading to sectoral bias, and the formu-lation of questions unnecessarily general. However, compared to a strategy of tailoring questions to the characteristics of the respondents, standardized questionnaires present the advantage of yielding sufficiently homogeneous information that can be analyzed by using standard statistical tools (Blinder et al. 1998). The questionnaires have a similar structure, organized in four broad sections (table 1.1).

Table 1.1 Common issues investigated in the national questionnaires

	AT	BE	FR	GE	IT	LU	NL	PT	SP
Part 1—General information on the economic environment									
Percentage of turnover due to the main product	X	X	X	X	X	X	X	X	X
Percentage of turnover in domestic and foreign markets	X	X	X	X	X	X	X	X	X
Market share	X			X	X	X	X	X	X
Number of competitors	X	X	X	X	X	X	X	X	X
Type of customer	X	X	X	X	X	X		X	X
Number of customers	X					X			
Relationships with customers: long-term versus occasional	X		X		X	X		X	X
Shape of the unit variable cost curve	X		X		X				
Factors affecting firms' competitiveness		X				X		X	
Part 2—Price determination									
Price discrimination across customers			X	X	X	X		X	X
Pricing to market				X		X		X	X
Price setting autonomy and price setting rule[a]	X	X	X	X	X	X	X	X	X
Contracts with customers	X			X				X	
Impact of competitors on firms' price					X	X	X		
Demand price elasticity	X	X			X	X		X	
Part 3—Price adjustment									
Time versus state dependence in price reviews	X	X		X	X	X	X	X	X
Frequency of price reviews	X	X	X		X	X	X	X	X
Information set considered in price reviews	X	X		X	X	X		X	X
Use of rule of thumb in price reviews		X				X		X	X
Factors hampering price adjustment	X	X	X	X	X	X	X	X	X
Frequency of price changes	X	X	X		X	X		X	X
Part 4—Asymmetries in price changes									
Factors causing a price increase and decrease	X	X	X	X	X	X	X	X	X
Speed of price reaction to changes in costs/demand	X		X			X		X	X

Source: National questionnaires reported in the Appendix to the book.
[a]In some questionnaires the two issues are addressed separately.

The first section collected information on product and market characteristics. In order to give respondents a precise reference for their answers, all surveys focused on the firm's "main product," defined in terms of the turnover it generates. Companies were also asked to indicate how representative the main product is in terms of their turnover; it turned out that the focus on the main product was not overly restrictive, as the latter accounted for around 60% or more of the turnover of the respondents for the euro area as a whole. Firms were then asked to indicate the main market for their primary product (domestic—eventually specifying whether national or local—or foreign). Concerning the structure of such a market, firms had to indicate both their market share and the number of competitors, two pieces of information used as proxies for the degree of competition. A few questions included in this section investigated the firm's relationships with customers, in particular the nature of the latter (other firms, public administration, final consumers, etc.) and whether the relationship was long term (longer than one year) or occasional. Finally, Belgium, Luxembourg, and Portugal added a set of questions on the main factors determining the competitiveness of the firm (e.g., quality of the product, price, delivery period).

The second section investigated how the price level is set. First, all questionnaires asked firms how they set their prices, that is, according to markup rules, following competitors' prices, and so on. Next, respondents had to provide an answer regarding the implementation of some forms of price discrimination across customers. In five questionnaires companies also had to give a numerical estimate of price elasticity. A few national questionnaires assessed the importance of firms' perceived competition, namely how the price level would differ if the firm did not have any competitor on the market, and the presence of an arrangement with the customers to offer the main product at a specific price for a certain period of time.

The third part of the questionnaires analyzed how prices are changed, focusing on whether time- or state-dependent pricing rules are followed and the frequency of price reviews and changes. Firms were also asked to report what type of information they take into account during price reviews, namely whether the review refers only to the past or whether expectations for the future are also considered. All questionnaires investigated the factors hampering price adjustments by asking firms to rank various theories of price rigidity.

The last section of the questionnaire focused on the possibility of asymmetric reactions of prices to shocks, namely whether adjustment differs in response to cost versus demand shocks, to positive versus negative ones, to large versus small shocks.

Besides these common questions, the individual questionnaires also analyzed particular aspects of the price setting process, in relation to the authors' specific research interests or the need for a more detailed analysis of aspects peculiar to the country considered (table 1.2). For instance, Austria and the Netherlands investigated the impact of the euro cash changeover; Belgium and Spain looked at pricing practices in markets other than that for

Table 1.2 Specific issues investigated in the national questionnaires

	AT	BE	FR	GE	IT	LU	NL	PT	SP
Impact of the euro cash changeover on prices	X						X		
Pricing behavior in markets other than the main one		X							X
Discount prices			X						X
Decreasing price during the product life-cycle				X					
Pro-cyclical unit margins				X					
Degree of competition in foreign markets						X			
Synchronization of cost and price changes						X			
Seasonality of price changes								X	X
Size of price changes			X					X	X
Information on wage setting								X	
Structure of production costs				X					

Source: National questionnaires reported in the Appendix to the book.

the main product; Germany, Luxembourg, Portugal, and Spain investigated the differences in pricing behavior in domestic and foreign markets; France and Spain analyzed to what extent customers can benefit from discount prices. Finally, Austria, France, Luxembourg, Portugal, and Spain raised specific questions aimed at collecting information on the time lapse between a change in cost or demand and a price change.

For each question, a list of possible answers expressed in simple terms was offered. In a few cases the respondents could also attach a score, that is, an assessment of degree of importance, choosing from among four categories: "1 = unimportant," "2 = of minor importance," "3 = important," and "4 = very important." This allowed the computation of mean scores and a comparison of the importance of the various factors from the firms' viewpoint.

How the Surveys Were Conducted

The interviews were conducted either by phone, traditional mail (or fax), or via the Internet, and eventually through a Web site; in France interviews could be done face to face (table 1.3). In most cases the contact in each firm was a senior manager; in a few countries a help desk was available to aid in filling out the questionnaire. To assess the ability of firms to provide meaningful answers to all questions, in most countries the questionnaires were pre-tested on a pilot sample.

Table 1.3 The main characteristics of the national surveys

Country	Time of the survey	Who conducted the survey	How the survey was conducted	Sample	Sample size	Response rate
AT	Jan.–Feb. 2004	WIFO (Austrian Institute of Economic Research)	Traditional mail	Existing sample of the Austrian Business Cycle Survey	≈2500	36%
BE	Feb.2004	Banque Nationale de Belgique	Traditional mail	Existing sample of the monthly business survey of the National Bank of Belgium	≈5600	35%
FR	Dec.2003–Feb. 2004	Banque de France branches	Traditional mail phone, face to face interviews	Existing sample of the monthly business survey of Banque de France	≈4300	38%
GE	June–July 2004	External institute (IFO)	Traditional mail	Existing sample of IFO monthly business survey	≈2740	46%
IT	Feb.–Mar. 2003	External company (Poster s.r.l.)	Internet (also fax)	Sample drawn from the existing sample of the quarterly survey on inflation expectations	729	46%
LU	Aug.–Nov. 2004	Banque centrale du Luxembourg	Traditional mail	Sample drawn from the National Statistical Institute	≈1100	30%
NL	May 2004	External institute (TNS-NIPO)	Internet	Panel of owners, higher/top level management	1870	67%
PT	May–Sept. 2004	Banco de Portugal	Traditional mail (also Internet)	Existing sample from the Banco de Portugal Central Balance-Sheet Database	2494	55%
SP	May–Sept. 2004	External company	Traditional mail (also fax and Internet)	Sample designed by Banco de España, stratified by sector and level of employment	≈3000	69%

Source: Authors' calculations.

There are pros and cons to the various methods of conducting the interviews. Face-to-face interviews (as in the study by Blinder et al. 1998) allow clarification of the questions, possibly minimizing the probability of missing or getting "silly" answers. Moreover, face-to-face interviews make it easier to assess whether the contact person is suitable. Finally, it is likely that the number of questions that can be raised through direct interviews is higher than that using other methods, due to lower time constraints on the side of the manager answering the questionnaire. However, this approach is costly, particularly for large samples, and the collection period can be longer than with other methods, so that firms might face a different economic outlook when they are interviewed.[5] On the contrary, the costs of carrying out the survey are much lower if indirect methods are used (in particular if national questionnaires can be completed over the Internet). In this case the sample can be larger and answers can be collected much faster.

An advantage of a standardized questionnaire without any filter by an interviewer is that answers are provided on a homogenous basis—that is, each participant the same questions—hence allowing a statistical analysis. This is not necessarily the case with face-to-face interviews, since each interviewer participating in the project can explain each question using different words, hence directing the respondents toward different answers.

The impact on the response rate of adopting an indirect method can be twofold. On the one hand, more questionnaires may be filled in, since respondents can complete them at their convenience (even at night if they wish); on the other hand, the absence of any contact with the interviewer may lead to nonresponses and missing answers when the questions are not clear. Nonetheless, the results reported in table 1.3 do not show a clear relationship between the response rate and the way information was collected.

Concerning the structure of the sample, the main differences across the national surveys refer to its size, its sectoral coverage, and the size of the firms included. The sample size is quite different across countries (table 1.3), ranging from around 750 in Italy to 5,600 in Belgium. In terms of response rate, three broad groups can be identified: Austria, Belgium, France, and Luxembourg with a response rate below 40%; Germany, Italy, and Portugal with around 50%; and Spain and the Netherlands with above 60%. All together, more than 11,000 companies in the euro area were surveyed.

The sectoral coverage was limited to manufacturing in Germany and in France; in the other countries, services firms were also considered (table 1.4).[6] Belgium, Italy, and Luxembourg had the largest sectoral coverage, including also firms operating in trade and construction, whereas Spain and the Netherlands included retailers but not firms in the construction sector. All in all, there appears to be a reasonably solid basis for comparing industry and services across countries. In the trade sector, which is covered by five national surveys, the number of firms surveyed is sufficiently high to allow a meaningful comparison. Conversely, the coverage of the construction sector is very poor, both in terms of countries and numbers of firms included in the samples.

Table 1.4 Sectoral coverage (percentages with number of respondents in brackets)

Sector	AT	BE	FR	GE	IT	LU	NL	PT	SP	EURO AREA[a]
Industry	76	38	100	100	65	20	18	84	44	62
	(661)	(753)	(1662)	(1228)	(215)	(67)	(219)	(1157)	(888)	(6850)
Trade	—	24	—	—	14	22	22	—	26	13
		(478)			(46)	(73)	(271)		(515)	(1383)
Other services	24	18	—	—	20	37	60	16	30	21
	(212)	(364)			(68)	(125)	(756)	(213)	(605)	(2343)
Construction	—	20	—	—	1	22	—	—	—	4
		(384)			(4)	(74)				(462)
Total	100	100	100	100	100	100	100	100	100	100
	(873)	(1979)	(1662)	(1228)	(333)	(339)	(1246)	(1370)	(2008)	(11038)

Source: Authors' calculations.
[a]Percentages for the euro area are computed on the basis of the absolute figures reported in brackets, which are the sum of the firms in each category over the nine countries.

Concerning firms' size, table 1.5 shows that for the euro area as a whole almost half of the firms have between 1 and 49 employees; this class of firm is represented in all national samples except Italy, where only firms with more than 50 employees are considered. The remaining firms in the samples are almost equally split, for the euro area as a whole, between two classes, 50 to 199 employees (29%) and more than 199 (24%); only the Netherlands included one-person firms.

In conclusion, the differences across countries, in terms of sample coverage and actual strategies of submitting the questionnaires, enhance the robustness of survey results. The same holds true with respect to the precise wording of the questions, their order, and the options available within a particular question, as well as the business cycle conditions under which the

Table 1.5 Firm size, based on the number of employees (percentages)

	AT	BE	FR	GE	IT	LU	NL[a]	PT	SP	EURO AREA[b]
1–49	53	75	18	29	—	46	81	39	42	47
50–199	28	17	43	35	39	43	19	38	23	29
≥200	19	8	39	36	61	11	—	23	35	24

Source: Authors' calculations.
[a]In the Netherlands, the size classes are defined as follows: 1–49; ≥50.
[b]Percentages for the euro area are computed on the basis of absolute figures, which are the sum of the firms in each category over the nine countries (not reported in the table).

Table 1.6 Macroeconomic indicators (percentages)

Country	Real GDP growth			Inflation (HICP)		
	2002	2003	2004	2002	2003	2004
Austria	1.0	1.4	2.4	1.7	1.3	2.0
Belgium	1.5	0.9	2.6	1.6	1.5	1.9
France	1.0	1.1	2.3	1.9	2.2	2.3
Germany	0.1	−0.2	1.6	1.4	1.0	1.8
Italy	0.3	0.0	1.1	2.6	2.8	2.3
Luxembourg	3.6	2.0	4.3	2.1	2.5	3.2
The Netherlands	0.1	−0.1	1.7	3.9	2.2	1.4
Portugal	0.8	−1.2	1.1	3.7	3.3	2.5
Spain	2.7	3.0	3.1	3.6	3.1	3.1
EURO AREA	0.9	0.7	2.1	2.2	2.1	2.1

Source: Eurostat.

survey was carried out (table 1.6). As chapter 2 shows, despite the above differences, results are pretty similar across countries. This lessens the potential significance of the drawbacks traditionally attached to the use of surveys: the qualitative nature of the information gathered, which sometimes makes it difficult to ascertain the precise importance of a given statement; the lack of a time dimension, which means that the surveys cannot be used to assess whether pricing patterns change over time; and the degree of uncertainty that surrounds the quality of the answers provided by the respondents.

NOTES

1. On asymmetries see also Buckle and Carlson (2000), Davies and Hamilton (2004), and Peltzman (2000).

2. European Commission surveys consist of a set a regular questions in which respondents—consumers and firms in two different surveys, respectively—have to indicate whether economic conditions have improved, remained unchanged, or deteriorated. Only a few questions are quantitative (for instance, that concerning capacity utilization); some are backward looking, others forward looking. For details, see European Central Bank (2004).

3. See Bils and Klenow (2004) for the United States and Dyhne et al. (2005) for the euro area. The quantitative empirical evidence for the euro area is also reported in chapter 14.

4. A partial exception is represented by Austria, where services firms received a questionnaire that differed from that sent to manufacturing firms in the wording of a few questions.

5. For instance, in the analysis by Blinder et al. (1998), information was collected through direct interviews over a period of about two years.

6. The industrial sector covers Sections D and E of the NACE Rev. 1 classification (manufacturing, electricity, gas, and water supply), while trade covers Section G (retail and wholesale trade) and services other than trade includes Sections H, I, and K (hotels and restaurants; transport, storage, and communication; real estate, renting, and business activities).

REFERENCES

Amirault, David, Carolyn Kwan, and Gordon Wilkinson. 2004. A survey of the price setting behaviour of Canadian firms. *Bank of Canada Review* Winter 2004–2005: 29–40.

Apel, Mikael, Richard Friberg, and Kerstin Hallsten. 2005. Microfoundations of macroeconomic price adjustment: Survey evidence from Swedish firms. *Journal of Money Credit and Banking* 37: 313–338.

Ball, Laurence, and Gregory N. Mankiw. 1994. Asymmetric price adjustment and economic fluctuations. *Economic Journal* 104: 247–262.

Bils, Mark, and Peter J. Klenow. 2004. Some evidence on the importance of sticky prices. *Journal of Political Economy* 112: 947–985.

Blanchard, Olivier J. 1987. Aggregate and individual price adjustment. *Brooking Papers on Economic Activity*: 57–122.

Blinder, Alan S. 1982. Inventories and sticky prices: More on the microfoundations of macroeconomics. *American Economic Review* 72: 334–48.

Blinder, Alan S. 1991. Why are prices sticky? Preliminary results from an interview study. *American Economic Review* 81: 89–100.

Blinder, Alan S., Elie R. D. Canetti, David E. Lebow, and Jeremy B. Rudd. 1998. *Asking about Prices: A New Approach to Understanding Price Stickiness*. New York: Russell Sage Foundation.

Buckle, Robert A., and John A. Carlson. 2000. Menu costs, firm size and price rigidity. *Economics Letters* 66: 59–63.

Caballero, Ricardo, and Eduardo M.R.A. Engel. 1993. Microeconomic rigidities and aggregate price dynamics. *European Economic Review* 37: 697–717.

Calvo, Guillermo. 1983. Staggered prices in a utility maximizing framework. *Journal of Monetary Economics* 12: 383–398.

Carlton, Dennis W. 1986. The theory and facts about how markets clear: Is industrial organization valuable for understanding macroeconomics? In *Handbook of Industrial Organization*, ed. Richard Schmalensee and Robert D. Willig. Amsterdam: North Holland.

Christiano, Lawrence, Martin Eichenbaum, and Charles Evans. 2005. Nominal rigidities and the dynamic effects of a shock to monetary policy. *Journal of Political Economy* 113: 1–45.

Clower, Robert. 1965. The Keynesian counterrevolution: A theoretical appraisal. In *The Theory of Interest Rates*, ed. Frank Hahn and Frank Brechling. London: Macmillan.

Davis, Michael C., and James D. Hamilton. 2004. Why are prices sticky? The dynamics of gasoline prices. *Journal of Money, Credit and Banking* 36: 17–37.

Dhyne, Emmanuel, Luis J. Álvarez, Hervé Le Bihan, Giovanni Veronese, Daniel Dias, Johannes Hoffmann, Nicole Jonker, Patrick Lünnemann, Fabio Rumler, and Jouko Vilmunen. 2005. Price setting in the euro area: Some stylised facts from individual consumer price data. European Central Bank Working Paper No. 524. Frankfurt am Main: European Central Bank.

Dotsey, Michael, Robert King, and Alexander L. Wolman. 1999. State-dependent pricing and the general equilibrium dynamics of money and output. *Quarterly Journal of Economics* 114: 655–690.

European Central Bank. 2004. Opinion surveys on activity, prices, and labour market developments in the euro area: Features and uses. *Monthly Bulletin*, January.

Fog, Bjarke. 1960. *Industrial Pricing Policies: An Analysis of Pricing Policies of Danish Manufacturers.* Amsterdam: North Holland.

Gabor, Andre, and Clive W. J. Granger. 1961. On price consciousness of consumers. *Applied Statistics* 10: 170–188.

Gabor, Andre, and Clive W.J. Granger. 1966. Price as an indicator of quality: Report on an inquiry. *Economica* 32: 43–70.

Gordon, Robert. 1981. Output fluctuations and gradual price adjustment. *Journal of Economic Literature* 19: 493–530.

Hall, Robert L., and Charles J. Hitch. 1939. Price theory and business behaviour. *Oxford Economic Papers* 2: 12–45.

Hall, Simon, Mark Walsh, and Antony Yates. 1997. How do UK companies set prices? Bank of England Working Paper No. 67. London: Bank of England.

Hall, Simon, Mark Walsh, and Antony Yates. 2000. Are UK companies' prices sticky? *Oxford Economic Papers* 52: 425–446.

Haynes, Warren W. 1962. *Pricing Decisions in Small Business.* Lexington, KY: University Press of Kentucky.

Holdershaw, John, Paul Gendall, and Robert Garland. 1997. The widespread use of odd pricing in the retail sector. *Marketing Bulletin* 7: 53–58.

Jobber, David, and Graham Hooley. 1987. Pricing behaviour in U.K. manufacturing and service industries. *Managerial and Decision Economics* 8: 167–171.

Kaplan, Adrian D. H., Joel B. Dirlam, and Robert F. Lanzillotti. 1958. *Pricing in Big Business: A Case Approach.* Washington D.C.: The Brookings Institution.

Köhler, A. 1996. Nominale Preisrigidität auf Gütermärkten: eine empirische Überprüfung neukeynesianischer Erklärungsansätze. CIRET-Studien No. 51. Munich: Centre for International Research on Economic Tendency Surveys.

Lanzillotti, Robert F. 1964. *Pricing, Production, and Marketing Policies of Small Manufacturers.* Seattle: University of Washington Press.

Leijonhufvud, Axel. 1968. *On Keynesian Economics and the Economics of Keynes.* New York: Oxford University Press.

Nakagawa, Shinobu, Hattori Ryota, and Izumi Tagagawa. 2000. Price setting behaviour of Japanese companies. Bank of Japan Research Paper. Tokyo: Bank of Japan.

Nowotny, Ewald, and Herbert Walther. 1978. The kinked demand curve: Some empirical observations. *Kyklos* 1: 53–67.

Okun, Arthur. 1981. *Prices and Quantities: A Macroeconomic Analysis.* Washington, D.C: The Brookings Institution.

Peltzman, Samuel. 2000. Prices rise faster than they fall. *Journal of Political Economy* 108: 466–502.

Rotemberg, Julio J. 2002. Consumer anger at price increases, time variation in the frequency of price changes, and monetary policy. National Bureau of Economic Research Working Paper No. 9320. Cambridge MA: National Bureau of Economic Research.

Rotemberg, Julio J. 2005. Customer anger at price increases, changes in the frequency of price adjustment, and monetary policy. *Journal of Monetary Economics* 52: 829–852.

Rotemberg, Julio J., and Garth Saloner. 1987. The relative rigidity of monopoly pricing. *American Economic Review* 77: 917–926.

Sheshinski, Eytan, and Yoram Weiss. 1977. Inflation and costs of price adjustment. *Review of Economic Studies* 44: 287–303.

Schindler, Robert M. 1991. Symbolic meaning of a price ending. *Advances in Consumer Research* 18: 794–801.

Smiley, Robert. 1988. Empirical evidence on strategic entry deterrence. *International Journal of Industrial Organization* 6: 513–529.

Taylor, John B. 1980. Aggregate dynamics and staggered contracts. *Journal of Political Economy* 88: 1–23.

Thaler, Richard. 1985. Mental accounting and consumer choice. *Marketing Science* 4: 199–214.

2

Summary of Results for the Euro Area

Silvia Fabiani, Claire Loupias, Martine Druant,
Ignacio Hernando, Claudia Kwapil, Bettina Landau,
Fernando Martins, Thomas Mathä, Roberto Sabbatini,
Harald Stahl, & Ad Stokman

This chapter provides evidence for the euro area on firms' pricing practices, summarizing the results of the surveys conducted in 2003 and 2004 by the national central banks of nine countries (Austria, Belgium, France, Germany, Italy, Luxembourg, the Netherlands, Portugal, and Spain) on a comparable basis. Details on each country are given in chapters 3 to 11. All together around 11,000 firms were surveyed in the euro area.

The organization of this chapter follows the different stages of the price adjustment process. The first section of the chapter describes the main characteristics of the markets in which firms operate. The second section deals with the price reviewing stage and provides evidence regarding the time- or state-dependent nature of firms' pricing policies, the information set used, and the frequency of price reviews. The third focuses on the stage at which firms actually change their prices and investigates the mechanism underlying price setting, the extent to which prices are not set uniformly across customers and markets, and the frequency of price changes. The fourth section explores the empirical support of alternative theories on price stickiness. The responses on the factors underlying price setting and asymmetries are analyzed in the fifth section. The final section presents our conclusions.

THE ECONOMIC ENVIRONMENT

The structure of the market in which firms operate is crucial for understanding the main features of their price setting and price adjustment practices. The surveys address issues such as the firm's main reference market and the relationships with its customers, both in terms of whether the latter mainly consist of other firms or final consumers and whether the relationships are long-standing or occasional in nature. Moreover, the degree of market competition is assessed on the basis of a range of indicators.

These aspects are, however, treated in a nonhomogeneous manner in the various national questionnaires. For example, there are some differences with respect to the definition of the firm's reference market. The respondents were requested to refer to their pricing behavior on their domestic market in Germany, France, Luxembourg, and Portugal, and on their main market in Belgium, Spain, Italy, and Austria. Clearly, to infer reliable results for the euro area as a whole, it is important that the responses of the majority of firms refer to their respective domestic (national) market or at least to the euro area. Table 2.1 shows that this is indeed the case for the industrial sector, and hence also very likely to be the case for all other sectors. However, the openness of individual countries is reflected by the fact that on average around 30% of the respondents reported the foreign market as their main one, in many cases another euro area country. As expected, this share is particularly high in Belgium and Luxembourg.

As for the type of customer, the majority of firms (75% on average) sell their main product predominantly to other firms, the share ranging from a minimum of 55% in Belgium to a maximum of almost 90% in Germany. This feature, which is clearly a reflection of the dominance of the industrial sector in most national samples, implies that the findings of the respective surveys

Table 2.1 Market structure (percentages)[a]

	AT	BE	FR	GE	IT	LU	NL	PT	SP	EURO AREA[b]
Reference market (industry)[c]										
domestic	69	55	64	78	73	58	72	67	85	73
foreign	31	45	36	22	27	42	28	33	15	27
Main customer										
other firms	84	56	66	89	73	—	—	84	58	75
consumers	9	40	30	7	25	—	—	13	39	21
public sector	7	4	4	4	2	—	—	3	3	3
Firm-customer relationships[d]										
long-term	81	78	54	57	98	85	—	83	86	70
occasional	19	22	46	43	2	15	—	17	14	30
Perceived competition[e]										
very low	20	18	19	19	10	15	5	8	27	17
low	18	22	17	23	25	17	25	21	19	21
high	30	30	38	34	37	37	49	39	24	35
very high	32	30	25	24	29	31	22	32	30	26

Source: Authors' calculations based on national data.
[a]Rescaled figures excluding nonresponses.
[b]Weighted average (GDP weights).
[c]Only the information on the reference market refers to the industrial sector.
[d]In the case of Belgium, France, and Italy, this refers to relationships with other firms.
[e]Measured by the importance a firm attaches to competitors' prices when considering reducing its own prices.

mostly refer to the behavior of prices in the business-to-business environment and thus producer prices rather than consumer prices.

The relationships between firms and customers are mostly of a long-term nature (on average for 70% of the firms interviewed). In the case of Italy the share is much higher, as it refers only to relationships with other firms and not to those with consumers.

The last piece of evidence presented in table 2.1 refers to the degree of market competition. This feature is proxied by the importance attributed by respondents to competitors' prices in triggering a reduction in their own prices. Although the majority of the firms perceive that competition is high or very high, the share of those firms operating in an environment of weak competition (very low and low) is on average just below 40%. It is worth remarking that firms were also asked to report other information on the market structure, such as the number of competitors in their main market or their market share. However, as not all surveys asked the same questions with regard to the market structure, but all surveys requested firms to provide direct information on how they judge the intensity of competition, we shall refer to the latter. The implications of the degree of competition on the price adjustment process in general and on the frequency of price changes in particular are controversial, and whereas the concept of perfect competition and price taking agents is well defined, there are a multitude of ways to model imperfect competition. Moreover, the fact that strategic complementarities strengthen price rigidity does not lend support to the often-made assertion that the larger the market power of a firm (defined as a low elasticity of demand), the stickier prices are. For a description of the importance of imperfect competition for the price adjustment process, see for example Andersen (1994) and chapter 13 in this book.

All in all, the evidence on the economic environment in which firms operate points to the prevalence of monopolistically competitive markets in which relationships between firms and customers are mostly of long-standing nature.

HOW AND HOW OFTEN FIRMS REVIEW THEIR PRICES

This section documents the main features of the first step of the price adjustment process, in which firms evaluate the price they want to set, taking into account the information at their disposal and checking whether the desired price coincides with the price they currently charge.

The assumption of instantaneous market clearing is part of the economist's toolkit. But individual firms do not continuously adjust their prices in response to all the relevant shocks in the economy. As extensively discussed in chapter 1, the literature considers mainly two types of behavior: time-dependent and state-dependent pricing rules. In the presence of frequent shocks, the former might lead to stickier prices than the latter, provided that the time frame is quite large and the cost of changing prices low enough.

Firms were asked to describe the method adopted for reviewing their prices, whether they mainly follow state-dependent, mainly time-dependent, or a combination of both rules. In the latter case, the idea is that they can follow time-dependent rules as an implementation of state-dependent ones under a stable environment (as in Sheshinski and Weiss 1977), rather than purely time-dependent rules. To distinguish between these two groups, some of the national questionnaires asked explicitly whether firms switched to state-dependent rules upon the occurrence of specific events.

Our analysis focuses on the share of firms following mainly time-dependent rules or both strategies, as these types of firms are expected, as stated above, to introduce more rigidity in the price transmission mechanism.

As shown in table 2.2, on average 34% of the interviewed firms follow purely time-dependent rules; around two-thirds adopt pricing rules with some element of state dependence. The share of time-dependent firms is around 35 to 40% in Austria, France, Italy, the Netherlands, Portugal, and Spain, whereas it is below 30% in Belgium, Germany, and Luxembourg. Among the group of firms characterized by elements of state dependence, those using a mixed strategy are dominant, except in Luxembourg, the Netherlands, Portugal, and Spain.

The share of firms following mainly time-dependent rules tends to increase slightly with the size of the firm when the number of employees is greater than 50; it is higher in services than in trade (except for Belgium and Luxembourg), and in trade than in industry (except for Italy and Luxembourg).

Table 2.2 Price reviewing rules (percentages)[a]

	Mainly time dependent				Both time and state dependent			
		Size class				Size class		
Country	Total	1–49	50–199	≥200	Total	1–49	50–199	≥200
Austria	41	43	33	35	32	30	39	44
Belgium	26	23	21	24	40	39	47	44
France[b]	39	—	—	—	55	—	—	—
Germany	26	24	29	28	55	56	53	58
Italy	40	—	39	42	46	—	47	38
Luxembourg	18	18	17	18	32	29	34	36
The Netherlands	36	34	42	—	18	17	24	—
Portugal	36	33	36	42	22	18	22	30
Spain	33	31	35	36	28	24	29	32
EURO AREA[c]	34				46			

Source: Authors' calculations based on national data.
[a]Rescaled figures excluding nonresponses.
[b]In the case of France, the issue has not been addressed directly; the information in the table has been estimated on the basis of the answers to other questions.
[c]Weighted average (GDP weights).

The Frequency of Price Reviews

All the firms indicating that they mainly carry out periodic price reviews and those adopting time-dependent pricing rules in normal circumstances were asked to mention the frequency of their price reviews. Typically, the respondents were given a choice among several categories (daily, weekly, monthly, quarterly, etc.). Belgium, Luxembourg, and Spain opted for a slightly different formulation, distinguishing between firms that review prices more than once a year, once a year, or less than once a year; within these categories respondents had to specify the typical number of times.[1]

Table 2.3 groups the results into three classes: "maximum three times a year," "between four and eleven times a year," and "at least twelve times a year." In all countries, the majority of firms fall into the first class, averaging 57% in the euro area as a whole. With respect to the median frequency, countries can be grouped into three categories: in Belgium, Italy, and Spain, the median firm reviews its price once a year; in Austria, France, and the Netherlands it does so on a quarterly basis; in Germany, Luxembourg, and Portugal the median firm falls in between.

Firms' size seems to have an effect on the frequency at which prices are reviewed: larger firms are found to carry out reviews significantly more often than smaller ones in Austria, Luxembourg, the Netherlands, and Spain. There are also some interesting differences across sectors. In five countries (Austria, Italy, Luxembourg, the Netherlands, and Portugal), services firms examine the optimality of their prices significantly less often than firms operating in other sectors. Albeit not statistically significant, this tendency can also be observed in Belgium and Spain. In Spain, Luxembourg, and the Netherlands, reviews are significantly more frequent in the trade sector than in manufacturing or other services. This is not the case for the other two countries that report results for trade (Belgium and Italy).[2]

There may be different reasons that price reviews happen with a relatively low frequency. On the one hand, the low frequency could be related to the (potentially sporadic) arrival of information. In other words, it may not

Table 2.3 Frequency of price reviews per year (percentages)[a]

Number of reviews per year	AT	BE	FR	GE	IT	LU	NL	PT	SP	EURO AREA[b]
≥12	29	4	31	30	28	26	37	5	7	26
4–11	25	8	22	17	14	20	19	26	7	17
≤3	46	88	47	53	57	54	44	69	86	57
Median[c]	4	1	4	3	1	2	4	2	1	

Source: Authors' calculations based on national data.
[a]Rescaled figures excluding nonresponses.
[b]Weighted average (GDP weights).
[c]Median number of price reviews per year.

make sense for firms to review their prices more often, as no additional information is available.[3] On the other hand, there may be informational costs associated with price reviews. In this case, it may be optimal for firms to forego obtaining the most topical information instead of incurring such costs. This issue is investigated later in this chapter.

Information Set Used for Price Reviews

To complete the evidence regarding the first stage of the price adjustment process, all surveys, except those conducted in France, Germany, and the Netherlands, enquire about the information set on which firms base their decisions when they review their prices. This is an important piece of evidence that reflects different degrees of optimality of price setting strategies. Companies applying rules of thumb (for instance, changing prices by a fixed percentage, or following a consumer price index [CPI] indexation rule) may end up charging a price that deviates substantially from the optimal one if a large shock occurs and hence behave nonoptimally. At the other extreme, price reviews are addressed in an optimal way if companies use a wide set of indicators relevant for profit maximization, including expectations about the future economic environment.

On average, 48% of the firms for which the information is available in the euro area evaluate their prices on the basis of an information set that includes expected economic conditions (table 2.4). There are some differences across countries in the share of forward-looking firms, which ranges from a minimum of 28% in Spain to a maximum of 68% in Italy. Moreover, a large fraction of firms, overall, does not behave optimally, either due to backward-looking mechanisms or to the adoption of rules of thumb. About one-third of firms take only historic data into account. For those surveys that included the rule-of-thumb option, the results indicate that this method is adopted by 37% of companies in Belgium, 33% in Spain, 30% in Luxembourg, and 25% in Portugal. Information available only for Luxembourg and Spain shows that smaller firms tend to be more backward-looking than larger ones and, conversely, larger firms tend to attach more importance than smaller ones to expectations about future conditions when assessing their prices.

Table 2.4 Information set for pricing decisions (percentages)

	AT	BE	IT	LU	PT	SP	EURO AREA[a]
Rule of thumb	—	37	—	30	23	33	
Past/Present context	37	29	32	26	30	39	34
Present/Future context	12	34	68	44	47	28	48
Past, present and future	51	—	—	—	—	—	

Source: Authors' calculations based on national data.
[a]Weighted average (GDP weights). Note that the percentages for the euro area do not add up to 100 as different answer categories were used in the various countries.

Overall, these results lend some support to the recent wave of estimations of hybrid versions of the New Keynesian Phillips Curve (see chapter 1 for more details).

HOW AND HOW OFTEN FIRMS CHANGE THEIR PRICES

This section focuses on the second stage of the price adjustment process, where firms actually change their prices. Three main aspects are considered, namely the mechanisms adopted by companies to set their price level, the extent to which they use alternative forms of price discrimination, and the frequency of price changes.

Price Setting

Markup and Other Price Setting Rules   All questionnaires address the issue of how companies set their prices. In Austria, Belgium, Luxembourg, the Netherlands, Portugal, and Spain firms were first asked to indicate whether they have an independent price setting policy or their price is regulated, set by the main company of the same group, or dictated by the main customer. Those with an independent policy were asked to specify whether their price is set as a margin (markup) on costs or depends on the price of their main competitor(s) or is set according to other strategies. This last option in some of the national questionnaires includes "regulated price" and "price set by customers." In the countries where no preliminary inquiry was made on the independence of the company's pricing policy, respondents were directly asked to indicate their price setting rule, choosing from among the above-mentioned alternatives.

The option that the price is set as a margin applied to costs requires some clarification. First, its formulation varies marginally across questionnaires. The main reason is that, whereas the theoretical literature refers to the concepts of markup and marginal costs, business people might not easily understand this terminology. In order to avoid confusion on the side of the respondents, the concept of markup has typically been translated into "profit margin" whereas the concept of marginal costs has been translated into a number of different expressions: "unit variable costs (cost of labor and of other inputs)," "(variable) unit costs," "unit variable production costs," or "variable production costs per unit."[4] Second, all questionnaires explore whether a markup rule is applied in general terms, except in Belgium, Germany, and the Netherlands, where a distinction is made between constant and variable markup. The Belgian survey introduces a further difference, between actual and desired markup. The latter concept is embedded in the specific wording used, which refers to a "completely self-determined profit margin" rather than to a profit margin in more general terms (for details, see the questionnaire reported in the Appendix to the book).[5]

Table 2.5 provides a summary of firms' price setting strategies by grouping the answers into three alternatives: "markup over costs," "price set according to competitors' prices," and "other." On average, in the euro area

Table 2.5 Price setting rules (percentages)[a]

Price rule	BE tot	const	var[b]	FR tot	GE tot	const	var	IT tot	NL const	var		PT[c]	SP	EURO AREA[d]
Markup	46	13	33	40	73	4	69	42	56	27	30	65	52	54
Competitors' price	36	—	—	38	17	—	—	32	22	—	—	13	27	27
Other	18	—	—	22	10	—	—	26	21	—	—	23	21	19

Source: Authors' calculations based on national data.
[a]Rescaled figures excluding nonresponses.
[b]Firms adopting a markup rule and responding "important" or "very important" to a least one of the theories concerning countercyclical markups.
[c]In the case of Portugal the issue was not addressed directly; the information reported in the table has been estimated on the basis of the answers to other questions.
[d]Weighted average (GDP weights).

more than half of the firms fix their price as a markup (fixed or variable) over costs. At the two extremes, French respondents reported the lowest share (40%), whereas German ones the highest (73%). For the countries (Belgium, Germany and the Netherlands) where a distinction is made between constant and variable markup, the latter dominates. In particular, in Germany only 4% of the companies apply a constant markup on calculated unit costs, whereas the share is higher in Belgium and the Netherlands (13% and 27%, respectively).

These results support the standard assumption in imperfectly competitive models that under quite general conditions, firms choose to charge a price that represents a markup over marginal cost and have therefore some lee-way for not adjusting prices when facing a variation in costs (see Andersen 1994 for a presentation of what standard models of imperfect competition imply for the adjustment of prices). Within these models, some assume time-varying markups, with important implications for business cycle fluctuations (see Rotemberg and Woodford 1994 for an overview of different models with exogenously and endogenously determined time-varying markups).

Turning to other price setting rules, on average almost one-third of the firms take the price of their competitors as a benchmark. They may be either price takers, or act in an oligopolistic market (being either followers or leaders with large market power that have to watch their competitors closely).

Finally, a minority of respondents set the price according to "other" rules (19% in the euro area as a whole). The share amounts to only 10% in Germany but it amounts to 26% in Italy, in the latter case reflecting a particularly high incidence of firms reporting their price being subject to some form of regulation in trade and services. If only the manufacturing sector is considered, the share for this country drops to 19%.

With respect to the firm size, smaller firms tend to rely more on markup rules than do larger firms. Partly, this could be a spurious result, as in the sample large firms are in general found to face a higher degree of competition (see chapter 13 for a focus on the relationship between market competition and pricing behavior). The percentage of companies following "other" rules is also generally higher in the case of larger firms than in that of smaller ones.

Price Discrimination and Pricing to Market   An additional important piece of information that complements the overall picture on price setting procedures pertains to the diffusion of price discrimination. This practice can take different forms: the price of a product may vary on the amount sold, the type of customer, the geographical area, or the distribution channel, to name but a few (see chapter 3 in Tirole 1988 for a detailed theoretical analysis of alternative forms of price discrimination). Several national questionnaires address this issue by asking firms whether they charge a uniform price to all their customers or whether their prices differ depending on the amount sold, are decided on a case-by-case basis, or differ depending on other criteria. The extent of price discrimination across geographical areas, known in the literature as pricing to market, is explored in the surveys conducted in Belgium, Luxembourg, Portugal, and Spain.

The findings generally reject the use of a uniform pricing scheme by euro area firms. In particular, the share of firms setting prices on a case-by-case basis or in accordance to the quantity of the product sold is, on average, around 80%. It ranges from 65% in Spain to 92% in Germany. In the other four countries where this evidence is available, that is France, Italy, Luxembourg, and Portugal, the figure is around 75% (see Fabiani et al. 2005).

In general, there is no clear relationship between the extent of price discrimination and the size of companies. If anything, smaller firms seem to make a slightly more frequent use of differentiated prices in France, Italy, and Portugal.

More significant differences are found across sectors, although on this point the evidence is limited to a few countries only. In particular, uniform pricing is, as expected, more common in the trade sector. In this sector, the share of firms charging the same prices to all customers is around 55% in Italy and Spain and 44% in Luxembourg. The corresponding figures for the overall samples in these countries are 19%, 35%, and 29%, respectively. At the other extreme, the share of firms setting their prices on a case-by-case basis or according to the quantity sold is highest in manufacturing, which may explain the high figure for Germany.

As for pricing to market, around half of the firms in Belgium and Spain are found to charge different prices in different countries. This is a high proportion, given that the exports of these countries are mostly directed towards the euro area, as pointed out for Belgium in chapter 4. Price discrimination is even more frequent on non–euro area markets. For example, 60% of Spanish exporters charge different prices across non–euro area countries. In the case of Portugal, the distinction between euro area and non–euro area markets is not possible, as the questions concerning pricing to market are only addressed to firms exporting outside the euro area, which were asked what would happen to the local price of their product on the foreign market if the euro appreciated by 5%. It turns out that more than half of them would either keep the price unchanged or increase it by less than 5%.

The questionnaires in the four countries ask firms to attach a score to some of the factors commonly identified in the literature as explanations of pricing to market models, such as competitors' prices, transportation costs, cyclical fluctuation in demand, structural market conditions, exchange rate fluctuations, and the tax system. The resulting ranking, obtained on the basis of mean scores, is strikingly similar across countries. In particular, the most relevant reasons are the prices charged by competitors on the local foreign markets and transportation costs; cyclical demand conditions rank immediately below. Exchange rate developments and structural features of the foreign markets are recognized as having a moderate importance. As expected, exchange rate movements receive a higher score from firms exporting outside the euro area. Nevertheless, even for these firms this factor is ranked below competitors' prices and demand. Finally, the local market tax system is singled out as the least important element. As Aucremanne and Druant (2005) indicate, this factor is more important in consumer oriented firms, for which differences in indirect taxation are presumably more relevant.

The Frequency of Price Changes

The surveys contribute to improve the quantitative assessment of the frequency with which companies change their prices; all of them, except that for Germany, address this issue.[6] In France, Italy, and Portugal, firms had to indicate the number of times they changed their prices in a given year, and in Austria, Belgium, Luxembourg, the Netherlands, and Spain they had to report the average yearly number of price changes over the recent past years.

Table 2.6 groups the answers into four categories: "at least four price changes," "two or three price changes," "one price change," and "less than

Table 2.6 Frequency of price changes per year (percentages)[a]

Number of changes per year	AT	BE	FR	GE	IT	LU	NL	PT	SP	EURO AREA[b]
≥ 4	11	8	9	21	11	27	11	12	14	14
2–3	15	18	24	21	19	27	19	14	15	20
1	51	55	46	14	50	31	60	51	57	39
<1	24	18	21	44	20	15	10	24	14	27
Median[c]	1	1	1	1	1	2	1	1	1	

Source: Authors' calculations based on national data.
[a]Rescaled figures excluding nonresponses.
[b]Weighted average (GDP weights).
[c]Median number of price changes per year.

one price change." The results are very homogenous across countries, with the exception of Germany, where a different data source—the Information and Forschung (IFO) Institute for Economic Research business survey for 2003—was used to obtain this specific information.[7] Overall, almost 40% of the firms in the euro area change their price once a year (the share rises to 51% if Germany is excluded from the computation of the euro area average). In all countries except Germany and Luxembourg, for approximately 70% of the respondents price adjustments take place a maximum of once a year.[8]

In all but one country, the median firm adjusts its price once a year. In Luxembourg, the exclusion of the construction industry, as is the case in the other countries, would also result in a median of one price change per year. On average, only 34% of the firms change prices more frequently than once a year. These results are consistent with the evidence based on micro quantitative evidence presented in chapter 14.

The size of the firm does not affect the frequency of price changes in most countries. However, the results for the Netherlands, the only survey that covers one-person firms, show that the latter have the lowest frequency of price changes (see chapter 9 and Hoeberichts and Stokman 2006).

Conversely, considerable differences across sectors, in line with the results obtained for price reviews, emerge from all the surveys that cover more than one sector. In four countries (Austria, Belgium, Italy, and Portugal), the services sector prices are changed less frequently than those in other sectors; in four countries (Italy, Luxembourg, the Netherlands, and Spain) adjustments are more frequent in the trade sector.

Taking into account only the companies that provided information on both the frequency of price reviews and that of price changes, the former appears to be higher than the latter. Even with the categorized data used here, at the euro area level the share of firms changing prices less than quarterly (a maximum number of three times per year) is 86%, compared with 57% of firms reviewing prices with the same frequency (table 2.7). Similar evidence is found in all but two countries.[9]

All in all, the evidence provided so far is consistent with the notion that price adjustment takes place in two stages. First, firms examine prices to check whether they are at the optimal level or need to be changed. As they do so at discrete time intervals (the majority less than four times per year),

Table 2.7 Price reviews and price changes per year (percentages)[a]

	AT	BE	FR	GE	IT	LU	NL	PT	SP	EURO AREA[b]
Price reviews ≤3	46	88	47	53	57	54	44	72	86	57
Price changes ≤3	90	91	91	79	89	73	89	88	88	86

Source: Authors' calculations based on national data.
[a]Rescaled figures excluding nonresponses.
[b]Weighted average (GDP weights).

some kind of stickiness already arises at this stage. Once the review has taken place, firms may change prices. However, they do so less frequently. This might be due either to the fact that there is no reason to implement an adjustment or to the existence of other factors effectively preventing a desired price change.[10]

WHY DO FIRMS HOLD PRICES CONSTANT?

The economic literature provides manifold explanations for sticky prices (see chapter 1). All national surveys present a list of theories chosen according to their relevance in the literature, as well as their rankings in the surveys already conducted for other countries (Apel et al. 2005, Blinder et al. 1998, Hall et al. 2000). Managers were asked a question along the following lines: "If there are reasons for changing the price of your main product, which of the following factors may well prevent an immediate price adjustment?" The respondents could indicate their degree of agreement with each theory, choosing from among four categories: "1 = unimportant," "2 = of minor importance," "3 = important," and "4 = very important," where the numbers indicate the scores attached to each category.[11]

Table 2.8 presents the mean scores obtained by ten theories, common across the various questionnaires, in each country and the corresponding euro area average. Based on this ranking, two groups can be distinguished: the first comprises those theories that receive an average score well above 2, whereas the second comprises the remaining ones. See chapter 12 for a comparison between the results for the euro area and those available for a number of other economies.

Reasons Perceived as Important by Decision Makers

Contracts, Either Explicit or Implicit   Contracts are one of the main reasons to postpone price adjustments. The theory of implicit contracts receives the highest average score (2.7) and ranks first in five countries; with an average score of 2.6, explicit contracts is the second most important theory at the euro area level and ranks as the most important in four countries. Discrepancies among euro area countries exist but are weak. The lowest score is 2.3 for explicit contracts in Spain, and the highest is 3.1 for implicit contracts in Portugal.

Both theories are based on the idea that firms establish long-run relationships with customers in order to make future sales more predictable. The high score they obtain is consistent with the finding that long-term relationships between firms and customers are very widespread in the euro area. In this respect, Okun (1981) argues that price increases that are due to cost increases are viewed as fair by customers, but price increases that are due to a tight market are regarded as unfair. If this is the case—and the results suggest that managers indeed share this perception—it would be more likely that firms increase their prices in response to cost shocks than to demand shocks (see the section on factors driving price changes and asymmetries for more details).

Table 2.8 The importance of theories explaining price stickiness (mean scores)

Theories	AT	BE	FR	GE	IT	LU	NL	PT	SP	EURO AREA[a]
Implicit contracts	3.0	2.5	2.2	—	—	2.7	2.7	3.1	2.6	2.7
Explicit contracts	3.0	2.4	2.7	2.4	3.0	2.8	2.5	2.6	2.3	2.6
Cost based pricing	2.6	2.4	2.5	—	—	2.7	—	2.7	—	2.6
Coordination failure	2.3	2.2	3.0	2.2	3.0	2.1	2.2	2.8	2.4	2.4
Judging quality by price	1.9	1.9	—	—	—	2.2	2.4	2.3	1.8	2.1
Temporary shocks	1.5	1.8	2.1	1.9	2.0	1.7	2.4	2.5	1.8	2.0
Change non price factors	1.7	1.7	—	—	—	1.9	1.9	—	1.3	1.7
Menu costs	1.5	1.5	1.4	1.4	2.0	1.8	1.7	1.9	1.4	1.6
Costly information	1.6	1.6	—	—	—	1.8	—	1.7	1.3	1.6
Pricing thresholds	1.3	1.7	1.6	—	1.0	1.8	1.8	1.8	1.5	1.6

Source: Authors' calculations based on national data.
[a]Unweighted average of countries' scores.

Price Setting Strategies   The theories cost-based pricing and coordination failure are ranked third and fourth, respectively, consistently with the price setting strategies discussed in the previous sections. The high score attached to the former confirms the fact that the majority of firms set their price as a markup over costs. In other words, relatively stable costs or the sluggishness of the price response to cost changes are an important explanation for sticky prices. Coordination failure relates instead to the interaction between firms on the same market. As shown above, nearly 30% of the firms follow competitors' prices when they decide upon their own. Together with the fear of a lack of coordination in price movements, this provides a further motivation of price stickiness, namely, that firms prefer not to change their prices as long as none of their competitors moves first.

These results do not depend on the survey methodology, the particular wording used, or the ordering of the answer categories, as the various national surveys were conducted in different ways (see chapter 1).[12] Each of the four theories receives a high score also in the studies available for non-euro area countries (see chapter 12).

Reasons Perceived as Not Important by Decision Makers

The remaining theories are on average not considered as important obstacles to price adjustment by euro area firms. This group includes prominent candidates such as physical menu costs and information costs. Although they are frequently advocated as explanations for price stickiness in the theoretical literature (e.g. Ball and Mankiw 1994), in practice they seem to be of minor importance.

As for the question of whether factors slowing down or preventing the process of price adjustment have a greater bearing on the first or the second stage of the process itself, our analysis suggests that for the majority of the firms, the main obstacles are not associated with price reviews but rather with price changes. In fact, the theory of information costs—that is, those associated with gathering and processing information for pricing decisions (stage one)—receives one of the lowest scores in all the country questionnaires that included this category. Overall, this finding is in line with the results of Zbaracki et al. (2004), who report quantitative estimates of the different costs of price adjustments, distinguishing between costs of producing and distributing price sheets (what we call menu costs), managerial costs (information costs in our terminology) and customer costs. They conclude that, although approximately one quarter of the overall costs of changing prices is due to the first two categories, three quarters arise because customers dislike price changes.[13]

FACTORS DRIVING PRICE CHANGES AND ASYMMETRIES OF PRICE REACTIONS

The empirical literature provides evidence that price increases and decreases do not occur with the same (conditional) probability. Dhyne et al. (2006) show that in the euro area price reductions are moderately less frequent than increases: four out of ten changes are reductions.[14] Analogous results are obtained by Lünnemann and Mathä (2005) using price index data. Asymmetries are also found with respect to the size of price changes, as average price increases tend to be smaller than decreases. The results for the United States are quite similar: Klenow and Kryvtsov (2005) report that 45% of all price changes are reductions.

The Determinants of Price Changes

In order to analyze what drives price changes and whether there are asymmetries depending on the direction of the adjustment, all national surveys include questions about the factors underlying price adjustments. Respondents were asked to assign scores between "1 = completely unimportant" and "4 = very important" to cost factors (labor costs, raw material costs, and financial costs) and market conditions (demand and competitors' prices) according to their importance in determining price increases and decreases, respectively.

Table 2.9 The importance of factors driving price changes (mean scores)

Factors	AT	BE	FR	GE	IT	LU	NL	PT	SP	EURO AREA[a]
INCREASE										
Labor costs	3.4	2.9	2.5	2.7	2.9	3.5	2.7	3.3	2.7	3.0
Costs of raw materials	3.1	2.9	3.0	3.4	3.3	—	2.5	3.6	3.1	3.1
Financial costs	1.9	2.2	—	1.9	2.3	3.0	2.1	2.5	1.8	2.2
Demand	1.9	2.2	2.0	2.2	2.4	2.3	2.3	2.5	2.4	2.2
Competitors' price	2.0	2.5	2.3	2.1	2.6	2.4	2.5	2.7	2.5	2.4
DECREASE										
Labor costs	1.3	2.1	1.9	1.9	2.4	2.6	2.1	3.0	2.0	2.1
Costs of raw materials	2.2	2.3	2.6	2.8	2.9	—	2	3.3	2.6	2.6
Financial costs	1.6	1.8	—	1.6	2.1	2.5	1.8	2.3	1.5	1.9
Demand	2.0	2.5	2.3	2.4	2.8	2.7	2.5	3.0	2.4	2.5
Competitors' price	2.6	2.9	2.8	2.6	2.8	2.8	2.7	2.9	2.7	2.8

Source: Authors' calculations based on national data.
[a]Unweighted average of countries' scores.

The results are presented in table 2.9, which contains the mean scores for each country as well as the euro area average in the last column. The costs of raw materials and labor are the most important factors in driving prices upward: they receive an average score of 3.0 and rank first and second in every country. As for price decreases, competitor's prices (with an average score of 2.8) appear the main driving force, followed by changes in demand conditions and costs of raw materials. Financial costs do not seem to be relevant. These results are not sensitive to differences in the firm's size.

In sum, euro area firms are more prompted to change their prices in response to shocks that lead to profit losses (rising costs of raw materials and labor, as well as a decrease in the competitor's prices) than to shocks leading to profit gains (decreasing labor and financial costs, as well as improving demand conditions and an increase in competitor's prices). This pattern does not depend on the economic outlook prevailing when the firms were interviewed, as the surveys were conducted in periods characterized by different gross domestic product (GDP) growth rates across countries.

An even clearer picture of the asymmetry in upward and downward price adjustment in relation to its underlying causes is provided by figure 2.1, which shows the difference between the scores attached to each factor as a determinant of price increases and of price decreases. The results reveal a

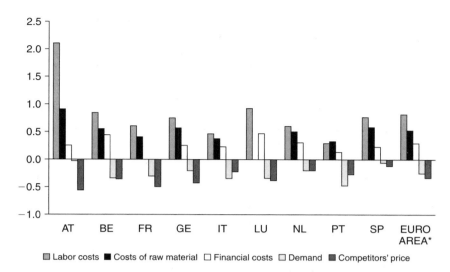

Figure 2.1 Asymmetries in factors driving price changes (difference between scores for price increases and decreases). *Source:* Calculations based on national data. *Unweighted average of countires' scores.

strikingly regular pattern of positive asymmetries for costs and negative ones for demand conditions and competitors' prices.

This evidence is in line with the conclusions from Peltzman (2000), who suggests that output prices respond asymmetrically to cost shocks depending on their directions. He shows that on average, prices respond faster to input price increases than to decreases and that the immediate response after a positive cost shock is at least twice the response to a negative one. The role of implicit contracts as an explanation for price stickiness, revealed in the previous section, may provide a rationale for this asymmetry. If, as argued by Okun's customer market theory, customers view price increases due to cost increases as fair and price increases due to rising demand as unfair, firms should be more likely to raise their prices in response to cost shocks than to demand shocks, as they try to avoid jeopardizing customer relationships. Although Peltzman (2000) only focuses on the asymmetry with regard to cost shocks, we additionally find that demand shocks also affect prices asymmetrically: negative demand shocks are more likely to induce price adjustments than positive ones.

Long-term Adjustment and Reaction Delay

Five countries (Austria, France, Luxembourg, Portugal, and Spain) investigated further the issue of price reactions after shocks, focusing on the time lag of the price response. Firms were asked whether they change their prices in reaction to a specific shock or not. In the case of a positive answer, they were requested to indicate the time (number of months) that elapses before the price change is implemented.

The results support the conclusion that lower demand is more likely to lead to price adjustments than higher demand, whereas the opposite is true for cost shocks; in addition, a larger share of firms adjust their price in reaction to increasing costs than to higher demand. Indeed, as far as demand shocks are concerned, the share of adjusting firms goes from 48% (in Austria) to 78% (in France) in the case of negative ones and from 37% (in Austria) to 77% (in France) in the case of positive ones. In the face of cost shocks, 92% of Austrian firms adjust their price against 82% in France when shocks are positive; when they are negative the highest and lowest shares are 81% (in Portugal) and 62% (in Austria), respectively. The gap between the share of adjusting firms after a positive and a negative cost shock is between 9 and 30 percentage points across countries. The difference between the share of firms reacting to positive cost shocks and to positive demand ones ranges between 5 (in France) and 55 percentage points (in Austria).

Table 2.10 presents the share of respondents, among those that change prices after a shock, that do it within a month, between one and three months, and after a period of more than three months. The median firm implements the price change one to three months after the shock has occurred in Austria,

Table 2.10 Speed of price adjustment after shocks (percentages)[a]

Mean lag	Higher demand	Lower demand	Higher costs	Lower costs
Austria				
<1 month	4	3	2	2
1–3 months	51	71	65	61
>3 months	45	26	33	37
France				
<1 month	35	37	34	31
1–3 months	34	35	27	29
>3 months	31	28	39	40
Luxembourg				
<1 month	34	42	47	40
1–3 months	24	31	25	28
>3 months	42	27	28	32
Portugal[b]				
<1 month	22	28	24	23
1–3 months	31	32	27	33
>3 months	47	40	49	44
Spain				
<1 month	18	21	15	13
1–3 months	17	21	18	18
>3 months	65	58	67	69

Source: Authors' calculations based on national data.
[a]Rescaled figures excluding nonresponses.
[b]In the case of Portugal, data only refers to firms adjusting their prices in the first year after a shock.

France, Luxembourg, and Portugal; in Spain the firm waits for more than three months. In general, in all countries at least one-third of the firms adjust their prices only after three months. Thus, if price adjustments were synchronized (which is not the case), these findings would justify the assumption of an adjustment process of one quarter in macro models for Austria, France, Luxembourg, and Portugal and of two or more quarters for Spain.

SUMMARY AND CONCLUSIONS

The main findings arising from the surveys on firms' pricing strategies, reviewed in this chapter, appear to be quite consistent across countries and allow drawing conclusions for the euro area as a whole, a summary of which is given below.

Two pieces of evidence from our surveys suggest that the model of perfect competition with the law of one price is not the blueprint for euro area markets. First, markup pricing is the dominant practice adopted by firms in setting prices. Second, price discrimination, across customers and markets, is very common.

As far as price adjustment is concerned, around one-third of the companies follow mainly time-dependent rules while the remaining two-thirds use pricing rules with some element of state dependence. When they review prices on a periodic basis, firms mostly do it with a frequency between one to three times per year. They tend to take into account a wide range of information, including expected economic developments; about one-third of them, however, adopt a purely backward-looking behavior.

Prices are actually changed even less frequently than they are reviewed: the median firm does so once a year. The evidence on the factors preventing a required price adjustment confirms indeed that the main obstacles to price flexibility arise at the second stage of price setting: in contrast to the suggestion of Ball and Mankiw (1994), the costs related to the collection of information do not seem to be among the most important impediments. Conversely, the fear that a price adjustment could jeopardize the relationships with customers (expressed in the theories on implicit and explicit contracts) is found to be much more crucial for price inertia, together with coordination failure.

Price movements in response to shocks are found to be asymmetrical, depending on the source and the sign of the shock. Price increases tend to be mostly affected by cost shocks, and price reductions mostly affected by changes in market conditions (demand and competitors' prices). Moreover, there seems to be higher nominal flexibility downward than upward in response to demand shocks, whereas the opposite holds for cost shocks.

NOTES

1. As table 2.3 shows, Belgium and Spain report significantly higher shares (nearly 90%) of respondents indicating that firms review their prices at most three times a year. This result suggests that the format of the answer categories might be relevant.

2. In Germany and France services are not covered.

3. Kashyap (1995) rejects this hypothesis. He observes different reviewing behavior also for products having similar cost and demand characteristics. However, if products are alike, then the arrival of the necessary information should also be correlated.

4. Overall, firms provide information on their average variable cost and not on their marginal cost.

5. The Belgian survey investigates indirectly whether desired markups are variable by testing the relevance of four theories that generate endogenously counter-cyclical movements in desired markups. The importance attached by the respondents to these theories allows the computation of the fraction of firms that apply (counter-cyclical) variable markups in the Belgian economy.

6. Over the last years the measurement of the unconditional degree of price stickiness in the euro area has also benefited from the availability of large scale datasets of individual consumer prices (see chapter 14).

7. The figures might be downward biased for Germany, since instead of the exact number of price changes the table reports the number of months in which a price change occurred. Nevertheless, this technical difference in itself cannot explain the huge gap between Germany and the other countries. Probably, part of the gap is due to the particularly weak cyclical demand outlook faced by German firms in 2003.

8. In Luxembourg, the finding that only 46% of the firms change their prices at this frequency is largely due to the inclusion of the construction sector and its relative share in the responses (22%).

9. Both in Belgium and in Spain the frequency of price reviews is only slightly higher than the frequency of price changes. As already mentioned, this might be partly explained by the format of the answer categories. In these two countries, firms were asked whether they review/change their prices more than once a year, once a year, or less than once a year. A substantial fraction indicates that they review/change their prices once a year. If these questions had been formulated allowing for more answer categories, the fraction of firms declaring a yearly frequency of reviews/changes might have been lower.

10. Although almost all national surveys address the issue of price reviews and price changes while referring to "normal conditions," in most cases it is not possible to control for the fact that the observed price behavior is in fact related to the occurrence of particular shocks, either of an idiosyncratic nature or a common one.

11. In the Dutch questionnaire, the scaling is more detailed (from 1 to 10). Results have been rescaled for comparability.

12. The ordering of the theories differs considerably across the various questionnaires. For example, in the Dutch questionnaire the theory of implicit contracts is the second answer category, whereas it appears in the ninth place in the Austrian questionnaire. Nevertheless, in both studies, the theory is regarded as the most important explanation. Overall, we do not find an association between the ordering of the answer categories and the scores given to theories.

13. Although our results suggest that menu costs and information costs are equally unimportant (in relation to other costs, especially customer costs), Zbaracki et al. (2004) estimate that managerial costs are six times the menu costs.

14. Some country surveys (France, the Netherlands, and Portugal) explicitly enquire about the share of price increases and decreases, which turn out to be around 70 and 30%, respectively.

REFERENCES

Andersen, Torben M. 1994. *Price Rigidity: Causes and Macroeconomic Implications*. Oxford: Clarendon Press.

Apel, Mikael, Richard Friberg, and Kerstin Hallsten. 2005. Microfoundations of macroeconomic price adjustment: Survey evidence from Swedish firms. *Journal of Money Credit and Banking* 37: 313–338.

Aucremanne, Luc, and Martine Druant. 2005. Price-setting behaviour in Belgium: What can be learned from an ad hoc survey? National Bank of Belgium Working Paper Research Series No. 65. Brussels: National Bank of Belgium.

Ball, Laurence, and Mankiw N. Gregory. 1994. A sticky-price manifesto. *Carnegie-Rochester Conference Series on Public Policy* 41: 127–151.

Blinder, Alan S., Elie R. D. Canetti, David E. Lebow, and Jeremy B. Rudd. 1998. *Asking about Prices: A New Approach to Understanding Price Stickiness*. New York: Russell Sage Foundation.

Dhyne, Emmanuel, Luis J. Álvarez, Hervé Le Bihan, Giovanni Veronese, Daniel Dias, Johannes Hoffmann, Nicole Jonker, Patrick Lünnemann, Fabio Rumler, and Jouko Vilmunen. 2006. Price changes in the euro area and the United States: Some facts from individual consumer price data. *Journal of Economic Perspectives* 20: 171–192.

Fabiani, Silvia, Martine Druant, Ignacio Hernando, Claudia Kwapil, Bettina Landau, Claire Loupias, Fernando Martins, Thomas Mathä, Roberto Sabbatini, and Ad Stokman. 2005. The pricing behaviour of firms in the Euro Area: New survey evidence. European Central Bank Working Paper No. 535. Frankfurt am Main: European Central Bank.

Hall, Simon, Mark Walsh, and Antony Yates. 2000. Are UK companies price sticky? *Oxford Economic Papers* 52: 425–446.

Hoeberichts, Marco, and Ad Stokman. 2006. Price setting behaviour in the Netherlands: Results of a survey. European Central Bank Working Paper No. 607. Frankfurt am Main: European Central Bank.

Kashyap, Anil K. 1995. Sticky prices: New evidence from retail catalogs. *Quarterly Journal of Economics* 110: 245–274.

Klenow, Peter J., and Oleksiy Kryvtsov. 2005. State-dependent or time-dependent pricing: Does it matter for recent U.S. inflation? Bank of Canada Working Paper No. 2005–4. Ottawa: Bank of Canada.

Lünnemann, Patrick, and Thomas Y. Mathä. 2005. Regulated and services' prices and inflation persistence. European Central Bank Working Paper No. 466. Frankfurt am Main: European Central Bank.

Okun, Arthur. 1981. *Prices and Quantities: A Macroeconomic Analysis*. Washington, D.C: The Brookings Institution.

Peltzman, Samuel. 2000. Prices rise faster than they fall. *Journal of Political Economy* 108: 466–502.

Rotemberg, Julio J., and Michael Woodford. 1994. Dynamic general equilibrium models with imperfectly competitive products markets. In *Frontiers of Business Cycle Research*, ed. Thomas F. Cooley. Princeton: Princeton University Press.

Sheshinski, Eytan, and Yoram Weiss. 1977. Inflation and costs of price adjustment. *Review of Economic Studies* 44: 287–303.

Tirole, Jean. 1988. *The Theory of Industrial Organization*. Cambridge MA: MIT Press.

Zbaracki, Mark J., Mark Ritson, Daniel Levy, Shantanu Dutta, and Mark Bergen. 2004. Managerial and customer costs of price adjustment: Direct evidence from industrial markets. *Review of Economics and Statistics* 86: 514–533.

Part II

Country-Specific Findings

3

Price Reactions to Demand and Cost Shocks

Survey Evidence from Austrian Firms

Claudia Kwapil, Josef Baumgartner, & Johann Scharler

We present some more details on the price setting process of Austrian firms as a complement to the findings summarized in chapter 2 for the euro area. In the first section we discuss data collection and the structure of the questionnaire. In the second section we describe the economic situation when the survey was conducted, along with some characteristics of the market structure the firms operate in. We investigate the properties of price adjustments in reaction to demand and cost shocks in the third section. In the final section we summarize our findings.

THE SURVEY

The survey on the price setting behavior of firms in Austria was carried out through a questionnaire that was sent as a supplement with the monthly business cycle survey (BCS) of the Austrian Institute of Economic Research (WIFO) in January 2004. In total, we contacted a sample of 2,427 firms from manufacturing and industry-related services (hereafter referred to as services) sectors, and 873 firms participated in the survey. We mailed the questionnaires to company decision makers (owners, CEOs, or their assistants). In the first week of February 2004, a reminder letter was sent to approximately 1,800 firms that had not responded by the end of January. We obtained an overall response rate of 36% by the end of February, which can be regarded as reasonably high, given the complexity of the issue and the length of the questionnaire, as the latter consists in total of 79 detailed questions (see the Appendix to the book).

When asking about price setting, one has to deal with the fact that many firms sell several types of goods in different (domestic or foreign) markets. In order to operationalize this issue, we asked the respondents to refer to their "main product or service" (in terms of turnover) in their main market. This was to prevent the respondents from losing focus and switching between different products when answering the questionnaire. We also decided to exclude some sectors a priori because the concept of main product was less suitable for them (e.g., construction, retailing), as pointed out by Hall et al. (2000). In addition, some sectors had to be disregarded because they are not included in the WIFO-BCS sample. Overall, the sectors included represent 42% of Austria's value added in 2001. In terms of the NACE two-digit classification, the following sectors are covered: manufacturing (15, 17 to 36) and some industry-related services (60, 63, 70 to 74, and 90).[1]

Response rates vary considerably across sectors and according to firm size (see table 3.A.1 in the Appendix to this chapter). More manufacturing firms participated in the survey than services firms. The WIFO-BCS sample was established as a stratified sample in the 1970s and has been re-stratified several times since then. The sample and the actual responses show a bias: industrial firms (producing intermediate and capital goods) and large (well established and successful) firms are overrepresented in terms of number of firms and employees, which is a common characteristic in longitudinal data sets of this kind (see Figure 3.A.1 in the Appendix to this chapter). In the sample, no newly founded firms are represented. In addition, firms that did not respond four times in a row (e.g., because of bankruptcy) are excluded from the WIFO-BCS. To correct for these effects, we poststratify the answers according to the sector of activity and the size class each firm belongs to.

The questionnaire covers different types of information about the participating firms.[2] In the first part of the questionnaire (section A), several characteristics of the responding firms are covered. The price setting process is the content of section B of the questionnaire. With questions B1 to B7, we focus on time- versus state-dependent pricing, price reviews, and price changes. To assess the importance of different theories about sticky prices, we translated eleven theoretical concepts into questions in everyday language (questions B8 and B9). Kwapil et al. (2005a) discuss these issues in full detail. In question B11, we ask about the reasons for price changes (e.g., labor costs and intermediate goods price changes). The asymmetries of price adjustments (increases versus decreases), price reactions to different kinds of shocks (demand versus cost shocks and transitory versus permanent shocks), and the influence of the size of a shock (small versus large shocks) are addressed in questions B10 and B13, respectively. In the third section of this chapter and in Kwapil et al. (2005b) results on these issues are presented.

According to the answers to question B1, 82% of the respondents are able to set prices by themselves, and we therefore restrict the analysis to those 715 firms.[3]

ECONOMIC SITUATION AND MARKET STRUCTURE

When filling in the questionnaire, the respondents were asked to answer either in a general way (i.e., how they usually react) or by indicating how they acted in recent years. Their responses are thus snapshots depending,

Table 3.1 Market and competition characteristics (percentages)

	Total	Manufacturing	Services[a]
Domestic turnover share (%)			
0	1.4	2.6	0.5
1–19	4.9	9.2	1.6
20–39	5.5	9.4	2.6
40–59	8.0	8.9	7.3
60–79	9.7	10.6	9.0
80–99	33.7	30.6	36.1
100	36.8	28.7	42.9
Main customer			
Wholesalers	11.9	26.7	—
Retailers	5.1	11.4	—
Within group	6.0	2.9	8.4
Other companies	59.6	44.2	71.8
Government	5.4	2.9	7.4
Consumers	8.7	10.9	7.0
Others	3.5	1.0	5.5
Market share (%)			
0–5	44.8	37.6	50.4
6–10	15.0	15.0	14.9
11–20	11.5	13.1	10.3
21–30	8.3	11.2	6.0
31–50	8.7	11.6	6.5
>50	11.7	11.5	11.9
Number of competitors			
None	1.5	0.8	2.0
<5	16.0	23.0	10.5
5–20	40.2	46.8	35.0
>20	42.3	29.4	52.5
Number of customers			
≤20	14.3	14.1	14.5
21–100	20.4	21.9	19.2
101–500	24.3	25.3	23.5
501–1,000	9.1	10.7	7.8
>1,000	31.9	28.0	34.9
Share of regular customers (%)			
≤20	2.1	3.1	1.3
21–40	3.5	4.1	3.0
41–60	7.4	6.9	7.7
61–80	35.8	26.3	43.2
>80	51.3	59.6	44.8

Source: Authors' calculations.
[a]Industry-related services.

among other things, on the economic situation in Austria and the market environment at the time the survey was conducted.

With an international business cycle downturn, economic growth in Austria lost its momentum after 2000. Following growth rates (in real terms) well above 3%, the economy slowed markedly to rates below 1%. Inflation was on the rise until May 2001 (3.4%) and declined afterward to 1.3% in 2003. The weak economic environment after 2000 also led to an increase in unemployment. A fragile labor market and a low rate of inflation resulted in moderate wage increases.

Questions A1 to A8 are aimed at providing information on the market environment in which the firm runs its business. Table 3.1 shows that in our sample 70 (88)% of the manufacturing (services) sector firms operate mainly in the domestic market. The latter is regarded as their main market if they earn more than 60% of their turnover there. The firms describe their market environment as quite competitive. For the manufacturing (services) sector 53 (65)% of the firms have a market share of less than 10% and 76 (88)% of the firms have more than five competitors. Approximately 80% of the respondents deal primarily with other firms. Just 9% deal directly with consumers and 5% report the government as their main customer. This reflects the fact that almost all firms in our sample belong to the industrial sector. Moreover, regular customers account for more than 60% of turnover in 87% of the respondents. These numbers indicate that the price setting strategies we are investigating refer to producer or wholesale prices. It also seems that an environment of imperfect competition might be a good proxy for the characterization of the market situation.

THE REACTION OF PRICES TO SHOCKS

Time Lag of Price Reactions

In order to investigate the issue of price stickiness, we analyzed the time lag of price adjustments. Firms had to indicate whether they change prices in reaction to shocks or not. In the case of affirmative answer, they were asked to provide the number of months elapsing before the price change. We distinguished between large and small, positive and negative, cost and demand shocks.[4] The results are summarized in Table 3.2, which reports in the first column the fraction of firms holding their prices constant in response to a shock and, in the third one, the mean number of months elapsing between the occurrence of the shock and the price reaction.

The average time lag of price reactions after shocks is four to six months. The answers range from a price adjustment within the same month to a time span of 24 months. The distribution is thus skewed to the right and the median firm waits for three to four months until it changes its price. In reaction to a small positive demand shock the median firm's response time is four months; for all other shocks it is three months. A comparison with the results from Blinder et al. (1998), shown in the fifth column, indicates that

Table 3.2 Speed of price reaction after shocks

Type of shock	Firms holding the price constant		Mean lag		Blinder's mean lag
	%	t-stat	Months	t-stat	Months
Panel A: Small and large shocks					
Small positive demand shock	82	7.26	6.1	5.22	
Large positive demand shock	65		4.6		2.9
Small negative demand shock	79	10.10	4.6	4.50	
Large negative demand shock	52		3.6		2.9
Small cost push shock	39	11.17	4.8	5.86	
Large cost push shock	8		3.8		2.8
Small decreasing cost shock	70	9.67	4.8	4.15	
Large decreasing cost shock	38		4.2		3.3
Panel B: Positive and negative shocks					
Small positive demand shock	82		4.6	-1.48	
Small negative demand shock	82	0.20	5.3		
Large positive demand shock	62		4.1	0.61	
Large negative demand shock	52	2.96	3.8		
Small cost push shock	40		4.5	-2.40	
Small decreasing cost shock	71	-10.19	4.9		
Large cost push shock	8		3.5	-5.05	
Large decreasing cost shock	36	-9.39	4.2		
Panel C: Demand and cost shocks					
Small positive demand shock	81	12.30	6.0	1.25	
Small cost push shock	39		5.2		
Small negative demand shock	80	2.57	4.2	-0.67	
Small decreasing cost shock	72		4.4		
Large positive demand shock	62	16.27	4.6	4.39	
Large cost push shock	9		3.7		
Large negative demand shock	48	1.83	3.6	-2.08	
Large decreasing cost shock	39		4.1		

Source: Tables 1 to 3 in Kwapil et al. (2005b) and authors' calculations.

the mean lag with which Austrian firms react to shocks is slightly longer than that of United States firms, for which it is approximately three months.

We draw the following conclusions, based on statistically significant tests (at the 5% level), reported in table 3.2.

First, more firms change their prices in reaction to large shocks than to small ones, and the reaction is faster for large shocks, as shown in panel A.

Second, a larger share of firms adjust their prices in response to a negative large demand change than to a positive one, as shown in panel B.[5] Conversely, for cost shocks (regardless of the size), more firms react to an increase than to a decrease, with a faster reaction to

upward than to downward shocks. This evidence is in line with
Blinder et al. (1998), who find that price reductions come with a half
month longer lag than price increases.

Finally, results in panel C indicate that significantly more firms react to
cost shocks than to demand shocks (regardless of the size and the
sign of the shock).

All in all, these results partly contradict the common view that prices
adjust more rapidly upward than downward. In fact, the degree and direction of price rigidity seems to depend on the source of the shock. In the face
of significant demand shocks, prices are stickier upward, whereas they are
stickier downward in the face of significant cost shocks. Moreover, prices are
on average stickier in response to shifts in demand than in costs.

Factors Explaining Price Reactions after Shocks

In this subsection we present results from probit regressions to gain some additional insights on how firms in Austria react to shocks and thus on the sources
of price stickiness. In particular, we try to link the reaction to shocks to various
firm's characteristics and to other factors investigated in the questionnaire.

The dependent variable in our regressions records whether a firm has
indicated in the survey that it reacts to shocks by adjusting prices or not, as
described in the previous subsection. We analyze the reaction of firms to
positive and negative demand, as well as to cost shocks. Moreover, we
distinguish between small and large shocks. The different types of shocks
are dealt with separately in our analysis.

For all the estimations carried out in this section, the dependent variable
y_i can take two values: it is equal to unity if a firm has indicated that it
changes its price in response to a given shock, and is zero otherwise. For
this type of dependent variable, a probit model represents an appropriate
framework. In general, the model can be written as

$$P(y_i = 1) = \Phi(x_i'\beta)$$

where β is a vector of coefficients, x_i is a vector of explanatory variables, and
$\Phi(\cdot)$ denotes the cumulative normal distribution function.

Following Small and Yates (1999), we start by including proxies for the
overall degree of competitiveness, such as the market share of the firm and
the number of competitors, as explanatory variables. We also include a
variable that indicates the shape of the marginal cost curve, since a flat shape
can be an explanation for constant prices in response to demand shocks in
the presence of constant markups. Since the relationship between firms and
customers might be important, we include the percentage of sales to regular
customers and to consumers. Customers may incur search and information
costs to make optimal purchases, and these costs might in turn influence the
price setting behavior of producers. Moreover, costumer relationships may
be more important when dealing with consumers as opposed to other
firms (or the government). Pricing to market has also been emphasized as a

potential source of price stickiness. If firms are active in foreign markets, they may set a price that reflects foreign market conditions.

The variables are constructed as follows: for market share we construct a dummy variable (*market*) that takes the value 1 if the market share of the main product is above 30%, and 0 otherwise. The number of competitors (*comp*) is also a dummy that takes the value 1 if a firm has at least five competitors, and 0 otherwise. The slope of the marginal cost curve is captured by the dummy *mc* that takes the value 1 if the firm has indicated that it faces constant marginal costs in question B5 of the questionnaire, and 0 otherwise. Furthermore, we include the fraction of sales achieved through regular customers (*regular*) and the percentage of sales that is generated by selling directly to consumers (*con*) and the variable *export*, which is the share of turnover of the main product generated outside Austria.

We also explore whether the probability of a price change is influenced by explicit contracts and menu costs. For this purpose, we create the dummy variable *explicit* that takes the value 1 if firms make arrangements that guarantee a specific price for a certain period of time. Similarly, the dummy *menu* indicates whether respondents rated menu costs as applicable or higher (grades 3 or 4) for preventing price increases and price reductions.

Finally, we include a set of dummies to capture industry and firm size effects. Firm size is continuous and measured by the number of employees, *emp*. The dummy variable *service* takes on the value unity for firms in the services sector, and 0 otherwise.

In table 3.3, panel A shows the results for demand shocks. From the included proxies for the overall degree of competition, only the number of competitors turns out to be significantly different from 0. It appears that firms having at least five competitors are more likely to adjust prices in reaction to large demand shocks regardless of the sign of the shock. We also find that firms with a large fraction of regular customers are less likely to adjust their prices, whereas firms with a large export share are characterized by a higher probability of reacting to large demand shocks. In the case of small shocks the picture is somewhat different. The fraction of regular customers is still highly significant and negative for both decreases and increases in demand. However, sales to consumers and the shape of the marginal cost curve are also significantly and negatively related to the probability of a price adjustment. This evidence supports the presence of asymmetries in the reaction to positive and negative demand shocks.

In panel B, table 3.3 shows the results for cost shocks. For increases, none of our explanatory variables turns out to be different from zero at conventional significance levels. For decreases, however, we find that firms in the services sector are more likely to react by changing prices. Moreover, with large decreases in costs, firms with a high share of sales to consumers are more likely to adjust their prices.

As a check for robustness, we repeated all our calculations with an alternative definition of the dependent variable. In particular, we defined $y_i = 1$ if the firm indicated that it changes its price within a period of three

Table 3.3 Price reaction to small and large shocks (probit regression)

Variable	Positive shock				Negative shock			
	Small		Large		Small		Large	
	coeff.	p-value	coeff.	p-value	coeff.	p-value	coeff.	p-value
Panel A: Demand shock								
market	0.08	0.75	−0.34	0.12	0.03	0.89	−0.00	0.99
comp	0.41	0.11	0.45	0.03	0.16	0.46	0.57	0.01
mc	−0.15	0.41	0.00	0.99	−0.41	0.03	0.09	0.59
con	−0.01	0.14	−0.00	0.64	−0.01	0.03	0.00	0.69
regular	−0.01	0.00	−0.01	0.01	−0.02	0.00	−0.02	0.00
export	0.00	0.35	0.01	0.01	−0.00	0.55	0.01	0.06
explicit	−0.12	0.58	0.22	0.27	0.13	0.55	0.07	0.75
menu	−0.18	0.54	−0.19	0.54	0.03	0.92	−0.13	0.67
service	−0.04	0.84	0.01	0.94	−0.09	0.64	−0.19	0.28
emp	0.00	0.69	0.00	0.73	0.00	0.86	0.00	0.77
constant	0.01	0.98	0.17	0.71	0.60	0.17	1.06	0.03
Number of obs.	490		476		498		434	
$F_{(10,466)}$	1.75		2.95		2.50		3.05	
Prob>F	0.07		0.00		0.01		0.00	
Panel B: Cost shock								
market	−0.02	0.94	−0.05	0.80	−0.14	0.53	−0.36	0.11
comp	−0.08	0.69	0.34	0.13	0.09	0.70	0.16	0.45
mc	−0.19	0.25	−0.29	0.33	0.26	0.14	−0.05	0.78
con	−0.00	0.37	0.01	0.25	0.00	0.63	0.01	0.00
regular	−0.01	0.27	0.00	0.26	0.01	0.32	0.01	0.03
export	0.00	0.62	−0.00	0.58	0.00	0.80	−0.00	0.40
explicit	0.22	0.26	−0.32	0.30	0.04	0.82	0.17	0.48
menu	−0.35	0.19	−0.47	0.17	−0.01	0.96	−0.32	0.31
service	0.12	0.49	0.32	0.28	1.33	0.00	0.74	0.00
emp	0.00	0.29	0.00	0.84	−0.00	0.20	0.00	0.65
constant	0.78	0.07	1.22	0.00	−1.02	0.04	−0.45	0.33
Number of obs.	487		491		502		476	
$F_{(10,466)}$	0.76		3.07		7.80		4.74	
Prob>F	0.67		0.00		0.00		0.00	

Source: Authors' calculations.

months after the shock, and $y_i = 0$ otherwise. We estimated different versions of our regressions, which include only one indicator of the overall degree of competition, that is, either *market* or *comp*. Our results appear robust to these modifications.[6]

To sum up, we find that in case of demand shocks, a high share of regular customers decreases the probability of a price change, regardless of the size and the sign of the shocks. Since implicit contracts are likely to play an important role when firms deal with regular customers, this outcome is also consistent with the findings reported in Kwapil et al. (2005a), indicating that implicit contracts are a key explanation for price stickiness in our sample. With large demand shocks, a higher number of competitors increases the probability of a price adjustment. Furthermore, firms with a higher share of exports are more likely to change their price in response to large demand shocks. In the case of cost push shocks, there is no statistical evidence for any difference in pricing behavior across firms. Note that this is in line with the result that 92% of all firms adjust their prices in response to a large cost push shock, reported in table 3.2. For a decrease in costs, we find that the services sector is more likely to react with a price adjustment.

Other Adjustment Mechanisms to Demand Shocks

Although the main focus of our survey was to investigate the sluggish adjustment of prices in reaction to a shock, we also enquired about other adjustment mechanisms in response to demand shocks. In question B13 we asked: "If the demand for your main product *decreased temporarily*, what would your first reaction be?" With a set of four questions asked along this line, we tried to distinguish between temporary and permanent, as well as positive and negative shocks. We allowed as answers eight (six) different adjustment mechanisms for demand decreases (increases), and the respondents could choose several items from the list. The numbers given in figure 3.1 represent the fraction of respondents that chose each answer.

As can be seen from the figure, price adjustment is not the principal reaction to a demand shock. As Kwapil et al. (2005a) point out, as explicit and implicit contracts are the major reasons for price stickiness in Austria, only a small fraction of firms is able to adjust its prices in the short run. By and large, this supports the evidence from table 3.2, where also a low fraction of firms reported changing its prices in reaction to a demand shock.[7]

How do firms adjust to demand shocks? Surprisingly, for negative (figure 3.1, panel A) as well as for positive (panel B) shocks (and even for temporary ones), 60 to 80% of firms report adjusting their factor inputs (labor and investment). The buffer function of inventories plays a minor role in Austria. For falls in demand, promotional sales and product innovations are also important strategies. As expected, a comparison of reactions to temporary versus permanent shocks shows that for the latter the adjustment is more pronounced.

SUMMARY

In this chapter, we presented details on how the survey was conducted in Austria and briefly discussed the content of the questionnaire. We also investigated the reaction of prices to cost and demand shocks.

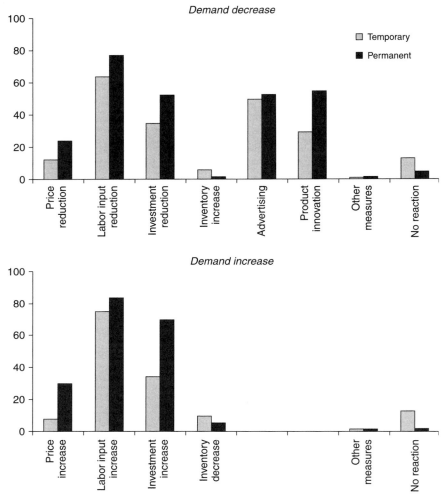

Figure 3.1 Adjustments in reaction to a demand shock (percentages).
Source: Authors' calculations.

The average time lag between a shock and the price adjustment is four to six months. Furthermore, firms react asymmetrically to cost and demand shocks: prices are stickier downward than upward in the face of cost shocks and the opposite is true in the case of large demand shocks.

Concerning demand shocks, regardless of the size and the sign of the shocks, we find that having a high share of regular customers reduces the probability of a firm's making a price change. Consistently with the observation of sluggish price behavior, a majority of firms report that they adjust factor inputs in reaction to such shocks.

If we interpret a monetary policy shock as a demand shock, it follows that monetary policy has an asymmetric impact on the Austrian economy. The price reaction to a monetary contraction should be more pronounced than to an expansionary monetary policy shock.

APPENDIX

This appendix reports detailed elements on the weighting and the response rates.

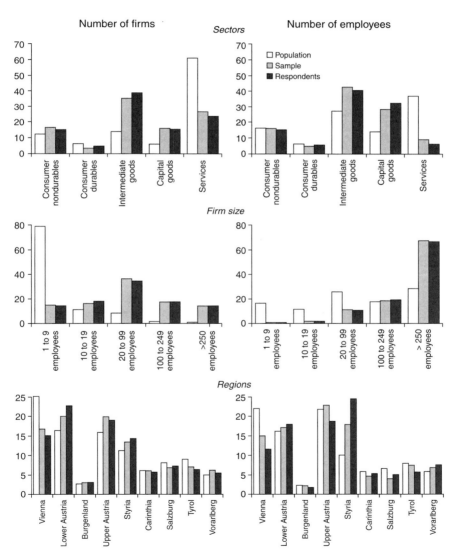

Figure 3.A.1 Comparison of population, sample, and respondents' characteristics (percentages). *Source:* Authors' calculations.

Table 3.A.1 Post-stratification weights and response rates[a]

Sector		Strata		Population		Respondents		Weights	Response rate
	h	Size	Z_h	Z_h/Z %	z_h^r	z_h^r/z^r %	w_h	n_h^r/n_h^g %
Food and	1	1	41,749	5.01	1,711	1.29	1.15	45.9
beverages	2	2	28,346	3.40	6,583	4.96	0.20	33.9
(15)								
Textile and	3	1	13,391	1.61	1,019	0.77	0.62	29.9
leather	4	2	19,403	2.33	5,619	4.23	0.16	33.3
(17–19)								
Wood products	5	1	18,632	2.24	1,656	1.25	0.53	47.9
(20)	6	2	13,863	1.66	2,506	1.89	0.26	23.3
Paper products	7	1	18,978	2.28	678	0.51	1.32	21.3
(21–22)	8	2	20,433	2.45	8,758	6.60	0.11	39.3
Coke and	9	1	16,544	1.99	966	0.73	0.81	33.7
chemicals	10	2	35,425	4.25	10,034	7.56	0.17	34.0
(23–25)								
Mineral products	11	1	11,655	1.40	1,352	1.02	0.41	46.6
(26)	12	2	15,144	1.82	4,938	3.72	0.14	33.3
Metal products	13	1	3,543	0.43	358	0.27	0.47	42.1
(27)	14	2	27,358	3.28	9,957	7.50	0.13	47.8
Fabricated metal	15	1	36,982	4.44	1,819	1.37	0.96	35.4
(28)	16	2	29,644	3.56	9,894	7.45	0.14	34.1
Machinery (29)	17	1	21,810	2.62	1,369	1.03	0.75	30.7
	18	2	36,578	4.39	20,063	15.11	0.09	39.8
Machinery	19	1	16,683	2.00	1,151	0.87	0.68	41.2
equipment	20	2	41,550	4.99	8,727	6.57	0.22	36.2
(30–33)								
Vehicles (34–35)	21	1	4,001	0.48	75	0.06	2.51	18.8
	22	2	14,868	1.78	18,874	14.22	0.04	48.5
Manufacturing	23	1	25,090	3.01	1,085	0.82	1.09	44.4
n.e.c. (36)	24	2	13,372	1.60	5,696	4.29	0.11	50.0
Transport	25	1	63,696	7.64	906	0.68	3.31	32.9
(60–63)	26	2	24,370	2.92	695	0.52	1.65	35.7
Real estate and	27	1	30,682	3.68	739	0.56	1.96	27.4
business	28	2	11,515	1.38	1,337	1.01	0.41	38.1
(70–73)								
Other business	29	1	117,488	14.10	2,185	1.65	2.53	36.8
activities (74)	30	2	54,767	6.57	1,751	1.32	1.47	14.8

Table 3.A.1

Sector	Strata h	Size	Population Z_h	Z_h/Z %	Respondents z_h^r	z_h^r/z^r %	Weights w_h	Response rate n_h^r/n_h^g %
Sewage and	31	1	4,345	0.52	149	0.11	1.37	18.9
refuse (90)	32	2	1,307	0.16	110	0.08	0.56	33.3
			Z		z^r			
Total			833,210	100.00	132,760	100.00	26.3	36.0

Source: Social security accounts, WIFO-BCS, and WIFO-OeNB PSB surveys.
[a]Sectors: NACE two-digit sector (or the sum of them); Size 1 (2): firms with less than 100 (100 or more) employees; Z_h: number of employees in the population stratum h; Z: number of employees in the population; z_h^r number of employees of the responding firms; z_h^r: number of firms that responded in stratum h; $z_g^g_h$: number of firms in the gross sample in stratum h; $wh = (Z_h/Z)/(z_h^r/z_h) \times \varphi$: post-stratification weight for stratum h, with $\varphi = 3.88$ being a constant rescaling factor to ensure that the total number of firms after post-stratification equals $N = 873$, the total number of respondents.

Acknowledgments We are grateful to the IPN participants for their useful comments and suggestions. Special thanks go to Gerhard Schwarz and Martina Geider for excellent research assistance in conducting the survey.

NOTES

1. NACE stands for "Nomenclature générale des Activités économiques dans le Communautés Européennes", which is the standard industrial classification for economic activities used by EUROSTAT.

2. We sent slightly different versions of the questionnaires to manufacturing and services firms. The original German versions of the questionnaires can be obtained from the authors upon request.

3. The alternative answers were that, for instance, the parent company, the main client, or a regulatory authority determines prices.

4. We did not distinguish between temporary and permanent shocks in this set of questions. However, in question B13 we focused on temporary versus permanent demand shocks and how firms react to them.

5. We did not ask explicitly whether firms adjust their prices upward or downward. However, we assume that they reduce their prices in response to shrinking demand and increase their prices in response to boosted demand. The answers to question B13, where we investigate how firms react to demand shocks (e.g., with price or with output changes), justify this assumption, as not a single firm indicated that it would increase prices in the face of falling demand.

6. Detailed results are available upon request.

7. A direct comparison of the numbers for decreases and increases in demand is not meaningful, as the number of response categories is different.

REFERENCES

Blinder, Alan S., Elie R. D. Canetti, David E. Lebow, and Jeremy B. Rudd. 1998. *Asking about Prices: A New Approach to Understanding Price Stickiness*. New York: Russell Sage Foundation.

Kwapil, Claudia, Josef Baumgartner, and Johann Scharler. 2005a. The price-setting behavior of Austrian firms. Some survey evidence. European Central Bank Working Paper No. 464. Frankfurt am Main: European Central Bank.

Kwapil, Claudia, Johann Scharler, and Josef Baumgartner. 2005b. How are prices adjusted in response to shocks? Some survey evidence from Austrian firms. Mimeo. Vienna: Oesterreichische Nationalbank.

Small, Ian, and Antony Yates. 1999. What makes prices sticky? Some survey evidence for the United Kingdom. *Bank of England Quarterly Bulletin* 39: 262–271.

4

Why Are Prices Sticky?

Evidence from an Ad Hoc Survey in Belgium

Luc Aucremanne & Martine Druant

This chapter reports the results of an ad hoc survey, conducted among some 2,000 Belgian firms active in industry, construction, trade, and business services. The sectors covered by the survey together represent 60% of GDP. Its content is based to a large extent on similar surveys conducted by Blinder et al. (1998) in the United States, Hall et al. (2000) in the United Kingdom, and Apel et al. (2005) in Sweden and has benefited from discussions within the Eurosystem Inflation Persistence Network.

The main purpose of the survey is to help describe the price rigidity prevailing in the economy. This, in turn, provides valuable information for understanding the dynamic reaction of output and inflation to shocks, as well as the transmission mechanism of monetary policy. The structure of the survey (and of this chapter) has its roots in the crucial role played by price rigidities in the New Keynesian literature, as it is for instance reviewed by Taylor (1999). The survey mainly addresses the qualitative aspects of pricing mentioned by Taylor. These relate to (1) the role of market power as a necessary condition for price stickiness to be a temporary equilibrium, (2) the question of whether price adjustment is mainly time- or state-dependent, (3) aspects related to the information used when reviewing prices, and (4) the relative role of nominal and real rigidities. Taylor characterizes the two latter aspects as two main factors that can help understand the persistence puzzle, that is, the fact that standard sticky price models have difficulties in generating sufficient inertia in both output movements and inflation, relative to what is observed empirically.

The survey has the major advantage of being capable of providing qualitative information on these issues and is, therefore, a complement to recent quantitative analysis of price rigidities based on producer or consumer prices (see for instance Aucremanne and Dhyne 2004 and 2005 for Belgium, and Dhyne et al. 2005 for the euro area). A survey indeed allows for a distinction to be made between price reviews and price changes, whereas observed price data will only reveal the final outcome of the price setting process, that is, the changes. Addressing the price reviewing stage explicitly also allows for an examination of the nature of the information set used.

This is particularly relevant, as the use of backward-looking information may be a supplementary cause of inflation persistence. Finally, survey results are probably the only source of information on the basis of which it is possible to get an answer to the question of whether the infrequent adjustment of prices is due to the existence of price adjustment costs (nominal rigidities) or to the fact that the frictionless real (or relative) price does not change or changes only marginally when aggregate output fluctuates (real rigidity) or is due to a combination of both.

The rest of this chapter is organized as follows. After a brief description of the survey design and its representativeness in the first section, the main results with respect to the context of the firms' activity are presented in the second section. The third section addresses the timing and frequency of price adjustments, as well as the nature of the information set used. The fourth section examines the various causes of price rigidity, namely the existence of several sorts of nominal and real rigidities. Finally, the fifth section summarizes the main conclusions.

DESIGN AND REPRESENTATIVENESS OF THE SURVEY

The National Bank of Belgium (NBB) took on the task of designing the questionnaire and organizing the survey. An initial draft questionnaire was sent out in December 2003 to 20 industrial firms. Fourteen firms took part in this pilot study. Based on their reactions, the original questionnaire was slightly adapted. In February 2004, the final questionnaire was sent out to all firms in the sample. They had three weeks in which to reply.

The questionnaire (see the Appendix to the book) contains three types of questions. In the first, participants are asked to indicate the importance of a particular statement by selecting "1 = unimportant," "2 = of minor importance," "3 = important," "4 = very important," or "? = I don't know." This analysis gives the average scores for the first four options, disregarding question marks and nonresponses. Based on the mean scores, statements have been ranked in descending order. Moreover, for each pair of statements, a Wilcoxon signed rank test has been carried out, in order to know whether or not the importance attached by respondents to the first statement is significantly different from the importance attached to the second statement and so on. In the second type of question, participants had to check off just one answer in a list. In the third, which was only used in a few cases, they had to enter exact figures.

The sample of firms is the same as that for the NBB's monthly business survey (table 4.1). It comprises 5,600 firms active in industry, construction, trade, and business services. The sectors covered represent 60% of GDP. Nearly 2,000 firms replied to the survey. This represents a 35% overall response rate, ranging from 32% in construction to 38% in industry. Starting from the number of firms participating in the survey, specific response rates

Table 4.1 The sample

	Population size[a]	Sample size[b]	Number of respondents	Response rate (%)	Weighting based on turnover
Total	394,339	5,600	1,979	35	100.0
Industry	44,439	2,000	753	38	30.9
Construction	70,685	1,200	384	32	5.0
Trade	132,292	1,400	478	34	36.7
Business services	146,923	1,000	364	36	27.4

Source: National Bank of Belgium.
[a]Firms liable for VAT, belonging to the sectors covered by the survey; 2001 data.
[b]The sample is the same as that for the monthly business survey.

were calculated for each question. All of these response rates exceeded 90%, except for the (difficult) question on the price elasticity of demand. Here, the response rate amounted to 47% (question A6).

In the original sample for the business survey, which was composed in close collaboration with the business federations, large firms are overrepresented. In order to make the results representative for the population of firms as a whole, stratification was subsequently carried out for the ad hoc survey. For this purpose, the population was divided into twelve strata according to the sector of activity and size class in terms of the number of employees. Next, weighting coefficients were calculated per stratum on the basis of turnover. In the remainder of this chapter we present turnover-weighted results.

Two other aspects regarding the representative nature of the survey are worth mentioning. First, it was found that 82% of the participating firms set their prices independently, whereas the remaining 18% have their prices set by the parent company or by the government (question A8). This means that, for the majority of firms, the decision-making process associated with pricing takes place entirely within the firm itself. These firms were therefore able to answer the whole of the questionnaire, including all the questions on the qualitative aspects of price setting. The other firms were only able to answer a shorter list of questions focusing mainly on the frequency of price changes. That information can, in fact, always be supplied, even if the price is not actually set by the firm. Second, firms were asked to answer the questions by considering their "main product." The usefulness of this lies in the fact that the firms have to concentrate on a specific product in order to give reliable answers to the questions on price adjustment, but at the same time there must be no doubt about the representative nature of the product for the firm as a whole. It turned out that the survey answers are also quite representative in this respect, as, on average, 69% of turnover is generated by the main product (question A2).

CONTEXT OF THE FIRMS' ACTIVITY: MARKET STRUCTURE AND DEGREE OF COMPETITION

The market structure and level of competition are crucial external factors for price setting behavior. A certain level of market power is necessary for a firm's decisions on pricing to make sense, because without market power (perfect competition), the price always corresponds to the marginal costs and no markup is applied. In such an environment, price rigidity does not exist. The survey therefore assesses these external factors in depth. The results are summarized in table 4.2.

Over half of the industrial firms replied that the Belgian market is the main market for their main product (question A3). Firms in construction, trade, and business services are exclusively active on the Belgian market. The survey puts the emphasis on the main market for the same reason as that

Table 4.2 Market structure and level of competition (percentages unless otherwise stated)

	Industry	Construction	Trade	Business services	Total
1. Main market for the main product					
Domestic market	55	—	—	—	—
Foreign market	45	—	—	—	—
2. Relationship with customers					
Long-term	64	21	27	56	41
Other	36	79	73	44	56
3. Firms with more than 20 competitors	16	44	26	45	29
4. If you were to increase the price by 10%, by what percentage would the turnover of your main product fall?[a]	50	58	33	35	40
5. Price setting method [b]					
We set our price fully according to our costs and a completely self-determined profit margin	2.9	3.5	3.0	3.1	3.0[c]
We set our price according to the price of our main competitor(s), meaning that we do not determine our profit margin ourselves	2.9	2.6	2.8	2.7	2.8
6. Firms practicing pricing to market	60	—	—	—	—

Source: National Bank of Belgium.
[a] Average percentage of turnover.
[b] Average scores (1 = unimportant, 2 = of minor importance, 3 = important, 4 = very important).
[c] A Wilcoxon signed rank test rejects the hypothesis that the statement has the same overall importance as the one below at the 5% level of significance.

justifying the choice of the main product, namely the desire to achieve sufficiently specific responses.

On average, approximately 40% of turnover comes from other firms with whom there is a long-term relationship (question A5). Industry and business services are the sectors where this proportion is highest, amounting to around 60%. Conversely, construction and trade are geared more toward direct sale to consumers.

Firms with over 20 competitors are least numerous in industry, where they total only 16%, against almost 45% in construction and business services (question A4). The main implication of this is probably that the industrial firms taking part in the survey as well as their competitors are mainly large firms, rather than implying that the actual level of competition is lower in industry. The price elasticity question (question A6) may provide additional information on the level of competition. On average, a 10% price increase causes turnover to fall by 40%; after conversion to quantities, this implies an average demand elasticity of 4.5. Elasticity is highest in construction and industry and lowest in trade. These elasticities indicate a fairly high level of competition, particularly in construction and industry. However, the results clearly deviate from a situation of perfect competition (infinitely large elasticity).

The ability of firms to determine their profit margin entirely independently also gives some indication of their market power. This issue is addressed by question A9, in which a score had to be given to two statements: namely, "We set our price fully according to our costs and a completely self-determined profit margin," and "We set our price according to the price of our main competitor(s), meaning that we do not determine our profit margin ourselves." The average score for the first option is 3.0, slightly higher than for the second option (2.8), and the importance attached to each possibility differs at the 5% level of significance. As one might expect, the scores obtained by the two statements show a negative correlation in the individual responses. The correlation is −0.29 and is, given the large number of firms, significantly different from zero from a statistical point of view. This correlation is, however, relatively low in economic terms, indicating that a nonnegligible number of firms had difficulties in clearly expressing a preference in favor of one of the statements. Nevertheless, the results obtained tend to suggest that, on average and to a small extent, Belgian firms are rather price makers than price takers, except in industry, where both statements receive the same average score. This is another indication that competition is strongest in industry.

In view of the openness of the Belgian economy, the main market is probably not the only market for industrial firms. Section C of the survey tries to find out about pricing practices in other markets. Almost 60% of industrial firms apply pricing to market (question C1). That is a very high percentage, given that payments within the euro area are effected in a common currency and the bulk of Belgian exports is destined for euro area countries. In industry, 73% of turnover comes from other countries, namely

54% from the euro area and 19% from elsewhere. The primary reason for applying pricing to market is to take account of competitors' prices (question C2). Finally, over 60% of participants said that competition is keener in the foreign market (question C3).

All in all, the results relating to market structure and the degree of competition clearly deviate from a situation of perfect competition. They are, however, also different from the monopolistic competition situation used in modern macroeconomic models; they tend rather to indicate an oligopolistic market structure. Results also indicate that industry faces the fiercest competition. The price elasticity of demand is greater there, and industrial firms are more price takers than the average. They also state that they have less market power abroad than in the home market and that competitors' prices are the main reason for applying pricing to market.

TIMING AND FREQUENCY OF PRICE ADJUSTMENTS

From the preceding section, it appears that firms have some market power and, therefore, conditions are met to make the pricing decision meaningful. Price stickiness can thus be a (temporary) equilibrium. Whether this is the case or not can be assessed by asking questions about the timing and frequency of price adjustments.

The price adjustment process generally takes place in two stages: the review stage and the price adjustment stage. In the review stage, the firm examines its scheme for maximizing profits in order to determine the price that it would like to charge. As this process entails costs, firms are unlikely to assess their prices continuously; it is therefore useful to check how often this review process is carried out. Moreover, addressing explicitly the review stage also allows for checking which type of information is used when reviewing prices. If the desired price resulting from the review process is different from that actually charged, the price may be altered, but not necessarily. Price reviews and changes are not necessarily carried out simultaneously, and reviews are probably more frequent, since supplementary specific costs are associated with an actual change of price. It is therefore important to address the frequency of actual price changes as well, separately from that of the price reviews. This phased method also implies that price reviews will be more likely to take place at regular intervals than price changes. That means that it is appropriate to investigate in the first phase of the adjustment process—in other words, the price reviews—whether the process is time dependent or state dependent.

Regarding this particular aspect, the survey participants were asked to specify when they review their prices, and were offered the following options (question B1a): "at specific time intervals" (interpreted as time dependent), "in reaction to specific events" (interpreted as state dependent), and "mainly at specific time intervals, but also in reaction to specific events" (interpreted as essentially time dependent, but possibly state dependent if a sufficiently significant event occurs). Price review that is purely time

Table 4.3 Time-dependent and state-dependent price reviews (percentages)

	Normal situation	Specific events
Time dependent	65.7	25.7
State dependent	34.3	74.3

Source: National Bank of Belgium.

dependent (i.e., even when a sufficiently significant event occurs) covers 26% of firms (table 4.3), whereas 34% of firms use purely state-dependent reviewing (even when the situation is normal). For 40% of firms, the price review process is normally time dependent but may be state dependent if a sufficiently significant event occurs. This means that if the situation is normal, most firms (66%) adopt time-dependent reviewing. However, when a significant event occurs, 40% of firms will shift to state-dependent price reviewing, implying that 74% of firms will adopt a state-dependent behavior. This pattern was found relatively homogenously across sectors.

The existence of a combination of time-dependent and state-dependent price setting was also observed in the micro prices underlying the Belgian consumer price index (CPI) (Aucremanne and Dhyne 2004, 2005). The above figures are very similar to the Swedish results of the survey by Apel et al. (2005). Moreover, the fraction of state-dependent firms is far more pronounced than suggested by the breakdown in Klenow and Kryvtsov (2006), as they found that only 10% of the variance of the United States CPI inflation stems from state-dependent factors, whereas the bulk of the variance is associated to time-dependent behavior. Our results therefore shed a different light on the macroeconomic models currently used, which are generally based on time-dependent price setting.

In principle, when setting its price, a firm takes account of all the relevant information for maximizing its profits, thus including expectations concerning the future, since, in the case of price rigidity, the new price will remain in force for some time. However, a firm may behave in a different way, because there is a cost involved in collecting all the relevant information. In that case, the pricing is no longer optimal from a macroeconomic point of view, and as the price setting becomes less forward looking, it gives rise to additional inflation persistence.

As regards the information used when reviewing prices (questions B2a and B2b), the survey gives firms a choice between two options, namely the application of a rule of thumb (e.g., a change equal to a fixed amount or percentage, indexation on the basis of the consumer price index, etc.) or the consideration of a wide range of information (demand, costs, competitors' price, etc.) relevant for profit maximization. Firms choosing the second option had to state whether this information concerns the present context or both the present and future context in which they operate. Only this last pricing method, which uses the fullest set of information, is associated with totally optimizing behavior.

These questions refer to the last time the price was reviewed, as the pilot study showed that it was not easy to ascertain the general behavior of firms on this issue. It is in fact entirely possible that they may apply a rule of thumb during a particular period and, after a certain time, switch to an optimal form of behavior when they realize that their price is too far away from its optimal level.

It turns out that 34% of firms optimized their prices (table 4.4). Another one-third of firms adopted an intermediate position by taking account of a wide range of information but only in relation to the current economic situation. Around 37% applied a rule of thumb. This means that, to a large extent, the pricing behavior is not optimal and this friction in price setting may be a significant source of inflation persistence. Industry achieves the highest score in terms of totally optimizing behavior (45% of firms consider a wide range of information that also takes account of the future) and the lowest score as regards the use of rules of thumb (only 29%). This sector, in fact, faces greater competition and is therefore more inclined to adopt an optimal pricing approach than the other sectors, because a miscalculated price here has a greater impact on demand. The use of a rule of thumb, such as simple price indexation based on the consumer price index, is most common in the business services sector.

The firms applying some form of time-dependent price reviewing were asked to specify how often they review their prices (question B1b). Moreover, all firms were asked to indicate how often they actually change their prices (question B5). The two questions give an idea of the frequency of price adjustment and permit calculation of the average implicit duration in months between two successive price reviews and two successive price changes.

The average duration between two successive price reviews is 10 months (only available for firms applying some form of time dependence), against almost 13 months between two successive price changes (available for all firms). When the latter duration is computed by using the same subsample of firms answering the price review question (i.e., only those applying some

Table 4.4 How did you review the price of your main product last time? (percentages)

	Industry	Construction	Trade	Business services	Total
We applied a rule of thumb	28.7	35.8	35.0	46.1	36.6
We considered a wide range of information					
related to the present context	26.6	38.5	34.6	22.9	29.4
related to the present and the future context	44.7	25.7	30.4	30.9	34.0

Source: National Bank of Belgium.

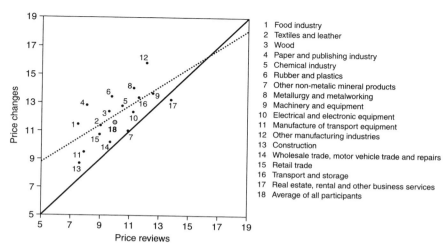

Figure 4.1 Price reviews and changes by subsector (average duration between two successive reviews or changes). Survey participants with time-dependent price reviews only. *Source:* National Bank of Belgium.

form of time dependence), it amounts to 12 months (figure 4.1). This subsample also allows us to make a coherent comparison between the two types of duration at the subsector level. Apart from real estate, rental, and other business services, we find in all subsectors that prices are reviewed a little more frequently than they are changed. The lower frequency of price changes tends to confirm the existence of specific costs related to the price change process. Moreover, there is a positive correlation between the two phenomena: firms with a short period between two reviews generally have a short period between two changes, and vice versa.

Overall, we find a relatively high degree of price stickiness, which corroborates the findings in Aucremanne and Dhyne (2004, 2005). The average intervals between reviews and between price changes are longest in business services and shortest in construction. Industry and trade are in an intermediate position. Although we clearly find that prices are reviewed fairly infrequently, the available evidence does not necessarily imply that the most important friction lies in this stage of the pricing process. Indeed, optimal behavior at the firm level can lead to infrequent price reviews, merely as a result of the knowledge that prices can only be changed infrequently. The positive correlation between both phenomena supports this interpretation.

CAUSES OF PRICE RIGIDITY

The survey also made it possible to examine the reasons for rigid pricing. For this purpose, a fairly long list of fifteen possible explanations for price rigidity was included in the questionnaire, and participants were asked to give a score corresponding to the importance of each of them (question B4). This list concerns both nominal and real price rigidities, as the recent literature emphasizes precisely the interplay between both types of rigidity as an important factor in shaping observed inflation and output dynamics.

According to the survey results, the explanations ranked at the top are implicit and explicit contracts (table 4.5). This is in line with the results already mentioned in regard to the main customers, which showed that a large part of the turnover (over 40% on average) comes from customers with whom there is a long-term relationship. In industry and business services, where the score of implicit and explicit contracts is slightly above average, the share of this type of customer relationship is actually close to 60%. Although it is obvious to consider explicit contracts as a source of nominal rigidity, it is less so in the case of implicit contracts, although the particular wording of the question (e.g., the notion "even if our competitors also change their price") refers to changing nominal rather than real prices. Other explanations connected with theories on nominal rigidities—namely judging quality by price, the risk of having to readjust the price in the opposite direction, and changing non–price elements—rank much lower. Psychological price thresholds, information gathering costs, and even physical menu costs come at the bottom of the list.

The low score attached to information gathering costs seems to be at odds with the fact that the price reviewing process occurs relatively infrequently and is not always based on a full range of relevant information. However, as already mentioned, the infrequent reviewing could be induced by the knowledge that prices cannot be changed continuously, rather than caused by high information gathering costs. The relatively low score could also reflect the fact that these costs relate in some cases to a limited information set used for nonoptimal price setting.

Price inertia is also due to a large extent to real rigidities, i.e. the fact that firms, provided that they can change their price, are reluctant to adapt their real or relative price in reaction to changes in aggregate output. One reason may be that the marginal-costs curve is flat, implying that the incentive to change prices over the business cycle is substantially reduced. This explanation is ranked third in the list of fifteen theories. Another possibility is that the incentive to adjust real prices is reduced by countercyclical shifts in the real marginal-costs curve. The survey tests two explanations. First, in the case of thick market effects on the supply side, the costs of attracting customers are reduced in a period of prosperity, and this keeps prices at a low level. Second, the theory of countercyclical financing costs states that owing to capital market imperfections, external financing becomes more expensive during recessions. This keeps marginal costs, and hence prices, at a high level. Both explanations are, however, ranked relatively low in the list of factors hampering price adjustment.

Yet another factor that can reduce the incentive to adjust relative prices over the business cycle is the fact that desired markups show countercyclical movements. The survey tests four possibilities in this respect. The first one

Table 4.5 Ranking of the possible explanations for price rigidity (mean scores)

	Type of rigidity[a]	Industry	Construction	Trade	Business services	Total[b]
Implicit contracts	N	2.6	2.5	2.4	2.6	2.5
Explicit contracts	N	2.9	2.9	1.8	2.7	2.4
Flat marginal costs curve	R/A	2.3	2.6	2.4	2.5	2.4
Importance of fixed costs/liquidity constraints	R/B	2.2	2.4	2.2	2.2	2.2
Kinked demand curve	R/B	2.4	2.0	2.3	2.0	2.2
Shifting customer clientele	R/B	1.9	2.1	2.2	2.1	2.1
Thick market demand	R/B	2.0	1.9	2.3	1.8	2.0
Judging quality by price	N	1.7	1.9	2.1	2.0	1.9
Thick market supply	R/C	1.7	1.8	1.9	1.7	1.8
Risk of having to readjust price in the opposite direction	N	1.8	1.6	1.8	1.7	1.8
Changing non price elements	N	1.9	2.0	1.6	1.6	1.7
Countercyclical financing costs	R/C	1.6	1.8	1.7	1.7	1.7
Psychological price thresholds	N	1.4	1.6	2.0	1.6	1.7
Information gathering costs	N	1.6	1.7	1.6	1.6	1.6
Physical menu costs	N	1.5	1.5	1.6	1.4	1.5

Source: National Bank of Belgium.

[a]N: nominal rigidity; R/A: real rigidity/flat real marginal costs curve; R/B: real rigidity/countercyclical movements in desired markups; R/C: real rigidity/countercyclical shifts in the real marginal costs curve.

[b]The dotted lines indicate that a Wilcoxon signed rank test rejects the hypothesis that the statements immediately above and below the line have the same overall importance at the 5% level of significance.

puts the emphasis on the importance of fixed costs or liquidity constraints or on a combination of both. According to the theory, during a recession, when cash flow is low, the price has to be maintained (which means increasing the markup) in order to continue to have sufficient liquidity. Two elements are in fact combined, namely that customers only respond gradually to a price reduction and that it therefore takes some time for the reduction to generate an increase in turnover, and that there are capital market imperfections that lead to liquidity constraints. The latter are due to a reduction in cash flow combined with the fact that a (major) part of the costs remains constant.

The second statement describing a situation in which the desired markup is countercyclical relates to the kinked demand curve theory, according to which firms are not tempted to be the first to change their prices. They are afraid that their competitors will not follow suit with a (relative) price increase and that they will thus lose market share. A (relative) reduction in price could spark a process prejudicial to all the market players. In both cases, firms prefer to wait for their competitors to act before then doing the same. Meanwhile, they prefer to adjust their markup downward (or upward) when marginal costs increase (or fall) during an upturn (or downturn) in economic activity.

The third theoretical concept is related to shifting customer clientele, based on two types of customers. On the one hand, are the loyal customers with low demand elasticity, and on the other hand are the customers who are less loyal, thereby presenting higher demand elasticity. Since the loyal ones remain customers during a recession, the price elasticity of demand is lower than during boom periods. Consequently, the markup increases during a recession, so that the price can remain unchanged or only a small reduction is needed. During a boom, the opposite happens: higher elasticity, lower markup, and prices unchanged or only slightly increased.

The last explanation concerning countercyclical markups relates to thick market effects on the demand side. It is worded as follows in the questionnaire: "When our customers buy a lot, they are more interested in comparing prices than when they do not buy a lot. They are more sensitive to price changes in booms than in recessions." This implies that the elasticity of demand is greater during periods of expansion, which counteracts cyclical increases in marginal costs by a reduction in the markup. During recessions, the elasticity of demand is lower and the markup is higher, thus preventing prices from falling.

These four explanations relating to the countercyclical character of markups are ranked fourth to seventh in the list of theories, and their ranks are statistically significantly different from those assigned to quite a number of the lower-ranked nominal rigidities already discussed. These high ranks are, moreover, fairly comparable to those obtained in the Swedish survey of Apel et al. (2005), where the first three statements take the sixth, fourth, and eighth place, respectively, in a list of thirteen. Only the explanation relating to the thick market on the demand side is an exception, ranking twelfth in the Swedish survey, whereas it ranks seventh in the Belgian survey.

These findings conform to recent economic theory, in which the interaction between nominal and real rigidities is specifically proposed as an explanation for inertia in price setting.

CONCLUSIONS

Belgian firms evidently operate in a context different from perfect competition. Firms do have some market power, and it is greater in the domestic market than abroad. The majority of industrial firms apply a pricing-to-market strategy. Several survey results suggest that the environment in which industrial firms operate is generally more competitive than it is for the other sectors. It seems that all the conditions are met for the price decision-making process to be meaningful and for price rigidity to be a (temporary) equilibrium situation.

As regards the frequency and timing of price adjustments, the survey results indicate a relatively high degree of price rigidity. The average time elapsing between two successive price reviews totals 10 months, and between two successive price changes it is 13 months. The highest degree of price rigidity is found in business services, and the lowest in construction. In the majority of firms, price reviews are time dependent when the situation is normal. If sufficiently significant economic shocks occur, however, the process becomes largely state dependent. These findings are in line with those obtained on the basis of quantitative micro data on consumer prices (Aucremanne and Dhyne 2004, 2005 for Belgium; Dhyne et al. 2005 for the euro area).

The explanations for price rigidity concern both nominal and real rigidities. Nominal rigidities are essentially connected with the existence of implicit and explicit contracts, whereas physical menu costs and costs related to the gathering of information relevant for the price setting decision play only a minor role. Real rigidities concern mainly a flat cyclical marginal costs curve and various sources of countercyclical movements in desired markups. These aspects of real rigidities both rank relatively high among the factors hampering price adjustment and are more important than quite a number of sources of nominal rigidity. These findings conform to recent economic theory, in which the interaction between the two types of rigidities is specifically proposed as an explanation for inertia in price setting.

Moreover, it was found that only one-third of firms conducted their last price review on the basis of a full set of information that also incorporated expectations concerning the future, whereas the other firms based their decisions on more limited information or applied a rule of thumb. Industry's approach to pricing focused more on the future, whereas business services made greater use of rules of thumb. The fact that a significant proportion of firms applied pricing that is not geared to the future may be an additional source of inertia in the inflation process.

REFERENCES

Apel, Mikael, Richard Friberg, and Kerstin Hallsten. 2005. Microfoundations of macroeconomic price adjustment: Survey evidence from Swedish firms. *Journal of Money Credit and Banking* 37: 313–338.

Aucremanne, Luc, and Emmanuel Dhyne. 2004. How frequently do prices change? Empirical evidence based on the micro data underlying the Belgian CPI. National Bank of Belgium Working Paper Research Series No. 44. Brussels: National Bank of Belgium.

Aucremanne, Luc, and Emmanuel Dhyne. 2005. Time-dependent versus state-dependent pricing: A panel data approach to the determinants of Belgian consumer price changes. National Bank of Belgium Working Paper Research Series No. 66. Brussels: National Bank of Belgium.

Blinder, Alan S., Elie R. D. Canetti, David E. Lebow, and Jeremy B. Rudd. 1998. *Asking about Prices: A New Approach to Understanding Price Stickiness*. New York: Russell Sage Foundation.

Dhyne, Emmanuel, Luis J. Álvarez, Hervè Le Bihan, Giovanni Veronese, Daniel Dias, Johannes Hoffmann, Nicole Jonker, Patrick Lünnemann, Fabio Rumler, and Juko Vilmunen. 2005. Price setting in the euro area: Some stylized facts from individual consumer price data. European Central Bank Working Paper No. 524. Frankfurt am Main: European Central Bank.

Hall, Simon, Mark Walsh, and Antony Yates. 2000. Are UK companies' prices sticky? *Oxford Economic Papers* 52: 425–446.

Klenow, Peter, and Oleksiy Kryvtsov. 2006. State-dependent or time-dependent pricing: Does it matter for recent U.S. inflation? NBER Working Paper No. 11043. Cambridge MA: National Bureau of Economic Research.

Taylor, John B. 1999. Staggered price and wage setting in macroeconomics. In *Handbook of Macroeconomics*, ed. John B. Taylor and Michael Woodford. Amsterdam: North-Holland.

5

Asymmetries in Price Setting

Some Evidence from French Survey Data

Claire Loupias & Roland Ricart

This chapter investigates asymmetries in the price setting behavior of French manufacturing firms. The results are based on a survey conducted by the Banque de France during Winter 2003–2004. The survey was carried out by the Survey Division of the Banque de France, in collaboration with local branches. The population belonging to the original sample was the same as that listed by the Banque de France for the manufacturing monthly business survey (around 4,300 firms). Firms were allowed to answer either in face-to-face interviews or by phone and mail, depending on their preference and the organization of the local Banque de France's branch collecting the answers. The questionnaires were answered mainly by CEOs and CFOs; overall, 1,662 firms answered, amounting to a global response rate of around 40%. The survey refers to the firms' "main product," defined as the one that generated the highest turnover in 2003. All statistics computed are weighted. Information on the structure of the questionnaire, how data were collected, the main characteristics of the interviewed firms, price rigidity, and the main factors underlying price stickiness can be found in Loupias and Ricart (2006). The whole questionnaire is reproduced in the Appendix to the book.

The potential asymmetries in price adjustment vary with the type of shock. As far as demand is concerned, the Blanchard and Fischer (1989) textbook reports traditional explanations for kinked demand curves. In this view, if a firm decreases its price, its competitors follow suit, whereas if it increases its price, it is not necessarily followed by others. This would lead to more sensitive price to downward demand shocks than to upward shocks. This is confirmed by our data. As far as cost shocks are concerned, several empirical papers (see for example, Peltzman 2000 on quite a large sample of diverse products, and Davis and Hamilton 2004 on gasoline prices) report that output prices tend to respond faster to input increases than to decreases. This is also consistent with our data.

Asymmetries are studied here from three points of view. The first section of the chapter presents the percentage of firms changing their price in 2003 and the magnitude of price changes. The second section examines how firms perceive the opportunity to change prices in response to four types of shocks: increase/decrease in demand/costs. The third section is devoted to the differences induced by firms' characteristics, market structure, and so on in the responses to shocks. The fourth section concludes.

MAGNITUDE AND ASYMMETRIES IN PRICE CHANGES

Size of Individual Price Changes

Individual price changes over the year 2003 are huge compared to the aggregate production price index (PPI) increase: −5% (+3%) for the median decrease (increase), against 0.3% for the PPI.

Table 5.1 reports the percentage of firms changing their price and the magnitude of price changes; as the magnitude is known only between the beginning and the end of the year, it considers only the price change between January and December 2003. The last column documents the evolution of the French PPI by type of good in the same period for reference purposes.

The total magnitude of price changes over the year increases with the number of price changes but not smoothly (see table 5.1): it is higher for one price change compared to two, but lower for one or two price changes compared to three to twelve.

If one assumes that all the price changes within a year for one firm are of the same sign, one can compute the average magnitude of price changes per firm in 2003 (see the last row in table 5.1). The first (third) quartile of the average magnitude of price increases (decreases) is +1% (−2%). Obviously, these figures are smaller than the total price changes, but their magnitude is still sizable compared to the average inflation rate for 2003 (+0.3%).

There is a considerable degree of heterogeneity in the price setting behavior depending on the type of good (see table 5.1). This applies both to the decisions to change prices and the magnitude of price changes: the magnitude is the highest for capital goods and the lowest for motor vehicles. As far as decisions to change prices are concerned, prices for intermediate goods change more frequently than those for consumer goods. This might be due to the fact that intermediate goods are sold to firms and not to households. Firms are probably less afraid to "antagonize" other firms with price variations, as they can explain to them why these variations are justified.[1] Zbaracki et al. (2004) study managerial and customer costs of price adjustment by using data from a large United States industrial manufacturer and its customers and offer qualitative evidence of customer "antagonization" costs. This is consistent with the fact that price changes at an intermediate level are not passed on to customers.

This large magnitude of price changes would argue in favor of menu cost (such as Mankiw 1985) against quadratic adjustment costs (such as Rotemberg 1982). However, Loupias and Ricart (2006) report that the menu cost theory is not supported at all by French decision makers. Zbaracki et al. (2004) find that adjustment costs are the sum of three types of costs: menu,

Table 5.1 Frequency and magnitude of price changes in 2003 (percentages)

	Firms changing their price[b]	Firms decreasing their price[c]	Firms increasing their price[d]	Price increases over total price changes	Size of negative price change[e]			Size of positive price change[e]			PPI change[e]
					1st quartile	median	3rd quartile	1st quartile	median	3rd quartile	
Total[a]	75.8	20.8	55.0	72.5	−10	−5	−3	2	3	6	0.3
By type of good											
Food, beverages, tobacco	82.1	7.3	74.7	91.0	−7	−5	−4	2	4	6	2.5
Consumer goods	61.6	22.5	39.1	63.4	−10	−7	−5	2	3	7	−0.1
Motor vehicles	86.7	9.9	76.9	88.6	−3	−2	−2	1	1	1	0.7
Capital goods	74.6	19.9	54.7	73.3	−14	−10	−3	2	5	20	−0.1
Intermediate goods	77.7	27.9	49.8	64.1	−11	−5	−2	2	3	5	0.1
By number of price changes per firm											
1	93.1	21.4	71.7	77.0	−10	−4	−2	2	3	4	
2	95.4	13.2	82.3	86.2	−8	−3	−2	1	1	3	
3 to 6	93.6	63.5	30.1	32.1	−14	−12	−5	5	10	20	
7 to 12	84.3	35.4	48.8	57.9	−15	−14	−1	3	5	8	
over 12	91.0	39.4	51.6	56.7	−25	−15	−7	4	13	30	
Average magnitude of price changes in 2003[f]					−6	−3	−2	1	2	4	

Source: Authors' calculations and INSEE.

[a] Total of manufacturing, including food but excluding energy.
[b] Percentage of firms for which the price of their main product at the end of 2003 is different than at the beginning.
[c] Percentage of firms for which the price of their main product at the end of 2003 is lower than at the beginning.
[d] Percentage of firms for which the price of their main product at the end of 2003 is higher than at the beginning.
[e] Magnitude of price change is defined as the rate of price change between the beginning and the end of 2003.
[f] Defined as percentage of price variation between the beginning and the end of 2003 over the number of price changes in 2003.

managerial, and customer costs. Their relative weights in total price adjustment are 4%, 23%, and 73%, respectively; menu costs are not found to be convex, whereas many components of managerial and customer costs are. This should lead to small and numerous price changes. But the firm they studied follows a once-a-year price adjustment policy despite ample opportunities to change prices at other times during the year. The firm's managers report that pricing activities are deeply embedded in the existing social structure, and that customers would not stand more than one price change per year.[2] It thus seems that this firm has to deal with convex costs under a once-a-year price adjustment constraint. This would be consistent with our data: large infrequent changes despite a very bad score of the menu cost theory.

Asymmetries in Price Changes and Downward Nominal Rigidity

Price increases are more likely than price decreases: they account for around 70% of total changes (see table 5.1). These results are in line with those obtained by Martins for Portugal in chapter 10. The magnitude of positive price changes is lower than for negative ones: +3% for the median increase and −5% for the median decrease for the whole of year 2003. Thus, the PPI growth rate observed in manufacturing reflects the higher frequency of price increases compared to price decreases and not the higher magnitude of price increases compared to price decreases.

These results may also be compared to those obtained by Baudry et al. (2007) from the price records used for computing the French CPI, even though they are based on different sources and relate to different periods (2003 instead of July 1994 to February 2003). Baudry et al. find that price increases account for 60% of total changes and that the magnitude of the median increase (+4%) is also smaller than that for the median decrease (−5%). It seems that the gap in the frequency of price increases between the survey and individual price records arises from the differences in techniques (Martins, in chapter 10, reports similar evidence for Portugal).

ASYMMETRIES IN RESPONSES TO SHOCKS

Survey respondents were also asked to specify whether or not they were able to change their price in the case of a major and lasting event, and if so, how long after the shock. As far as total price adjustment is concerned, prices are found to be more rigid downward than upward in the case of cost shocks; the opposite is true for demand shocks. Regarding the speed of adjustment, firms react faster to a demand decrease than to an increase, whereas there is no evidence of different responses for cost shocks. Firms are found to react faster to demand than to cost shocks. Details are given below.

Asymmetries in the Final Responses to Shocks

To allow comparisons in the frequency of price changes, we restrict our analysis to the firms that have faced the four types of shocks considered

Table 5.2 Do you modify the price of your main product in reaction to a shock? (percentages)[a]

	Higher demand or lower competition (1)	Lower demand or higher competition (2)	Higher unit variable production costs (3)	Lower unit variable production costs (4)
Yes	77.1	78.3	81.7	73.3
fully	*72.1*	*80.4*	*59.3*	*71.6*
partly	*27.9*	*19.6*	*40.7*	*28.4*
No	22.9	21.7	18.3	26.7
Total	100	100	100	100
No. of observations	963	963	963	963

Source: Authors' calculations.
[a]For the significance of proportion differences, see the Appendix to this chapter.

(increase/decrease in demand/costs) during the two years preceding the survey, in order to have the same sample of firms in each case.

We are left with 963 observations (see table 5.2). Our comments focus on the share of respondents that report to adjust prices. More firms change their prices when they face a decrease rather than an increase in demand (the difference amounts to 1.2 percentage points).[3] On the other hand, many more firms change their prices when they face higher than lower costs (8.4 percentage points). The comparison among types of shocks is uneasy. It seems that the share of firms that modify their price in response to shocks is the highest for increasing cost shocks (82% of the firms respond at least partly), and the lowest for decreasing cost shocks (73%). In the middle comes the share of firms that modify their price in response to negative (78%) and positive (77%) demand shocks.[4]

It is hard to comment on the amplitude of reactions to shocks. When firms respond to shocks, more seem to do so fully in the case of lower demand (80%) than in the case of increased demand (72%). Things are the same for cost shocks: more firms respond fully in the case of lower costs than in the case of higher ones.

Asymmetries in the Speed of Adjustment

To allow comparisons between the speed of adjustment, we restrict our analysis to the firms that answered that they were able to change prices in response to the four types of shocks. We are left with 335 firms, covering 55% of the manufacturing value added.[5] Results are given in table 5.3. Firms react faster to a decrease in demand (37.2% react within one month) than to an increase (34.7%), whereas there is no evidence of asymmetries in the speed of the response to cost changes.[6]

Table 5.3 How long does it take to change prices in reaction to a shock?
(percentages)[a]

Delay	Higher demand or lower competition (1)	Lower demand or higher competition (2)	Higher unit variable production costs (3)	Lower unit variable production costs (4)
Shorter than 1 month	34.7	37.2	33.4	31.2
Between 1 and 3 months	34.5	34.9	27.4	29.3
Longer than 3 months	30.8	28.0	39.2	39.5
No. of observations	335	335	335	335

Source: Authors' calculations.
[a]For the significance of proportion differences, see the Appendix to this chapter.

Blinder et al. (1998) do not find any evidence for the United States that firms respond more rapidly to cost shocks than to demand shocks. French manufacturing firms, however, are found to respond more rapidly to demand shocks than to cost shocks. This is true for both positive and negative shocks.

ASYMMETRIES IN PRICE REACTION TO DEMAND AND COST SHOCKS: MORE DETAILS

Loupias and Ricart (2006) report that ratings of the price stickiness theories by French decision makers are different depending on whether the response to shocks should lead to an increase in price or to a decrease. Furthermore, differences are not the same for cost shocks and demand shocks. Indeed, the average score (on a four-point scale) given by firms' decision makers on the importance of changing price after a shock is 2.5 for an increase in labor costs but only 1.9 for a decrease. As far as demand shocks are concerned, however, the score is 2.3 for decreases but only 2.0 for increases. Prices are therefore more rigid downward than upward for cost shocks, while the reverse is true for demand shocks.

In this section we try to determine which factors might increase the probability to change prices in reaction to a demand or labor cost shock. The empirical model directly follows the approach presented in Small and Yates (1999). The model tries to explain why firms consider that an increase (decrease) in labor cost or demand is a reason to raise (lower) the price of their main product. Four dummies (0, 1) are created (from question 13) to capture the probability that firms would raise or lower prices in response to a change in demand or labor costs (pud, pld, puc, plc).[7] Five kinds of explanations are considered: the degree of market competition, the type of customer relationship, the cost structure, the existence of public price regulation schemes, and the exposure to foreign markets. The degree of market competition is measured by four dummies—*Rivals_none, Rivals_5, Rivals_20,* and *Rivals_more_ than_ 20*—constructed from question 3 and measuring the fact that the firm has no competitors at all, less than five, between five and twenty, or more than twenty competitors. Relationships with customers are summarized by two dummies: *Customer_firms* and *Price_no_discr.* The first measures whether or not more than 60% of the turnover generated by the main product is sold to other firms (question 4), and the second measures whether or not the price is the same for all customers (question 6). Regulation of market price is measured by *Price_reg,* which is equal to 1 if the price is regulated (question 9) and 0 otherwise. The dummy for cost structure, *Mc,* captures whether or not the marginal cost is constant (question 8). The impact of pricing to market on price stickiness is gauged by two different measures of the exposure to foreign market: *Ext_mkt* and *Exp_share.* The two dummies equal 1 if foreign markets are the most important for the firm and if the firm's export turnover is higher than 40%, respectively. These two almost tautological variables come from two different parts of the questionnaire (preliminary requirements and question 2) and so do not exactly reflect the same information.

Finally, we decided to control for the type of manufacture (five dummies), the size (six dummies constructed from the number of employees), and the geographical area (five dummies) of the firm.

Six regressions were run, one for each of the four dependent variables mentioned above: price response to positive/negative demand/cost shocks, and two pooled regressions (with either negative or positive shocks) on demand and costs. In these last two cases, a dummy was introduced to identify whether or not the shock is positive. In order to get comparable results, we ran our regressions on a common sample; due to missing values, this consisted of 882 observations. Probit estimates are given in tables 5.4 to 5.6.

Our main results are as follows. First, market structure affects price stickiness. The variable measuring that a firm is in competition with less than five firms *(Rivals_5)* significantly reduces the likelihood that prices will rise (decrease) in response to an increase (decrease) in demand; this also holds, as expected, when demand shocks are pooled. This result is consistent with those obtained by Small and Yates (1999) for the United Kingdom. If we look at the regressions concerning the responsiveness of prices to a change in costs, we find that market structure matters only in the case of a positive shock *(Rivals_5* and *Rivals_20* are both significant). It is not significant or wrongly signed in the case of the United Kingdom.

Second, the variable indicating whether firms' marginal cost is flat *(Mc)* does not significantly affect the likelihood that prices will rise (decrease) in response to an increase (decrease) in demand. It was significantly negatively signed for an increase in demand in the United Kingdom.

Third, the type of customers and the pricing strategy by type of customers modify price stickiness in the following way. The fact that the firm does not discriminate prices *(Price_no_discr)* decreases the probability of adjusting prices in response to a demand shock (either positive or negative) but the type of customer *(Customer_firms)* has no impact. As far as cost shocks (either

Table 5.4 Price adjustment in response to a demand shock (probit estimates)

	Reduce price in response to a fall in demand				Raise price in response to an increase in demand			
	(1)		(2)		(3)		(4)	
Constant	0.08	0.72	0.29	0.04	0.13	0.56	0.11	0.48
Rivals_none	0.14	0.54			0.05	0.83		
Rivals_5	−0.48	0.00	−0.59	0.00	−0.49	0.00	−0.49	0.00
Rivals_20	0.16	0.26			−0.02	0.88		
Rivals_more_ than_20	ref				ref			
Mc	0.12	0.22			0.08	0.42		
Customer_firms	0.05	0.66			−0.04	0.69		
Price_no_discr	−0.57	0.00	−0.62	0.00	−0.53	0.00	−0.56	0.00
Price_reg	−4.92	0.97			−4.39	0.96		
Ext_mkt	0.02	0.90			0.22	0.11	0.30	0.00
Exp_share	0.02	0.89			0.13	0.33		
Food	0.00	0.99	−0.02	0.87	−0.20	0.22	−0.20	0.21
Consumer goods	−0.14	0.34	−0.29	0.03	−0.32	0.04	−0.47	0.00
Motor vehicles	0.20	0.40	0.26	0.25	0.11	0.64	0.20	0.40
Capital goods	0.43	0.00	0.41	0.00	−0.08	0.52	−0.07	0.59
Intermediate goods	ref		ref		ref		ref	
Paris area	−0.33	0.05	−0.32	0.05	−0.67	0.00	−0.62	0.00
North-west	−0.51	0.00	−0.54	0.00	−0.41	0.01	−0.43	0.00
North-east	−0.20	0.16	−0.24	0.07	−0.25	0.08	−0.24	0.09
South-west	−0.33	0.06	−0.33	0.05	−0.12	0.48	−0.10	0.58
South-east	ref		ref		ref		ref	
0–19 employees	−1.21	0.07	−1.24	0.06	−1.57	0.06	−1.56	0.06
20–49 employees	0.60	0.01	0.59	0.00	−0.49	0.06	−0.50	0.05
50–99 employees	0.05	0.79	0.09	0.63	−0.37	0.08	−0.32	0.11
100–249 employees	−0.15	0.24	−0.10	0.39	−0.28	0.04	−0.24	0.07
250–499 employees	0.27	0.04	0.29	0.02	0.03	0.82	0.05	0.67
at least 500 employees	ref		ref		ref		ref	
Number of obs.	882		882		882		882	
Weight	0.86		0.86		0.86		0.86	
Log L	−509.1		−518.9		−452.7		−459.9	
Pseudo R²	0.211		0.185		0.189		0.168	
Chi-Square (d.o.f.)	147.9(22)	0.00	128.4(15)	0.00	123.1(22)	0.00	108.6(16)	0.00

Source: Authors' calculations.
Notes: Weighted estimates. Values in italics are the estimated p-values of the test statistics. Columns (1) and (3) present results obtained including all the variables in regressions; columns (2) and (4) present those obtained with only the significant ones. Ref stands for reference and indicates the variable to which each sign of coefficients must be interpreted relatively.

Table 5.5 Price adjustment in response to a cost shock (probit estimates)

	Reduce price in response to a fall in costs				Raise price in response to a rise in costs			
	(1)		(2)		(3)		(4)	
Constant	−0.81	*0.00*	−0.84	*0.00*	−0.41	*0.05*	−0.41	*0.05*
Rivals_none	0.30	*0.22*			0.44	*0.07*	0.43	*0.07*
Rivals_5	−0.03	*0.87*			−0.32	*0.03*	−0.32	*0.02*
Rivals_20	0.00	*1.00*			−0.28	*0.05*	−0.28	*0.05*
Rivals_more_ than_20	ref				ref		ref	
Customer_firms	−0.45	*0.00*	−0.46	*0.00*	−0.56	*0.00*	−0.56	*0.00*
Price_no_discr	0.03	*0.84*			−0.03	*0.83*		
Price_reg	−0.97	*0.005*	−0.93	*0.01*	−1.57	*0.00*	−1.58	*0.00*
Ext_mkt	−0.13	*0.36*			−0.24	*0.09*	−0.24	*0.09*
Exp_share	0.23	*0.08*	0.18	*0.11*	0.23	*0.07*	0.23	*0.07*
Food	0.09	*0.61*	0.10	*0.54*	0.12	*0.45*	0.11	*0.46*
Consumer goods	0.30	*0.05*	0.30	*0.05*	0.49	*0.00*	0.48	*0.00*
Motor vehicles	1.12	*0.00*	1.19	*0.00*	0.32	*0.20*	0.32	*0.20*
Capital goods	0.51	*0.00*	0.52	*0.00*	0.49	*0.00*	0.49	*0.00*
Intermediate goods	ref		ref		ref		ref	
Paris area	−0.29	*0.13*	−0.26	*0.16*	−0.28	*0.11*	−0.28	*0.11*
North-west	0.26	*0.10*	0.26	*0.10*	0.34	*0.03*	0.34	*0.03*
North-east	0.01	*0.94*	0.02	*0.89*	0.35	*0.02*	0.35	*0.02*
South-west	−0.27	*0.17*	−0.24	*0.22*	0.16	*0.35*	0.16	*0.35*
South-east	ref		ref		ref		ref	
0–19 employees	−0.47	*0.53*	−0.45	*0.55*	−0.30	*0.64*	−0.30	*0.64*
20–49 employees	−0.20	*0.48*	−0.20	*0.46*	0.20	*0.39*	0.20	*0.38*
50–99 employees	0.23	*0.26*	0.27	*0.17*	0.88	*0.00*	0.88	*0.00*
100–249 employees	0.14	*0.31*	0.15	*0.27*	0.64	*0.00*	0.64	*0.00*
250–499 employees	0.14	*0.30*	0.13	*0.32*	0.46	*0.00*	0.46	*0.00*
at least 500 employees	ref		ref		ref		ref	
Number of obs.	882		882		882		882	
Weight	0.86		0.86		0.86		0.86	
Log L	−423.7		−425.3		−500.8		−500.8	
Pseudo R^2	0.143		0.138		0.224		0.224	
Chi-Square (d.o.f.)	86.5 (21)	*0.00*	83.3(16)	*0.00*	157.9(21)	*0.00*	157.8(20)	*0.00*

Source: Authors' calculations.

Notes: Weighted estimates. Values in italics are the estimated p-values of the test statistics. Columns (1) and (3) present results obtained including all the variables in regressions; columns (2) and (4) present those obtained with only the significant ones. Ref stands for reference and indicates the variable to which each sign of coefficients must be interpreted relatively.

Table 5.6 Price adjustment: pooling positive and negative shocks (probit estimates)

	Change price in response to a change in demand				Change price in response to a change in costs			
	(1)		(2)		(3)		(4)	
Constant	0.27	0.23	0.36	0.03	−0.87	0.00	−0.99	0.00
Demand_up/ Cost_up	−0.38	0.00	−0.71	0.00	0.52	0.00	0.51	0.00
Rivals_none	0.11	0.64			0.36	0.12		
Rivals_5	−0.46	0.00	−0.53	0.00	−0.19	0.21	−0.16	0.11
Rivals_20	0.08	0.57			−0.15	0.31		
Rivals_more_ than_20	ref				ref			
Mc	0.10	0.32						
Customer_firms	0.01	0.95			−0.51	0.00	−0.51	0.00
Price_no_discr	−0.55	0.00	−0.59	0.00	−0.004	0.97		
Price_reg	−4.74	0.97			−1.28	0.00	−1.20	0.00
Ext_mkt	0.12	0.40	0.17	0.13	−0.18	0.20		
Exp_share	0.07	0.60			0.23	0.08	0.17	0.12
Food	−0.09	0.55	−0.10	0.50	0.11	0.49	0.13	0.42
Consumer goods	−0.23	0.13	−0.38	0.01	0.38	0.01	0.37	0.01
Motor vehicles	0.16	0.50	0.24	0.30	0.73	0.00	0.84	0.00
Capital goods	0.18	0.14	0.18	0.15	0.49	0.00	0.52	0.00
Intermediate goods	ref		ref		ref		ref	
Paris area	−0.47	0.01	−0.43	0.01	−0.28	0.13	−0.24	0.19

positive or negative) are concerned, the fact that customers are mainly firms (*Customer_firms*) lowers the likelihood of a price adjustment.

Fourth, price regulation (*Price_reg*) decreases the probability to change prices in response to a cost shock (either positive or negative) and has no impact in the case of a demand shock.

Fifth, pricing to market has an impact on price stickiness. The fact that the main market is foreign (*Ext_mkt*) increases the probability of raising prices in response to a rise in demand, but not when demand falls (neither *Ext_mkt* nor *Exp_share* is significant). The fact that the firm's export turnover is more than 40% (*Exp_share*) increases the probability of adjustment in response to a cost shock (either positive or negative). This is the opposite of what is

Table 5.6

| | Change price in response to a change in demand | | | | Change price in response to a change in costs | | | |
	(1)		(2)		(3)		(4)	
North-west	−0.46	*0.00*	−0.48	*0.00*	0.31	*0.05*	0.31	*0.04*
North-east	−0.22	*0.12*	−0.24	*0.09*	0.19	*0.20*	0.20	*0.18*
South-west	−0.23	*0.18*	−0.22	*0.21*	−0.03	*0.88*	0.02	*0.91*
South-east	ref		ref		ref		ref	
0–19 employees	−1.36	*0.06*	−1.36	*0.06*	−0.39	*0.57*	−0.38	*0.58*
20–49 employees	0.15	*0.48*	0.15	*0.48*	0.02	*0.93*	0.06	*0.81*
50–99 employees	−0.14	*0.47*	−0.09	*0.63*	0.57	*0.003*	0.64	*0.00*
100–249 employees	−0.21	*0.11*	−0.16	*0.21*	0.41	*0.002*	0.42	*0.00*
250–499 employees	0.15	*0.24*	0.18	*0.16*	0.31	*0.02*	0.32	*0.02*
at least 500 employees	ref		ref		ref		ref	
Number of obs.	1764		1764		1764		1764	
Weight	0.86		0.86		0.86		0.86	
Log L	−490.7		−498.8		−472.4		−476.1	
Pseudo R^2	0.152		0.134		0.155		0.146	
Chi-Square (d.o.f.)	130.1 (23)	*0.00*	114.1 (17)	*0.00*	129.1 (22)	*0.00*	121.7 (18)	*0.00*

Source: Authors' calculations.
Notes: Weighted estimates. Values in italics are the estimated p-values of the test statistics. Columns (1) and (3) present results obtained including all the variables in regressions; columns (2) and (4) present those obtained with only the significant ones. Ref stands for reference and indicates the variable to which each sign of coefficients must be interpreted relatively.

obtained for the United Kingdom, where the share of exports decreases the probability of changing prices in response to a rise or a decrease in costs. The dummy *Ext_mkt* is not significant in the case of a fall in costs but is significantly negative when costs rise. So this last effect probably offsets part of the previous one.

Results obtained with the pooled regressions confirm the descriptive statistics discussed above: whereas a demand increase is significantly less likely to induce a price response than a demand decrease, a cost increase is significantly more likely to induce a price change than a cost decrease. These results are consistent with those obtained for the United Kingdom.

CONCLUSIONS

This chapter investigates asymmetries in the price setting behavior of French manufacturing companies. The data were collected from a specific survey conducted by the Banque de France during Winter 2003–2004. Prices adjust infrequently but the size of the adjustment is quite large. Among firms that modified the price of their main product between the beginning and the end of 2003, 70% increased it, whereas 30% decreased it. The magnitude of price decreases is higher than that of price increases. Thus, there is no sign of downward price rigidity in French manufacturing.

Asymmetries in price stickiness are found to be different for cost shocks compared to demand shocks: prices are more rigid downward than upward for cost shocks, but the reverse is true for demand shocks. Although these findings are very robust, the magnitude of these phenomena is quite small. Whether small asymmetries may be magnified by other phenomena to have large effects is an issue that is left for further research.

APPENDIX: SIGNIFICANCE TESTS

Table 5.A.1 reports results of tests for the significance of pairwise reaction to shocks reported in tables 5.2 and 5.3. The figures contained in the table are the p-values related to the null hypothesis H0: proportion differences are not significant.

Table 5.A.1 Significance tests of reaction to shock differences in tables 5.2 and 5.3

	(1)/(2)	(3)/(4)	(1)/(3)	(1)/(4)	(2)/(3)	(2)/(4)
Table 5.2						
Yes fully	0.00	0.01	0.00	0.10	0.00	0.00
Yes partly	0.00	0.00	0.00	0.66	0.00	0.00
No	0.04	0.00	0.00	0.01	0.01	0.00
Table 5.3						
a delay shorter than 1 month	0.01	0.16	0.18	0.01	0.00	0.00
a delay between 1 and 3 months	0.67	0.54	0.05	0.12	0.04	0.08
a delay longer than 3 months	0.01	0.52	0.00	0.00	0.00	0.00

Significance tests on table 5.2 are computed on the proportions below

	(1)	*(2)*	*(3)*	*(4)*
Yes fully	55.6	63.0	48.4	52.5
Yes partly	21.5	15.3	33.3	20.8
No	22.9	21.7	18.3	26.7
Total	100.0	100.0	100.0	100.0

Source: Authors' calculations.

Acknowledgments We would like to thank Bénédicte Fougier for her participation in setting the questionnaire. We are indebted to all participants to the IPN for very useful discussions on a previous version of this chapter, and more particularly to Hervé Le Bihan and Patrick Sevestre. We are also grateful to Serge Nakache, Laurent Baudry, and Sylvie Tarrieu for their wonderful research assistance. The usual disclaimer applies.

NOTES

1. Rotemberg (2005) has developed a model where consumers care about the fairness of prices and react negatively only when they become convinced that prices are unfair.

2. In Blinder et al. (1998), the first reason given by respondents for not changing prices more frequently than they do is that "it would antagonize or cause difficulties for their customers."

3. The equality of the two coefficients is statistically rejected at the 5% level; see table 5.A.1 in the Appendix to the chapter.

4. The equality of all these coefficients on a pairwise basis is statistically rejected at the 5% level.

5. This is not really unexpected, since one can envisage that many manufactures are not subject to contradictory lasting changes in their environment/production costs within any two-year period.

6. The equality of these two coefficients is statistically rejected at the 1% level.

7. *Pud* equals 1 if an increase in demand has an impact on price that is either "important" or "very important" and 0 otherwise. *Pld* equals 1 if a decrease in demand has an impact on price that is either "important" or "very important" and 0 otherwise. *Puc* equals 1 if an increase in costs (cost of labor) has an impact on price that is either "important" or "very important" and 0 otherwise. *Plc* equals 1 if a decrease in costs (cost of labor) has an impact on price that is either "important" or "very important" and 0 otherwise.

REFERENCES

Baudry, Laurent, Hervé Le Bihan, Patrick Sevestre, and Sylvie Tarrieu. 2007. What do thirteen million price records have to say about consumer price rigidity. *Oxford Bulletin of Economics and Statistics* forthcoming.

Blanchard, Olivier J., and Stanley Fischer. 1989. *Lectures on Macroeconomics.* Cambridge Mass.: MIT Press.

Blinder, Alan S., Elie R. D. Canetti, David E. Lebow, and Jeremy B. Rudd. 1998. *Asking about Prices: A New Approach to Understanding Price Stickiness.* New York: Russell Sage Foundation.

Davis, Michael C., and James D. Hamilton. 2004. Why are prices sticky? The dynamics of wholesale gasoline prices. *Journal of Money, Credit, and Banking* 36: 17–37.

Loupias, Claire, and Roland Ricart. 2006. Price setting in the French manufacturing sector: New Evidence from Survey Data. *Revue d'Economie Politique* 4: 541–554.

Mankiw, N. Gregory. 1985. Small menu costs and large business cycles: A macroeconomic model of monopoly. *Quarterly Journal of Economics* 100: 529–538.

Peltzman, Sam. 2000. Prices rise faster than they fall. *Journal of Political Economy* 108: 466–502.

Rotemberg, Julio J. 1982. Sticky prices in the United States. *Journal of Political Economy* 90: 1187–1211.

Rotemberg, Julio J. 2005. Customer anger at price increases: Changes in the frequency of price adjustment and monetary policy. *Journal of Monetary Economics* 52: 829–852.

Small, Ian, and Antony Yates. 1999. What makes prices sticky? Some survey evidence for the United Kingdom. *Bank of England Quarterly Bulletin* 39: 262–271.

Zbaracki, Mark J., Mark Ritson, Daniel Levy, Shantanu Dutta, and Mark Bergen. 2004. Managerial and customer costs of price adjustment: Direct evidence from industrial markets. *Review of Economics and Statistics* 86: 514–533.

6

Price Setting in German Manufacturing

Evidence from New Survey Data

Harald Stahl

This chapter presents the results of a survey conducted in June 2004 on price setting behavior on a sample of 1,200 German manufacturing firms. The firms reported why they respond with a delay to shocks and how they adjust their prices. The chapter is organized as follows. The first section starts with a description of the survey. The second section investigates how prices are set and, in particular, whether firms have price setting power. The third section analyzes factors that hamper price changes, and the fourth section discusses why firms adjust prices. The fifth section reports the results of a cluster analysis, aimed at identifying groups of firms with distinct reasons for price stickiness. The sixth and final section summarizes the findings and offers conclusions. For the questionnaire, see the Appendix to the book.

THE SURVEY

The German survey on producer price setting was carried out on behalf of the Deutsche Bundesbank by the IFO Institute in Munich, which sent out the questionnaire to the 2,500 participants of its monthly business cycle survey in manufacturing. The enclosed letter stated that the questionnaire was part of the business cycle survey and intended to enable the matching of cross-sectional and time-series information at the plant level. This approach also avoided a duplication of questions that might otherwise have annoyed participants.

The sample of the business cycle survey developed historically and is *by purpose*.[1] Large firms are overrepresented. Firms report for product groups, which in most cases coincide with plants. Most firms are single plant firms. Larger plants may reply for several product groups. In these cases the largest product group was selected for the special survey. The name of the product group was mentioned at the beginning of the questionnaire. Eventually,

1,200 firms or 47% of all firms participated, mainly those that participate regularly in the business cycle survey. All descriptive results are weighted with poststratification weights, based on the number of plants according to the two-digit NACE classification and size class.

The questionnaire consists of two parts: "general information" and "information regarding price formation." The first part mainly concerns the market the firm operates in. In the second part firms are asked how they set their prices, and, on a four-point scale, whether price setting and price reviewing follow a time- or a state-dependent pattern, whether companies are forward or backward looking, what causes price changes, and what the likely reasons for a postponement of price changes are. The questionnaire states that the scale goes from "1 = minor importance" to "4 = great importance." In the tables and text of the present analysis, the numeric scale is translated as follows: "1 = not important," "2 = moderately important," "3 = important," and "4 = very important."

The questionnaire focuses on domestic sales prices as opposed to price setting in foreign markets. This turned out not to be a major problem. According to the responses to questions 2 and 3, domestic price setting should apply for roughly 60% of firms and 95% of sales. This astonishingly high share is partly due to exports through wholesalers.

PRICE SETTING

Most sticky price models (e.g., Woodford 2003; Rotemberg 1982) postulate that firms are price setters and that they apply some type of markup pricing. However, these models do not generate the inflation persistence diagnosed by vector autoregression analysis. Two ways of mitigating this problem are to let a fraction of firms index their prices to another price or price index (Yun 1996; Christiano et al. 2005) and to assume that a fraction of firms follow a price leader with a lag, a form of strategic complementarity.

Table 6.1 shows that most of the firms (88%) report that they do have a certain margin for setting their prices (question 8). Markup pricing (73%) dominates the price setting of firms with market power.[2] There are only a few firms that set their prices by applying a constant markup on calculated unit costs (4%). These firms may be price leaders, that is, the most powerful firms. The majority of firms use a time-varying markup (69%). They use calculated unit costs as reference and take market conditions and competition into account. The second most common behavior of firms is to take the price of the main competitor as a benchmark. This is the case for 17% of price setters.[3] Most of them may be less powerful than their main competitor and therefore do not challenge him by undercutting his price. However, there may also be powerful firms in an oligopoly that have to watch their competitors closely. Indexation to another price is almost nonexistent.

Table 6.1 Types of price setting of firms with price setting power (percentages)[a]

Type of price setting	Share of firms
Constant markup on calculated unit costs	4.4
Taking calculated unit costs as a reference and varying the markup, accounting for market and competition conditions	69.4
Taking the price of the main competitor as a reference	16.9
Tying the price to another price (e.g. wage)	2.2 (5.0)[b]
Other	7.1 (11.9)[b]
Total	100.0 (106.9)[b]

Source: Author's calculations.
[a]Answers have been rescaled for missing responses.
[b]Values in brackets include double counts. For instance, 5.0% report tying their price to another price and applying another type of price setting.

REASONS FOR PRICE STICKINESS

This section investigates why firms do not adjust their prices immediately after shocks, even if they have some market power. Since the questionnaire was restricted to two pages, it includes only some of the theories presented in chapter 1 that were surveyed by other euro area countries. Theories that seemed a priori less important in manufacturing or had turned out to be of low importance in other studies were disregarded. Two examples are psychological pricing points and judging quality by price, proposed by Blinder et al. (1998), which ranked twenty-second and twenty-fifth out of 27 theories in Köhler's (1996) survey for Germany. Also, physical menu costs did not perform well in the two studies, but since this explanation is so prominent in the literature, it was included nonetheless. For transitory shocks, coordination failure, and the price elasticity of demand, different replies were possible depending on the direction of the price adjustment.

On average, explicit nominal contracts prohibiting a price change for a certain period of time are the most important reason for price stickiness at the plant level. One reason for this is that they are almost ubiquitous. A tabulation of the average importance of fixed nominal contracts by the duration of contracts indicates that firms do not feel hamstrung by short contracts but by those with a duration longer than half a year (see table 6.2).

Coordination failure achieved the second rank (table 6.3). With a mean score of 2.6 compared to 1.9, the fear that the firm will lose market share because competitors will not follow the price increase is larger than the fear to trigger a price war by a price reduction. Therefore, coordination failure causes, on average, more upward than downward stickiness.

The third rank is shared by three theories: price elasticity of demand, price change preferably at a fixed point of time, and price change preferably according to a fixed time interval.[4] A two sided t-test did not reject the hypothesis of

Table 6.2 Importance of written contracts according to contract length[a]

Duration in months	Average importance (mean score)	Share of firms[b] (%)	Average sales share[c] (%)
0	1.4	12.9	0.0
$1 < x \leq 3$	2.3	18.1	53.2
$3 < x \leq 6$	2.4	18.8	58.7
$6 < x \leq 9$	2.7	1.2	53.4
$9 < x \leq 12$	2.7	44.7	61.6
$12 < x$	2.6	3.3	57.1
Total (mean)	2.4	100.0	51.4

Source: Author's calculations.
[a]Answers have been rescaled for missing responses.
[b]18.1% of firms have written contracts lasting on average longer than one month but not longer than three months.
[c]The firms with written contracts lasting on average longer than one month but not longer than three months sell on average 53.2% of their sales under these contracts.

equality. The next in the list are transitory shocks and sluggish costs, that is, absence of a price change because there is no trend in costs. However, the average importance of these theories is not much lower than that of the theories ranked second and third. A clear difference shows up for physical menu costs. They earned the lowest rank, with an average score of 1.4.

Table 6.3 Average importance assigned to various reasons for price stickiness (mean scores)[a]

	Price increase	Price reduction	Total	Rank[b]
Nominal fixed term contract	—	—	2.4	1
Coordination failure	2.6	1.9	2.2	2
Price elasticity of demand	2.2	2.1	2.1	3
Regular date for price change	—	—	2.0	3
Regular time interval for price change	—	—	1.9	3
Transitory shock	1.8	2.0	1.9	6
Sluggish costs	—	—	1.8	7
Menu costs	—	—	1.4	8
Other	1.1	1.1	1.1	—

Source: Author's calculations.
[a]Answers have been rescaled for missing responses.
[b]A t-test at the level of 1% does not reject the hypothesis that the mean scores of the reasons with rank 3 are equal.

REASONS FOR PRICE ADJUSTMENT

Whereas the previous section focused on reasons for postponing a price change, this section focuses on reactions to cost and demand shocks and to price changes by competitors, and it investigates whether these reactions are symmetric or not. In question 16, firms had to grade several shocks on a four-point scale of importance for a price increase or a price reduction. On the cost side, increases in labor costs were split into permanent and transitory increases because the face-to-face interviews revealed that the firms' understanding of labor costs referred to permanent increases in hourly wages. Firms claimed that reductions in wage costs never happen. The same distinction for reductions of labor costs was prevented by space constraints.

The question for demand changes contains a double asymmetry. Firms were not only asked what importance they attach to demand increases for price increases and demand decreases for price reductions but also whether demand decreases are important for price increases or demand increases for price reductions. The second asymmetry is motivated by the fact that with a high share of fixed unit costs, prices should decrease with an increase in demand and vice versa. Further, it is frequently argued that marginal costs decrease because discounts grow in line with the quantity purchased.

It turned out that the most important motivation for price changes is the cost of materials (see table 6.4). The impact of these is larger for price rises than for price reductions. Labor costs matter in the event of permanent wage increases, but transitory increases, as well as reductions of labor costs, have only a modest impact. For reductions of labor costs, permanent changes may likewise be more important than transitory changes. This could explain why the average grade for reductions lies between the grades for permanent and transitory increases. Financing costs are not important either. An increase in financing costs is more likely passed on to customers than a reduction. An increase in productivity, which can be seen as a permanent cost reduction, received an average score of 2.4. Thus, firms are more likely to react to cost increases than to cost reductions. For demand shocks, there are almost no differences in mean grades between the four alternatives, due to double asymmetries: they range from 2.0 to 2.3. Yet it is questionable as to whether all firms understood the double dichotomy. On the one hand, approximately 25% attached a grade of 3 or 4 to the importance of a demand decrease for a price increase as well as for a price reduction. On the other hand, when asked for the reasons for a price increase (reduction), about 10% of firms assigned a high grade to a demand decrease (increase) and a low grade to a demand increase (decrease). These may be firms with high fixed costs.

An asymmetric reaction can be observed for competitors' price changes. Firms react strongly to price reductions by competitors but to a lesser extent to price increases, in accordance with the theory of coordination failure. A chi-square and a likelihood ratio test reject the null hypotheses of symmetry for all reactions.

Table 6.4 Asymmetric reactions of price changes to shocks (mean scores)[a]

Type of shock	Price		p-values[b]	
	Increase	Reduction	χ^2	LR
Increase (reduction) of costs of materials	3.4	2.8	0.00	0.00
Permanent increase of labor costs (e.g. negotiated wage increase)	2.7	—	—	—
Transitory increase of labor costs (e.g. overtime hours, bonuses)	1.5	—	—	—
Reduction of labor costs (e.g. bonuses, lay offs)	—	1.9	—	—
Increase (reduction) of financing costs	1.9	1.6	0.00	0.00
Increase in productivity	—	2.4	—	—
Product improvement	2.3	—	—	—
Demand increase (reduction)	2.2	2.3	0.00	0.00
Demand reduction (increase)	2.2	2.0	0.00	0.00
Price increase (reduction) by a competitor	2.1	2.6	0.00	0.00
Other	1.9	1.8	0.89	0.89

Source: Author's calculations.
[a]Answers have been rescaled for missing responses.
[b]Let m_{ij} $(i, j = 1, \ldots, r)$ denote the expected frequency of cell ij in a $(r \times r)$ contingency table. Let n_{ij} denote the respective empirical frequency. The ML-estimate for the expected frequency under the null hypotheses of symmetry $(H_0 : m_{ij} = m_{ji})$ is $(n_{ij} + n_{ji})/2$. The statistic for the χ^2 test is

$$\chi^2 = \sum_{i=1}^{r} \sum_{j=1}^{r} (n_{ij} - (n_{ij} + n_{ji})/2)^2/((n_{ij} + n_{ji})/2) = \sum_{i>j} (n_{ij} - n_{ji})^2/(n_{ij} + n_{ji}) \text{ and } LR = 2 \sum_{i \neq j} n_{ij} \cdot \ln (2 \cdot n_{ij})/(n_{ij} + n_{ji})$$

is the statistic for the Likelihood ratio test. Under H_0 both test statistics have asymptotically a χ^2 distribution with $r(r-1)/2$ degrees of freedom.

A cross-tabulation of type of price setter with the importance of several reasons for price increases and reductions confirms the results obtained in the section on price setting. Firms with a constant markup respond to cost changes but rarely to demand changes, and are less likely than other firms to respond to competitors' price reductions. Firms that take the price of their main competitor as a reference are more likely to react to competitors' price changes and to demand changes than other firms. These firms may take demand changes as an indirect indication of price changes by their competitors. This would also explain why they are less likely to react to permanent wage increases than do other firms. They react to permanent wage increases only insofar as they react to their competitors' reaction to permanent wage increases. Another explanation for the stronger reaction to demand increases is that these firms are price followers most of the time but occasionally they have to act as price leaders to avoid being punished by their competitors. Thus, from time to time, they have to sacrifice some market share that is least detrimental to their profits at times of exceptional demand. Firms with a variable markup are caught in the middle between firms with a constant markup and firms that take the price of their main competitor as a reference.

Firms that follow indexation schemes raise their prices more often in response to cost increases than do other firms. It is irrelevant whether these increases are costs of materials, permanent wage increases, or financing costs. In the case of cost reductions, these firms behave like other firms. Yet indexation does not necessarily imply that prices are adjusted continuously in the way macro models typically assume. Indexation may also be lump sum.[5] This is obvious, considering indexation to wage contracts. Another example was offered by a manufacturer of car parts in a face-to-face interview; one of his customers usually makes a proposal for a one-time price adjustment if input prices have increased more than expected.

CLUSTERING OF FIRMS

The analysis of the importance of various reasons for postponing a price change in the previous section yielded no dominant explanation. We will therefore need to use a more complex model. One possibility may be a model with several groups of firms, each group facing a simple but distinct explanation for its behavior. A cluster analysis may identify such groups; this section reports the results of this analysis, based on the answers to questions 16 and 17, that is, the reasons for changing a price and for postponing a price change. The analysis reveals that it is difficult to identify different homogeneous groups of firms. Instead, firms may be grouped by increasing complexity of reasons for price stickiness. The results suggest that eventually it would be more appropriate to use an alternative model in which each firm has many reasons to postpone a price change, and not just one or a few. Such a model has to be developed in the future.

The aim of the specific cluster analysis carried out here is to partition the firms into a distinct number of nonoverlapping clusters. In the words of Kendall (1980: 32), a cluster is "a group scattered around some central value, possibly condensing in a nuclear set, not necessarily spherical but not excessively elongated into a rod-like shape." Within clusters, the objects should be as similar as possible, yet the distance between the central values of the different clusters should be as great as possible. The cluster analysis thus requests a measure of similarity or dissimilarity. Here we understand the distance of the object to its central value as a residual and use the Euclidean distance or the sum of squared residuals as a dissimilarity measure, depending on the clustering method.[6]

As preparation for the cluster analysis, we must clarify first whether the variables used are comparable. This may not be the case because there might be some latent variables that are under- or overrepresented. For example, there are two variables to measure the importance of transitory shocks for postponing a price change—one for a price increase and the other for a price cut—but only one to measure the importance of sluggish costs. Without any correction, transitory shocks would be overrepresented in the analysis, which would be likely to lead to biased central values and distances.[7] A factor analysis is therefore used to identify a few (latent) variables for changing a price or representing the reasons for postponing a price change. For the cluster analysis, the variables are grouped together according to their assignment to the factors. This step is often called "weighting." Details on factor analysis can be found in Stahl (2005). Readers who are not interested in the weighting procedure may skip the next subsection.

Weighting

The factor analysis for the reasons of postponing a price change shows two factors with an eigenvalue larger than one, where the second is only slightly larger than one. Thus, the Kaiser criterion favors at most two factors. A sizeable drop in the eigenvalue occurs between the first and the second factor and between the second and the third factor, so that again at most two factors should be retained. The first factor already explains 73% of the total variance. The two-factor solution explains slightly more than the total variance, thereby indicating that some variables are assigned to both factors, which is undesirable. Hence, from a formal point of view a one-factor solution might even be preferable to the two-factor one. However, the interpretation of the outcome of the one-factor solution is almost impossible and the residual variances of most variables are too large. Therefore, we choose two factors.

The discussion starts with the second factor, as this is easier to interpret.[8] It is named "time dependence" because the variables "price change preferably at a specific point of time" and "price change preferably after a specific period of time" are assigned uniquely to this factor. A negative loading shows up for the variable "price change in advance if possible." This negative sign is interpreted as reflecting state-dependent price setting because state dependence is the opposite of time dependence. However, this variable should not be assigned exclusively to the second factor because it displays a positive loading for the first factor that is not much smaller than the one for the second. The menu cost variable shows similar behavior. It loads positively with the time-dependent factor yet also correlates with the first factor. All the other reasons can be assigned to the first factor. The price elasticity of demand, transitory shocks, and coordination failure are the variables that mainly constitute the first factor. Since there is no good catchword for the first factor, yet price elasticity of demand and coordination failure are related to competition, the first factor is called "competition." Two of the reasons for postponing a price change have not been mentioned so far: nominal fixed term contracts and sluggish costs. For these two reasons the two-factor model is a poor fit.[9]

Although two interpretable factors were identified, the exercise reveals several serious problems. First, the assignment of the items to the factors is not unique: physical menu costs are one example. Second, the communalities of several items are very low.[10] For example, both factors explain only 1% of the variance of sluggish costs. In other words, the number of explanations for price stickiness cannot be reduced to a small number of possibly latent reasons by a factor analysis. This would lead to a substantial loss of information. For the cluster analysis we therefore use a set of reasons for postponing a price change that is slightly more detailed than the two factors.[11] However, the factor analysis suggests that the question of time dependence versus state dependence and the remaining reasons are two distinct issues, which is an interesting outcome.

The factor analysis for the reasons for price changes again gives us two factors, "costs" and "demand." However, the fit of the model does not favor the use of factors for data analysis in general. Their use should be restricted to cases where simplicity is preferable to a good fit. For the cluster analysis, the variables are grouped together according to their assignment to the factors.[12]

Summarizing the results of both factor analyses, we get eight groups of variables. For each firm, we calculate the averages of each group and then cluster the firms by these averages.[13]

Clustering

Next, we have to choose a method for clustering. We use Ward's method, which is an agglomerative hierarchical clustering method, and, as an alternative, the k-means method. Both methods start by considering each observation as a separate group. The closest two groups are combined, and this process continues until all observations belong to the same group. Ward's method joins the two groups that result in the minimum increase in the error sum of squares. Once created, clusters are no longer dissolved in a further step of clustering. Although this results in a reduced statistical fit, it makes it easier to choose the number of clusters. In the $k+1$ cluster solution just one cluster of the k cluster solution is split into two clusters. Hence, the comparison of both outcomes is easy.

The k-means method starts by selecting k observations as the centers of k clusters. Each observation is assigned to a specific cluster by minimizing the squared Euclidean distance. New cluster centers are calculated and the process is iterated. The method is nonhierarchical. Firms that have been assigned to a specific cluster in an earlier step can be assigned to different clusters in a more advanced step. The iteration stops if no observation is reallocated. Through reallocation, k-means clustering allows a better statistical fit than Ward's method. Hence, we use Ward's method in a first step to choose the number of clusters, and we use the k-means method in a second step to improve the assignment of the individual firms to the different clusters.

The preferred outcome of the analysis is four clusters (see table 6.5). The assignment of the individual firms to the four clusters of Ward's method and the k-means method coincides for 556 (the sum of the diagonal in table 6.5) out of 850 firms (the sum of all firms in table 6.5), that is, for two out of three firms. Differences occur in the assignment to the first and fourth cluster, which will be discussed below.

Table 6.5 Comparison of the assignment using the Ward's and the k-means methods (number of firms)[a]

| K-means method | Ward's method | | | | |
	Cluster 1	Cluster 2	Cluster 3	Cluster 4	Total
Cluster 1	76	64	1	36	177
Cluster 2	37	178	23	3	241
Cluster 3	1	9	186	42	238
Cluster 4	33	9	36	116	194
Total	147	260	246	197	850

Source: Author's calculations.
[a]Unweighted figures.

Table 6.6 Average importance assigned to various reasons for price stickiness (mean scores)[a,b]

| Variable[c] | k-means clusters | | | | Ward's method clusters | | | |
	1	2	3	4	1	2	3	4
Nominal fixed-term contract	1.4	1.4	3.5	3.2	1.6	1.4	3.4	3.3
Coordination failure (+)	2.0	2.5	2.6	2.9	2.2	2.4	2.6	2.8
Coordination failure (−)	1.6	1.9	1.8	2.3	1.8	1.8	1.9	2.0
Price elasticity of demand (+)	1.7	2.2	2.2	2.4	1.9	2.1	2.2	2.3
Price elasticity of demand (−)	1.6	2.2	2.2	2.3	1.9	2.1	2.2	2.1
Transitory shock (+)	1.5	2.0	1.8	2.0	1.7	1.9	1.8	1.7
Transitory shock (−)	1.6	2.0	1.8	2.3	2.0	1.9	1.9	2.0
Sluggish costs	1.5	1.8	1.9	2.0	1.7	1.7	2.0	1.9
Menu costs	1.3	1.3	1.2	1.6	1.5	1.4	1.2	1.4
Fixed point of time	2.2	1.4	1.4	3.1	3.1	1.4	1.5	2.4
Fixed time interval	1.9	1.5	1.3	3.2	3.1	1.3	1.6	2.4
Price change in advance	1.4	3.1	3.1	2.2	2.3	2.7	3.3	1.8
Share of firms (%)	21	28	28	23	13	35	31	21

Source: Author's calculations.
[a]Answers have been rescaled for missing responses.
[b]Average scores greater than 2.0 are in italics.
[c](+) positive shock; (−) negative shock.

Do these four clusters describe four distinct groups of firms where for each group just one reason for postponing a price change matters? The outcome is mixed. Two out of four clusters, the first and the second, seem to represent distinct groups in this sense (see table 6.6). The k-means method separates these clusters even better than Ward's method.

Cluster one represents firms that do not feel much hampered in their price adjustment. If they feel hampered at all, it is because of time-dependent price setting. The share of these firms is smaller in the case of Ward's method (13%) compared to the k-means method (21%), but the firms in the first cluster of Ward's method feel more hindered (3.1) than the firms in the respective k-means cluster (2.1). However, coordination failure plays some role in the first cluster of both methods.

Cluster two represents firms that feel hampered by coordination failure and the price elasticity of demand. These firms may face a kinked demand curve. They change prices in advance, if possible.

Cluster three is similar to cluster two. However, nominal fixed-term contracts are very important, in addition to the already important kinked demand curve. The firms in the third cluster feel more vulnerable than those in the second cluster. However, this is not because a reason that already had an above average importance in the second cluster has become even more important, but because a reason that was of only minor importance in the second cluster has now become more important.

In cluster four, time-dependent price setting increases the complexity further.

Hence, a research strategy may be to start with a simple model for some of the firms and subsequently increase the complexity of the model.

SUMMARY

The survey of 1,200 German manufacturing firms taken in 2004 reveals that almost all of them (88%) have a certain margin for price setting. Most firms set their prices relative to the prices of their main competitors and apply markup pricing. This confirms the basic assumptions of widespread sticky price models. Yet indexation is rejected by the data.

Asked why they postpone a price adjustment, firms attached the greatest importance, on average, to fixed nominal contracts, followed by coordination failure as the second most likely source of price rigidity. Coordination failure results in more upward than downward stickiness. No single theory can explain delayed price adjustment. A model has to take into account several reasons for postponing a price change for each firm. However, for almost 50% of firms, price stickiness may be explained by a relatively simple model, whereas for the other half a quite complex model is necessary.

In accordance with markup pricing, firms are most likely to change prices in response to changes in the costs of materials. Such an impact is greater for price increases than for price reductions. Labor costs matter in the event of permanent wage increases. Transitory increases, as well as reductions of labor costs, have only a modest impact. In accordance with coordination failure, firms react strongly to price reductions by competitors but to a lesser extent to price increases.

Acknowledgments I am indebted to all participants to the IPN and to J. Döpke, J. Gali, A. Levin, H. Herrmann, J. Hoffmann, and W. Lemke for their useful comments on a previous version of this chapter.

NOTES

1. Germany had no register of firms before 1995, so no random sampling was possible. Instead, researchers had to decide deliberately which firms to ask, for example, based on published sales figures. This is called sampling by purpose or purposive sampling. In recent years, the sample has been refreshed to make it more representative.

2. The questionnaire does not specify whether firms apply the markup to marginal cost or to average cost. It is not at all clear whether firms calculate marginal cost. After all, if they fix prices for a certain time, the markup should be applied to average expected marginal costs. Further, if the markup is not constant but instead is related to other factors, the distinction between marginal cost and average cost is probably no longer important.

3. Although the question was addressed only to price setters, a substantial share of price takers provided an answer to it. Therefore, some estimation can be provided for price takers, too. If it is assumed that those who did not answer question number 8 set their price differently (item 5 of question 8), then 28% follow their main competitor.

4. If a firm changes its price once a year and always during the same month, say in January, the answers to both questions have to coincide. However, if there is an exceptional price change, say in April, then the firm that preferably changes its price at a fixed point in time should next change its price again in January, whereas a firm that preferably changes its price after a fixed time interval should next change its price in April of the following year.

5. Indexation needed special permission before EMU.

6. Someone who is not familiar with cluster analysis should think of it as of assigning firms to groups by minimizing the within-variance and maximizing the between-variance.

7. Bacher (1994). For example, to cluster people by income, it should be ensured that only one person per household is asked. Otherwise the income by household should be averaged, which may even reduce measurement error. The factor analysis is intended to determine which items belong to one and the same household.

8. After rotation, the ordering of the factors no longer has any intrinsic meaning.

9. In fact, if one allows for four factors, nominal fixed-term contracts show up as a distinct factor.

10. The communality is the percentage of the variance of the item that is explained by the factors.

11. The set of reasons for postponing a price change are (1) regular date and regular time interval, (2) coordination failure, price elasticity of demand, and transitory shock, (3) foreseeable price change in advance, (4) menu costs, (5) nominal fixed-term contracts, and (6) sluggish costs.

12. The reasons for changing a price are (1) demand change, change of price by a competitor, and product improvement, and (2) all remaining items.

13. In the cluster analysis, all variables are standardized by using their theoretical values for mean (2.5) and standard deviation (1.25).

REFERENCES

Bacher, Johann. 1994. *Clusteranalyse: Anwendungsorientierte Einführung*. München: R. Oldenbourg Verlag GmbH.

Blinder, Alan S., Elie R. D. Canetti, David E. Lebow, and Jeremy B. Rudd. 1998. *Asking about Prices: A New Approach to Understanding Price Stickiness*. New York: Russell Sage Foundation.

Christiano, Laurence, J., Martin Eichenbaum, and Charles L. Evans. 2005. Nominal rigidities and the dynamic effects of a shock to monetary policy. *Journal of Political Economy* 113: 1–45.

Kendall, Maurice. 1980. *Multivariate Analysis*. London and High Wycombe: Charles Griffin & Company Ltd.

Köhler, Annette G. 1996. Nominale Preisrigiditäten auf Gütermärkten: Eine Empirische Überprüfung Neukeynesianischer Erklärungsansätze. Ciret-Studien 51. München: IFO Institut für Wirtschaftsforschung.

Rotemberg, Julio J. 1982. Monopolistic price adjustment and aggregate output. *Review of Economic Studies* 44: 517–531.

Stahl, Harald. 2005. Price setting in German manufacturing: New evidence from new survey data. Deutsche Bundesbank Discussion Paper Series 1: Economic Studies No. 43/2005. Frankfurt am Main: Deutsche Bundesbank.

Woodford, Michael. 2003. *Interest and Prices*. Princeton: Princeton University Press.

Yun, Tack. 1996. Nominal price rigidity, money supply endogeneity, and business cycles. *Journal of Monetary Economics* 37: 345–370.

7

The Pricing Behavior of Italian Firms

New Survey Evidence on Price Stickiness

Silvia Fabiani, Angela Gattulli, & Roberto Sabbatini

This chapter presents the empirical evidence on a number of aspects of pricing behavior in Italy based on the questionnaire responses of a sample of around 350 industrial and services firms at the beginning of 2003. The first section briefly presents the structure of the questionnaire, how data were collected, and the main characteristics of the interviewed firm. The second section addresses the issue of how the firm sets its price. The third explores how rigid this price is, when and how it changes, and what are the main factors underlying its stickiness. The presence of any asymmetry in price adjustment in reaction to demand and cost shocks is investigated in the fourth section. The fifth section offers our conclusions.

THE SURVEY AND THE CHARACTERISTICS OF THE RESPONDENTS

The survey, coordinated by the Banca d'Italia, was outsourced to a private company and carried out in February and March 2003 on the basis of a questionnaire elaborated by the Banca d'Italia and a list of firms extracted from the sample used by the bank itself for its quarterly survey of inflation expectations. The questionnaire was pretested on a pilot sample, which provided useful indications on how to carry out the survey. Some of the questions were modified as a result. In September 2004, a few issues that had not been analyzed satisfactorily in the initial questionnaire were investigated again by submitting, through the same private company, an additional brief questionnaire to a sample of firms drawn from the same population as the original survey.[1]

The population from which the sample was drawn consists of firms with more than 50 employees, belonging to almost all sectors but excluding the public sector, agriculture, banking, insurance, transport, and housing services, as well as a small number of other areas in the services sector. The questionnaire was not suitable for firms belonging to these sectors, in particular because of the difficulty related to identification of the main product. The survey refers, in fact, to the firms' "main product or service," defined as the one that generated the highest turnover in 2002. Since for around 75% of the responding firms such a product accounts for more than 40% of turnover, the decision to focus on pricing strategies for the main product does not seem to be overrestrictive.

The population was stratified according to size and geographical area, but not with respect to the sector of activity, in order to avoid cells with too few observations. The answers provided by each firm were weighted with the ratio between the number of firms in the population belonging to each cell and the number of respondents in the same cell. Hence, all the results presented in this chapter are analyzed and reported as estimated proportions of the population. For most answers, results are presented both for the total sample and with a sectoral breakdown in order to highlight eventual differences in pricing behavior across industries.[2]

Of the initial list of 729 firms that received the questionnaire, 333 completed it. A response rate of 45.7% is deemed acceptable, given the complexity of the questionnaire, and it is, moreover, in line with other similar studies. Around 90% of the companies in the initial sample were contacted by e-mail (the rest by fax) and were able to complete the questionnaire directly on a Web site.[3] Firms were also contacted by telephone to check as to whether they were intending to participate in the survey.

Around two-thirds of the respondents belong to the industrial sector. The underrepresentation of the services sector is due both to the fact that a few areas had to be excluded and to the lower response rate among services firms (37.1% and 40.2% in retail and other services, respectively) compared to manufacturing firms (48.5%).[4] Differences in the response rate by firm size and geographical area were more limited.

The questions were mostly multiple choice. In some cases the possible answers were coded on a four-point scale ("1 = unimportant," "2 = minor importance," "3 = important," "4 = very important"); in others, respondents could provide open answers, expressing their views in their own words. Only a limited number of questions required a precise quantitative answer.

The questionnaire was organized in four sections (for details, see the Appendix to the book). The first section collects general information on the market in which the firm operates and some features of its relationships with customers. The second focuses on the price setting mechanism and, in particular, on the determinants of the price level. The third deals with the main aspects concerning price reviews and price changes. The final part of the questionnaire tries to assess whether firms facing different kinds of shocks behave asymmetrically when the price has to be increased or decreased.

Table 7.1 displays the main characteristics of the firms covered in the survey, in particular the market in which they operate, their role in such a market, and their interaction with other firms and with customers.

For most firms (around 80%), the reference market is the domestic one (question A4); only in the manufacturing sector did a significant proportion of respondents (around 25%) indicate foreign markets as being most important for their sales.

Table 7.1 The main characteristics of the firms interviewed (percentages)[a]

		Sector				
	Total	Manufacturing excl. food	Food	Construction	Retail	Other services
What is the most important market (in terms of turnover) for your main product?						
Local	26.2	11.4	31.5	36.5	60.9	36.1
National	56.8	61.9	56.1	63.5	36.2	59.4
Other euro area countries	9.6	16.3	6.4	0.0	0.0	1.0
Non-euro area countries	7.3	10.4	5.9	0.0	2.9	3.5
On the domestic market your firm is:						
The first	13.7	13.9	15.4	0.0	24.1	4.9
Among the first 4	36.4	43.2	26.2	3.2	36.1	24.2
Among the first 10	27.8	24.2	28.2	0.0	30.1	39.2
Not among the first 10	22.0	18.7	30.2	96.8	9.7	31.7
What is the number of your competitors on the domestic market?						
None	0.1	0.2	0.0	0.0	0.0	0.1
<5	20.4	20.2	6.3	0.0	21.6	29.8
Between 5 and 20	46.1	52.8	29.8	0.0	43.0	39.6
>20	33.3	26.7	63.9	100.0	35.5	30.5
The price of your main product is:						
The same for all customers	18.5	8.7	26.3	0	54.8	17.3
Different depending on quantity	41.0	52.6	42.1	0	24.0	22.7
Decided case by case	40.5	38.7	31.5	100.0	21.2	60.0

Source: Authors' calculations.
[a]Answers have been rescaled for missing responses.

In order to understand the role played by competitive pressures, firms were asked to provide information on their market share (question A6 in the questionnaire) and on the number of their competitors (question A7). Only around 20% are not among the first ten companies in the relevant market; 12% reported being the first firm, 31% reported being among the first four. This picture, confirmed by the information concerning the number of competitors (question A7), is not surprising, given that the survey covers only firms with more than 50 employees and that they were asked to focus on a very narrowly defined category of products (the main product). This could partly explain why the degree of market power, as captured by the above indicator, is higher in the manufacturing and retail sectors than in services.

Around half of the firms interviewed sell their main product principally to other firms (question A8), thus suggesting that the pricing strategies we are investigating refer mostly to producer or wholesale prices. Firms tend to have long-term relationships (longer than one year) with their customers (question A9); occasional relationships have considerable importance only in the retail and services sector. This is reflected in the presence of some form of price discrimination according to the type of customer or to the quantity of product sold, or both (question B1). There are, however, differences across sectors: in retailing the price is mostly the same for all customers; in manufacturing and services it tends either to differ according to the quantity sold or to be decided case by case. In particular, services firms tend to set their price on the basis of a certain degree of direct negotiation, which includes aspects that go beyond quantity (e.g., after sales assistance). In construction, not surprisingly, the price is mostly decided case by case.

PRICE SETTING

In the second part of the questionnaire, companies were asked to indicate how they set the price of their main product (question B2). They could either indicate that they use a markup rule, or that their price is mostly based on their competitors' price, or that it is determined by customers, or, finally, that it is subject to some form of regulation. Markup price setting dominates in all sectors (on average, it is adopted by 49% of firms; table 7.2), although the role of competitors (25%) and of customers (19%) turns out to be quite relevant. As for sectoral differences, competitors' pricing strategies are significantly more important for manufacturing than for services firms, whereas regulation appears to be particularly stringent in the retail sector.

The importance of competitors' prices is confirmed by the answers to question B3, where firms indicated how different their price would be if they had

Table 7.2 Price setting rules (percentages)[a]

	A markup is applied to unit variable costs	The price is determined by competitors' price	The price is set by customers	The price is regulated
Total	49.1	24.6	18.6	7.8
Manufacturing excl. food	54.0	26.9	17.5	1.6
Food	66.8	10.5	9.3	13.4
Construction	7.5	41.3	51.2	0.0
Retail	34.6	25.2	24.5	15.7
Other services	48.5	22.0	15.8	13.6

Source: Authors' calculations.
[a]Answers have been rescaled for missing responses.

no rivals. Prices would be either "very different" or "fairly different" for more than half of the respondents, and "slightly different" for a further 37% of them. Also in this case there is a remarkable dispersion across sectors: whereas only 6.5% of manufacturing firms would leave their price unchanged even if they had no rivals, this percentage rises to around 20% in the retail and services industries. This might be due to the fact that these latter firms operate mostly in local markets or under more severe price regulation.

PRICE ADJUSTMENT

How and How Often Price Adjustment Occurs

Following the theoretical setting presented in chapter 1, the process of price adjustment can take place according to either time-dependent rules, in which prices are reviewed periodically at given intervals, or state-dependent rules, in which prices are adjusted when their deviation from the optimal level becomes large enough to make the gain in profit from adjustment outweigh the related cost. A further possibility is that firms typically follow time-dependent rules but switch to state dependence at times of major shocks.

In order to discriminate between these different options, firms were asked to qualify their strategy of price review (question C1). Although the majority of them (46%; table 7.3) seem to adopt a mixture of both time- and state-dependent rules, among those that do not, time dependence dominates (38% as compared to 15% of firms following purely state-dependent rules).

In addition to the type of rule firms follow for their price reviews, the information set they evaluate at this pricing stage is another important element for assessing the microfoundations of macroeconomic models (question C2). When asked about this issue, in particular whether they refer to past information only or also to expected developments, around 68% of the firms reported some form of forward-looking behavior, where expectations affect pricing strategies (table 7.3). Only around 30% of respondents seem to take only the past into account when revising their prices.

More than half of the firms that adopt time-dependent rules typically review their price once a year, 15% at quarterly intervals, 14% at monthly intervals, and around 15% every week or more often (figure 7.1). In the food, retail, and services sectors, price reviews tend to take place more frequently: around one-third of food-producing firms and 8.5% of retailers evaluate their prices every week, whereas around 17% of services firms report a daily frequency of price reviews.

After assessing how and how often prices are reviewed, the questionnaire focuses on the second step of the price adjustment process, asking firms how many times they had actually changed the price of their main product in 2001 and 2002 (questions C7 and C8). Results are similar in the two years and point to a certain degree of stickiness in all sectors (differences are not statistically significant): the majority of respondents apparently changed their price only once a year, around 10% twice, fewer than 10% more than every two months.

Table 7.3 The rules and the information set underlying price changes (percentages)[a]

	Total	Manufacturing excl. food	Food	Construction	Retail	Other services
			Sector			

How do you review the price of your main product (without necessarily changing it)?

	Total	Manufacturing excl. food	Food	Construction	Retail	Other services
At predetermined time intervals	38.1	36.4	36.0	5.6	42.4	41.2
Mainly at predetermined time intervals, but also in reaction to specific events	46.4	52.3	58.3	89.0	42.8	25.7
In reaction to specific events	15.4	11.3	5.7	5.4	14.8	33.1

The information set you consider when you review the price of your main product is related to[b]

	Total	Manufacturing excl. food	Food	Construction	Retail	Other services
Only past relevant information	31.6	31.2	37.8	11	33.3	29.5
Also current and expected relevant information	68.4	68.8	62.2	89	66.7	70.5

Source: Authors' calculations.
[a]Answers have been rescaled for missing responses.
[b]Supplementary survey conducted in September 2004.

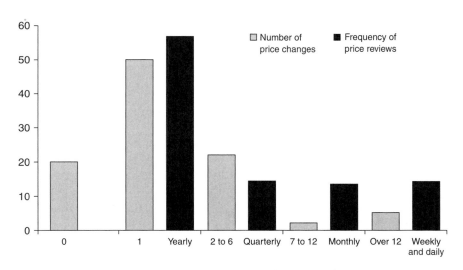

Figure 7.1 Number of price changes in a year and frequency of price reviews (percentages). The figure is based on the answers to questions C1 and C7.
Source: Authors' calculations.

The comparison between the frequency of price reviews and of price changes provided in figure 7.1 suggests that changes tend to be slightly less frequent than reviews: almost 60% of the respondents typically review their price once a year, whereas about 50% of them actually change their price with that frequency.

Why Are Prices Sticky?

Having ascertained that firms do not review their prices continuously and that they change them even less frequently, this section addresses the actual importance of the alternative theoretical explanations that may lead a firm to temporarily deviate from its profit-maximizing price, overviewed in chapter 1. For this purpose, firms were asked to evaluate the relevance they attached to each of the various explanations (question C3), on a scale from "1 = unimportant" to "4 = very important."

The resulting ranking, presented in table 7.4, shows that the presence of explicit contracts is the most important reason behind a firm's decision to postpone a required price change. As expected, there is some dispersion across sectors: the rank is quite high in the services sector and much lower in retailing.

Table 7.4 Factors that might delay price adjustments (mean scores)

		Sector				
	Total	Manufacturing excl. food	Food	Construction	Retail	Other services
Coordination failure	2.6	2.6	2.7	3.0	2.7	2.3
Explicit contracts	2.6	2.7	2.8	3.3	1.9	3.0
Temporary shocks	2.0	1.9	2.2	1.1	2.0	1.9
Pricing thresholds	1.4	1.2	1.8	1.4	2.0	1.3
Menu costs	1.6	1.5	1.7	1.1	1.8	1.6
Bureaucratic rigidities	1.3	1.2	1.6	1.1	1.4	1.2
The fear of losing the most loyal customers[a]	3.2	3.2	3.3	3.0	3.2	3.3

Source: Authors' calculations.

[a]Supplementary survey conducted in September 2004. As mentioned before, the firms interviewed at this stage overlap only partly with those surveyed in the original sample. Hence, the results concerning this specific factor underlying price stickiness cannot be analyzed as if they referred to the same sample; this implies, in particular, that the importance of the "fear of losing the most loyal customer" cannot be ranked with the other theories listed in the table, though it receives a very high mean score.

The theory that received the second highest rank is coordination failure, implying that a firm does not change its price because it fears that doing so will trigger a price war. This evidence is consistent with the importance that companies attribute to rival prices, a point that emerged earlier in the analysis.

The third most relevant explanation of the inertial behavior of prices is the fact that firms do not react in response to a shock because they perceive the shock as temporary.[5] In particular, this factor was considered important or very important by about 30% of retailers and food producers.

The possibility that firms delay a price adjustment because they fear the reaction of their most loyal customers (question C4) was investigated only at a later stage, on a different sample of firms, and turned out to be important or very important for the majority of respondents. Although we cannot compare its position in the overall ranking of theories considered above, the fact that 80% of firms indeed care about the reaction of their customers to a price change is an important qualitative indication that this element is very relevant in pricing behavior.

As in other similar surveys, price setting at attractive thresholds (which implies a discontinuous relationship between price and demand) and menu costs (physical and information costs involved in the adjustment process), as well as bureaucratic rigidities, were ranked quite low overall by Italian firms (the mean scores are 1.4, 1.6, and 1.3, respectively). As expected, however, both pricing thresholds and menu costs were recognized more widely in retailing than in the other sectors. In the case of pricing thresholds, in particular, around 33% of respondents in the retail industry considered this aspect important or very important, against 11% in manufacturing, 32% in the food industry and 9% in services.[6]

ASYMMETRIES IN PRICE ADJUSTMENT

The last section of the questionnaire focuses on whether firms facing a shock behave symmetrically irrespective of the source of the shock or whether prices have to be increased or decreased. For a given demand or cost shock, firms might, in fact, react differently if they have to adjust their price upward or downward in relation to the direction of the shock. Moreover, irrespective of that, they might respond differently to demand and cost shocks.

Firms were asked to evaluate the relevance of a number of factors (cost of labor and of raw materials, financial costs, demand conditions, competitors' strategies) as driving forces behind upward (question D1) or downward (question D3) price movements. Overall, firms judge cost shocks (of labor and other inputs) to be rather important in driving their prices upward and downward (table 7.5). The impact, however, is relatively more important when prices have to be increased than when they have to be reduced. Financial costs do not appear among the major sources of price adjustments, particularly downward. As for changes in demand conditions, only around

Table 7.5 Factors behind a price increase/decrease (mean scores)

	Increase	Decrease
Increase/decrease in the cost of labor	2.9	2.4
Increase/decrease in the cost of raw materials	3.3	2.9
Increase/decrease in financial costs	2.3	2.1
Rise/fall in demand	2.4	2.8
Price increase/decrease by competitors	2.6	2.8

Source: Authors' calculations.

42% of firms reported this factor as being "important" or "very important" in determining price increases. Conversely, demand shocks seem to exert much stronger pressure when prices have to be decreased. Also, the influence of competitors' behavior, which already emerged in the previous sections, although generally quite high, seems to be slightly stronger in driving prices downward than upward.

The remainder of this section describes the results of an empirical exercise similar to that presented in Small and Yates (1999), which further explores the factors behind the response of prices to shocks, focusing in particular on the presence of asymmetries in price adjustment.

We estimated a probit model of the form:

$$P(y_j=1)=F(b_1x_{1j}+\cdots+b_mx_{mj})$$

where y_j is a zero one dummy based on the firms' answers on the factors underlying negative and positive price changes. Specifically, we created four dummy variables, which capture whether firms increase their price in response to an increase in demand or costs (*pud* and *puc*) or lower it in response to a fall in demand or costs (*pld* and *plc*). The set x_{ij} contains i explanatory variables for firm j, which might influence the way in which prices react to shocks. These variables were chosen in order to reflect a number of propositions advanced in the theoretical literature on price stickiness.

First, we explored the possibility that, as Ball and Romer (1990) argue, nominal prices are stickier in a market where firms' profits do not change much in the face of shocks—in other words, that real rigidities magnify nominal rigidities. According to this idea, the more sensitive profits are to shocks (with prices unchanged), the more likely it is that firms react by changing prices.

Among the factors determining the degree of real rigidity, we first considered market competition. In principle, the more competitive the market, the more likely it is that a firm will adjust its price in response to shocks in order to avoid a fall in profits. Hence, for given nominal rigidity (due, for instance, to the presence of menu costs), stronger competition should induce a greater responsiveness of prices to cost and demand shocks (Martin 1993; Small and Yates 1999). On the basis of our survey we con-structed a number of variables capturing the degree of market competition: the firm's reported market share (*mkt_shr*), the number of its competitors (*rivals*), and how the firm would set its prices if it had no rivals (*comp_press*).

A further feature affecting the degree of real rigidity is the nature of the relationship between the firm and its customers. A firm can sell its main product to other firms or directly to final consumers. In the first case it is likely that lower search costs are sustained by customers to collect the information needed to act optimally. Therefore, the probability that the firm will adjust its price in response to shocks is greater than in the case in which the firm deals mainly with final consumers, which face higher search costs. Similarly, the existence of a long-term relationship between the firm and its customers is likely to generate a resistance to continuous price changes so as to avoid antagonizing the customers (Small and Yates 1999). To capture the nature of the firm's relationship with its customers we constructed a dummy variable reflecting the fact that the firm deals mainly with other firms (*customer*) and one that identifies whether the firm discriminates the price depending on the customer (*price_discr*). We also created a dummy allowing for the possibility that the price is subject to some form of regulation (*price_reg*).

The last proxy for real rigidity is a variable that records whether the firm's marginal cost curve is flat (*mc*). As Hall (1986) recognizes, variable marginal costs should make price adjustments more likely in the face of a shock.

An additional reason that a firm might not adjust its prices in response to shocks is that it mainly sells its products abroad and therefore adopts some form of pricing to market; to investigate this we constructed two dummies: the first identifies whether the firm's share of turnover due to exports is above 40% (*exp_share*); the second records whether the firm identifies the foreign market as being the principal one for its main product (*ext_mkt*).

We also included among the regressors control variables for the type of economic activity, the size of the firm, and the geographical area in which it is based, which account for unobserved characteristics of the firm that might have an impact on price behavior but are not captured by the previous explanatory variables.[7]

To gauge the presence of asymmetries in pricing behavior when prices have to be adjusted upward or downward, we estimated the above model separately for demand and cost shocks; for each type of shock we carried out separate regressions for upward and downward shocks. Table 7.6 reports the results of the model specification, including only the variables that turned out to be significant or to significantly affect the overall equation.[8]

As far as demand shocks are concerned, market structure, as captured by the degree of competitive pressure perceived by the firm (*comp_press*), significantly affects the probability of price adjustments in the face of a shock, whether positive or negative: as expected, prices tend to change

Table 7.6 Factors underlying price flexibility (main results of probit analysis)[a]

	Demand increase (pud)	Demand decrease (pld)	Costs increase (puc)	Costs decrease (plc)
High competition	+	+	−	−
Variable marginal costs	+	no		
Low search costs	+	no	no	no
Regulated price	no	no	−	no
High export share	no	no	−	−

Source: Authors' calculations; Fabiani et al. (2004).
[a]A plus (+) denotes that the factor is positively and significantly related to the probability of a price increase/decrease in response to an increase/decrease in demand/costs; a minus (−) denotes that the factor is negatively and significantly related to the probability of a price increase/decrease in response to an increase/decrease in demand/costs; "no" denotes that the factor is not significantly related to the probability of a price increase/decrease in response to an increase/decrease in demand/costs.

more promptly in a more competitive environment. The probability of raising prices when faced by a positive demand shock is significantly lower for firms with a flat marginal cost function (*mc*), but this feature does not have an impact in the case of a negative shock. Similarly, the fact that the firm's customers incur lower search costs (*customer*) is positively correlated with the responsiveness of prices to a demand increase, although it has no significant effect in the case of a fall in demand. There is no evidence supporting what is theoretically postulated by pricing to market models.

As for the reaction of prices to cost changes, table 7.6 shows that the probability of lowering prices in response to a decrease in costs is significantly and inversely correlated with the degree of market power (*mkt_shr*), and it is not affected by search costs (*customer*).[9] The same effects appear also in the case of cost increases. The latter seem also to be more easily translated into prices when there is some form of price regulation. Firms mainly operating in foreign markets (*ext_mkt*) seem to have a significantly lower price responsiveness to both positive and negative cost shocks, and this supports the hypothesis of some form of nominal rigidity due to pricing to market behavior.

As a final piece of evidence, we pooled the increases and decreases and estimated two separate regressions for demand and cost shocks, testing the significance of an "increase" dummy in both cases (table 7.7). This exercise confirms an important form of asymmetry in the responsiveness of prices to changes in cost and demand: whereas a rise in demand is less likely to induce a price change than a fall, a cost increase is more likely to prompt a price change than a cost reduction.

Table 7.7 Price adjustment: pooling positive and negative shocks (probit estimates)[a]

	Change price in response to a change in demand		Change price in response to a change in costs	
Constant	1.40	(0.63)	1.64	(0.65)
Demand_up/ Cost_up	−0.51**	(0.18)	1.02**	(0.25)
mkt_shr1	−0.64**	(0.31)	−1.43**	(0.37)
mkt_shr4	−0.34	(0.26)	−0.14	(0.33)
mkt_shr10	−0.45*	(0.26)	−0.24	(0.32)
customer	0.46**	(0.20)		
price_discr			1.09**	(0.33)
mc	−0.38*	(0.24)		
exp_share	0.26	(0.26)		
ext_mkt			−1.05**	(0.29)
price_reg	−0.63**	(0.29)		
manufacturing	0.11	(0.66)	−0.02	(0.63)
retail	0.39	(0.70)	−0.09	(0.70)
other services	−0.30	(0.68)	−0.34	(0.67)
food	0.61	(0.68)	−1.10*	(0.67)
north-west	−0.72**	(0.29)	−0.29	(0.34)
north-east	−0.51*	(0.31)	−0.31	(0.36)
centre	−0.57*	(0.32)	−0.11	(0.38)
up to 199 employees	−0.48**	(0.21)	0.06	(0.31)
200–999 employees	−0.40**	(0.21)	0.43	(0.31)
Number of obs.	433		503	
LogL	−264.5		−140.8	
Pseudo R^2	0.12		0.27	
χ^2 (d.o.f.)	48.1 (15)	[0.000]	74.8 (15)	[0.000]

Source: Authors' calculations; Fabiani et al. (2004).
[a]Weighted estimates. ** and * indicate statistical significance at the 5% and 10% significance level, respectively. Values in round brackets are the estimated standard errors. Values in square brackets are the estimated p-values of the test statistics.

CONCLUSIONS

The results of our survey of manufacturing and services firms point to the existence of stickiness in price adjustment in the Italian economy, which is related both to the stage in which firms evaluate their pricing strategies and to that in which they actually implement price changes. In reviewing their prices, firms mostly follow a combination of time- and state-dependent rules, also taking into account expected developments in the relevant factors. The frequency of price reviews is pretty low; the median firm reviews its prices once a year. Price changes are less frequent than price reviews.

Among the proposed explanations behind nominal price rigidity, three are ranked highest by the firms interviewed: explicit contracts, coordination failure, and their perception of the temporary nature of shocks. There is also evidence that the fear of a reaction from the firms' most loyal customers to a price adjustment is a very relevant factor underlying the postponement of a price change.

The results point to the existence of asymmetries in the adjustment of prices to positive and negative shocks, in particular on the demand side. First, real rigidities, as captured by a flat marginal cost curve and by the fact that customers incur high search costs, reduce the responsiveness of nominal prices to a positive change in demand but not to a negative one. Second, both market structure, as measured by the firm's degree of market power, and some form of pricing-to-market rigidity seem to enhance nominal price stickiness in response to cost shocks. Finally, price responsiveness to changes in costs is greater when the changes are positive than when they are negative, whereas in the case of demand changes, prices seem to be more rigid upward than downward.

Acknowledgments We are indebted to all participants to the IPN for their useful comments on a previous version of this chapter. We are also grateful to Luigi Guiso, Marco Magnani, and to the participants on the 2004 National Bureau of Economic Research Summer Institute meeting for their comments.

NOTES

1. In particular, questions B2 and C1 in the original questionnaire were submitted again with a different phrasing and list of possible answers; the new questions C2 and C4 were added, following what was done in other countries. On the one hand, since the firms interviewed in the two stages overlap only partly, the results related to the four questions in the second survey cannot be interpreted and analyzed as though they referred to the same sample as the original survey. Their use is, however, problematic only in the econometric exercise presented at the end of the chapter. On the other hand, the fact that both samples were drawn from the same population means that the additional information collected in September 2004 can be considered for the descriptive analysis as a piece of evidence on pricing behavior in Italy that fits adequately with the overall findings.

2. The significance of sectoral differences was assessed formally through standard statistical tests; results are available upon request from the authors or can be found in Fabiani et al. (2004).

3. A call center was available to firms requiring additional information. The use of the Internet, which speeded up the whole procedure and helped contain the cost of the survey, was also motivated by the fact that the survey was outsourced to the

same company that has been carrying out the quarterly Banca d'Italia survey of inflation expectations over the last years. This is conducted through the Internet.

4. The questionnaire was found to be better suited for manufacturing firms and less suited for those in the services sector, mostly because it is more difficult for the latter to identify a main product and define the pricing strategy related to it. Other problematic aspects are related to the difficulties in identifying the main product on the basis of turnover for firms producing several goods and to the lack of an autonomous pricing strategy for firms with only one customer, for branches of foreign firms, and for those producing items subject to price controls. Also, firms selling their products by public tender follow pricing rules different from market strategies.

5. In practice, the importance of this behavior might change in relation to the sector and to the nature of the shocks affecting the firm's optimal price, in particular whether these shocks are perceived as global or as firm specific. The survey allows one to draw some conclusions about the former aspect (type of sector) but not the latter (type of shock).

6. The low ranking of pricing thresholds contrasts somewhat with the evidence provided by other studies based on Italian micro consumer prices, which show instead that this pricing behavior is extremely widespread (Mostacci and Sabbatini 2003). However, the two pieces of evidence can be reconciled considering that, as the prices analyzed in the survey are likely to be mostly producer prices, it is quite reasonable that attractive thresholds play a limited role at the early stage of the distribution chain.

7. The complete list of variables is reported in Fabiani et al. (2004).

8. The full set of results is reported in Fabiani et al. (2004).

9. Small and Yates (1999) find similar results for search costs but no significant effect for market competition.

REFERENCES

Ball, Laurence, and David H. Romer. 1990. Real rigidities and the non-neutrality of money. *Review of Economic Studies* 57: 183–203.

Fabiani, Silvia, Angela Gattulli, and Roberto Sabbatini. 2004. The pricing behavior of Italian firms: New survey evidence on price stickiness. European Central Bank Working Paper No. 333. Frankfurt am Main: European Central Bank.

Hall, Robert. 1986. Market structure and macroeconomic fluctuations. *Brookings Papers on Economic Activity* 2: 285–322.

Martin, Stephen. 1993. Price adjustment and market structure. *Economics Letters* 41: 139–143.

Mostacci, Franco, and Roberto Sabbatini. 2003. L'euro ha creato inflazione? Changeover e arrotondamenti dei prezzi al consumo in Italia nel 2002. *Moneta e Credito* 221: 45–95.

Small, Ian, and Antony Yates. 1999. What makes prices sticky? Some survey evidence for the United Kingdom. *Bank of England Quarterly Bulletin* 39: 262–271.

8

A Survey of Price Setting Practices of Luxembourg Firms

Patrick Lünnemann & Thomas Mathä

This chapter reports the findings of a survey on the price setting behavior of Luxembourg firms. In the second half of 2004, more than 1,000 firms from the construction, industry, and services sector (including retail) were contacted. Firms were requested to disclose key characteristics of their market environment, as well as main elements of their price setting practices, such as the adoption of time- and state-dependent rules, the role of forward-looking and backward-looking behavior, the speed of adjustment in response to both demand and cost shocks, as well as the determinants of price increases and decreases. Finally, the survey aimed at identifying the obstacles to faster price adjustment.

The first section of the chapter discusses the survey design and the sample selection. The second section discusses the main characteristics of the market in which firms operate. The third section presents the key features of the price setting behavior both at the price review and at the price setting stage. The fourth section studies the reasons underlying the postponement of price adjustment. The fifth section analyzes the determinants of price changes in more depth. The sixth section summarizes our findings on the speed of adjustment and the seventh section offers our conclusions.

SURVEY DESIGN

The Questionnaire

The survey, which was carried out by the Banque centrale du Luxembourg (BCL) in the second half of 2004, is designed in close correspondence with those used by Blinder et al. (1998), Hall et al. (2000), Apel et al. (2005), and those developed in the context of the Inflation Persistence Network (IPN). The questionnaire is provided in the Appendix to the book. In order to achieve the highest response rates, questionnaires in both French and German were attached to a letter signed by a board member of the BCL emphasizing the importance of this survey. Questions were designed in such a way as to reduce the administrative burden of the respondents by requesting qualitative information and offering respondents a selection of predefined answers (such as a four-point scale: "1 = unimportant," "2 = minor importance," "3 = important," and "4 = very important"). To the extent possible, firms were offered a choice of ranges (e.g., on the market share). Only in few cases were they asked to provide quantitative information (e.g., on turnover). Firms had to respond by mail (a free-of-charge return envelope was enclosed); they were given telephone and e-mail contacts for assistance.[1]

In the following, we distinguish between four different sectors: construction, industry, trade, and services. We further distinguish between three firm size classes: namely, 25 employees or less (small firms hereafter), 26–75 employees (medium sized firms), and more than 75 employees (large firms).

The Sample

To obtain information across a relatively wide range of size and sector strata and at the same time to have a minimum number of replies for each of these strata, specific sampling weights were used. In general, sectors in which firms were not expected to set prices autonomously were not considered (e.g., agriculture, hunting and forestry, health, public administration and defense, and compulsory social security). Furthermore, we excluded the sector of financial intermediation as well as companies with fewer than five employees. Within each of the strata considered, firms were chosen randomly.[2]

In total, 1,133 companies encompassing the sectors of trade, (other) services, industry, and construction were contacted. Out of these firms, 367 participated in the survey, resulting in an overall response rate of 32%. Contrary to what done in most of the other euro area surveys, though, this survey was not attached to already existing ones (such as business cycle surveys), directed to a sample of firms that had revealed a sound willingness to participate in surveys in the past. Table 8.1 suggests the presence of a

Table 8.1 Population versus sample (percentages)[a]

	Population	Sample sent out	Sample received	Response rate
Agriculture	2	0	0	—
Construction	10	20	21	33
Industry	5	20	23	36
Services	60	38	36	30
Trade	24	22	21	31
Small	90	38	28	24
Medium	6	33	36	35
Large	4	30	37	40
Total				32

Source: Authors' calculations.
[a]Rows may not sum to 100 due to rounding.

sample bias. Both the composition of the firms contacted and the structure of those participating in the survey are not perfectly representative of the company structure in Luxembourg, a fact often reported in this type of studies.[3] In particular, small companies are underrepresented, whereas firms in construction, industry and services other than trade tend to be overrepresented. To adjust for the sample bias, the replies are poststratified with respect to both economic activity and size class.

MAIN MARKET CHARACTERISTICS

Market Location and Client Structure

Most respondents indicated that the main market is Luxembourg; overall, 87% of turnover is generated in the domestic market. Almost the entire remainder is generated in the euro area, and less than 1% outside it (table 8.2). As expected, foreign markets are more important for industrial firms, 67% of their turnover being generated abroad. With the exception of large industrial firms, Luxembourg is the main market for the main product irrespective of the size class or field of activity. For industrial firms, the fraction of those serving mainly Luxembourg declines as the firm size increases. The peculiarity of this sector reflects the fact that industrial products are essentially tradables, while construction and services are hardly so. Other factors are economies of scale and the small domestic Luxembourg market.

The survey reveals that 76% of firms generate the largest share of their turnover with longstanding customer relationships (relationships lasting more than one year; question 9). This is irrespective of the size and the sector. The role of long-term relationships with customers is particularly important for industrial firms, but less so for construction firms; it generally increases with firm size.

The Competitive Environment

Competition is key to price theory and an important determinant of price flexibility.[4] Several theoretical contributions suggest a negative relationship between competition and price rigidity (e.g. Rotemberg and Saloner 1987; Dornbusch 1987). On the empirical front Carlton (1986) has shown that price rigidity is strongly correlated with industry-level concentration. Similarly, survey evidence for several euro area countries has suggested that competitors' prices are an important factor for firms to reduce their own prices (chapter 2). Using micro price data from domestic supermarkets, Lünnemann and Mathä (2005a) have shown that the frequency of price change is affected by both the number of competitors with regard to a narrow product category and their overall market share.

The survey incorporates several questions related to competition among firms. First, companies were asked to indicate the number of competitors for their main product in the domestic market (question 7). Overall,

Table 8.2 Market environment of Luxembourg firms (percentages)

	Construction	Industry	Services	Trade	Small	Medium	Large	Total
Share of total domestic turnover	94	67	84	86	88	80	77	87
Firms for which LU is main market	100	66	77	85	88	81	78	87
Firms with mainly long-term customers	64	91	77	85	74	88	90	76
Firms with more than 10 competitors in the domestic market	72	32	61	61	64	49	46	61
Firms with market share below 5%	53	34	65	47	55	35	26	51
Firms that would increase the price by 5% or more in the absence of a direct competitor in the domestic market	64	23	42	54	51	49	49	51

Source: Authors' calculations.

approximately 60% of all firms have more than ten competitors (table 8.2), whereas approximately 10% estimate the number of their competitors to lie between one and four, and between five and ten. Less than 2% of all firms say they have no competitors. In general, the share of firms facing more than ten competitors decreases with the firm size. The corresponding shares for construction and industry are roughly 70% and 30%, respectively. In industry, 45% have fewer than five competitors.

Second, Luxembourg firms typically have a low market share (question 8). An absolute majority of firms estimate their market share to be less than or equal to 5% (table 8.2). Low market shares are particularly frequent with services firms (65%) but relatively infrequent for industrial firms (34%). Still, market shares of 5% or less have been the modal response for all four sectors considered.

Third, firms were asked to assess the impact of competition on their product's price. Overall, approximately 50% of them report that their prices would rise by at least 5% in the absence of a direct competitor (question 15). More than 40% of respondents expect the price of their main product to increase by 5% to 10%; approximately a further 10% estimate the price increase to be larger than or equal to 10%. More than 30% of firms expect the price of their main product not to change at all in the absence of an immediate competitor. Table 8.2 illustrates the substantial variation across size classes and sectors with respect to the expected impact of immediate competition on prices. The share of firms envisaging an increase of at least 5% on their main product's price in the absence of a direct competitor is below the average for industrial and services firms and above the average for construction and trade firms.

Fourth, as firms do not only compete in prices, but also engage in non–price competition in a number of dimensions (e.g., product quality/or customer service), they were asked to assess the importance of several predefined factors for their overall competitiveness according to a rank scale ranging from "1 = unimportant" to "4 = very important" (question 11). The strongest recognition was obtained by the quality of the product (table 8.3); this applies to all size and sector strata, except for large construction firms, which consider quality second to the price. Overall, the price ranks second. The degree of product differentiation and after-sales service received below average recognition. The delivery lag is considered the least important factor. On average, almost all criteria are considered at least important.

The importance assigned to the different factors for competitiveness varies substantially across sectors and size classes. The degree of product differentiation receives strong support from services firms but limited support from industrial firms. The latter, contrary to all other sectors, also assign relatively strong recognition to delivery lags. An interesting finding is that customer service receives the smallest recognition by services firms (midway between unimportant and important).

Table 8.3 Factors affecting firms' competitiveness (mean scores)

	Construction	Industry	Service	Trade	Small	Medium	Large	Total
Quality of product	3.7	3.8	3.9	3.8	3.8	3.7	3.7	3.8
Price of product	3.5	3.3	3.4	3.4	3.4	3.4	3.6	3.4
Long-term relationship	3.2	3.5	3.4	3.3	3.3	3.4	3.3	3.3
Customer service	3.4	3.1	2.6	3.2	3.1	3.1	2.8	3.1
Product differentiation	3.0	2.9	3.3	3.0	3.0	3.1	3.0	3.0
Delivery lags	2.9	3.3	2.8	2.9	2.9	3.1	3.2	2.9
Mean	3.3	3.3	3.2	3.2	3.3	3.3	3.3	3.3

Source: Authors' calculations.

PRICE SETTING BEHAVIOR

Who Sets the Price

Almost 80% of firms set the price of their main product autonomously, whereas 8% and 5% report it to be determined at the group level or by a public institution (question 14). Across all firm-size classes and all sectors, autonomous price setting is by far the most frequent response chosen. Substantial differences prevail however: whereas 99% of construction firms are in a position to set prices autonomously, the same applies to only 46% of trade firms. In contrast, the share of firms setting prices autonomously is by and large independent of the firm size. It is interesting that the fraction of those whose price setting is subject to public regulation is highest for large firms (note that almost 25% of trade firms responded that their prices would be subject to public regulation).

Price Review Stage

Firms that set prices autonomously were requested to disclose how often they revise and change them, whether they follow time- or state-dependent rules (question 16), and whether they are forward- or backward-looking price setters.

Whereas 20% of firms review prices at regular intervals (time dependence hereafter), 48% do so in response to specific events (state dependence), and 22% review prices generally at specific intervals, but also in response to shocks (see table 8.4). Hence, about 70% of the respondents apply some form of state-dependent rule when reviewing prices, thus stressing the

Table 8.4 Price reviews (percentages)

	Time versus state dependence				Backward versus forward looking		
	Time	State	Both	Don't know	Backward	Forward	Rule of thumb
Construction	9	59	18	15	48	20	32
Industry	20	59	19	2	19	40	41
Services	15	50	27	8	35	30	35
Trade	28	40	22	9	30	42	29
Small	21	49	19	10	36	31	33
Medium	16	45	35	5	20	55	24
Large	17	42	37	4	26	52	22
Total	20	48	22	10	34	34	32

Source: Authors' calculations.

importance of being able to react swiftly to changes in relevant economic conditions. Table 8.4 illustrates that for all sectors and size classes, the exclusive use of state-dependent rules is more frequently encountered than the exclusive use of time-dependent rules. The share of companies exclusively adopting state-dependent rules decreases with firm size.

Question 18 requested firms to disclose whether their most recent price review took into consideration information exclusively referring to present and future (forward looking) or past and present (backward looking) developments in business conditions. If neither was applicable firms could still choose a third alternative reflecting the use of a predefined rule (rule-of-thumb behavior).

Overall, our results suggest an almost uniform distribution between forward- and backward-looking firms and those applying rules of thumb (table 8.4). With 48% (20%), backward-looking behavior is relatively more (less) frequently applied by construction (industrial) firms. In general, small firms tend to rely more on backward-looking practices than medium sized and large companies. The largest shares of forward-looking firms are found in the trade (42%) and industry (40%) sectors, whereas construction firms (20%) are the least forward looking. Around 40% of industrial firms apply rules of thumb.

Firms responding that they review prices at regular intervals were subsequently asked how often they do so (question 17). The median over all firms is twice a year; 76% of firms review their prices at quarterly frequency or less often, whereas the remaining 24% do so monthly or more often. Only 1% of all firms review prices at a daily frequency, mostly medium-sized ones in construction and trade. Daily reviews are applied by neither small nor industrial firms.

Table 8.5 Frequency of price reviews (percentages)

	Construction	Industry	Services	Trade	Total
Daily	1	0	1	2	1
Weekly	1	1	0	46	19
Monthly	1	17	8	1	3
Quarterly	33	23	18	1	17
Half yearly	32	27	40	2	21
Yearly	32	12	32	47	36
Less than yearly	0	21	1	0	2
Total	100	100	100	100	100
Median[a]	2	2	2	4	2

Source: Authors' calculations.
[a]Median number of price reviews per year.

Overall, the share of firms reviewing prices more than once a year is about 60%. The corresponding share for construction, industry, and services is 67% for each sector, whereas it is only 52% for trade (table 8.5). The modal frequency of price review is annual in trade, semi-annual in services and industry, and quarterly in construction. The median is twice a year in construction, industry, and services, but it is four times a year in the trade sector. For time-dependent firms reviewing their prices annually, a clear seasonal pattern emerges; more than 50% perform their review in January. Within the trade sector, a clear bimodal distribution is discernible: 46% of companies review prices weekly, whereas 47% do so on an annual basis only.

Price Setting

Price Discrimination Question 12 asked whether firms charge identical prices or not. Price discrimination could take two forms, either setting prices as a function of the quantity sold but according to a uniform price list, or on a case-by-case basis. The share of firms charging identical prices is approximately 35%, whereas 65% of firms apply some sort of discrimination. Overall, charging an identical price is the modal outcome for all sectors except construction.

The share of companies charging identical prices is particularly high for services and trade (both around 50%) and lowest for construction (15%). In services and construction the share of firms charging identical prices shrinks with size, but this is not the case for industry and trade.

Approximately 30% of all firms fix the price according to the quantity sold. This option is the modal response for medium-sized and large industrial firms only. Of all firms, the remaining 35% sell their main product at prices varying case by case; there is substantial variation across sectors, spanning from 17% in trade to 55% in construction.

Pricing to Market   As Luxembourg is a very small market, firms start operating internationally at a very early stage in order to grow. Companies serving foreign markets were asked whether they price to market and, if so, they were requested to assess the importance of seven potentially relevant factors (e.g., variations in the exchange rate, tax system, transport costs) according to a rank scale ranging from "1 = unimportant" to "4 = very important." Almost 70% of firms apply identical prices in all markets, a figure fairly high compared to other countries (see chapter 2); 4% charge identical prices across euro area countries, whereas 27% responded that prices differ across markets. The share of price discrimination across markets increases with firm size.

The most important reasons for pricing to market are transportation costs and the price charged by competitors, followed by the level of regulation, the tax system, and structural market conditions (table 8.6). Exchange rate developments are, on the contrary, only of minor importance, thus reflecting the fact that most internationally active firms operate mostly in neighboring European Monetary Union (EMU) countries. Consistent with this interpretation, the importance of exchange rate variations increases with firm size.

Frequency of Price Change   Overall, the median firm changes its price twice a year; 28% of respondents change prices exactly once a year. The frequency of price adjustment varies considerably across sectors and size classes (table 8.7). Companies operating in construction and trade change their price more often than those in industry and in services, where only 13% and 15% of firms, respectively, do it more than twice a year. The median frequency

Table 8.6 Factors affecting pricing to market (mean scores)

	Construction	Industry	Service	Trade	Small	Medium	Large	Total
Transport costs	3.0	3.5	2.9	3.1	3.0	3.7	3.5	3.1
Price of competitors	2.1	2.1	3.0	3.4	2.6	3.1	3.1	2.7
Level of regulation	2.0	3.0	2.5	2.2	2.4	1.6	2.7	2.4
Tax system	1.1	3.4	2.9	2.4	2.3	1.3	3.3	2.2
Structural market conditions	1.1	2.5	2.5	2.9	1.9	3.6	3.2	2.1
Cyclical demand changes	1.1	2.1	3.3	2.4	1.9	2.9	2.9	2.1
Variations in exchange rates	1.0	2.4	1.0	1.8	1.2	1.2	2.1	1.2

Source: Authors' calculations.

Table 8.7 Frequency of price changes (percentages)

	Construction	Industry	Services	Trade	Total
Daily	16	0	3	2	7
Weekly	8	1	0	22	10
Monthly	8	7	3	5	6
Quarterly	9	5	9	14	10
Half yearly	33	29	36	28	32
Yearly	17	41	37	28	28
Less than yearly	7	17	11	1	8
Total	100	100	100	100	100
Median[a]	2	1	1	2	2

Source: Authors' calculations.
[a]Median number of price changes per year.

of two price changes a year is identical to the median frequency of two price reviews a year; it is higher than the median reported in other euro area countries. This may partly be related to the inclusion of the construction sector in our survey.

THEORIES EXPLAINING PRICE STICKINESS

As a key complement to the study of inflation persistence at the aggregate and the sectoral level as well as to the analysis of consumer prices at the micro level (Lünnemann and Mathä 2005a, 2005b), the survey aimed at identifying the most important obstacles to faster price adjustment. It proposed fifteen reasons for prices to deviate from their optimum level, based on the seminal work by Blinder et al. (1998). Firms were asked to assess the importance of each of these reasons according to a scale ranging from "1 = unimportant" to "4 = very important."

The results indicate that firms consider implicit contracts the most important obstacle to price adjustment (table 8.8); the theory of constant marginal costs comes second in our ranked table of theories, and explicit contracts rank third. These three theories have also received strong recognition in studies for other countries. Three further theories of price stickiness receiving substantial recognition from Luxembourg firms are procyclical elasticity, thick markets (demand side), and liquidity constraints, ranked four to six, with no substantial differences across sectors and size classes.

However, our results are much less supportive with respect to temporary shock (rank 11), external finance (12), menu costs (13), non–price factors (14), and costly information gathering (15). Similar to findings from other

Table 8.8 Theories explaining price stickiness (ranking)

	Construction	Industry	Service	Trade	Small	Medium	Large	Total
Implicit contracts	2	3	4	3	1	1	2	1
Constant marginal cost	3	1	1	4	2	3	3	2
Explicit contracts	1	4	7	8	5	2	1	3
Procyclical demand	6	5	3	2	4	4	5	4
Thick markets—demand	4	6	8	1	3	6	7	5
Fixed costs/liquidity constraints	5	2	5	9	6	5	4	6
Judging quality by price	7	10	2	10	8	7	8	7
Thick markets—supply	8	9	6	7	7	9	11	8
Coordination failure	12	7	9	6	9	8	6	9
Threshold pricing	15	15	14	5	10	15	13	10
Temporary shock	14	13	13	11	11	13	14	11
External finance	10	11	11	13	12	11	10	12
Menu cost	11	12	10	14	13	12	9	13
Non-price factors	9	8	12	15	14	10	12	14
Costly information	13	14	15	12	15	14	15	15

Source: Authors' calculations.

surveys, we find some variation in the relevance of theories across firms. Small and medium-sized firms assign strongest relevance to the implicit contracts, whereas large firms judge explicit contracts the most important obstacle to flexible prices. Constant marginal costs as well as judging price by quality are particularly relevant for services, but trade firms rank thick markets (demand) in the first and attractive prices in the fifth place; the latter never scores better than the tenth place in the other sectors. Finally, liquidity constraints are judged to be the second most important impediment to faster price adjustment for industrial firms.

DETERMINANTS OF PRICE CHANGES

Recent empirical evidence shows that price increases occur more frequently than price decreases: for the euro area countries, as well as for Luxembourg, this asymmetry is about 60% to 40% for unprocessed food, processed food, energy, and non-energy industrial goods, whereas it is more pronounced and closer to 80% to 20% for services (Dhyne et al. 2005; Lünnemann and Mathä 2005a, 2005b). Peltzman (2000) also provides evidence that prices respond asymmetrically to cost shocks.

To assess whether there is any asymmetry related to the direction of price adjustment, firms were requested to indicate the relevance of specific cost factors (such as labor, financial, and other costs), of productivity change, and of market conditions (such as demand and competitors' behavior) for the decision to adjust the price of their main product (questions 21 and 22). They were asked to assess the importance of the above factors according to a rank scale ranging from "1 = unimportant" to "4 = very important." The results indicate very clearly that increases in labor costs are considered the most important factor for price increases, followed by increases in other costs (figure 8.1). Below average recognition is obtained for increases in demand, price increases by competitors, productivity decreases, and capital costs. The average recognition is not independent of the firm's size. Productivity, capital costs, indexation, and wage costs all turn out to be more important for small firms than for medium-sized ones and, even more so, large firms. Instead, differences across sectors are moderate.

With regard to price reductions, the most important underlying factors are price cuts by competitors and declining wage costs; declining capital costs and productivity increases were assigned relatively low importance (question 22). There are very moderate differences across sectors and size classes: construction firms, in particular large ones, consider declining demand as the most important factor for price reductions, a scenario probably not recorded in Luxembourg for a decade or two. Contrary to the case of price increases, no single factor receives an average recognition equivalent to "important" or higher.

All factors considered (except for price of competitors and demand fluctuations) were assigned a higher recognition as drivers of price increases than of price reductions.

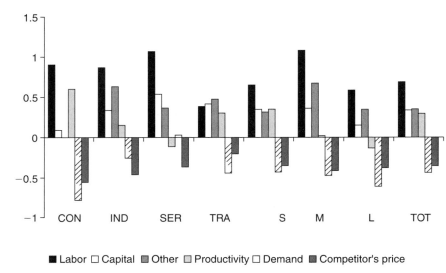

Figure 8.1 Factors' relevance: price increase relative to price decrease (mean scores). *Legend:* CON = construction, IND = industry, SER = services, TRA = trade, S = small, M = medium, L = large, TOT = total. *Source:* Authors' calculations.

SPEED OF PRICE ADJUSTMENTS

In assessing the degree of price stickiness, it is essential not only to know the obstacles to immediate price adjustments, but also to quantify the degree of sluggishness. As the latter may differ in response to specific types of shock, question 19 investigates the speed of price adjustment in response to cost and demand shocks. In order to capture potential asymmetries with regard to the direction of the price change, a distinction is made between positive and negative shocks. Firms were asked to assess the speed of adjustment according to a rank scale ranging from "1 = less than 1 week" to "6 = the price remains unchanged."

Our results indeed suggest that the speed of price adjustment depends on the type and direction of the shock (figure 8.2). Three main results emerge: first, firms raise prices relatively soon in response to an increase in production costs. Approximately 30% and 50% of firms adjust their main product's price within a single week and within a single month, respectively. Small firms react faster in response to increasing costs. In addition, we find large discrepancies across sectors. Whereas approximately 70% of trade firms adjust prices within a single month, an equally rapid adjustment is carried out by about 30% of industrial and services firms. In fact, the median lag of price adjustment is between three to six months in industry, but less than one month in trade.

Second, firms seem to adjust prices much less rapidly in response to an increase in demand. Overall, 17% of them react within a one-month period; for

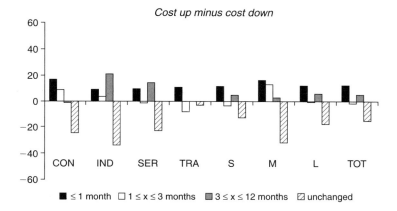

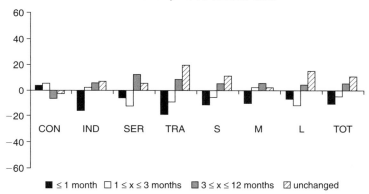

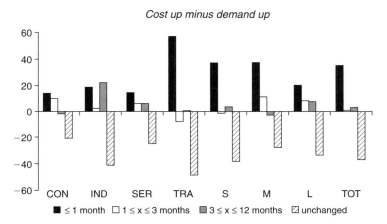

Figure 8.2 Differences in adjustment speed (percentages). The figures on the vertical axis represent the difference (in percentage points) between the fractions of firms adjusting their price in response to the shocks indicated in the title of each figure within the time span reported in the key. *Legend:* CON = construction, IND = industry, SER = services, TRA = trade, S = small, M = medium, L = large, TOT = total. *Source:* Authors' calculations.

16% the adjustment takes place after three or more months only. The corresponding share is particularly high in services (around 30%), but relatively small in trade (less than 10%). The share of firms not adjusting prices following an increase in demand is 47%; it is particularly sizeable in the trade sector (59%).

Third, the speed of adjustment is much less asymmetric in the case of weakening demand and declining costs. Overall, 37% (25%) of all firms do not adjust prices at all following a reduction of demand (declining costs). This share is particularly high in industry (about 45%). Trade firms seem to adjust prices relatively fast, with approximately 20% (29%) of them reacting within a single week. The corresponding shares for the other sectors are much lower (always below 10%).

All in all, firms adjust their price very rapidly in response to increasing costs and very sluggishly in response to strengthening demand.

CONCLUSIONS

Our survey shows that, in general, Luxembourg firms generate around 90% of their turnover in the domestic market, have a low market share, face a relatively large number of competitors, and typically maintain longstanding customer relationships.

In assessing the relevance of different factors driving their competitiveness, firms assigned strongest recognition to the quality of their product. With regard to price setting practices, almost 80% of companies set prices autonomously. Backward-looking, forward-looking, and rules-of-thumb mechanisms are found to be equally important.

About 20% of firms review prices at regular intervals, whereas 48% of them do so in response to specific events. The others adopt both rules. The median frequency of price review and of price change is twice a year. Around two-thirds of firms apply some sort of price discrimination across customers, but pricing to market does not seem to be particularly relevant.

Increases in labor costs are the most important factor for price increases, followed by increases in other costs whereas price reductions are driven mainly by reductions in competitors' prices and declining wage costs.

The speed of price adjustment depends on the type and direction of the shock. Firms seem to raise prices relatively soon in response to an increase in production costs: approximately half of them react within a single month. They adjust prices much less rapidly in response to an increase in demand, almost half of them not reacting at all. The speed of adjustment is much less asymmetric in the case of declining costs and shrinking demand.

Implicit contracts are considered the most important obstacle to price adjustment, followed by constant marginal costs and explicit contracts.

Acknowledgments We would like to thank Nico Weydert from STATEC for granting us access to the company register and for sampling the firms surveyed; Martine Druant and Bettina Landau for their critical review of the questionnaire; Olivier

Marty, Guy Premont, and Ladislav Wintr for assistance in data processing; and Claudia Kwapil and other IPN members for their constructive help and criticism received. Finally, we would like to thank the participating firms, without whom this undertaking would have been impossible.

NOTES

1. Firms that did not reply by September 2004 were reminded to do so by the end of October.
2. The sampling was undertaken by the national statistical institute STATEC. Numerical differences to chapter 2 are primarily due to a different weighting scheme adopted.
3. See also chapter 3 on this point.
4. For a survey on the relationship between competition and inflation see for example Asplund and Friberg (1998).

REFERENCES

Apel, Mikael, Richard Friberg, and Kerstin Hallsten. 2005. Micro foundations of macroeconomic price adjustment: Survey evidence from Swedish firms. *Journal of Money, Credit, and Banking* 37: 313–338.

Asplund, Markus, and Richard Friberg. 1998. Links between competition and inflation. *Sveriges Riksbank Quarterly Review* 3: 50–73.

Blinder, Alan S., Elie R. D. Canetti, David E. Lebow, and Jeremy B. Rudd. 1998. *Asking About Prices: A New Approach to Understanding Price Stickiness*. New York: Russell Sage Foundation.

Carlton, Dennis W. 1986. The rigidity of prices. *American Economic Review* 76: 637–658.

Dhyne, Emmanuel, Luis J. Álvarez, Hervé Le Bihan, Giovanni Veronese, Daniel Dias, Johannes Hoffmann, Nicole Jonker, Patrick Lünnemann, Fabio Rumler, and Jouko Vulminen. 2005. Price setting in the euro area: Some stylized facts from individual consumer price data. European Central Bank Working Paper No. 524. Frankfurt am Main: European Central Bank.

Dornbusch, Rudiger. 1987. Exchange rates and prices. *American Economic Review* 77: 93–106.

Hall, Simon, Mark Walsh, and Anthony Yates. 2000. Are UK companies' prices sticky? *Oxford Economic Papers* 52: 425–446.

Lünnemann, Patrick, and Thomas Y. Mathä. 2005(a). Consumer price behavior in Luxembourg: Evidence from micro CPI data. European Central Bank Working Paper No. 541. Frankfurt am Main: European Central Bank.

Lünnemann, Patrick, and Thomas Y. Mathä. 2005(b). Regulated and services' prices and inflation persistence. European Central Bank Working Paper No. 466. Frankfurt am Main: European Central Bank.

Peltzman, Sam. 2000. Prices rise faster than they fall. *Journal of Political Economy* 108: 466–502.

Rotemberg, Julio J., and Garth Saloner. 1987. The relative rigidity of monopoly pricing. *American Economic Review* 77: 917–926.

9

The Pricing Behavior of Dutch Firms

Survey Evidence on Price Stickiness

Marco Hoeberichts & Ad Stokman

This chapter analyzes price setting policies of firms in the Netherlands. The study is based on information from a survey commissioned by de Nederlandsche Bank in May 2004. This survey is the first attempt to capture the characteristics of price setting for a broad range of companies in the Netherlands.

The main results of this analysis can be compared to those provided by Jonker et al. (2004), who examine the degree of nominal rigidities of consumer prices in the Dutch economy using a large database with monthly price quotes of 49 items during the period 1998–2003. Though the two studies are based on different sets of information, a number of interesting similarities arise. They both provide strong evidence that prices are stickiest in small firms and most flexible in large firms. The median price duration arising from the survey is 12 months, against 9 months in the study on price records. The reason for this difference might be that the survey covers a broader set of prices, both consumer and business-to-business prices, finding that the latter change much less frequently than the former. Both studies find that price increases occur more often than decreases and that the magnitude of decreases is larger, although in the survey this difference is more pronounced. Finally, Dutch price setters are found to follow both time- and state-dependent pricing strategies. One difference that emerges from the two analyses concerns the speed of price adjustment of one-person firms: although the micro study concludes that these firms change prices almost as quickly as large ones, here we do not find such similarity. This may be due to the fact that in the survey one-person firms cover a much wider range of activities, including business-to-business transactions.

Dutch firms were interviewed about several aspects of their price setting, ranging from frequency of price changes and price reviews, to how they set their prices and why they change them or not. Several theories of price stickiness were investigated. The main finding is that stickiness is a significant feature of price setting in the Netherlands. It is strongest among small firms, those providing business-to-business services, and those facing weak competition.

The chapter is organized as follows. In the first section, we briefly describe the survey setup. In the second section, we analyze and discuss the outcomes of the survey, focusing on the frequency of price reviews and price changes, price setting rules, reasons for price stickiness, and the existence of asymmetries in pricing behavior. In the third section we offer our conclusions.

SURVEY SETUP

The survey was carried out by a private company (TNS-NIPO) in May 2004, on the basis of a questionnaire prepared by de Nederlandsche Bank (see the Appendix to the book). The sample was drawn from a panel of 12,000 company owners, directors, and high-level managers responsible for marketing, sales, or finance. The questionnaire was sent by e-mail to almost 1,900 selected employees, employers, and self-employed, in most cases to their home e-mail addresses. This approach has the advantage that people can pick their own time to reply. The questionnaire was pretested on a pilot sample of 200 firms. In total, TNS-NIPO received 1,246 responses. The overall response rate was 67%, quite high considering the nature of the survey. The response rate of large companies was the lowest (36%), but still satisfactory when compared to other surveys in the same field. The high response rate demonstrates the suitability of the business panel for our purpose.

An important feature of the panel is its broad coverage of the Dutch business community. For our investigation into price stickiness this was crucial. The main part of our sample refers to the services sector, both because the latter is the dominant economic activity in the Netherlands and because we expect price stickiness to be particularly relevant for certain types of services. The need for a broad spectrum also applies to company size, measured in our survey by the number of employees; we distinguish seven size classes (question 0.3): one employee (including owner), 2 to 4, 5 to 9, 10 to 19, 20 to 49, 50 to 99, and 100 or more employees. To our knowledge, our survey is unique in that it also provides detailed information on price setting behavior of firms with fewer than 50 employees (for detailed results on the survey and price setting in small companies, see Hoeberichts and Stokman 2006). About half of the respondents are small companies with at most 9 employees, representing over 90% of the business community. In terms of employment figures, their share is much smaller, but still quite substantial with 32% of total employment (Jakulj et al. 2003). Excluded from the survey are the government, construction, the financial sector, the energy sector, and farming. The sample is stratified in seven sectors and seven size classes. We used this stratification to weight the results and make the analysis representative for the Dutch economy.

Respondents were requested to fill in the survey with respect to the "main product," or one typical product sold by the company. Picking a specific product was convenient especially for companies adopting a variety of pricing strategies for different goods and services. Moreover, with this instruction we prevented the respondent from switching from one product to another, thereby safeguarding internal consistency throughout the questionnaire.

In order to get an impression of the scope of our survey, firms were asked whether they adopt a unique pricing policy for their products or not. On average, 28% of the respondents reported that their price setting is basically the same for all products, 24% that they adopt one pricing strategy for the greater part of their assortment, and 44% stated that price setting may vary substantially with the type of product. Not surprising, price setting by large companies is more diversified than for smaller ones (53% against 37%). All in all, these figures suggest that the scope of the survey is broader than what might perhaps be expected from the single product approach.

SURVEY OUTCOMES

Table 9.1 shows the main characteristics of the firms in our sample, after we applied the poststratification weighting scheme. About half of the firms indicated the national market as the most important one for their main product; the local market is the most relevant for 23% of the firms, the international one for 18%. This seems rather low for an open economy such as the Netherlands. However, it has to be borne in mind that we only asked about the "most important" market, so that a firm that trades 60% internally and 40% abroad is counted as a firm that sells most of its main product on the national market. For the remaining 10% of firms the regional market is the point of reference. There are some striking differences across sectors: on the one hand, the international market is very important for manufacturing firms and, to a lesser extent, for those in the transport sector; the local market, on the other hand, is particularly relevant for retailers (especially food) and hotels and restaurants.

The degree of competition is another important characteristic of the market in which firms operate. It is also notoriously hard to measure. As a rule, we expect competitive pressure to rise with the number of competitors. But this measure has its shortcomings. For example, in oligopolistic markets with a small number of large firms, competition may be strong as well. Therefore, we included two measures of the degree of competition in our questionnaire: the number of competitors (in five categories: none, 1, 2 to 5, 6 to 20, more than 20) and the degree of perceived competition (in four categories: not at all, weak, strong, very strong). For most sectors, both measures point in the same direction but for some there are differences. In the business-to-business services sector, 32% of the firms reported more than 20 competitors (20% for the total sample), whereas only 18% reported very strong perceived competition (26% for the total). At the other extreme, only 17% of the firms in the transport sector reported more than 20 competitors, but 41% perceive very strong competition. This probably reflects the fact that the transport sector provides a more homogeneous product than does the business-to-business services sector, making it more difficult for a firm to

Table 9.1 The main characteristics of the interviewed firms (percentages)[a]

	Total	Sector						
		Manufacturing	Retail food	Retail non-food	Wholesale	Transport	Hotel and restaurant	Other services
1. What is the most important market (in terms of turnover) for your main product?								
Local	23.1	5.4	70.4	41.4	9.6	19.2	50.6	14.9
Regional	8.8	4.9	1.1	8.7	8.9	6.6	6.4	14.3
National	49.9	47.9	22.5	42.0	66.2	49.7	34.5	59.6
International	18.3	41.8	6.0	7.8	15.3	24.6	8.5	11.3
2. How do you perceive competition in your market?								
Very strong	26.3	26.4	37.8	33.6	35.5	41.1	14.3	18.3
Strong	50.0	52.6	50.1	47.1	47.4	33.9	47.1	55.5
Weak	19.6	19.9	8.3	18.1	15.3	16.5	28.4	20.8
Not at all	4.1	1.0	3.8	1.1	1.8	8.4	10.2	5.4
3. On the domestic market, could you indicate the number of your competitors?								
None	6.3	8.7	2.6	1.9	2.9	14.0	11.2	5.2
1	3.9	5.7	0.0	1.0	3.3	0.9	8.0	4.0
Between 2 and 5	38.3	50.5	49.8	43.8	25.7	37.7	38.8	29.0
Between 5 and 20	31.6	26.0	33.6	32.4	46.5	30.9	29.8	30.1
>20	19.9	9.1	14.0	20.9	21.6	16.5	12.2	31.8

Source: Authors' calculations.
[a] Answers have been rescaled for missing responses.

charge a price that is higher than the one charged by competitors, even when the latter are only few.

Price Reviews and Changes

In questions 2.3 and 2.4 we asked firms about the frequency of price reviews and changes. In tables 9.2 and 9.3, results on these issues are shown for different sectors and firm sizes. It is clear that in all sectors price reviews occur more frequently than changes and that the degree of stickiness differs substantially across sectors. Price reviews are most frequently observed in wholesale and retail, especially food, and also in manufacturing. Firms in these sectors, except manufacturers, also change prices most frequently. Within the services sector, the prices of business services are the most rigid.

Two out of three Dutch firms review their prices more than once a year, and one out of three actually changes them more than once a year. In manufacturing, 70% of the firms reported that they review prices more than once a year but still only 26% change them with the same frequency. Prices in business services appear to be the most rigid: about half of all firms review and less than 20% change their prices more than once a year. The hotel and restaurant sector also has relatively sticky prices.

As already mentioned, our survey has a broad coverage of firm sizes. Table 9.3 shows how the frequency of price reviews and changes varies with firm size. Clearly, small firms with only one employee have the most rigid prices: only 37% of them review and only 24% change prices more than once a year. The low frequency of price reviews for the smallest firms really stands out: of firms that are only slightly larger and have from 2 to 4 employees, 51% review more than once a year. Large firms tend to review very frequently (69% of them more often than once a year), but still only 36% change prices more than once a year.

Table 9.2 Price reviews and price changes per sector (percentages)[a]

Sector	Firms that review more than once a year	Firms that change more than once a year
Manufacturing	70.8	26.2
Wholesale	73.1	48.4
Retail food	86.0	67.6
Retail non-food	78.4	58.5
Hotel and restaurant	57.5	27.2
Transport	61.9	34.8
Business services	47.5	18.5
Total	64.1	33.6

Source: Authors' calculations.
[a]Answers have been rescaled for missing responses.

Table 9.3 Price reviews and price changes by size class (percentages)

Firm size (employees)	Firms that review more than once a year	Firms that change more than once a year
1	37.4	24.2
2–4	50.7	30.3
5–9	60.6	36.2
10–19	64.8	29.4
20–49	60.7	27.4
50–99	72.6	38.7
>100	69.4	36.2
Total	64.1	33.6

Source: Authors' calculations.

Overall, the higher frequency of price reviews compared to price changes suggests that the costs of collecting information are not so crucial.

Price Determination

We asked companies how they determine the price for their main product. In the Appendix to the book (question 2.7), all possible answers are listed. Here we focus on the five most important answer categories, distinguishing, as in the previous section, by sector and by size. Table 9.4 reports the results

Table 9.4 Price setting rules (percentages)[a]

	A fixed markup is applied to unit variable costs	A variable markup is applied to unit variable costs	The price is determined by competitors	The price is set by customers	The price is linked to another price (e.g. wage or fuel)
Total	24.6	36.4	21.9	6.0	11.1
Manufacturing	27.9	39.2	21.1	3.3	8.4
Retail food	24.5	30.7	40.9	2.0	1.9
Retail non-food	31.2	28.1	28.6	10.2	1.9
Wholesale	25.0	52.5	21.1	1.4	0.0
Transport	21.9	21.5	16.0	15.4	25.2
Hotel and restaurant	27.5	35.1	19.7	5.9	11.8
Other services	18.2	36.9	18.6	6.2	20.2

Source: Authors' calculations.
[a]Answers have been rescaled for missing responses.

by sector. One-quarter of firms apply a fixed markup to their costs. The largest group (36%) applies a variable markup to unit variable costs, without specifying the details of the market conditions that determine the markup. Another 22% applies a markup that varies with the price that competitors charge; 11% link the price to another price, such as wages or fuel, and for 6% of the firms the price is determined by the main customer.

It is clear that firms in the retail non-food sector and in the hotel and restaurant sector have a preference for applying a fixed markup to their costs. The variable markup, depending on market conditions, is the most frequent way of determining prices in manufacturing, wholesale, transport, and other services.

As with the frequency of price changes and reviews, the one-employee firms stand out in the way they determine prices. Where the general picture shows that smaller firms tend to apply a fixed markup and large ones a variable markup, one-employee firms appear to determine their price mostly by looking at their competitors' prices.

Firms can change the price that they charge for their product at regular time intervals or in response to specific events. We asked them (question 2.2) how they determine when it is time to adjust their price. Table 9.5 reports the results for the economy as a whole and by sector. About one out of three firms applies purely time-dependent pricing at regular intervals longer than one day. In the transport sector this share is much larger, at 55%. Another 38% of firms reported that they apply purely state-dependent pricing, only reacting to specific events. Daily adjustments are applied by 6% of companies, mainly concentrated in the retail food and wholesale sectors.

Reasons for Price Stickiness

Firms may have many reasons not to change prices immediately. In question 2.10 we asked which factors might delay carrying out a price adjustment for the main product. Respondents attributed a value from "1 = irrelevant" to "4 = very important" to each of eight theories of price stickiness often found in the literature. The results, reported in table 9.6, are in line with those obtained for other euro area countries (see chapter 2), showing that implicit and explicit contracts play an important role, whereas menu costs and attractive pricing appear to be relatively unimportant. The picture is broadly the same across sectors, but we also observe some noticeable differences. For the hotel and restaurant sector, for instance, the fear that lowering prices might mistakenly be interpreted as lower quality is the most important reason for delaying price adjustments. As expected, attractive pricing and menu costs are relatively relevant in the retail sector. We also find a difference between small and large firms: for large firms, explicit rather than implicit contracts are the most important reason not to change prices, whereas for small firms implicit contracts are more relevant.

Asymmetries

In this section we discuss asymmetric price responses of Dutch firms to shocks. The literature provides a number of explanations for asymmetries.

Table 9.5 The rules underlying price changes (percentages)[a]

	Total	Manufacturing	Retail food	Retail non-food	Wholesale	Transport	Hotel and restaurant	Other services
				Sector				
Do you adjust the price you want to charge for your main product at fixed time intervals?								
Yes, every day	6.1	1.7	28.6	8.6	15.8	1.9	6.6	1.8
At predetermined intervals	32.9	32.7	15.8	23.4	30.0	55.0	30.3	37.7
Mainly at predetermined intervals, but also in reaction to specific events	22.9	25.4	30.2	24.0	16.5	20.2	25.8	21.3
No, only in reaction to specific events	38.1	40.2	25.4	44.0	37.7	22.9	37.3	39.2

Source: Authors' calculations.
[a] Answers have been rescaled for missing responses.

Table 9.6 Importance of theoretical explanations in delaying price changes (mean scores)

					Sector				
	Total	Manufacturing	Retail food	Retail non-food	Wholesale	Transport	Hotel and restaurant	Other services	
Customers expect us to keep prices as stable as possible	2.7	2.7	2.6	2.5	2.7	2.9	2.6	2.7	
Prices can only be changed when contract is renegotiated	2.6	2.7	2.6	2.2	2.7	2.8	2.2	2.7	
Lowering prices might mistakenly be interpreted as quality loss	2.4	2.3	2.7	2.4	2.2	2.2	2.6	2.4	
We fear that we may need to revise the price in the opposite direction	2.4	2.3	2.5	2.3	2.3	2.2	2.4	2.4	
We fear that competing firms will not change their price	2.2	2.3	2.3	2.4	2.3	2.0	2.1	2.2	
Instead of changing prices, we prefer to change other conditions	2.1	2.2	2.0	2.1	2.1	2.1	1.8	1.9	
We set prices at attractive thresholds	1.8	1.7	2.2	2.3	1.8	1.8	1.8	1.7	
Presence of high menu costs of changing prices	1.7	1.6	1.9	2.1	1.8	1.9	1.9	1.6	

Source: Authors' calculations.

They might arise because of strategic interaction between firms (Rotemberg and Saloner 1987), the presence of menu costs (Ball and Mankiw 1994), search costs (Small and Yates 1999), or capacity constraints (Finn 1996). According to Ball and Romer (1990), nominal prices are stickier in a market where firms' profits do not change much in the face of shocks.

As described above, menu costs seem to play a very limited role in pricing decisions. Unfortunately, we do not have information about search costs. Furthermore, as the economy had just started to recover from a recession at the time the firms were surveyed, we do not expect capacity constraints to be particularly relevant. In the following we take a closer look at the role of competition. Next, as the smallest firms are found to be the most rigid price setters and are well represented in our survey, we focus on one-person companies in greater detail.

In questions 2.8 and 2.9, respondents were asked to attribute a value from "1 = irrelevant" to "4 = very important" to factors leading to price increases and decreases. According to the results, asymmetric responses to shocks are a general feature of price behavior in the Dutch business sector (table 9.7). Rising costs have a significantly larger upward effect on prices than declining costs have in the opposite direction. Asymmetric responses are strongest for labor cost shocks. If we group firms according to the degree of competition they face, from severe to weak, responses to cost shocks, both positive and negative, are strongest for the first group. To put it differently, price setting is more flexible in a competitive environment. Moreover, for firms perceiving weak competition, reported cost asymmetries are significantly larger. Similar results are found in most other countries (see Hall et al. 2000 for the United Kingdom and chapter 2 for the euro area).

Asymmetric price responses are also widespread when market conditions change. In competitive markets, company prices respond more strongly to conditions such as weakening demand and lower competitors' prices, leading to price decreases, than to shocks in the opposite direction. With weak competition, asymmetries vanish. These results may have important implications for monetary policymaking and are also very interesting for macroeconomic model building, in which asymmetries are often ignored.

Table 9.7 Factors likely to cause a price increase/decrease (mean scores)

	Increase	Decrease
An increase/decrease in labor costs	2.9	2.2
An increase/decrease in raw materials costs	2.6	2.1
An increase/decrease in financial costs	2.2	1.9
A rise/fall in demand	2.4	2.6
Price increase/decrease by competitors	2.6	2.7

Source: Authors' calculations.

Compared to the surveys in other countries, the Dutch survey contains detailed information about small firms, including the smallest one-person firms that in the Netherlands account for around 40% of the business population (in terms of value added their weight is smaller but nevertheless significant). The share of business-to-business services in one-person firms is 60%; the shares of those in retail non-food, in wholesale or transport, and in retail food are 13%, 12%, and 3%, respectively. One-person companies exhibit peculiarities not only in comparison to large firms but also with respect to the other small firms. Price responses to cost shocks by one-person companies are by far the weakest, both in the case of downward and upward pressures; the response to changes in demand or competitors' prices is stronger, however, especially under worsening market conditions, and is more in line with that of larger companies. This behavior can be explained by a number of features. As the employer and employee is one and the same person, these firms are relatively insensitive to labor cost shocks. Moreover, for many one-person firms raw materials are of little importance. Finally, the weak responsiveness to financial costs can be explained by the fact they rely to a great extent on internal financial resources.

To sum up, most one-person companies change their prices only occasionally, but when they do they set the prices in accordance with market conditions.

CONCLUSIONS

Our survey provides interesting new insights into the price setting behavior of Dutch companies. Because of its broad coverage, we were able to identify some basic characteristics of sticky price companies. First, the degree of competition is very important in shaping firms' pricing behavior: with weak competition, producer prices become much stickier. Company size is also found to be relevant. Our study is the first that sheds light on pricing behavior of small companies (from 1 to 9 employees), which represent a significant part of the business community. One-person firms are by far the stickiest price setters.

Besides size and competition, sectoral differences also matter: trade firms (wholesale and retail) adopt relatively flexible pricing policies, whereas prices in the business services and hotel and restaurant sectors are the most rigid.

Finally, there is clear evidence of asymmetries in price adjustment, depending on the type of shock (to costs or to market conditions). Among the motives for not changing or delaying price changes, informal and explicit contracts are the most relevant. Menu costs and attractive prices are unimportant. This is in line with the finding for other European countries.

REFERENCES

Ball, Laurence, and N. Gregory Mankiw. 1994. A sticky-price manifesto. *Carnegie-Rochester Conference Series on Public Policy* 41: 127–151.

Ball, Laurence, and David Romer. 1990. Real rigidities and the non-neutrality of money. *Review of Economic Studies* 57: 183–203.

Finn, Mary G. 1996. A theory of the capacity utilization/inflation relationship. *Federal Reserve Bank of Richmond Economic Quarterly* 82: 67–86.

Hall, Simon, Antony Yates, and Mark Walsh. 2000. Are UK companies' prices sticky? *Oxford Economic Papers* 52: 425–446.

Hoeberichts, Marco, and Ad Stokman. 2006. Price setting behaviour in the Netherlands: Results of a survey. European Central Bank Working Paper No. 607. Frankfurt am Main: European Central Bank.

Jakulj, Jelena, Nicole Jonker, and Marga Peeters. 2003. Employment dynamics within small, medium and large establishments in the Netherlands at the end of the 1990: Where and to what extent did job creation and job destruction occur? DNB Research Memorandum No. 742. Amsterdam: De Nederlandsche Bank.

Jonker, Nicole, Harry Blijenburg, and Carsten Folkertsma. 2004. An empirical analysis of price setting behaviour in the Netherlands in the period 1998–2003 using micro data. European Central Bank Working Paper No. 413. Frankfurt am Main: European Central Bank.

Rotemberg, Julio J., and Garth Saloner. 1987. The relative rigidity of monopoly pricing. *American Economic Review* 77: 917–926.

Small, Ian, and Antony Yates. 1999. What makes prices sticky? Some survey evidence for the United Kingdom. *Bank of England Quarterly Bulletin* 39: 262–271.

10

How Portuguese Firms Set Their Prices

Evidence from Survey Data

Fernando Martins

This chapter summarizes the main results from a survey conducted by the Banco de Portugal between May and September 2004 on a sample of 1,370 firms, mostly from manufacturing, with the purpose of investigating price setting in Portugal. The analysis was structured around three main questions. What is the degree of price stickiness in Portugal? What are the main reasons that prevent firms from adjusting their prices more promptly in response to significant changes in their costs or demand? To what extent does the qualitative evidence coming from the survey support the results stemming from micro quantitative data?

The chapter is organized as follows. The first section summarizes the main features of the sample selection and the survey design. The second section presents a number of characteristics of the market where firms operate that are important for their pricing decisions. The third section assesses the degree of price stickiness in Portugal on the basis of a number of indicators, including the frequency of price reviews and price changes, the speed of price changes in response to shocks, and the share of firms following time-dependent and state-dependent pricing rules. The fourth section examines the main theories of price stickiness put forward in the literature. The fifth section investigates the reaction of prices to demand and cost shocks, and the sixth section presents some concluding remarks.

SAMPLE AND SURVEY DESIGN

The survey was conducted by the Banco de Portugal between May and September 2004 on the basis of a sample covering mostly manufacturing but also a number of services sectors. Some sectors, such as construction or retailing, were excluded, mostly because of the difficulty in identifying a "main product." Almost 2,500 firms were contacted to participate. These were selected predominantly from the Central Balance Sheet Database (*Central de Balanços*, CB).[1] The sample was stratified by sector and size. The whole population of firms for the selected sectors was first split into two groups according to the number of employees: one group (small firms) contained firms with 20 to 50 employees, and the other group (large firms) included firms with 50 or more employees. It was decided that 40% of firms would be drawn from the first group and the remaining 60% would be drawn from the second. A cross-tabulation of these two groups with the selected 31 NACE two-digit sectors that were selected gave rise to 62 mutually exclusive strata. The number of firms to be drawn from each stratum was selected according to the relative frequency of every stratum in the Ministry of Employment Personnel Database (*Quadros de Pessoal*, QP), an annual mandatory survey conducted by the Portuguese Ministry of Employment, which is the best proxy for the population of Portuguese firms. At the end, the sample included 2,099 firms from manufacturing, 10 from energy, and 382 from services. These firms accounted for about 17% of total employment in Portugal.

The questionnaire was organized in six sections containing a total of 31 questions (see the Appendix to the book). For the sake of comparability, a large share of these questions was taken from other similar surveys conducted in other euro area countries. An attempt was made to phrase the questions as much as possible in nontechnical language that could be understood by a nonspecialist.

After the sample had been selected and a first draft of the survey had been designed, a small scale pilot survey was carried out on a sample of 20 firms at the end of May 2004. This provided a very useful mechanism for an ex ante assessment of firms' reaction to the survey. Following the analysis of responses and after contacting some of the surveyed firms by phone, a number of questions were either reformulated or even eliminated in order to make the survey shorter and simpler. Expressions like "marginal costs" or "firms with a lower elasticity of demand" were replaced by less technical terms such as "changes in costs" or "firms that are less sensitive to changes in prices." The pilot survey was also very helpful in terms of choosing the best way to contact firms.

In July 2004, a revised version of the questionnaire was sent by traditional mail to the whole sample of firms, making clear inter alia that the survey was supposed to be answered by someone well informed about the firm's price setting (senior managers in most cases). Firms were allowed to answer within 15 working days either by traditional mail or through a specially created Web site. A help desk was also created to support firms, either by phone, fax, or e-mail. By mid August, a reminder was sent to firms that had not responded. At the end, 1,370 valid questionnaires were received. A response rate of 55% was rather pleasing, given that for most firms it was the first time they were facing this kind of survey and some of the questions were not particularly easy to answer.

MAIN MARKET CHARACTERISTICS

There are a number of market characteristics that are important determinants of firms' pricing behavior. These include the location of their main market (domestic or foreign), the degree of competition they face, and the kind of relationship they have with their customers. In this section, each of these market characteristics is analyzed.

Main Product and Main Market

The survey focused on firms' "main product," either a good or a service, referred to as the product with the highest turnover in 2003. The main objective was to minimize the potential problem of firms considering different products and price strategies in their answers. It would appear that this was not a very restrictive limitation to the survey, as the main product accounted on average for about 80% of firms' total turnover (table 10.1).[2] This was broadly expected, since the sample excluded sectors for which a main product was particularly difficult to identify. The representative nature of the main product is higher in services and for smaller firms.

Regarding firms' main market, three-quarters sell their main product mostly to domestic customers. The location of firms' main market is important because price setting strategies might be different in domestic and foreign markets. As expected, this share is higher in services and for smaller firms. The higher degree of openness found in manufacturing and among larger firms is consistent with the results obtained when exporting firms were asked about the percentage of their turnover that was due to exports.

Finally, the type of price setting behavior under analysis seems to refer predominantly to producer prices. Indeed, most firms sell their main product to other firms, whereas only about 13% sell it directly to consumers.

Table 10.1 Some market characteristics (percentages)

	Total	Manufacturing	Services	Small firms	Large firms
Share of main product in total turnover	81.1	77.6	88.3	82.5	77.2
Main market:					
Portugal	75.0	67.4	88.7	83.0	62.8
Other EU-12	19.7	24.7	9.4	14.0	27.7
Other	5.4	7.9	1.9	3.0	9.5
Share of exports in total turnover	26.7	36.3	10.6	19.8	39.6
Main destination of sales:					
Other companies	84.2	91.9	39.7	83.0	84.4
Public administration	3.3	2.3	10.3	3.8	3.3
Directly to consumers	12.5	5.8	50.0	13.1	12.2

Source: Author's calculations.

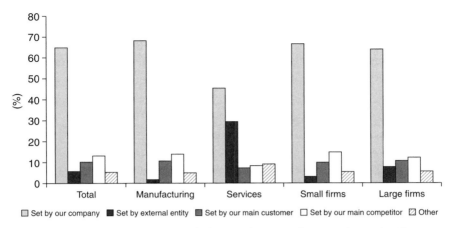

Figure 10.1 Price setting autonomy (Who sets the price of your main product? question 16). *Source:* Author's calculations.

Relationship with Customers and Competitive Pressures

The kind of relationship that firms have with their customers—that is, whether it is long-standing or only occasional—can have a bearing on their price strategies. Results show that slightly more than 80% of firms have a long-term relationship with their customers. This share is higher in manufacturing. Firms also reported that their sales to longer-term customers account for about three-quarters of their total sales.

Competitive pressure is another important variable affecting firms' price setting decisions. Under normal circumstances, the lower the competitive pressure faced by firms, the higher the room for not adjusting prices instantaneously in response to relevant shocks. The survey contains a number of questions that try to capture the degree of competition. In questions 6 and 7, firms were asked about the number of competitors they have in the Portuguese market and about their market share. Even though the coverage of our sample has a bias toward larger firms, in general markets appear to be very competitive: 56% of firms have more than 20 competitors in their main market and 53% have a market share of less than 5%. As expected, the degree of competition is somewhat weaker for larger firms irrespective of which of the two proxies is used.

However, even though most firms seem to operate in highly competitive markets, about two-thirds of them reported that they still have some autonomy over their price (figure 10.1). This is a key condition for the presence of some degree of price stickiness: if firms were pure price takers, their prices would simply equal marginal costs and markups and price rigidities would not exist.

MEASURING PRICE STICKINESS

In this section, the degree of price stickiness is assessed on the basis of five indicators: (1) the share of firms following time-dependent pricing rules vis-à-vis the share of firms following state-dependent pricing rules, (2) the frequency of price reviews, (3) the frequency of price changes, (4) the share of firms that take into account expectations about future economic developments when reviewing their prices, and (5) the speed of price responses following cost or demand shocks.

How Firms Review Their Prices: Time-Dependent and State-Dependent Pricing Rules

Under normal circumstances, firms review their prices before they decide whether to change them or not. Price reviews can be carried out in several ways. Firms can review at regular intervals and independently of market conditions, for instance at the beginning of every month; these firms follow what is usually called a time-dependent price reviewing rule. Alternatively, prices can be reviewed whenever firms consider that there has been a sufficiently large shift in the underlying determinants of prices, such as input costs or competitors' prices. These are the so-called state-dependent rules. In the presence of shocks, time-dependent rules would in principle lead to greater price stickiness than would state-dependent rules.

To test the relative importance of both approaches, firms were asked whether their prices are generally reviewed at a well-defined frequency or in response to market conditions. The survey also included a "hybrid option" in order to consider firms that may want to follow a combination of the two strategies, that is, to review prices regularly but also to allow for some flexibility whenever this is considered necessary due to changing market conditions. Results show that under normal circumstances 55% of firms follow time-dependent rules (table 10.2). In the event of specific shocks, 19% of firms change to state-dependent price reviewing. This is in line with the results reported in chapter 2, which show that in the euro area the percentage of firms following pure time-dependent pricing is 34%. In manufacturing, most firms seem to follow state-dependent rules, whereas in services the bulk of firms prefer to review their prices at regular time intervals.

Backward-Looking and Forward-Looking Price Setting: The Role of Information

In macroeconomic theory, there has been extensive discussion on whether inflation should be modeled primarily as a backward-looking variable, as in

Table 10.2 Price reviewing rules (percentages)

	Total	Manufacturing	Services	Small firms	Large firms
Time-dependent	35.4	31.7	63.4	33.0	38.3
Mixed	19.2	23.2	17.1	18.1	25.1
State-dependent	45.4	45.1	19.4	48.9	36.7

Source: Author's calculations.

the traditional expectations augmented Philips curve, or as a forward-looking variable, as in the New Keynesian Philips curve. The central point lies in the behavior of inflation in the short run and its implications for monetary policy (see, for instance, Galí et al. 2001).

Survey analysis could shed some light on this debate by asking firms directly which information they take into account when reviewing their prices. If they do it only on the basis of past developments, using for instance a rule-of-thumb mechanism, and simply ignore the expected future behavior in the main determinants of prices, this could be an additional source of price stickiness. According to the evidence collected, about 40% of firms review their prices taking into account a wide range of information, including expectations about future economic developments (table 10.3). However, a large fraction build price decisions without looking at economic projections, whereas about one-quarter of them simply adopt a rule-of-thumb approach based, for instance, on the overall consumer price index or on wage growth. Results also indicate that manufacturing and larger firms seem to be more forward looking. The evidence supports the recent preference for the use of hybrid versions of the Philips curve that also include backward-looking or rule-of-thumb terms (see, for instance, Fuhrer 1997).

The Frequency of Price Reviews and Price Changes

Another important indication of price stickiness could be obtained through the analysis of the frequencies of price reviews and price changes. The recent availability of large-scale datasets for consumer and producer price indices has contributed to the measurement of the analysis of the frequency of price changes and of the duration of price spells (see Dias et al. 2004, for the analysis of the Portuguese CPI and PPI micro datasets). However, survey results are still useful as a way of cross-checking the evidence obtained from the quantitative datasets.

In the survey, the firms that follow time-dependent rules, either strictly or only when there are no large shifts in market conditions, were first asked to mention the normal frequency of their price reviews. If the costs incurred by firms to collect the relevant information for pricing decisions were negligible, it would be expected that firms review their prices quite regularly.

Table 10.3 Information set used in price reviews (percentages)

	Total	Manufacturing	Services	Small firms	Large firms
Only past information	33.1	31.7	20.6	35.7	26.4
Rule of thumb	24.6	20.0	41.7	24.5	22.4
Includes expectations about future developments	42.3	48.3	37.7	39.8	51.2

Source: Author's calculations.

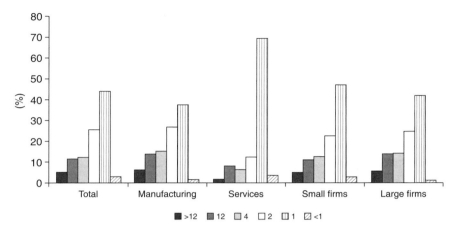

Figure 10.2 Frequency of price reviews (number of times per year; question 19). Average frequency: Total = 4.2; Manufacturing = 4.6; Manufacturing + Energy = 4.6; Services = 2.5; Small firms = 3.9; Large firms (>50) = 4.4. *Source:* Author's calculations.

However, results show that only about 5% of firms do it more than once a month (figure 10.2). This indicates that price reviews are probably not costless. Firms may fear that the possible gains resulting from reviewing prices every day or every week, for instance, might not be large enough when compared to the costs they have to bear to update almost on a continuous basis the background information for pricing decisions.[3] The size of these information costs seems to be such that about 50% of firms adopting time dependent rules review their prices no more than once a year. Comparing results across sectors, evidence shows that price reviews are more frequent in manufacturing than in services firms.

Having analyzed the frequency of price reviews, the next step was to ask firms how often they actually changed their prices. Comparing results for firms that responded both to the question on price reviews and the one on price changes, the evidence shows that, as expected, price changes are less frequent than price reviews: about three-quarters of firms change their prices no more than once a year (figure 10.3). As for price reviews, the findings concerning price changes suggest that services firms adjusted their prices less frequently than do other sectors.[4]

How Quickly Firms React to Cost and Demand Shocks

As Blinder et al. (1998) pointed out, the analysis of the frequencies of price reviews and price changes is not sufficient to measure the degree of price stickiness: infrequent price changes may reflect infrequent cost and demand shocks. In this light, firms were asked to report the time that elapses on average between a significant demand or cost shock and the corresponding price change.

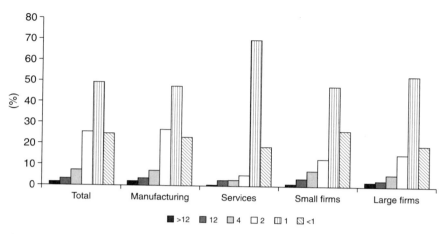

Figure 10.3 Frequency of price changes (number of times per year; question 20). Average frequency: Total = 2.0; Manufacturing = 2.1; Manufacturing + Energy = 2.1; Services = 1.5; Small firms = 1.9; Large firms = 2.1. *Source:* Author's calculations.

Respondents had six options: less than one week; from one week to one month; from one to three months; from three to six months; from six months to one year; the price remains unchanged. Regarding the latter option, it should be interpreted as referring to the short-run rigidity in response to a shock firms consider as permanent. If for instance firms interpret a significant rise in costs as permanent, then any answer that does not include a change in prices will not make sense. Thus the last option indicates that firms do not adjust their prices in the first year after the occurrence of a given shock.

Table 10.4 reports the percentage of firms that maintain their prices unchanged in the six months after a shock. There is no evidence that prices move faster upward than downward. However, firms seem to respond faster to cost shocks, in particular when they are positive, than to demand shocks. About 38% of firms maintain their prices unchanged in the first

Table 10.4 Firms that do not change their prices in the first six months after a shock (percentages)

	Total	Manufacturing	Services	Small firms	Large firms
Positive demand shock	54.5	50.4	81.2	53.1	56.0
Positive cost shock	37.7	31.8	67.0	36.6	36.8
Negative demand shock	44.0	38.5	73.0	42.8	43.9
Negative cost shock	42.6	37.6	76.1	41.6	44.0

Source: Author's calculations.

six months after a positive cost shock, 55% after a positive demand shock. Moreover, the speed of price adjustment is considerably higher in manufacturing than in services, which is in line with the conclusions coming from the frequency analysis.

DIRECTION AND MAGNITUDE OF PRICE CHANGES: SURVEY EVIDENCE VERSUS MICRO QUANTITATIVE EVIDENCE

As mentioned before, one important objective of this study was to investigate to what extent the results stemming from the quantitative micro data is supported (or not) by the qualitative evidence provided by the survey. Dias et al. (2004) pioneered the study of price setting behavior in Portugal by using the micro datasets underlying the consumer and producer price indices. In their paper and taking the period from 1992 to 2001 as a reference, they concluded inter alia that (1) price decreases account for around 40% of total price changes, (2) the magnitude of price increases is broadly similar to that of price decreases, (3) consumer prices seem to change more frequently than producer prices, something that is valid both for price increases and decreases. However, this comparison should be carried out with care. The analysis in Dias et al. was based on monthly data covering the period 1992–2001, whereas in this survey, firms were simply asked about their last price changes (the last ten price changes was suggested as a benchmark).

Survey results confirm the finding that price decreases are more common than it is usually believed: on average, slightly more than 30% of total price changes are reductions (table 10.5), a share smaller than the one reported in Dias et al. (2004) but in line, for instance, with the result obtained by Loupias and Ricart for France (chapter 5). Downward price rigidity is apparently higher in services: only one price change out of five is a reduction. However, given that the services sector has typically a larger labor input share, this could be explained by downward nominal wage rigidity.

Table 10.5 Direction and magnitude of price changes (percentages)

	Total	Manufacturing	Services	Small firms	Large firms
Share of price increases in most recent price changes	67.5	65.5	80.1	67.4	68.1
Average magnitude of most recent price changes:					
Increases	3.1	3.2	3.3	3.2	3.2
Decreases	3.7	3.8	3.5	3.9	3.6

Source: Author's calculations.

As to the magnitude of price changes, survey results reveal that the magnitude of price decreases is on average about 0.5 percentage points higher than that of price increases. These results suggest that the positive inflation witnessed at the aggregate level is apparently the result of a higher frequency of price increases and not of differences in magnitude between price increases and decreases.

REASONS FOR PRICE STICKINESS

The process of adjusting prices is typically divided into two stages: the price review and the price change. Results from the last section suggest that firms review their prices at discrete intervals and not continuously, thus pointing to the presence of some kind of stickiness at the first stage of the process. Once the price review has been made, firms decide whether they want to change their price or not. Results also show that price changes are less frequent than price reviews. This could happen either because the evidence coming from the price review does not support the need for a price change or because once firms decide to incur the informational costs of reviewing their prices, they recognize that there are extra costs associated with a price change that could possibly outweigh their benefits. In this section, the possible origin of these costs is analyzed. This is done by asking firms the following question: "Firms sometimes decide to postpone price changes or to change their price only slightly. This is generally due to various factors. Some of them are listed below. Please indicate their importance in your company." The list contained twelve theories of price stickiness, all explained in a language that could be broadly understandable. A detailed description of these theories can be found in chapter 1.

Respondents were asked to indicate their degree of agreement with each option on a scale ranging from "1 = unimportant" to "4 = very important." The theories were not mutually exclusive: firms could, and did in many cases, consider several of the options as very important. Table 10.6 ranks the theories by mean scores.

Results suggest that the implicit contracts theory is the most important explanation for infrequent price adjustments. It is in firms' own interest to establish a long-term relationship with their customers in order to make their sales more predictable. To do so, they try to capture and retain the loyalty of their customers by changing their prices infrequently. This is also favorable to customers because more stable prices minimize search costs (e.g., saving shopping time). This result is consistent with the fact reported above that most firms have a long-term relationship with their customers, and it may also justify why they are more likely to increase their prices in response to cost shocks than to demand shocks, as they try not to threaten customer relationships. The mean rank attached to this theory is surprisingly high given the traditional magnitude of mean scores in similar studies, which on a comparable scale do not normally exceed 3.

Table 10.6 Theories of price stickiness (mean scores)

	Total	Manufacturing	Services	Small firms	Large firms
Implicit contracts	3.1	3.2	3.0	3.2	3.1
Coordination failure	2.8	2.9	2.7	2.8	2.9
High fixed costs	2.8	2.8	2.8	2.9	2.8
Cost based pricing	2.7	2.7	2.7	2.8	2.6
Explicit contract	2.6	2.6	2.8	2.6	2.7
Procyclical elasticity of demand	2.6	2.6	2.5	2.8	2.5
Time lag in price adjustments	2.5	2.5	2.5	2.4	2.5
Temporary shock	2.5	2.5	2.2	2.5	2.4
Judging quality by price	2.3	2.3	2.2	2.4	2.2
Menu costs	1.9	1.9	1.9	1.9	1.9
Pricing threshold	1.8	1.8	1.9	1.8	1.8
Costly information	1.7	1.7	1.7	1.7	1.7

Source: Author's calculations.

The coordination failure and the high fixed costs theories are the next two in the ranking, with similar (not statistically different) mean scores. The first refers to the fact that it may not be in a firm's interest to change its price if its main competitors do not change their prices as well, and the second refers to the constraint that the presence of high fixed costs puts on a firm's decision to change its price. Constant marginal costs, explicit contracts, and procyclical elasticity of demand complete the group of theories that exceed the neutral score of 2.5. If marginal costs do not change by much, there is no reason to change prices frequently. This is the reasoning behind the theory of constant marginal costs. The existence of explicit (written) contracts implies that prices can only change when the contracts are renegotiated. Finally, if firms' elasticity of demand is procyclical (i.e., their markup is countercyclical), their demand curve becomes less elastic as it shifts down, which means that when demand decreases, firms lose first their "less loyal" customers and retain those who are less sensitive to price, thus implying that the price can be kept basically unchanged.

The remaining theories have a limited relevance for explaining the inertia observed in prices. In particular, physical menu costs, that is, the amount of resources needed to implement a price change, are not so important in deterring firms from adjusting their prices more frequently. The same holds for pricing thresholds, that is, the fact that some firms may want to quote their prices according to certain psychological thresholds (for example, pricing at 4.99 euros instead of 5 euros) if they believe that increasing them above these thresholds will lead to a disproportionate fall in demand. Finally, the theory of costly information, which focuses on the costs of collecting the relevant information to decide whether the current price is right or not, also received a low score. Hence, the evidence suggests that the main sources of price stickiness are not in the first but in the second stage of price setting.

CONCLUDING REMARKS

In this chapter, price stickiness in Portugal was analyzed on the basis of qualitative data coming from a survey conducted by the Banco de Portugal. The main conclusions are the following.

First, results point to the presence of a considerable degree of price persistence. Most firms do not review or change their prices more than once a year. Time lags in price adjustments were found to be significant. Slightly more than half of the firms follow time-dependent price reviewing, although only one-third stick to this practice after the occurrence of specific shocks. And, finally, more than half of the firms build their price decisions taking into account only historical data.

Second, the degree of price stickiness seems to be higher in services than in manufacturing, a finding that is also identified for the euro area as a whole. The higher degree of price persistence observed in services could reflect the higher labor share, which in general is associated with lower frequencies of price changes.

Third, prices seem to go down more frequently than is normally assumed: slightly more than 30% of total price changes are reductions. This result is in line with the evidence from the quantitative data, both for Portugal and for the euro area as a whole. Moreover, the absolute size of price decreases seems to be larger than that of price increases.

Finally, customers' preference for stable prices, which take the form of implicit contracts, is apparently the main reason for the persistence observed in prices. Other relevant sources were also found: coordination problems, the constraint imposed by a high proportion of fixed costs, marginal costs that vary little, and the presence of formal contracts that are costly to renegotiate.

Acknowledgments I am extremely grateful to Pedro Neves, who was mainly responsible for setting up this project. I would also like to thank the participants of the IPN as well as my colleagues from the research department of the Banco de Portugal, Carlos Robalo Marques, Daniel Dias, Isabel Horta Correia, João Santos Silva, Mário Centeno, Nuno Alves, Pedro Portugal, and José Machado, for their very helpful comments and suggestions. Special thanks also go to Leonardo Gonçalves from Universidade Lusíada de Lisboa for his excellent research assistance. I am also indebted to Fátima Teodoro, Pedro Luís, Maria Lucena Vieira, and Fernanda Carvalho for their computing support in several stages of the project and also to Guilherme Pinto and António Garcia from the statistics department for sharing experience gained from other surveys conducted by the Banco de Portugal.

NOTES

1. An annual survey conducted by the Banco de Portugal that gathers important economic and financial information on firms.

2. To account for possible biases in the response structure, all the results reported in this chapter are weighted. For details on the weighting procedure, see Martins (2005).

3. A different explanation could stem from the possibility that some firms may consider more frequent review of their prices impractical because new relevant information arrives at a low frequency rate.

4. Survey results also revealed that firms that sell their product mostly to other firms, our best proxy for the behavior of producer prices, seem to change their prices more frequently than those that sell their product mostly to final consumers.

REFERENCES

Blinder, Alan S., Elie R. D. Canetti, David E. Lebow, and Jeremy B. Rudd. 1998. *Asking about Prices: A New Approach to Understanding Price Stickiness*. New York: Russell Sage Foundation.

Dias, Mónica, Daniel Dias, and Pedro D. Neves. 2004. Stylised features of price setting behaviour in Portugal: 1992–2001. European Central Bank Working Paper No. 332. Frankfurt am Main: European Central Bank.

Fuhrer, Jeffrey. 1997. The (un)importance of forward-looking behavior in price setting. *Journal of Money, Credit and Banking* 29: 338–350.

Galí, Jordi, Mark Gertler, and J. David López-Salido. 2001. European inflation dynamics. *European Economic Review* 45: 1237–1270.

Martins, Fernando. 2005. The price setting behaviour of Portuguese firms: Evidence from survey data. European Central Bank Working Paper No. 562. Frankfurt am Main: European Central Bank.

11

The Pricing Behavior of Spanish Firms

Luis J. Álvarez & Ignacio Hernando

This chapter presents a summary of results of a survey on price setting behavior carried out by the Banco de España in 2004 on a sample of 2,008 industrial and services firms. This survey complements the recent empirical evidence on price setting behavior in Spain based on micro CPI (consumer price index) and PPI (producer price index) data (Álvarez and Hernando 2006; Álvarez et al. 2005). Given the wide sectoral coverage of our sample in comparison to other countries, in this chapter we focus on the differences in pricing behavior across sectors and refer the interested reader to Álvarez and Hernando (2005) for the full set of results. The organization of the remainder of the chapter is as follows. The first section presents the sample and the structure of the questionnaire. The second section describes the environment in which firms operate. The third section presents results on pricing policies, and the fourth section analyzes the main factors underlying price changes. The fifth section explores the relevance of different theories on price stickiness. The sixth section investigates the potential role of a number of factors to explain differences in the degree of price stickiness across firms, and, finally, the last section offers our conclusions.

THE SURVEY DESIGN: SAMPLE AND QUESTIONNAIRE

The survey was carried out by a private company (Dephimatica, S.A.) between May and September 2004 on the basis of a questionnaire and a stratified random sample provided by the *Banco de España*. The questionnaire was directed (where possible) to firms' top managers. It was sent on paper via traditional mail, and firms were given the option of answering by traditional mail, telephone, fax, or the Internet.

The population from which the sample was drawn consists of firms with more than five employees belonging to the following sectors (two-digit NACE classification): manufacturing (NACE 15 to 37), energy (NACE 40 and 41), trade (NACE 50 to 52), hotels and restaurants (NACE 55), and transport and communications (NACE 60 to 64). The coverage in terms of gross value added (GVA) is complete for manufacturing and energy, and is 52.3% for market services. The survey thus covers 51.3% of Spanish GVA.

An initial sample of 2,905 firms was chosen via stratified random sampling. Strata were defined in terms of two-digit NACE branch of activity and size class, based on employment, and firms were randomly selected within each stratum.[1] Once the field work was completed, 2,008 valid questionnaires were obtained, implying a response rate of 69.1%. Despite a high homogeneity of response rates across branches and size classes, we have poststratified the answers according to population weights. These are based on the share of GVA for each sector and the share in total employment within a given sector for each size class. All results refer to weighted data.

The design of the questionnaire (see the Appendix to the book) draws upon previous literature (e.g., Blinder et al. 1998) and work conducted in the context of the Inflation Persistence Network (IPN). The questionnaire was phrased in plain Spanish so that it could be understood by a wide range of managers of very heterogeneous companies, and a slightly different version of the questionnaire was sent to retailers and restaurant and bar owners to accommodate some of their particularities. The questionnaire was pretested on a small pilot sample, with the result that some questions were slightly redrafted. There are four parts with a total of 22 questions. Part A collects information on the main product sold by the firm and on the markets in which it operates. Part B refers to information on the firm's pricing policies. Part C analyzes the main driving factors explaining price changes, and part D refers to the relevance attached by the firm to different theories on price stickiness.

To properly identify cross-industry differences in pricing behavior, we have used a detailed sectoral classification. In particular, we distinguish twelve sectors: four groups of manufacturing industries (food products, non-food consumer goods, intermediate goods, and capital goods), energy, three trade groups (food, energy, other goods), and four aggregates of other services (hotels and travel agents, bars and restaurants, transport and communications).[2] The correspondence between the classification used and the three-digit NACE is in Álvarez and Hernando (2005).

MAIN CHARACTERISTICS OF THE MARKETS

Part A of the questionnaire collects information on characteristics of the market, such as the geographical location, the degree of competition, and the type of customers. All these features are key determinants of firms' pricing policies.

Regarding the geographical dimension, firms were questioned on the geographical distribution of their sales (question A2). It is found that they mostly operate in the domestic market. In fact, most of their turnover is generated in Spain (87%), whereas sales to the euro area account for 9% and those to the rest of the world for 4%. The fraction of turnover due to exports is higher for manufacturing firms (20%) and, particularly, for those producing capital goods (30%). In turn, external sales are almost negligible for firms in the energy, non-food trade, bars and restaurants, and communications sectors. Firms were also asked about the geographical scope of their main market (question A5). Most of them refer to the domestic market as the main one (90%). The national market is the most important for around 40% of companies, whereas 22% and 26% declare that their main market is regional or local, respectively. As expected, regional and local markets are significantly more relevant for firms in the trade sector and restaurants. In turn, the share of companies with a main international market is highest in manufacturing, particularly for producers of capital and intermediate goods.

The questionnaire included two questions directly related to the degree of competition faced by the firm. Specifically, firms were asked to report on their market share (question A6) and on the number of competitors (question A7). These two measures have some shortcomings. For instance, there may be a very high degree of competition in some oligopolistic markets with a small number of big firms (e.g., telecommunications). Moreover, some sectors may have a large number of competitors but still maintain local market power (e.g., bars). For this reason, we indirectly measure the degree of competition faced by a firm by the importance attached by the firm to changes in competitors' prices in explaining its own price cuts (question C1). Hoeberichts and Stokman (2006) report that this measure is closely linked to the degree of perceived competition directly reported by firms.

More precisely, we consider that a firm faces intense competition if it reports that competitors' prices are important or very important in determining a reduction in its own price. According to this definition, around 55% of firms face intense competition (figure 11.1). Some noteworthy differences are found across sectors. The degree of perceived competition is lowest in energy-related sectors, where regulation is important. At the other extreme, the share of companies facing intense competitive pressures is highest in communications (69%), hotels and travel agents (66%), and food trade (65%).

To investigate the relationship with customers, firms were asked about the distribution of their turnover by type of customer (question A8). Around 58% of them sell their products predominantly to other firms, almost 40% to consumers and 3% to the public sector. Important differences across sectors can be seen. Manufacturing companies sell primarily to other companies, whereas consumers account for most of the turnover of firms in energy, trade, and bars and restaurants. The public sector is the main customer for 11% of energy firms.

Firms were also asked whether most of their customers are regular or occasional (question A9). The results show the relevance of long-term relationships, since 86% of firms report that most customers are regular. This is especially the case in manufacturing, energy, food trade, and communications sectors (over 90%). In energy trade, hotels, and bars and restaurants, the share of companies selling mainly to regular customers is lower, but still over 60%.

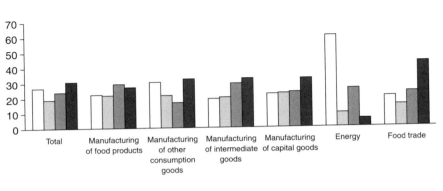

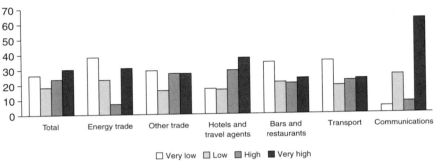

☐ Very low   ☐ Low   ▨ High   ■ Very high

Figure 11.1 Perceived competition: importance of changes in competitors' price to explain price decreases (question C2_8). *Source:* Authors' calculations.

PRICE SETTING BEHAVIOR

This section explores the main features of the pricing policies of Spanish firms. Question B1 addresses the issue of who sets the price of the "main product." Most firms (80%) declare having an autonomous price setting policy, even though they face nonnegligible competition and, hence, enjoy limited market power. This feature is found in all sectors except in energy, where the public sector directly sets the price for one-third of firms and sets it jointly with the company for 40% of them. Public intervention in price setting is also relevant in the transport sector. In addition, the parent company determines the price in 5% of cases, especially in trade and in capital goods manufacturing. Finally, main customers only directly set the prices of their suppliers in 2% of cases.

Time-Dependent versus State-Dependent Pricing Rules

To model the fact that firms do not continuously adjust prices when there are changes in the economic environment, the literature has considered two alternative types of price setting behavior: time-dependent and state-dependent pricing rules (see chapter 1). To assess the empirical importance of both types of rules, firms were asked for the strategy they follow when

Table 11.1 Rules and information set used in price setting (percentages)

Sector	Rules[a]			Information set		
	Time dependent[b]	Mixed[c]	State dependent[d]	Rule of thumb[e]	Current-looking[f]	Forward-looking[g]
Total	33.4	28.1	38.5	32.6	39.5	27.9
Manufacturing of food products	24.8	31.9	43.3	25.2	43.0	31.8
Manufacturing of other consumption goods	42.3	28.6	29.1	34.9	35.5	29.6
Manufacturing of intermediate goods	18.2	22.7	59.2	25.3	43.5	31.2
Manufacturing of capital goods	22.6	28.7	48.6	32.8	42.8	24.4
Energy	45.7	16.7	37.6	27.9	44.6	27.6
Food trade	26.0	23.1	50.9	29.6	57.4	13.0
Energy trade	41.6	31.5	27.0	0.0	83.8	16.2
Other trade	34.8	24.5	40.7	35.1	45.0	20.0
Hotels and travel agents	52.1	38.1	9.8	27.6	29.1	43.3
Bars and restaurants	35.0	31.9	33.1	46.6	40.0	13.4
Transport	40.3	35.0	24.7	47.0	29.2	23.8
Communications	26.4	28.6	45.0	17.2	18.4	64.5

Source: Authors' calculations.
[a]Percentages have been rescaled to sum to 100 after disregarding firms choosing response 54 in question B4.
[b]Response 51 to question B4.
[c]Response 52 to question B4.
[d]Response 53 to question B4.
[e]Response 71 to question B6.
[f]Response 72 to question B6.
[g]Response 73 to question B6.

reviewing prices (question B4). State-dependent rules are used by around 38% of firms, whereas around one-third follow purely time-dependent ones (table 11.1). The remaining 30% of companies use a mixed strategy, in the sense that they use a time-dependent rule under normal circumstances but change prices when a sufficiently large shock occurs.

Some differences across sectors in the type of pricing rules used are observed. The share of firms following a purely time-dependent rule is higher in hotels and travel agents and also in energy, where many prices are regulated. By contrast, this share is lower among manufacturers of intermediate and capital goods and communication companies, where state-dependent rules are clearly predominant. In the trade sector, state-dependent rules dominate, with the exception of energy trade; they are also more common both in the production and trading of food products than in the rest of consumer goods.

An interesting finding is that the higher (lower) the degree of perceived competition is, the lower (higher) the share of companies using purely time-dependent rules.

Information Set Used in Price Revisions

An element that has relevant implications for price sluggishness is the information set used by firms to take pricing decisions. To address this issue, firms were asked how they examine the price they would like to charge (question B6). On the whole, around 33% of firms apply a rule of thumb when reviewing prices, whereas the rest follow some type of optimizing behavior, in the sense that they assess different pieces of information on the economic environment (table 11.1). Slightly less than one-third display some type of forward-looking behavior, since they take into account expected future developments. It is found that rule-of-thumb price setters are more common among transport firms, bars and restaurants, and firms facing a low degree of competition. On the contrary, the share of forward-looking price setters is higher among communication firms and those operating in a very competitive environment. As will be later discussed, this result is consistent with the idea that prices of firms facing more intense competition are more likely to react to changes in their environment.

The Frequency of Price Reviews and Changes

Firms following either a purely time-dependent rule or a mixed strategy were asked about the frequency of price reviews (question B5). Around 70% declare reviewing prices once a year or less frequently, 16% of companies do it two or three times a year, and 14% four or more times a year. The median firm reviews prices once a year. Wholesale and retail trade companies, especially those selling food and energy products, seem to review their prices more often, thus reflecting the frequent changes in the cost of inputs and sales periods. All energy trade firms and around 75% of food trade firms review prices more than once a year, as compared to 30% for the whole sample. At the other extreme, all firms in the energy sector report at most one review a year and only 15% of manufacturers of capital goods report more than one.

All firms were asked how often they actually change their prices (question B7). On average, they do so once a year and around one-third of them at least twice a year (table 11.2). It is found that the frequency of price changes is highest for companies trading food and energy products, in line with the evidence on micro CPI data (e.g., Dhyne et al. 2006). All companies in energy trade and 73% in food trade change their prices at least twice a year, whereas the corresponding fraction is just 9% for bars and restaurants, 13%

Table 11.2 Price flexibility indicators

Sector	Average duration[a] (months)	Firms with at least two changes[b] (%)	Fast response demand increase[c] (%)	Fast response cost increase[c] (%)	Fast response demand decline[c] (%)	Fast response cost decline[c] (%)
Total	12.2	28.9	24.3	28.1	32.3	23.2
Manufacturing (food)	10.3	33.2	36.9	34.1	42.0	26.0
Manufacturing (other consumption)	13.1	21.0	11.3	19.4	18.1	14.7
Manufacturing (intermediate goods)	13.2	21.2	24.0	29.0	32.6	23.1
Manufacturing (capital goods)	13.3	16.5	16.8	27.9	20.5	21.4
Energy	23.4	20.2	9.5	18.7	9.5	18.7
Food trade	5.1	73.4	56.9	55.7	67.1	48.0
Energy trade	0.3	100.0	66.9	83.5	66.9	66.9
Other trade	10.4	36.7	26.7	33.9	34.2	28.2
Hotels and travel agents	9.1	40.7	32.9	17.8	49.7	19.1
Bars and restaurants	13.6	9.4	6.5	21.0	11.3	15.0
Transport	13.1	13.2	15.6	17.9	24.6	11.2
Communications	13.1	44.5	35.6	36.6	48.3	35.7

Source: Authors' calculations.

[a] Average time (in months) elapsed between two consecutive price changes. Computed from responses to question B7.
[b] Firms changing their prices at least twice a year. Obtained from responses to question B7.
[c] Firms changing their prices within a period of three months after the shock. Computed from responses to question C2.

for transport companies, and 16% for capital goods manufacturers. This low frequency of price changes for capital goods manufacturers is consistent with the results obtained from micro producer price data by Álvarez et al. (2005). It is also observed that the frequency of price changes for manufacturers of food products is higher than for manufacturers of other consumption goods, again in line with micro PPI data.

The frequency of price changes is higher for firms facing a high degree of competition. In fact, the share of companies changing their prices more than once a year is 43% for those facing the highest degree of competition, whereas it is only 13% for those facing low competitive pressures.

Price Discrimination

Question B3 addresses the issue of price discrimination. It is found that the use of uniform pricing schemes is not widespread. Only around one-third of firms charge the same price to all customers. Moreover, around one-fourth report that their price depends on the amount sold, 30% declare that it is decided on a case-by-case basis, and 11% mention other criteria to justify differences in the price charged. Some interesting differences arise in a sectoral analysis. Uniform pricing is significantly more common in trade and in bars and restaurants (50% and 79%, respectively). The use of price discrimination is instead particularly widespread among manufacturing companies, especially manufacturers of intermediate products and capital goods. Overall, in most sectors there are significant fractions of firms discriminating prices both on the basis of the quantity sold and on other criteria.

A particular form of price discrimination is known as pricing to market and consists in setting different prices in different geographical areas. In question A3, firms that sell some of their products outside Spain were asked whether the price charged in different countries is the same or not. The responses to this question show that 53% of exporting firms do apply some form of pricing to market and almost 60% of those exporting outside the euro area charge different prices across countries. This pricing strategy is more common in transport and communications.

THE DETERMINANTS OF PRICE CHANGES

This section deals with the main factors driving price changes. To address this issue, two types of questions were included in the questionnaire. First, firms were asked to assess the importance of several factors that could lead to price increases and decreases (question C1) and, second, they were questioned on the speed with which they react to different shocks (question C2). Available micro evidence for Spain (Álvarez and Hernando 2006 for the CPI and Álvarez et al. 2005 for the PPI) points to a high degree of heterogeneity in the frequency of price adjustment across types of products. Nevertheless, these results might reflect either a genuine difference across sectors in the degree of price stickiness or a different frequency of cost and demand shocks across sectors. The purpose of this section is to discriminate between these two possible explanations.

Main Driving Factors of Price Changes

The list of factors causing a price increase or decrease (question C1) includes changes in costs (labor, financial, raw materials, energy, and other costs of production), productivity changes, changes in demand, changes in competitors' price, improvements in quality, and attempts to gain market share (table 11.3).

The same ranking of driving factors behind price changes is obtained in terms of mean scores and of the percentage of companies indicating that a given factor is important or very important. Specifically, cost of raw materials and labor costs are the main determinants of price increases. By contrast, the most important factors causing a price decrease are changes in competitors' prices, the cost of raw materials, and in demand. Financial costs and productivity changes are among the lowest ranked, both for price increases and decreases.

Table 11.3 Driving factors of price increases and decreases

	Mean scores[a]	p-value[b]	Importance[c] (%)
Price increases			
Change in the cost of raw materials	3.1	0.00	72.6
Change in labor costs	2.7	0.00	56.8
Change in competitors' prices	2.5	0.00	52.1
Change in demand	2.4	0.00	43.5
Change in energy and fuel prices	2.2	0.00	35.3
Change in other production costs	2.1	0.89	32.0
Improvement in design quality or product range	2.1	0.00	34.0
Change in productivity	1.9	0.00	27.3
Change in financial costs	1.8	—	19.4
Attempt to gain market share	—	—	—
Price decreases			
Change in competitors' prices	2.7	0.08	57.2
Change in the cost of raw materials	2.5	0.00	51.7
Change in demand	2.4	0.00	48.1
Attempt to gain market share	2.2	0.00	40.1
Change in labor costs	2.0	0.00	29.3
Change in productivity	1.8	0.01	25.9
Change in energy and fuel prices	1.8	1.00	23.1
Change in other production costs	1.8	0.00	23.5
Change in financial costs	1.5	—	13.4
Improvement in design quality or product range	—	—	—

Source: Authors' calculations.
[a]Respondents are asked in question C1 to indicate the importance of each factor, the alternative scores being: 1 = unimportant, 2 = of minor importance, 3 = important, 4 = very important.
[b]Refers to the null hypothesis that the factor's mean score is equal to the score of the theory just ranked below.
[c]Fraction of firms rating the factor as important or very important.

It is interesting that for most explanatory factors, the mean score and the share of firms reporting that each factor is important are higher for price increases than for price decreases, with two exceptions: changes in competitors' prices and demand seem to be more relevant in driving price reductions than for price increases. Overall, these results point to the existence of asymmetries in the behavior of prices: changes in costs are the main factor underlying price increases, whereas changes in market conditions (demand and competitors' prices) are the driving forces behind price reductions.

There are some differences by sector. Upward movements in prices reflect mainly high costs of non-energy raw materials in most sectors, although there are some exceptions: in energy and transport, energy inputs are the most relevant factor; competitors' prices have a prominent role in energy trade and communications; changes in demand are the main driving factor for hotels and travel agents.

The Speed of Price Adjustment after Shocks

Firms were asked to report the average time elapsed between the occurrence of a significant event and the corresponding price reaction (question C2). Although median lags tend to fall in the six months to one-year range in all cases, the comparison of reactions to different shocks provides some interesting patterns.

First, prices seem to be more flexible downward than upward in response to demand shocks. In fact, we find that the share of firms adjusting prices within three months in response to a drop in demand is larger than to an increase in demand (table 11.2). Similarly, the fraction of firms keeping their price constant after a drop in demand is lower than after an increase. Moreover, the average lag of the response is significantly shorter after a demand contraction than after an expansion. Second, prices seem to be more flexible upward than downward in the face of cost shocks, a result in line with the evidence for the United States (Peltzman 2000). Specifically, we find that the fraction of companies changing prices within three months in the face of an increase in costs is larger than in response to a fall. Analogously, the share of firms not reacting to a cost increase is lower than to a cost decrease, and the average response is faster in reaction to increases than to decreases.

By sector, the main differences are that energy producers and bars and restaurants tend to be relatively slow in reacting to shocks, whereas the trade sector, especially that of food and energy products, is relatively quick in adjusting prices.

EVIDENCE ON THEORIES OF PRICE STICKINESS

To help discriminate among different price stickiness models, we proposed a list of nine theories for managers to assess (question D1), which are described in chapter 1.

Table 11.4 summarizes the empirical relevance attached by respondents to the different theories, according to their mean scores. Rankings of theories

Table 11.4 Theories of price stickiness: factors leading to a delay in price adjustment

| | Reasons for deferring | | | | | |
| | An increase in price | | | A reduction in price | | |
	Mean score[a]	p-value[b]	Importance[c] (%)	Mean score[a]	p-value[b]	Importance[c] (%)
Implicit contracts	2.6	0.00	57.8	—	—	—
Coordination failure	2.4	0.00	47.6	2.2	0.00	38.6
Explicit contracts	2.2	0.00	42.3	2.1	0.00	36.1
Temporary shocks	1.8	0.00	23.5	1.8	0.91	24.0
Quality signal	—	—	—	1.8	0.00	23.9
Pricing points	1.5	0.00	14.3	1.4	0.32	11.8
Menu costs	1.4	0.00	11.2	1.4	0.01	10.7
Change non-price factors	1.3	0.40	8.5	1.3	0.06	8.5
Information costs	1.3	—	8.2	1.3	—	7.1

Source: Authors' calculations.
[a]Respondents are asked in question D1 to indicate the importance of each theory, the alternative scores being: 1 = unimportant, 2 = of minor importance, 3 = important, 4 = very important.
[b]Refers to the null hypothesis that the factor's mean score is equal to the score of the theory just ranked below.
[c]Fraction of firms rating the theory as important or very important.

to explain delays in price increases and decreases are remarkably similar. The three theories that receive the highest support are implicit contracts, coordination failure, and explicit contracts. The first obtains the highest average score (2.6), being regarded as important by almost 60% of firms. The underlying idea behind it is that firms build up long-term relationships with their customers that they want to preserve by keeping their prices stable as long as possible. This result is consistent with the above-mentioned fact that a very high fraction of companies declare that most of their turnover is generated from regular customers. Moreover, the empirical support received by this theory is also consistent with the results of Zbaracki et al. (2004), who conclude that the overall cost of changing prices is mostly due to the cost of antagonizing customers. The relevance of long-term relationships with customers also explains the high scores obtained by the theory of explicit contracts, which ranks third and is considered as important by around 40% of firms. The importance of this explanation is higher for companies selling predominantly to other firms and especially for those whose main customer is the public sector. The theory of coordination failure is ranked second, being relatively more relevant for price increases (50%) than for price decreases (40%). Firms are reluctant to raise prices when their competitors' prices are unchanged to avoid losing customers. Similarly, the possibility of triggering a price war prevents companies from reducing prices. This theory obtains a higher score for companies that operate in competitive environments.

The theories of temporary shocks and quality signals are in an intermediate position. In both cases, their average score is slightly above 1.8, and they are highly ranked by around 25% of firms. The remaining four theories (pricing points, menu costs, information costs, changes in non-price factors) cannot be considered as relevant to explain delays in the adjustment of prices. This is remarkable, given that this group includes some of the theories (menu costs or information costs) that are among the most widely used in the theoretical literature to support price stickiness.

A comparison of the ranking across sectors does not show substantial differences. The top three theories are highly ranked in all sectors, with the exception of explicit contracts, which are less relevant in trade and in bars and restaurants, while the theories in the bottom group receive low scores in all sectors. Nevertheless, some differences may be singled out. Pricing points and menu costs receive higher scores in trade, hotels, and bars and restaurants; explicit contracts rank first in hotels, transport, and communications; the theory of quality signals obtains a high score in hotels and bars and restaurants.

DETERMINANTS OF PRICE STICKINESS

In this section, we explore the potential role of a number of factors to explain differences in the degree of price stickiness across firms. We mainly focus on the cost structure of the different industries and their prevailing competitive environments, although we also consider some other variables. We first analyze the influence of these factors on the reported frequency of price changes by means of a log-linear model and then estimate probit models to assess the incidence of these factors in the speed of adjustment to different shocks.[3]

Determinants of the Frequency of Price Changes

To summarize the cost structure of the different sectors, we consider the share of labor and of energy inputs in total costs.[4] Given that wage changes typically take place once a year, we expect more (less) labor-intensive industries to carry out price revisions less (more) frequently. On the contrary, given that prices of oil products change very often, firms that are highly (lowly) intensive in the use of energy inputs in the production process are expected to adjust their prices more (less) often. We also expect a higher frequency of price change by those firms operating in more competitive environments. To this end, we consider both direct measures of competition such as concentration indices and number of competitors in a sector and indirect measures such as the relevance attached by firms to changes in competitors' prices to explain their own price decreases. We also consider the information set used by the firm in order to change prices. In particular, we expect those firms applying rules of thumb in price setting to be less flexible than firms that take into account a wide range of current and expected variables to adjust prices. Other variables that may help explain the frequency of price adjustment are the size of the firm, the existence of government-set prices, and the relevance of attractive prices. We expect the latter two factors to result in more sluggish price adjustment, whereas we expect a positive correlation between the size of the firm and the frequency of price adjustment.

Our main results are the following (table 11.5). First, the cost structure is a determinant of the frequency of price adjustment. In particular, the coefficient of the labor share is negative and that of energy inputs is positive. Second, a higher degree of competition results in a higher frequency of price adjustment. Specifically, the relevance attached by firms to changes in competitors' prices to explain their own price decreases is significant in line with the evidence by Carlton (1986) and Geroski (1995).[5] Furthermore, we find an additional effect for the relevance attached by firms to changes in demand conditions to explain price changes. Third, firms applying rules of thumb change their prices less often than those that consider a wide range of current and expected variables to reset prices. Finally, small firms tend to be more sluggish in price setting than bigger ones; sectors where prices are set by the government are characterized by a lower frequency of adjustment; the use of attractive prices is associated with more sluggish price adjustments.

Determinants of the Speed of Adjustment

We estimate probit models to analyze the speed of reaction of firms to positive and negative demand and cost shocks. The dependent variable is set to one if the firm declares that it changes its price within a period of three months after the shock, and zero otherwise. We consider the same set of potential explanatory variables as we do in the analysis of the determinants of the frequency of price changes.

Our results indicate the following (table 11.5). First, the cost structure affects the speed of adjustment. In particular, the higher the labor share, the slower the price response to both types of shocks. Moreover, the higher the share of energy input costs, the higher the probability of a fast price adjustment, although this effect is not significant in the case of cost shocks. Regarding the influence of the degree of competition and demand conditions, we find that a higher degree of competition is associated with a faster response to a negative demand shock, suggesting that a slow price reaction to a contraction of demand might result in a substantial loss of market share. However, competitive pressures do not seem to affect the speed of reaction to other shocks. In addition, the relevance attached by firms to changes in

Table 11.5 Determinants of the frequency of price change and of the speed of adjustment to shocks

Explanatory variables[e]	Frequency of price change[a] (loglinear regression)		Speed of adjustment to shocks[b] (probit regression)							
	Coefficient	p-value[c]	Increase in demand		Fall in demand		Increase in costs		Fall in costs	
			Marginal effect[d]	p-value	Marginal effect[d]	p-value	Marginal effect[d]	p-value	Marginal effect[d]	p-value
Labor	−0.67	0.00	−0.25	0.01	−0.37	0.00	−0.40	0.00	−0.41	0.00
Energy	0.03	0.01	0.01	0.01	0.01	0.01	0.00	0.24	0.00	0.19
Competition	0.12	0.05	0.02	0.32	0.09	0.00	−0.03	0.15	−0.01	0.61
Demand conditions	0.08	0.00	0.05	0.00	0.05	0.00	0.02	0.00	0.02	0.00
Rule of thumb	−0.15	0.00	−0.06	0.00	−0.04	0.10	−0.03	0.16	−0.01	0.78
Small firm	−0.01	0.00	0.00	0.03	0.00	0.03	0.00	0.29	0.00	0.25
Regulated price	−0.34	0.01	−0.12	0.00	−0.19	0.00	−0.21	0.00	−0.15	0.00
Attractive price	−0.03	0.02	−0.01	0.11	0.01	0.44	0.01	0.12	0.01	0.09
Food	0.14	0.26	0.11	0.02	0.12	0.02	0.04	0.35	0.04	0.33
Consumer non food	−0.29	0.00	−0.06	0.07	−0.05	0.25	−0.03	0.52	0.00	0.97
Intermediate	−0.32	0.00	−0.02	0.50	0.02	0.64	0.02	0.62	0.02	0.52
Capital goods	−0.19	0.03	−0.02	0.66	−0.01	0.78	0.06	0.22	0.06	0.17
Energy	−0.40	0.04	−0.17	0.00	−0.25	0.00	−0.07	0.49	−0.05	0.58
Food trade	1.37	0.00	0.24	0.00	0.26	0.00	0.21	0.00	0.20	0.00

	Model 1		Model 2		Model 3		Model 4		Model 5	
Energy trade	3.01	0.00	0.32	0.02	0.16	0.26	0.18	0.22	0.25	0.07
Hotels and travel agents	0.23	0.06	0.13	0.07	0.30	0.00	0.01	0.86	0.10	0.16
Bars and restaurants	−0.25	0.00	−0.09	0.02	−0.09	0.06	0.00	0.99	0.01	0.92
Transport	−0.35	0.00	−0.05	0.16	−0.03	0.58	−0.05	0.31	−0.03	0.48
Communications	−0.21	0.14	−0.01	0.93	0.09	0.29	0.07	0.41	0.10	0.19
Constant[f]	0.33	0.00	—		—		—		—	
Number of observations	1869		1861		1862		1862		1862	
Log likelihood	−2568.01		−798.61		−925.64		−979.92		−882.93	
AIC	5176.01		1637.22		1891.27		1999.84		1805.85	
BIC	5286.68		1747.79		2001.86		2110.43		1916.44	

Source: Authors' calculations; Industrial, Trade and Services Surveys; National Statistical Institute (input-output tables).

[a] Dependent variable: log of the annual frequency of price changes.

[b] The dependent variable in the probit model takes a value of 1 if the firm changes its price in reaction to a shock within three months.

[c] Computed with Huber-White robust standard errors.

[d] Marginal effect computed at sample averages.

[e] Definition of explanatory variables: Labor (labor costs as a percentage of labor and intermediate input costs); NACE 3-digit level. Energy (energy costs as a percentage of labor and intermediate inputs costs); NACE 3-digit level. Competition (dummy variable equal to 1 if response equals 4 in question C.1.8.2). Demand conditions (sum of questions C.1.7.1 and C.1.7.2); NACE 2-digit level. Rule of thumb (dummy variable equal to one if response 71 in question B.6.A). Small firm (firms with less than 50 employees; question 0.D). Regulated price (dummy variable equal to 1 if response 14 in question B.1). Attractive price (dummy variable equal to one if response equals 3 or 4 in question D.1.4).

[f] The marginal effect is not defined for the intercept term.

demand in explaining price changes impact positively on the probability of fast price adjustment. The sign and significance of the effects of the rest of the variables are in line with those obtained for the frequency of price adjustment, with the exception of attractive pricing that does not seem to affect the speed of adjustment. Firms that use simple rules to review their prices are more likely to display a slow adjustment after shocks, especially in the case of positive demand shocks. Second, a very significant effect is found for the variable indicating the intervention of the public sector in the price setting process: firms whose prices are set by the government are characterized by a lower probability of displaying a fast price reaction. As regards differences across industries, we find that the probability of a fast adjustment is consistently highest for firms in the food and energy trade sectors, in reaction to both demand and costs shocks. By contrast, the speed of reaction after demand shocks is likely to be lowest in the production of energy and in bars and restaurants.

CONCLUSIONS

Our results indicate that almost 80% of Spanish companies in the survey have an autonomous price setting policy. Most of them adopt elements of state dependence and follow some type of optimizing behavior when resetting their prices. The median firm changes its price once a year, although there are substantial differences across industries in the frequency of price adjustment.

The use of some form of price discrimination is a common practice. Changes in costs are the main factor underlying price increases, whereas changes in market conditions (demand and competitors' prices) are the driving forces behind price reductions. Moreover, prices seem to be more flexible downward than upward in response to demand shocks, whereas the opposite holds in the face of cost shocks. Among the theories proposed in the literature to explain nominal price stickiness, the highest empirical support is obtained for the existence of implicit contracts, coordination failure, and explicit contracts.

Cost structure and a competitive environment stand out among the factors determining the degree of price flexibility. In particular, the higher the labor costs for firms, the lower the frequency of price changes and the slower the response to demand shocks. Moreover, prices tend to be more flexible the higher the share of energy inputs over total costs, the more competitive the environment in which firms operate, and the more importance firms attach to demand conditions.

Finally, cross-industry differences in pricing behavior can be identified. Trade firms, manufacturers of food products, and communications companies employ more flexible price setting strategies, which give them a greater ability to react to relevant shocks. At the opposite extreme, energy, bars and restaurants, and transport are the sectors that follow more rigid pricing policies.

NOTES

1. The four size strata refer to firms with 6 to 9, 10 to 49, 50 to 199 and over 200 employees.

2. Note that our sectoral classification includes two energy-related industries: "energy" that refers to energy production and "energy trade" that refers to energy distribution.

3. In Álvarez and Hernando (2005), we check the robustness of results by considering two count data models (Poisson and negative binomial regression) and two relative frequency models (the log odds ratio model and the Papke and Wooldridge procedure 1996). Results are robust across estimation methods.

4. Precise definitions and sources of the variables used in the analysis are provided in the notes to table 11.5.

5. Alternative direct measures of competition such as the average markup, the cumulative share in employment of leading firms, Herfindahl, Rosenbluth, Hannan Khay, or Gini indices, or an entropy measure are never significantly negative. This probably reflects the fact that there are some competitive markets where a few firms have high market shares. On the contrary, there are also markets where a high number of firms with low market shares enjoy market power at the local level.

REFERENCES

Álvarez, Luis J., Pablo Burriel, and Ignacio Hernando. 2005. Price setting behavior in Spain: Evidence from micro PPI data. Banco de España Working Paper No. 0527. Madrid: Banco de España.

Álvarez, Luis J., and Ignacio Hernando. 2005. The price setting behavior of Spanish firms: Evidence from survey data. Banco de España Working Paper No. 0537. Madrid: Banco de España.

Álvarez, Luis J., and Ignacio Hernando. 2006. Price setting behavior in Spain: Stylized facts using consumer price micro data. *Economic Modelling* 23: 699–716.

Blinder, Alan S., Elie R. D. Canetti, David E. Lebow, and Jeremy B. Rudd. 1998. *Asking about Prices: A New Approach to Understand Price Stickiness*. New York: Russell Sage Foundation.

Carlton, Dennis W. 1986. The rigidity of prices. *American Economic Review* 76: 637–658.

Dhyne, Emmanuel, Luis J. Álvarez, Hervé Le Bihan, Giovanni Veronese, Daniel Dias, Joannes Hoffman, Nicole Jonker, Patrick Lunnemann, Fabio Rumler, and Juko Vilmunen. 2006. Price setting in the euro area: Some stylized facts from individual consumer price data. *Journal of Economic Perspectives* 20: 171–192.

Geroski, Paul A. 1995. Price dynamics in UK manufacturing: A microeconomic view. *Economica* 59: 403–419.

Hoeberichts, Marco, and Ad Stokman. 2006. Price setting behaviour in the Netherlands: Results of a survey. European Central Bank Working Paper No. 607. Frankfurt am Main: European Central Bank.

Papke, Leslie E., and Jeffrey M. Wooldridge. 1996. Econometric methods for fractional response with an Application to 401(K) Plan Participation Rates. *Journal of Applied Econometrics* 11: 619–632.

Peltzman, Sam. 2000. Prices rise faster than they fall. *Journal of Political Economy* 108: 466–502.

Zbaracki, Mark J., Mark Ritson, Daniel Levy, Shantanu Dutta, and Mark Bergen. 2004. Managerial and customer costs of price adjustment: Direct evidence from industrial markets. *Review of Economics and Statistics* 86: 514–533.

Part III

Comparative Analysis

12

A Comparison Based on International Survey Evidence

Patrick Lünnemann & Thomas Mathä

The seminal work by Blinder et al. (Blinder 1991; Blinder et al. 1998), based on a survey of firms' price setting behavior in the United States, was followed by similar analyses for Canada (Amirault et al. 2004), Japan (Nakagawa et al. 2000), Sweden (Apel et al. 2005), and the United Kingdom (Hall et al. 1996; 2000), besides those for the euro area countries presented in the previous chapters. These studies have vastly improved our understanding of general aspects of firms' price setting and complemented the existing quantitative empirical evidence on the issue.

The aim of this chapter is to compare the results for the various economies. The comparison focuses on the following aspects: the survey design (first section), price setting and price reviewing (second section), the adjustment speed and the drivers of price adjustment (third section), and the reasons underlying the postponement of price adjustments (fourth section).

SURVEY DESIGN

Table 12.1 summarizes the main features of the surveys considered here, such as the sample size, the response rate, the time period, and the sectoral coverage. In the United States and Canada surveys were based on face-to-face interviews covering a relatively low number of firms (200 and 170, respectively). In contrast, most of the other studies chose to mainly rely on questionnaires mailed to a relatively large sample of firms (in a couple of cases firms were offered the option to answer via the Internet or by phone). The actual number of respondents varies widely across countries. In the euro area, a total of more than 11,000 firms were interviewed as a whole, ranging from 333 firms in Italy to about 2,000 in Belgium; in Japan, Sweden, and the United Kingdom, around 600 firms participated in the survey. The response rates vary substantially; the surveys for Canada and the United States received the highest response rates (above 60%), for the euro area, Japan and Sweden, it varied but exceeded 45%.

In most surveys, the interviews were carried out directly by the central banks, with a few exceptions in which they were outsourced to external

Table 12.1 The individual surveys

	Euro Area	Canada	Japan	Sweden	United Kingdom	United States
Main source	Fabiani et al. (2005); Chapter 2	Amirault et al. (2004)	Nakagawa et al. (2000)	Apel et al. (2005)	Hall et al. (2000)	Blinder et al. (1998)
Auxiliary sources	Chapters 3–11			Apel et al. (2001)	Small and Yates (1999) Hall et al. (1996)	Blinder (1991; 1994)
Form of survey	Mailed questionnaires, phone, face to face, Internet	Structured face to face interviews	Mailed questionnaire	Mailed questionnaire	Mailed questionnaire	Structured face to face interviews
Date or timing	Feb. 2003–Nov. 2004	July 2002–March 2003	April–May 2000	March–May 2000	Sept. 1995	April 1990–March 1992
Conducted by	4 National Central Banks (BE, FR, LU, PT); 5 external agencies (DE, ES, IT, NL, AT)	Bank of Canada regional branch offices	Bank of Japan	Statistics Sweden	Bank of England Network of regional agents and Business Finance Division	Princeton graduates students
Firms contacted	24,248	255	1,206	1,285	1,100	350
Replies	11,039	170	630	626	654	200

Response rate	46%	67%	52%	49%	59%	61%
Random sample	No	No	No	Yes: sample stratified according to size	No	Yes
Sectoral coverage	Manufacturing 62% Construction 4% Other services 21% Trade 13%	Manufacturing 26% Construction 10% Other services 49% Trade 14%	Manufacturing 65% Constr. & real estate 10% Other services 12% Trade 13%	Manufacturing 50% Services 50%	Manufacturing 68% Construction 6% Other services 13% Trade 13%	Manufacturing 35% Mining & Constr. 11% Other services 27% Trade 18% Other 9%
Representative of the firm size distribution	No	Yes	No	Yes	No	No
Firm size coverage	1–49 employees 47% 50–199 employees 29% ≥200 employees 24%	20–99 employees 32% 100–499 employees 28% ≥500 employees 40%	Unknown	5–19 employees 31% 20–199 employees 31% ≥200 employees 39%	1–100 employees 19% 101–500 employees 39% >500 employees 42%	USD 10M–24.9M 20% USD 25M–49.9M 3% ≥USD 50M 67%
Reference price	Main product	One of main business lines	Not specified	Main product	Main product or product group	Not specified

Source: Authors' calculations based on results reported in: Fabiani et al. (2005); Amirault et al. (2004); Nakagawa et al. (2000); Apel et al. (2005); Hall et al. (2000); Blinder et al. (1998).

companies. In the United States, the interviews were conducted by Princeton graduate students.

An important difference across the various studies regards the timing at which the information was collected. For the nine euro area countries, the surveys were carried out between 2003 and 2004, but the other surveys cover quite different time periods. In the United States the interviews were conducted at the beginning of the 1990s; in the United Kingdom in 1995; in Japan and in Sweden in 2000; finally, in Canada in 2002–2003. As table 12.2 shows, there are important differences between key macroeconomic indicators in the years in which firms were surveyed. For the purpose of the interpretation of the results, the consequences can be twofold: on the one hand, this factor raises the possibility that differences in results may reflect, at least partly, the different cyclical conditions prevailing at the time the data were collected; on the other hand, it may enhance the robustness of common results emerging from the various studies, on which the remainder of this chapter shall focus.

As far as the sample design is concerned, Blinder et al. (1998) aimed at obtaining information representative of the private, unregulated, nonfarm, for-profit segment of the United States economy; a similar approach was adopted in the Canadian survey. On the contrary, Apel et al. (2005) opted for a sample representative of the entire Swedish firm population.[1] In the euro area, most national surveys focused on the manufacturing sector, although also services firms were considered in a number of countries (chapter 1). The construction and trade sectors, instead, were underrepresented. In other words, the euro area sample is not representative of the actual structure of the economy; in particular, the manufacturing sector is overrepresented, presumably due to the fact that this type of questionnaire is more suitable for industrial firms (see chapter 1 for further considerations on this issue).

Table 12.2 Macroeconomic data (percentages)

	Euro Area	Canada	Japan	Sweden	United Kingdom	United States
Survey period	Feb. 2003–Nov. 2004	July 2002–March 2003	April–May 2000	March–May 2000	Sept. 1995	April 1990–March 1992
Data reference period	2003–2004	2002–2003	2000	2000	1995	1990–1992
Inflation (GDP deflator)	1.9/2.1	1.0/3.4	−1.6	1.4	2.6	2.3/3.9
Real GDP growth	0.6/1.7	3.3/1.7	2.8	4.3	2.9	−0.2/3.3
Unemployment rate	8.8/8.9	7.7/7.6	4.7	4.7	7.7	5.6/7.5
Exchange rate variation	11.3/3.4	−2.1/8.9	11.8	−0.2	−4.3	−0.9/−5.7

Source: Authors' calculations on International Monetary Fund data.

However, as the level of detail of the results presented in the various studies does not allow us to properly take into account sectoral differences, the comparative analysis carried out here mostly refers to the whole sample on which each survey is based. This is an important caveat to bear in mind when interpreting diverging results across studies.

Finally, the structure of the various questionnaires differs. Although all surveys investigate similar aspects of firms' pricing behavior—such as the frequency of price reviews and changes, the relative importance of time- versus state-dependent rules, the relevance of factors that might impede faster or more frequent price changes, and so on—the actual list of questions, their wording, their order, to name but a few elements, are not homogeneous across studies.

All in all, the surveys were not designed to be compared to each other, with the exception of those for the euro area, which were conducted within the framework of the Inflation Persistence Network (IPN), with the specific aim of obtaining comparable evidence. Thus, to an extent that cannot be assessed accurately, a rigorous comparison of pricing behavior across countries is limited by the differences in the respective survey design and methodology. For this reason, the comparisons made in the following sections will mainly be of a qualitative rather than quantitative nature and will focus on the results that seem to hold across most surveys.

Some of the studies report information on aspects regarding the market environment in which firms operate, such as the export propensity, the

Table 12.3 Market environment of firms (percentages)

	Euro Area	Canada	Japan	Sweden	United Kingdom	United States
Firms with domestic market as the main one	73[a]	81	—	—	—	—
Firms with mainly long-term customers	70	—	—	86	—	85
Firms with at least 5 competitors in the domestic market	53–84[b]	60	—	47	67	—
Firms with market share below 10%	—	—	47	—	38	—
Main customer						
Other firms	75	—	—	77	—	70
Consumers	21	—	—	12	—	21
Other[a]	3	—	—	10	—	9

Source: Authors' calculation based on results reported in: Fabiani et al. (2005); Amirault et al. (2004); Nakagawa et al. (2000); Apel et al. (2005); Hall et al. (2000); Blinder et al. (1998).
[a]Only for industry.
[b]Range for individual countries; see individual chapters.

market share, the number of direct competitors, the customers, and the nature of the relationships between firms and their customers. In general, the firms participating in the surveys operate primarily on the domestic market, have more than five competitors in all countries but in Sweden, have a low market share, and are typically engaged in long-term relationships with their customers, predominantly other firms (table 12.3).[2]

PRICE SETTING AND REVIEWING

For modeling purposes, it is important to assess whether the assumption of perfect competition is realistic or, instead, whether firms operate in imperfectly competitive markets, in which they have some degree of market power. Almost all surveys include a general question on how firms set their prices. Overall, markup pricing seems to be the dominant form of price setting, although competitors' pricing strategies are also quite relevant. Results on price setting practices are explicitly reported only in the studies for the euro area, Japan, and the United Kingdom.[3] More than 50% of euro area respondents set prices on the basis of a markup—variable or fixed—over costs. According to the Japanese survey, 18% of firms apply a fixed markup, whereas 36% set the price at the highest level the market can bear, which can also be regarded as a particular form of markup pricing. Similarly, in the United Kingdom, 39% of the respondents set prices at the highest possible level and a further 37% adopt a variable (20%) or a fixed (17%) markup. The Swedish survey assumes markup pricing and focuses on its cyclical behavior, finding that firms attach the highest recognition to constant and procyclical markups. In the euro area, Japan, and the United Kingdom, a considerable share of firms (around or above 20%) set prices according to the level chosen by their competitors.

Turning to the frequency of price review, in the euro area the weighted and unweighted median number of price reviews per year is 2.7 and 2, respectively (table 12.4), which is between the median for Canada (four reviews per year) and the United States (two reviews per year). Also, it is higher than in Japan (one to two reviews per year) and in Sweden (one review per year). However, the median frequency of price review may hide substantial differences or similarities in the underlying distribution. For instance, 20% of British firms reviewing prices at a daily interval push the median up to 12 price reviews per year, whereas the low median for Swedish firms conceals that 19% of them review prices at a daily frequency. Focusing on the mode of price reviews, the differences observed across countries diminish substantially; in all individual country surveys the mode is one price review per year.

Compared to the results for the median frequency of price review, there is a certain degree of homogeneity across the euro area countries with regard to the frequency of price changes. Within the euro area as a whole, both the weighted and unweighted median is one price change per year (see chapter 2), which reveals a relatively low number of price changes compared to other countries. A similarly low frequency of price change has been reported for Sweden

Table 12.4 Price reviews versus price changes[a]

Number of	Euro Area	Canada	Japan	Sweden	United Kingdom	United States
Price reviews						
Median	2.7	–	1–2	1	12	2
Mode	1	–	1–2	1	1	1
Price changes						
Median	1	4	1–2	1	2	1.4
Mode	1	1	1–2	1	1	1

Source: Authors' calculation on the basis of results reported in: Fabiani et al. (2005); Amirault et al. (2004); Nakagawa et al. (2000); Apel et al. (2005); Hall et al. (2000); Blinder et al. (1998).
[a]Euro area results calculated by using national GDP weights (constant market prices in 2004). Results for Japan calculated by weighting results according to reported sample composition between manufacturing (65%) and non-manufacturing (35%) firms. Euro area, United States and Swedish results refer to firms with elements of time-dependent price review behavior.

only. In contrast, the median number of price changes for Canadian, British, and United States firms is higher (4, 2, and 1.4 price changes per year, respectively). The higher frequency of price changes in the United States compared to the euro area is consistent with results obtained from studies based on micro consumer prices (see chapter 14). In addition, the direct comparison between the euro area and Sweden, on the one hand, and the United Kingdom and the two North American economies, on the other hand, illustrates the presence of differences with regard to the fraction of firms with very low frequencies of price change. In particular, both in the euro area and in Sweden, about 25% of firms change their price less often than once a year. In Canada, the United Kingdom, and the United States, the corresponding share is much lower, at 8, 6, and 10%, respectively.

The frequency of price adjustment is positively related to the degree of market competition; this result is consistent across countries. The surveys for the United Kingdom, Canada, and Sweden show that the price change frequency is positively affected by the number of firms' direct competitors, whereas the surveys for the euro area also show that it is positively related to the importance that firms attach to their competitors' prices for their own pricing decisions.

To some extent, these results certainly also reflect the differences in the design, methodology, and timing of the respective surveys. In addition, because many of the surveys differ with respect to the sample coverage, it cannot be excluded that the above differences are partly related to the sectoral and size composition. Indeed, there is a considerable degree of heterogeneity across sectors and firm size in the frequency of price adjustment. In particular, the findings for most euro area countries, Canada, and the United Kingdom point to a significantly lower frequency of price adjustment in services as compared to manufacturing, whereas firms in the trade sector are found to change prices relatively often. Moreover, firms' size seems to

Table 12.5 Time- versus state-dependent price reviews

	Time	State	Both[b]	Don't know/Other
Euro Area	34	20	46	—
Canada	66	34	—	—
Japan	—	—	—	—
Sweden	42[a]	28	22	7
United States	60	30	10[c]	—
United Kingdom	79	11	10	—

Source: Authors' calculations based on results reported in: Fabiani et al. (2005); Amirault et al. (2004); Nakagawa et al. (2000); Apel et al. (2005); Hall et al. (2000); Blinder et al. (1998).
[a]The figure includes firms that answered reviewing prices at a daily frequency.
[b]Firms normally following time-dependent pricing rules but switching to state-dependent rules in case of major shocks.
[c]Periodic price reviews for some products but not for others.

matter, both in several euro area countries and in Canada and Sweden; larger firms tend to adjust prices more often than smaller ones. Notwithstanding these caveats, selected indicators suggest a remarkable congruence across countries. In particular, the median and mode of the price review and price change frequency are, with few exceptions, unexpectedly similar across countries.

As widely acknowledged in the preceding chapters, the type of rule followed by firms for price reviews has a bearing on the degree of nominal flexibility. Unfortunately, most surveys compared here differ from each other in their approach to this issue.[4] Nevertheless, the empirical evidence available only for the euro area and Sweden indicates that mixed strategies dominate over purely time- or state-dependent ones. In the United States, 10% of all firms report that they have periodic reviews for some products but not for others (Blinder et al. 1998, p. 90); in the United Kingdom, 10% use a mixture of time- and state-dependent price reviews. Focusing on pure strategies only, all surveys point toward dominance of periodic price reviews over state-dependent ones (table 12.5). From an empirical point of view, it would be very interesting to know whether it is time- or state-dependent firms that are, in the end, more flexible. Results available for Canada show that state-dependent firms change prices up to five times as often as time-dependent firms.

ADJUSTMENT SPEED AND FACTORS DRIVING PRICE ADJUSTMENT

The frequency of price reviews and changes may give an incomplete picture of the true flexibility of firms' price adjustment mechanisms. This may particularly be the case in a very stable business environment, where firms rarely have to review and change their prices. One alternative indication of price flexibility can be obtained by asking firms about the speed of their price reaction to major demand or cost changes, either positive or negative. Unfortunately, only few surveys investigated this particular aspect.

The analysis for the United States reveals that (1) prices are adjusted on average roughly three months after the shock, (2) there is essentially no evidence suggesting that prices react faster to shocks implying an upward than a downward movement, (3) and contrary to the common belief, firms do not respond more rapidly to cost than to demand shocks. If anything, the opposite is the case. The evidence available for five euro area countries (Austria, France, Luxembourg, Portugal, and Spain), reported in Fabiani et al. (2005), confirms the above finding on the average adjustment lag for those firms that (eventually) adjust prices (a substantial proportion of firms, however, do not adjust prices at all); in contrast, it indicates the presence of an asymmetry in the reaction to shocks implying price increases and decreases, and a substantial adjustment lag asymmetry with regard to cost and demand shocks .

In more detail, following a cost-increasing shock, an (unweighted) average of 88% of the firms of the five euro area countries adjust their prices, whereas only 62% react to a strengthening demand shock. The corresponding shares for a cost-decreasing shock and a weakening demand shock are 72% and 68%. A similar asymmetry is also reported by Small and Yates (1999) for the United Kingdom, where 88% of firms raise prices following a cost increase but only 55% reduce them following a cost reduction. On the demand side, the corresponding shares are 47% and 62% for rising and falling demand, respectively.

Focusing on those firms that eventually adjust their prices following a shock, the evidence reveals that in the five euro area countries the median firm does so within one to three months, regardless of the direction or the source of the shock. A similar finding is reported for the United States, where the median adjustment lag is one to three months, also regardless of the type and the direction of shock.

In sum, the comparison of the adjustment speed among euro area, British, and United States firms reveals marked differences. In the five euro area countries, as well as in the United Kingdom, there is substantial evidence pointing toward a double asymmetry in price adjustment following shocks. Firms are more likely to react if costs go up than when they go down, but the opposite is the case for demand; furthermore, price adjustments are much more likely when costs go up than when demand goes up. This does not seem to be the case in the United States.

The surveys conducted in the euro area countries and in the United Kingdom also investigate the main factors behind price increases and decreases and provide further evidence on asymmetries in firms' price setting behavior. While cost-increasing shocks (related to material and wages) are found to be particularly relevant for price increases, price decreases by competitors and weakening demand appear to be the main drivers of price reductions.[5] The surveys for Canada and Sweden refer to price changes without distinguishing between decreases and increases. Both confirm that competitors' price changes constitute the most important factor underlying firms' decisions to change prices. Shocks to non-labor costs are ranked second by firms. As far as demand shocks are concerned, they rank third in Canada and fourth in Sweden (table 12.6).

Table 12.6 Factors driving price changes (rankings)

	Euro Area	Canada	Japan	Sweden	United Kingdom	United States
Price increases:						
Price changes by competing firms	3				2	
Pressures from important customers						
Changes in demand	4				3	
Changes in input or material costs: imported goods domestic costs	1				1	
Changes in taxes and charges						
Exchange rate changes						
Changes in labor costs	2					
Changes in capital costs	4				5	
Prices never increase					4	
Higher market share					6	
Fall in productivity					7	
Price decreases:						
Price changes by competing firms	1				1	
Pressures from important customers						
Changes in demand	3				3	
Changes in input or material costs: imported goods domestic costs	2				2	
Changes in taxes and charges						
Exchange rate changes						
Changes in labor costs	4					
Changes in capital costs	5				7	
Prices never fall					4	
Lower market share					5	
Rise in productivity					6	
Price changes (either direction):						
Price changes by competing firms	2	1		1	2	
Pressures from important customers				3		
Changes in demand	4	3		4	3	

Table 12.6

	Euro Area	Canada	Japan	Sweden	United Kingdom	United States
Changes in input or material costs:	1				1	
imported goods				2		
domestic costs		2		5		
Changes in taxes and charges		5		6		
Exchange rate changes		6		8		
Changes in labor costs	3	4		9		
Change in capital costs	5			7	6	
Prices never rise/fall					4	
Higher/lower market share					5	
Fall/rise in productivity					7	

Source: Authors' calculation based on results reported in: Fabiani et al. (2005); Amirault et al. (2004); Nakagawa et al. (2000); Apel et al. (2005); Hall et al. (2000); Blinder et al. (1998). The ranking for price changes for the euro area and the United Kingdom are calculated by averaging the scores for price increase and decrease.

THEORIES UNDERLYING PRICE STICKINESS

Survey data are particularly suited to capture the impediments to faster price adjustment. All the surveys considered here follow a similar approach in investigating the actual relevance, from the firms' viewpoint, of various theoretical explanations for this behavior (see chapter 1 for details).[6]

Among the theories considered in at least five surveys, the existence of contracts, either implicit or explicit, is commonly recognized as the most important obstacle to faster price adjustment in the euro area, Sweden, and the United Kingdom (table 12.7). In the United States, implicit and explicit contracts rank fourth and fifth, respectively, and in Canada they rank fourth and second.[7] These findings may be related to the widespread diffusion of long-term relationships between firms and their customers, as reported by the majority of the firms surveyed in most countries.

Cost-based pricing and coordination failure (see chapter 1) are also among the most recognized explanations for price stickiness. The former ranks first in Canada, second in Sweden, the United Kingdom, and the United States, and third in the euro area, whereas the latter ranks first in the United States and Japan, third in the United Kingdom, and fourth in the euro area and Sweden.[8]

In all surveys except that for the United States, the role of menu costs and of pricing thresholds is not found to be particularly relevant by firms. The ranking of non-price elements varies substantially across countries. They are relatively unimportant in the euro area and in the United Kingdom, but they receive a higher ranking (third place) in the United States and in Canada.

Table 12.7 Theories of price stickiness (rank)[a]

Number of theories considered	Euro Area[b]	Canada	Japan	Sweden	United Kingdom	United States
	10	11	9	13	11	12
Main theories:						
Implicit contracts	1 (1)	7 (4)	2 (2)	1 (1)	5 (5)	4 (4)
Consumer anger/ customer relations		2				
Explicit contracts	2 (2)	3 (2)	3 (3)	3 (3)	1 (1)	5 (5)
Cost-based pricing (prices do not change until cost change)	3 (3)	1 (1)		2 (2)	2 (2)	2 (2)
Constant marginal costs					6	9
Coordination failure						
Price change	4 (4)		1 (1)	4 (4)	3 (3)	1 (1)
Price increase		5				
Price reduction		8				
Kinked demand curve						
Deviation from implicit collusion				9		
Quality judged by price	5		8		10	12
Temporary shocks	6					
Non-price elements	7 (5)	4 (3)	5 (5)		8 (6)	3 (3)
Delivery lag			9		7	10
Menu costs	8 (6)	10 (5)	7 (6)	11 (6)	11 (7)	6 (6)
Costly information gathering	9			13		
Pricing thresholds	10 (7)		4 (4)	7 (5)	4 (4)	8 (7)
Other theories:						
Procyclical elasticity			6	8	9	7
Hierarchical delays						11
Countercyclical cost of finance				5		
Liquidity constraints/ fixed costs				6		
Thick markets (supply)				10		
Thick markets (demand)				12		
Low inflation		6				
Factors unchanged		9				
Sticky information		11				

Source: Authors' calculation based on results reported in: Fabiani et al. (2005); Amirault et al. (2004); Nakagawa et al. (2000); Apel et al. (2005); Hall et al. (2000); Blinder et al. (1998).
[a]Ranks reported in the table refer to the whole sample. In brackets we report the "relative rank," that is, the one obtained by rescaling the original ranking considering only the theories which are common to at least five studies.
[b]Unweighted average of euro area countries scores. It may relate to a limited number of countries only and may not be sufficiently representative of the entire euro area.

The level of detail reported in the original country studies does not allow a thorough assessment of the sectoral dimension of these results. In the euro area, the importance attached to the theories varies only marginally across sectors. In Japan and in the United Kingdom, however, the sector-specific rankings differ markedly. Implicit contracts are the most important source of price stickiness for British manufacturing firms, but they receive average recognition only in the construction sector. Explicit contracts are ranked first in the Japanese construction sector, but appear as being relatively unpopular among retailers.

CONCLUDING REMARKS

This chapter compares the international survey evidence of firms' price setting behavior. Notwithstanding the fact that the surveys were not designed to be compared with each other and differ in numerous respects, such as methodology, sample coverage, and timing, some striking similarities emerge.

First, firms typically operate in imperfectly competitive markets, where they have a low market share, face a number of competitors, and are primarily engaged in long-term relationships with their customers, mainly other firms.

Second, a considerable proportion of firms adopt time-dependent price reviewing rules. However, in surveys that consider as an option the possibility for firms to switch from time- to state-dependent rules under special circumstances, this mixed strategy turns out to be the most widespread.

Third, the modal frequency of price review and price change is generally low and remarkably similar across countries (one per year for all surveys). The median firm, instead, reviews and changes prices more often in the United Kingdom, Canada, and the United States than in Sweden and in most euro area countries.

Fourth, in the euro area and in the United Kingdom, price adjustments are more likely after cost-increasing than cost-decreasing shocks. The opposite holds in the case of demand shocks. An additional asymmetry is found in the speed of the response of prices to shocks, which turns out to be higher for cost than for demand shocks.

Fifth, remarkable similarities across countries are found with regard to the economic explanations impeding immediate price adjustments after shocks. In general, implicit and explicit contracts, coordination failure, and cost-based pricing are recognized by firms as the most important elements to explain price rigidity in all surveys. At the other extreme, the theories of menu costs and pricing thresholds are not regarded as particularly relevant sources of delays in price adjustment.

Acknowledgments We would like to thank Richard Friberg, Tony Yates, Silvia Fabiani, and Roberto Sabbatini for their constructive comments and helpful suggestions on earlier drafts of this chapter.

NOTES

1. Firms with more than five employees, excluding sectors where the price setting is fully determined by political means or where products are not priced.

2. The survey for the United States does not ask any questions on the competitive environment of firms, whereas the Swedish survey asks firms how many competitors they have but does not report the figures.

3. In the questionnaires for the euro area, firms simply had to tick a box containing their preferred option; in the Japan and the United Kingdom surveys the possible answers had to be rated according to "appropriateness or relevance." The numbers reported in the text for Japan and the United Kingdom refer to top preferences, which were adjusted to sum to 100%.

4. The Blinder et al. (1998) survey simply asks whether "firms have a customary time interval . . . between price reviews for the most important products" (Blinder et al. 1998, p. 318). The possible answers are "No," "It varies by product," and "Yes." Hence, state dependence is only an implicit answer, whereas time dependence is explicitly mentioned. The British and Canadian surveys, in contrast, specify the option "in response to specific events," but mutually exclude time- and state-dependent options. Moreover, the question in the Swedish survey is specified as, "How often do you actively review the price of your main article or service and consider whether it should be changed or not?" (Apel et al. 2001, Appendix B), and the possible answers are "Daily or more often," "At specific time intervals," "Mainly at specific time intervals, but also in connection with special events . . . " and "In connection with special events.". The wording of the same questions in the nine euro area surveys is very similar and related to the wording of the Swedish survey.

5. Wage costs were not considered in the survey for United Kingdom.

6. Besides the common aspects, there are interesting differences. For example, the Canadian survey explicitly studies the role of low inflation; the questionnaire for the United States investigates the role of bureaucratic delays in slowing down decisions; in several euro area countries, the idea of firms avoiding price changes that have to be reverted soon afterward (temporary shocks) receives non-negligible recognition.

7. The low recognition received in Canada by implicit contracts may result from the fact that in this survey the fear of antagonizing the customers (which is not considered explicitly in the other analyses) is regarded as the second most important source of price stickiness, and it might not be mutually exclusive with the theory of implicit contracts.

8. The theory of cost-based pricing was not considered in the Japanese survey.

REFERENCES

Amirault, David, Carolyn Kwan, and Gordon Wilkinson. 2004. A survey of the price setting behaviour of Canadian firms. *Bank of Canada Review* Winter 2004–2005: 29–40.

Apel, Mikael, Richard Friberg, and Kerstin Hallsten. 2001. Micro foundations of macroeconomic price adjustment: Survey evidence from Swedish firms. Sveriges Riksbank Working Paper Series No. 128. Stockholm: Sveriges Riksbank.

Apel, Mikael, Richard Friberg, and Kerstin Hallsten. 2005. Micro foundations of macroeconomic price adjustment: Survey evidence from Swedish firms. *Journal of Money, Credit and Banking* 37: 313–338.

Blinder, Alan S. 1991. Why are prices sticky? Preliminary results from an interview study. *American Economic Review Papers and Proceedings* 81: 89–96.

Blinder, Alan S., Elie R. D. Canetti, David E. Lebow, and Jeremy B. Rudd. 1998. *Asking about Prices: A New Approach to Understand Price Stickiness*. New York: Russell Sage Foundation.

Fabiani, Silvia, Martine Druant, Ignacio Hernando, Claudia Kwapil, Bettina Landau, Claire Loupias, Fernando Martins, Thomas Mathä, Roberto Sabbatini, and Ad Stokman. 2005. The pricing behaviour of firms in the Euro Area: new survey evidence. ECB Working Paper No. 535. Frankfurt am Main: European Central Bank.

Hall, Simon, Mark Walsh, and Anthony Yates. 1996. How do UK companies set prices? *Bank of England Quarterly Bulletin* 6: 1–13.

Hall, Simon, Mark Walsh, and Anthony Yates. 2000. Are UK Companies' Prices Sticky? *Oxford Economic Papers* 52: 425–446.

Nakagawa, Shinobu, Hattori Ryota, and Izumi Tagagawa. 2000. Price setting behaviour of Japanese companies. Bank of Japan Research Paper. Tokyo: Bank of Japan.

Small, Ian, and Anthony Yates. 1999. What makes prices sticky? Some survey evidence for the United Kingdom. *Bank of England Quarterly Bulletin* 39: 262–271.

13

Competition and Price Adjustment in the Euro Area

Luis J. Álvarez & Ignacio Hernando

A crucial factor determining firms' pricing behavior is the degree of market competition. Since the early studies on price stickiness were undertaken using micro data, the relationship between market structure and pricing behavior has been a highly researched issue in industrial economics.[1] In particular, a great deal of attention has been devoted to the question of whether firms in competitive markets are more likely to change prices in response to shocks than firms enjoying significant market power (see, for instance, Ginsburgh and Michel 1988 and Martin 1993). Moreover, firms in more competitive industries, facing higher uncertainty about their future position in the market, may be more concerned with ensuring short-run returns, which leads to a higher responsiveness to current shocks (Encaoua and Geroski 1986). By contrast, firms facing less competition can place more emphasis on long-term returns and adopt pricing policies that smooth out expected fluctuations in costs and demand.[2] Oligopolists may prefer delays in adjusting prices in order to avoid breaking tacit pricing understandings (Stiglitz 1984).

There are also a number of empirical papers linking price stickiness and degree of market competition. For instance, Carlton (1986) and Hall et al. (2000) find that firms in competitive markets tend to adjust prices faster than companies facing a less elastic demand. Geroski (1992) shows that price responses to both supply and demand shocks are faster in more competitive industries. Similarly, Weiss (1995) finds that cost changes are more fully transmitted into prices in industries with low concentration ratios. Overall, the empirical evidence tends to favor the existence of a positive link between price flexibility and the degree of competition (see Dixon 1983; Encaoua and Geroski 1986; and Bedrossian and Moschos 1988), although there are also studies reporting the opposite result. For instance, Domberger (1979) finds a positive relationship between the speed of price adjustment and market concentration. He rationalizes this result by arguing that prices should react faster to cost shocks in concentrated industries, given that information is more easily gathered the higher the degree of concentration.[3]

More recently, renewed attention has been placed on the empirical relevance of the relationship between the degree of price stickiness and the intensity of market competition. For instance, the existence of a positive association between the frequency of price change and the degree of competition has been documented on the basis of individual producer prices for Spain and Belgium (see Álvarez et al. 2005 and Cornille and Dossche 2006, respectively) and for Luxembourg using consumer prices (Lünnemann and Mathä 2005). Furthermore, the qualitative information in the surveys on price setting behavior discussed in this book has provided an alternative source to assess the empirical significance of this relationship, which has been analyzed in several countries (see the second section below).

In this chapter, we analyze the relationship between price flexibility and competition, focusing on euro area manufacturing and services industries. The distinguishing features of our study are the consideration of the whole euro area, the use of survey data, and the inclusion of services sectors, which are generally neglected in this type of analysis. After this introduction, the remainder of the chapter is organized as follows: the first section discusses the measurement of the degree of market competition in surveys. The second section explores the main features of firms' pricing strategies in light of their competitive environment. The third section shows some evidence on the relationship between competition and the degree of price flexibility. The fourth section presents our econometric results on the determinants of price flexibility in the euro area, and the fifth section offers our conclusions.

MEASURING THE DEGREE OF MARKET COMPETITION

Measuring the degree of market competition is an extremely complex task that has received a lot of attention in the literature on industrial organization (see, for instance, Bresnahan 1989). In the context of the surveys on price setting discussed in this book, most national questionnaires included two questions directly related to the degree of competition faced by firms. Specifically, companies were asked to report on their market share and on the number of competitors. Unfortunately, these two measures have several shortcomings. First, both are highly subjective in the sense that different firms may use different criteria to define relevant markets or identify their potential competitors. Second, in some oligopolistic markets with a small number of big companies enjoying large market shares, there is a very high degree of competition (e.g., telecommunications). Third, some industries may have a large number of competitors but still maintain local market power (e.g., bars and restaurants).

For this reason, we infer the degree of competition faced by a firm from the importance it attaches to changes in competitors' prices in explaining its own price decreases. The rationale for this choice is that it can be expected that the more competitive the environment faced by a firm, the more its pricing strategy is likely to be affected by the behavior of its competitors. It is interesting that the results of the Dutch survey (chapter 9), which is the only survey to include a direct question on the degree of perceived competition, support the use of this measure to proxy market competition. The importance

Table 13.1 Degree of perceived competition[a] (percentages[b])

Country	Very low	Low	High	Very high
Austria	20.2	18.2	30.3	31.3
Belgium	17.6	21.8	30.4	30.1
France	19.5	17.3	38.4	24.9
Germany	19.0	23.4	34.0	23.6
Italy	9.8	24.6	37.0	28.5
Luxembourg	15.3	17.2	36.7	30.7
The Netherlands	4.6	24.6	48.8	22.0
Portugal	8.5	21.1	38.6	31.9
Spain	26.6	19.2	24.0	30.2
Euro Area[c]	17.1	21.5	35.2	26.2

Source: Calculations based on national data.
[a]Measured by the importance a firm attaches to competitors' prices when considering reducing its own prices.
[b]Rescaled figures excluding nonresponses.
[c]Weighted average (GDP weights).

attached by firms to changes in competitors' prices turns out to be highly correlated with the directly reported degree of perceived competition (Hoeberichts and Stokman 2006). This measure has the additional advantage that it is available for all countries. An additional measure that we use in the empirical analysis is the share of firms that set prices using a markup rule. We expect this share to be negatively related to the degree of market competition. Unfortunately, this information is not available for Austria and Luxembourg.

If we measure intense competition by considering those firms that report that competitors' prices are important or very important in determining a reduction in their own prices, it turns out that around 60% of firms in the euro area face intense competition (see table 13.1). This share ranges from 54% in Spain to 71% in the Netherlands, although it has to be borne in mind that these cross-country differences are affected by differences in the sectoral coverage of national surveys.[4]

COMPETITION AND FIRMS' PRICE SETTING STRATEGIES

As discussed in the introduction, the degree of market competition is an important factor in determining price setting behavior. In particular, it is reasonable to expect that firms facing a higher degree of competition will employ more flexible price determination strategies, which give them a greater ability to react to changes in market conditions.

In this section, we use the results of the national surveys to analyze differences in firms' price setting policies, according to the intensity of market competition. Specifically, we focus on the differences in some aspects of pricing strategies, such as the use of markup rules versus other policies, time versus state dependence, forward-looking behavior, and frequency of price reviews, in terms of the degree of competition faced by firms.

The various questionnaires address the issue of how firms set prices via slightly different formulations. Nevertheless, the results of the national

Table 13.2 Price setting policies by degree of perceived competition[a] (percentages[b])

Country	Markup	Competitors' price	Other
Belgium			
All firms	45.9	36.4	17.7
Low competition	—	—	—
High competition	—	—	—
France			
All firms	40.0	38.0	22.0
Low competition	49.8	24.4	25.9
High competition	36.0	47.6	16.4
Germany			
All firms	73.0	17.0	10.0
Low competition	78.9	9.4	11.7
High competition	69.8	22.5	7.6
Italy			
All firms	42.4	31.7	25.9
Low competition	57.6	14.5	27.9
High competition	33.6	42.6	23.7
The Netherlands			
All firms	56.4	22.3	21.3
Low competition	56.6	15.3	28.2
High competition	56.5	25.4	18.1
Portugal			
All firms	64.5	12.6	22.9
Low competition	78.7	2.9	18.4
High competition	59.9	17.6	22.4
Spain			
All firms	51.9	26.6	21.5
Low competition	61.3	11.8	27.0
High competition	44.1	40.5	15.3
Euro Area[c]			
All firms	54.3	27.1	18.7
Low competition	63.6	14.7	21.7
High competition	49.8	35.1	15.1

Source: Authors calculations based on national data.
[a]Measured by the importance a firm attaches to competitors' prices when considering reducing its own prices.
[b]Rescaled figures excluding nonresponses.
[c]Weighted average (GDP weights).

surveys, with the exception of those for Austria and Luxembourg, can be compared by grouping the answers into three alternatives: "markup over costs," "price set according to competitors' prices," and "other" (see chapter 2). Overall, the evidence, summarized in table 13.2, shows that a significant share of firms (54%) set their prices as a markup over marginal costs, suggesting that they enjoy a non-negligible degree of market power. The fraction of companies setting prices according to those of their competitors is 27%. Finally, around 19% of the companies state that they do not have autonomous price setting policies. For these firms, the final decision on the price charged is taken by a different economic agent, and this may be the public sector, the parent company, the main customers, or the suppliers.

There are interesting differences in these figures with respect to the degree of perceived competition. In particular, we find that the fraction of firms using markup rules is higher among those operating in low-competition environments: 64% as compared to 50% among firms facing intense competition. This result is qualitatively similar for all countries. In turn, only 15% of euro area firms operating in low competitive markets set prices taking into account competitors' prices, whereas 35% of them do so if they face strong competition. This pattern of results also holds for all countries.

State-dependent rules may lead to more flexible prices than time-dependent ones in the face of shocks; hence, we check whether pure state-dependent rules are more frequent among competitive firms. The evidence in favor of this hypothesis is rather weak: the fraction of euro area firms using pure state dependent rules is 27% among firms facing intense competition and 25% for firms operating in low competition environments.

The use of forward-looking strategies can also be expected to be more widespread in competitive environments. Evidence for Spain shows that price revisions among highly competitive firms do not usually involve the application of simple rules but are the result of an optimizing process in which expectations as to how market conditions may change are fairly frequently taken into account. The fraction of forward-looking price setters is 37% among firms operating in a competitive environment and 18% for companies facing low competition. Furthermore, the Spanish survey also shows that firms operating in competitive environments use active commercial policies to a greater extent.

There are also differences concerning the frequency of price reviews. As expected, firms operating in more competitive environments review their prices more frequently (figure 13.1). For the euro area as a whole, the fraction of firms reporting that competitors' prices are unimportant (very important) and reviewing prices at least 12 times per year is 23% (34%). Conversely, the share of companies reviewing prices at most three times per year is 68% (45%) for firms reporting that competitors' prices are unimportant (very important) on their pricing decisions. This positive relationship between the frequency of price reviews and the intensity of competition is observed in all countries.

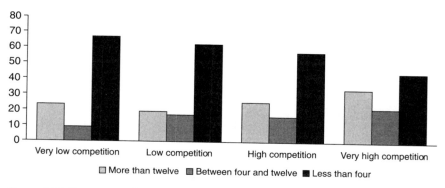

Figure 13.1 Frequency of price reviews by degree of perceived competition. Measured by the importance a firm attaches to competitors' prices when considering reducing its own prices. *Source:* Authors' calculations based on national data.

COMPETITION AND THE DEGREE OF PRICE FLEXIBILITY

Descriptive Statistics

A first approach to explore the relationship between competition and price stickiness consists in measuring the frequency of price adjustment for different groups of firms defined in terms of the degree of competition they face. As figure 13.2 shows, firms facing stronger competitive pressures display a higher frequency of price adjustment. For the euro area as a whole, the share of companies changing prices at least four times a year is 10% (26%) for firms reporting that competitors' prices are unimportant (very important) in their pricing decisions. Conversely, the fraction of firms changing prices at most once a year is 73% (50%) for firms indicating that competitors' prices are unimportant (very important) in price setting. This pattern of results is observed in all countries with the exception of Austria.

Table 13.3 reports the average implicit duration as obtained from interval grouped figures for the frequency of price changes for the different countries and degrees of competition.[5] For the euro area, prices remain unchanged on average for the most competitive firms for 9 months, whereas in more sheltered markets prices are maintained for 14 months. As can be seen from the table, the relationship between the degree of perceived competition and the average price duration is negative and monotonic in most countries.

Country-Specific Results

The link between the prevailing competitive environment and the degree of price flexibility has been explored in the different country-specific studies via a variety of methodological approaches. Some studies have analyzed the influence of the degree of market competition on the reported frequency of price changes. In particular, chapter 9 finds a positive impact from the perceived degree of competition on the frequency of price adjustment by

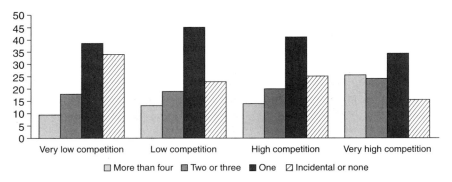

Figure 13.2 Frequency of price changes by degree of perceived competition. Measured by the importance a firm attaches to competitors' prices when considering reducing its own prices. *Source:* Authors' calculations based on national data.

Table 13.3 Average implicit price duration (in months[a]) by degree of perceived competition

Country	Degree of perceived competition[b]			
	Very low	Low	High	Very high
Austria	10.0	9.4	9.9	10.5
Belgium	12.7	11.9	12.0	10.8
France	14.0	11.7	11.3	7.9
Germany	15.9	12.2	14.1	11.4
Italy	12.7	13.1	11.8	7.6
Luxembourg	10.5	9.3	9.1	6.4
The Netherlands	10.6	11.9	10.5	9.2
Portugal	13.3	13.0	12.2	11.6
Spain	13.1	11.3	11.0	9.4
Euro Area[c]	13.8	12.0	12.1	9.4

Source: Authors' calculations based on national data.
[a]To obtain these implicit durations, the following assumptions have been made: for firms declaring "at least four price changes per year" it has been assumed a duration of 1.33 months (i.e., 8 price changes per year); for those declaring "two or three changes per year" a duration of 4.8 months (i.e., 2.5 price changes per year) has been considered; for those declaring "one change per year" a duration of 12 months has been considered; and, finally, for those declaring "less than one price change per year" a duration of 24 months has been assumed.
[b]Measured by the importance a firm attaches to competitors' prices when considering reducing its own prices.
[c]Weighted average (GDP weights).

using an ordered logit model. In a similar vein, chapter 11 reports a positive effect of the intensity of competition on the frequency of price changes in a log-linear regression model. In both cases, the estimated models control for other potential determinants of price flexibility. In turn, chapter 4 in a bivariate analysis finds that flexible firms—that is, firms with shorter average duration between two consecutive price changes—tend to experience more competition, as proxied by different indicators such as the number of competitors or the importance of competitors' prices to explain price changes.

The influence of the intensity of competition on the probability of price adjustments after shocks has been addressed for a larger number of countries by using probit models. The reaction to positive and negative demand as well as cost shocks has been considered. The general conclusion that arises from these country-specific studies is that the speed of response to demand shocks is significantly higher for firms operating in more competitive environments. In this type of analysis, the dependent variable is a binary variable that is set to 1 if the firm declares that it changes its price (within a specific period or without any time constraint) after the shock and 0 otherwise. In turn, the intensity of competition is proxied by the importance attached by companies to their competitors' prices, although there are country-specific differences as well.[6] Table 13.4 reports the sign of the estimated impact in the available country studies. Overall, results show that the higher the degree of market competition, the more flexible in response to demand shocks prices are. This finding holds across countries and independently of the direction of the shocks, although it is not significant for Portugal or, in the case of contractionary shocks, for Spain. These results suggest that a slow price

Table 13.4 Impact of market competition on the probability of adjustment after shocks (main results from probit analysis)[a,b]

| Country | Type of shock | | | |
	Increase in demand	Fall in demand	Increase in costs	Fall in costs
Austria	+	+	no	no
France	+	+	+	no
Italy	+	+	−	−
Portugal	no	no	no	no
Spain	+	no	no	no

Source: Calculations based on national data.
[a]A plus (+) denotes that competition is positively and significantly related to the probability of a price increase/decrease in response to an increase/decrease in demand/costs; a minus (−) denotes that competition is negatively and significantly related to the probability of a price increase/decrease in response to an increase/decrease in demand/costs; "no" denotes that competition is not significantly related to the probability of a price increase/decrease in response to an increase/decrease in demand/costs.
[b]The definition of the dependent variable in the probit analysis as well as of the competition variable may be found in the country specific studies.

reaction to demand contraction in a highly competitive sector may result in a substantial loss of market share. In contrast, the speed of adjustment to cost shocks does not seem to be significantly affected by the degree of competition.

DETERMINANTS OF PRICE FLEXIBILITY IN THE EURO AREA

In this section, we explore the potential role of a number of factors to explain differences in the degree of price flexibility across euro area industries. We focus on the competitive environment, the cost structure of the different industries, demand conditions, and product market regulations.

Data

We have put together a database with sectoral information from national surveys. Our starting point is the consideration of all NACE two-digit sectors, where we can broadly distinguish three groups of industries in terms of national coverage.[7] The first is manufacturing, which is covered in all country surveys; second, some market services (trade, hotels and restaurants, and transport and communications), which are covered in at least two big and two small euro area countries;[8] and third, the remaining sectors. Our full sample does not include this last group of sectors, since coverage in terms of countries is too limited to be considered informative for a euro area analysis.[9]

There are specific industries in some countries in which only a limited number of firms were surveyed. To ensure that our results are not driven by these observations, we also consider restricted samples made up of those sectors in which there are at least ten surveyed firms in a given country.[10] We refer to these samples as high representativity samples.

The variables considered in our econometric models are mostly derived from the country surveys. Therefore, the different variables refer to the same set of firms. To enhance the degree of comparability across countries, we employ the same definitions of variables as in Fabiani et al. (2005). The main variables we use are the following.

Price Flexibility   For the full set of countries, we have information on the number of price changes per year.[11] Specifically, for each country and industry we know the fractions of firms that change prices according to four different categories: (1) at least four price changes per year, (2) two or three price changes per year, (3) one price change per year, and (4) less than one price change. We use the fraction of firms that change prices at least four times a year as the dependent variable in the econometric analysis.

Perceived Competition   One measure of competition is obtained from the importance firms attribute to competitors' prices in influencing a reduction in their own prices. Information refers to a mean score of the following categories: "1 = unimportant," "2 = of minor importance," "3 = important," and "4 = very important."

Markup An alternative measure of competition for all countries, except Austria and Luxembourg, can be obtained from questions on price setting. In particular, we use the percentage of firms that declare employing markup over costs rules.

Labor Costs, Raw Materials Costs, and Demand All national surveys included questions about the factors that are important for changing prices upward or downward, including labor costs, raw material costs, and demand conditions. Respondents were asked to assign scores between "1 = completely unimportant" and "4 = very important" to each of them. In our analysis we consider, for each factor, the sum of scores for price increases and decreases.

Product Market Regulation We employ both objective and subjective measures of regulation.[12] For the former, which involve coding a variety of features of different laws and combining them into a single index, we use the estimates provided by Nicoletti et al. (1999). For the subjective measures, which involve coding responses to public opinion surveys of experts or of business people in which respondents are asked about the existence and impact of various regulations, we use the estimates by Pryor (2002). In both cases, measures refer to regulations at the national level, as information at the industry level is not available.

Sectoral Dummies We also consider dummies for groupings of manufacturing sectors (food, other consumer goods, intermediate products, and capital goods) and services sectors (trade, hotels and restaurants, and transport and communications).

Econometric Methodology

In our analysis, we model the fraction of firms (*freq*) that change prices frequently. Given that fractions are bounded between 0 and 1 and linear predictors can take any real value, linear models are inappropriate in this setting and the alternative of using a log-odds ratio model also has potential problems. First, the method is not valid if the fraction takes on the values 0 or 1, as is sometimes the case in our sample. Second, further assumptions are needed to recover the conditional expectation. To avoid these problems we use the quasi-maximum likelihood (QML) approach of Papke and Woolridge (1996), involving the estimation of a nonlinear model. Specifically, the observed frequency is expressed as a bounded nonlinear function (typically a cumulative distribution function) of explanatory variables (*x*), and a Bernoulli likelihood function is maximized. The corresponding estimator is consistent and asymptotically normal. In our estimates we use a logistic cumulative distribution function.[13] That is, we estimate

$$freq = \frac{e^{\alpha + \Sigma \beta_i x_i}}{1 + e^{\alpha + \Sigma \beta_i x_i}} \qquad freq \sim \text{Bernoulli}$$

Results

In this section, first we report the results for basic specifications in which we measure the degree of market competition by the importance attached by firms to competitors' prices in explaining their own price cuts and do not include any product market regulation variable. Second, we alternatively proxy competition by the variable *markup*. Finally, we estimate specifications including product market regulation variables. Throughout we present results for the full sample of manufacturing and services and also for manufacturing sectors only, since these data refer to all countries. In all cases, we check for robustness by using high representativity samples, where only those industries in which at least ten firms are surveyed in a given country are considered.

The first column in table 13.5 reports estimates for the complete set of manufacturing and services industries. As can be seen, price flexibility—as measured by the fraction of firms that change prices at least four times a year—is significantly and positively affected by the degree of market competition. Regarding the variables proxying the cost structure, we expect that those sectors where labor costs are highly relevant tend to contain a relatively small fraction of firms that change prices often. This is explained by the fact that wage changes typically take place once a year. On the other hand, those sectors where raw materials are highly relevant can be expected to show a high degree of price flexibility, since raw material prices change very often. In this specification, we estimate a negative coefficient on labor and a positive one on raw materials, although they are not significant. We also find a positive and significant effect of the demand variable, showing that in those sectors where demand conditions are important there is a high degree of price flexibility. Regarding country dummies, we find positive and significant coefficients for Austria, Germany, and Luxembourg. This is interesting, since Austria and Germany are two countries where product market regulation is low.[14] Finally, the transport and communications sector is found to be significantly less flexible than the other sectors.[15] The second column in table 13.5 restricts the sample to highly representative industries. The only difference with respect to the whole sample is that cost variables are now highly significant, although the demand variable is no longer significant. Considering only manufacturing industries (column 3), competition, cost structure, and demand variables are all significant, with the exception of the labor variable, which is only correctly signed. Finally, restricting the manufacturing sample to highly representative sectors, we find that competition and cost variables are highly significant, although this is no longer the case for the demand variable.

An alternative measure of competition is obtained by using the percentage of firms that employ markup rules. The main disadvantage of this measure is that it is not available for Austria and Luxembourg. Column 1 of table 13.6 reports the results for the full sample. It is found that competition, cost, and demand variables are all significant. These results also hold for the smaller sample of highly representative industries (column 2). Consideration

Table 13.5 Determinants of price flexibility[a,b] (perceived competition specifications)

Explanatory variables[c]	Manufacturing and services		Manufacturing	
	Full sample	High representativity sample	Full sample	High representativity sample
Perceived competition	0.69**	0.88***	0.85**	0.91***
Labor	−0.11	−0.56***	−0.18	−0.59***
Raw materials	0.22	0.27**	0.30*	0.32**
Demand	0.35*	0.25	0.34*	0.24
Austria	2.75***	2.61***	3.06***	2.76***
Belgium	0.23	−0.1	0.54	0.13
France	0.54	−0.39	0.58	−0.4
Germany	1.52***	0.70**	1.55***	0.67**
Italy	0.53	0.45	0.56	0.37
Luxembourg[d]	1.07**	1.57***	0.99	—
The Netherlands	0.64	0.43	—	—
Spain	0.45	−0.16	0.4	−0.3
Consumer non-food goods	−0.47	−0.2	−0.45	−0.19
Intermediate goods	−0.17	−0.21	−0.19	−0.22
Capital goods	−0.56	−0.38	−0.55	−0.39
Trade	0.66	0.28	—	—
Hotels and restaurants	−0.32	−0.25	—	—
Transport and communications	−1.08**	−1.18***	—	—
Constant	−6.68***	−4.38***	−7.26***	−4.53***
Number of obs.	162	133	137	113
Pseudo R squared	0.48	0.40	0.47	0.41
Log likelihood	−49.61	−39.78	−42.19	−33.83
AIC	137.22	117.56	114.39	95.65
BIC	195.89	172.47	158.19	133.84

Source: Authors' calculations.

[a]Dependent variable: fraction of firms that change prices at least four times a year.

[b]p-values: * = p < .1; ** = p < .05; *** = p < .01. Computed using Huber-White robust standard errors.

[c]Definition of explanatory variables: see the main text. The reference industry is Food in Portugal.

[d]The Luxembourg survey does not include any manufacturing industry in which more than ten firms were surveyed.

Table 13.6 Determinants of price flexibility[a,b](markup specification excluding product market regulation)

Explanatory variables[c]	Manufacturing and services		Manufacturing	
	Full sample	High representativity sample	Full sample	High representativity sample
Markup	−0.02***	−0.02***	−0.02***	−0.02**
Labor	−0.33*	−0.39**	−0.42**	−0.47**
Raw materials	0.37**	0.41***	0.45***	0.48***
Demand	0.32*	0.52***	0.32*	0.47***
Belgium	−0.11	−0.15	0.04	0.16
France	−0.32	−0.27	−0.47	−0.33
Germany	1.13***	1.00**	1.05**	0.86**
Italy	−0.27	−0.56	−0.33	−0.87*
The Netherlands	0.83*	0.38	—	—
Spain	−0.01	−0.12	−0.27	−0.28
Consumer non-food goods	−0.83**	−0.76**	−0.75**	−0.72**
Intermediate goods	−0.47	−0.64**	−0.48	−0.63**
Capital goods	−0.85**	−0.85**	−0.81**	−0.79**
Trade	−0.19	0.26	—	—
Hotels and restaurants	−0.79*	−0.57	—	—
Transport and communications	−1.45***	−1.62***	—	—
Constant	−2.6	−3.50**	−2.41	−3.41**
Number of obs.	122	108	104	93
Pseudo R squared	0.36	0.33	0.40	0.33
Log likelihood	−31.42	−27.46	−26.43	−23.46
AIC	96.84	88.92	78.87	72.92
BIC	144.51	134.51	113.24	105.84

Source: Authors' calculations.
[a]Dependent variable: fraction of firms that change prices at least four times per year.
[b]p values: * = $p < .1$; ** = $p < .05$; *** = $p < .01$. Computed using Huber-White robust standard errors.
[c]Definition of explanatory variables: see the main text. The reference industry is Food in Portugal.

of only manufacturing firms does not change the results (column 3), and these are also robust for the high representative sample (column 4).

Table 13.7 considers the addition of either objective or subjective measures of product market regulation to the specifications in table 13.6. Column 1 includes the objective measure of Nicoletti et al. (1999) for the

Table 13.7 Determinants of price flexibility[a,b] (markup specification including product market regulation)

Explanatory variables[c]	Manufacturing and services		Manufacturing	
	Objective regulation[d]	Subjective regulation[e]	Objective regulation[d]	Subjective regulation[e]
Markup	−0.02**	−0.02***	−0.02**	−0.02***
Labor	−0.45***	−0.37***	−0.51***	−0.37***
Raw materials	0.40***	0.41***	0.48**	0.43**
Demand	0.32**	0.33**	0.32*	0.35**
Product markets regulation	−2.51***	−2.45***	−2.48***	−2.79***
Consumer non-food goods	−0.75**	−0.81**	−0.72**	−0.81**
Intermediate goods	−0.45	−0.48*	−0.46*	−0.51*
Capital goods	−0.76**	−0.82**	−0.73**	−0.85**
Trade	−0.17	−0.34	—	—
Hotels and restaurants	−0.79*	−1.14***	—	—
Transport and communications	−1.39***	−1.52***	—	—
Constant	−0.49	−1.03	−0.64	−0.85
Number of obs.	122	122	104	104
Pseudo R squared	0.30	0.34	0.31	0.35
Log likelihood	−31.96	−31.64	−27.06	−26.73
AIC	87.92	87.28	72.11	71.45
BIC	121.57	120.93	95.91	95.25

Source: Authors' calculations.
[a]Dependent variable: fraction of firms that change prices at least four times a year.
[b]p values: * = $p < .1$; ** = $p < .05$; *** = $p < .01$. Computed using Huber-White robust standard errors.
[c]Definition of explanatory variables: see the main text. The reference industry is Food in Portugal.
[d]Objective product market regulation variable. Source: Nicoletti et al. (1999).
[e]Subjective product market regulation variable. Source: Pryor (2002).

whole sample of manufacturing and services industries. It is found that competition, cost structure, and demand variables are highly significant. Moreover, those countries in which product market regulation is more important display a lower degree of price flexibility. Column 2 reports results using the subjective measure by Pryor (2002) and shows that the results are robust to the change in the regulation variable. As an additional check, we consider just manufacturing sectors. The relevance of competition, cost structure, and demand variables are again found, regardless of the use of an objective (column 3) or subjective (column 4) measure of product market regulation.

CONCLUSIONS

Recent empirical studies on price setting behavior using micro data have shown a marked heterogeneity in the degree of price stickiness across industries. In this chapter, we have explored the role of a number of factors in explaining this heterogeneity, on the basis of the information provided by surveys on pricing behavior conducted in nine euro area countries. The main focus has been placed on the influence of the intensity of competition on the degree of price flexibility. Our results suggest that the pricing policies of firms operating in more competitive environments show greater flexibility in certain aspects. These firms carry out price revisions and changes substantially more often and tend to use markup rules to a lesser extent. Overall, the price setting strategies of the most competitive firms give them a greater capacity to react to shocks and, in practice, make for greater flexibility in their prices.

The direct influence of market competition on price flexibility is corroborated by a cross-country cross-industry econometric analysis based on the information provided by the surveys. This analysis also shows that the cost structure and demand conditions help to explain the degree of price flexibility. Finally, it suggests that countries in which product market regulation is more relevant are characterized by less price flexibility. Overall, these results are in line with the micro quantitative evidence on the determinants of the frequency of consumer and producer price changes (chapter 14).

Acknowledgments We are grateful to all members of the Eurosystem Inflation Persistence Network (IPN) and, particularly, Luc Aucremanne, Josef Baumgartner, Martine Druant, Silvia Fabiani, Angela Gattulli, Marco Hoeberichts, Claudia Kwapil, Bettina Landau, Claire Loupias, Patrick Lünnemann, Fernando Martins, Thomas Mathä, Pedro Neves, Roland Ricart, Roberto Sabbatini, Johann Scharler, Harald Stahl and Ad Stokman for helpful discussions and for providing industry data from their national surveys. We also acknowledge comments from Juan Peñalosa on a previous version of this chapter.

NOTES

1. See Mills (1927) and Means (1936) for early contributions on the behavior of individual prices, and Silberston (1970) and Carlton (1989) for surveys of theoretical and empirical work on the relationship between pricing behavior and market structure.

2. A similar argument is considered by Eichner (1973). Industries characterized by increasing returns to scale usually lead to a small number of competitors that carry out the necessary large irreversible investments. The pricing policies of these firms are more oriented by long-run objectives than by short-run costs or demand fluctuations.

3. This argument is consistent with Stigler's (1964) model, according to which the fewer the number of firms in an industry, the easier it is to monitor price cuts.

4. For instance, the degree of perceived competition in Spain is found to be lowest in energy (31%), energy trade (38%), and bars and restaurants (44%). At the other end

of the spectrum, the share of firms facing intense competitive pressures is highest in communications (69%), hotels and travel agents (66%), and food trade (65%).

5. To obtain these implicit durations, the following assumptions have been made. For firms declaring "at least four price changes per year," a duration of 1.33 months (that is, eight price changes per year) has been assumed; for those declaring "two or three changes per year," a duration of 4.8 months (that is, 2.5 price changes per year); for those declaring "one change per year" a duration of 12 months; and, finally, for those declaring "less than one price change per year," a duration of 24 months.

6. The precise definitions used in the different countries both for the binary dependent variable and for the proxies of competition can be found in the country specific studies.

7. Available data for the Netherlands correspond to the aggregate of manufacturing and five different services groupings. For Belgium, we have information on 17 aggregates that group NACE sectors.

8. These industries are covered in the Italian and Spanish surveys.

9. Specifically, we cover the NACE two-digit sectors coded 15, 17–22, 24–36, 51–60, 64. The remaining sectors do not satisfy the minimum coverage rule of two big countries and two small countries. The exclusion of the sector "Coke and refined petroleum" is due to its markedly different pricing behavior.

10. Given its special characteristics, we have not applied the ten firms minimum for the sector "Office machinery and computers" (NACE 30).

11. Specifically, five national surveys (for Belgium, Spain, Luxembourg, the Netherlands, and Austria) refer to the average number of price changes per year in recent years, whereas three (for Italy, France and Portugal) refer to the number of price changes in a precise year. For Germany, the figures we use refer to the number of price changes, as reported by the same firms in the IFO business survey in 2003, given that the German questionnaire did not include a question on the number of price changes.

12. See Nicoletti and Pryor (2006) for a comparative study of several quantitative indicators of regulation in OECD nations.

13. In our robustness analyses we have also considered a standard Gaussian distribution and a complementary log-log distribution. Results are not affected by the specific function used.

14. No information for Luxembourg is available.

15. According to the results from country-specific studies (see, for instance, chapter 11), this result is most likely driven by the high stickiness of pricing policies of transport firms.

REFERENCES

Álvarez, Luis J., Pablo Burriel, and Ignacio Hernando. 2005. Price setting behaviour in Spain: Evidence from micro PPI data. Banco de España Working Paper No. 0527. Madrid: Banco de España.

Bedrossian, Arakel, and Demetrios Moschos. 1988. Industrial structure, concentration, and the speed of price adjustment. *Journal of Industrial Economics* 36: 459–475.

Bresnahan, Timothy F. 1989. Empirical studies of industries with market power. In *Handbook of Industrial Economics*, ed. Richard Schmalensee and Robert Willig. Amsterdam: North-Holland.

Carlton, Dennis W. 1986. The rigidity of prices. *American Economic Review* 76: 637–658.

Carlton, Dennis W. 1989. The theory and facts about how markets clear. Is industrial organization valuable for understanding macroeconomics? In *Handbook of Industrial Economics*, ed. Richard Schmalensee and Robert Willig. Amsterdam: North-Holland.

Cornille, David, and Maarten Dossche. 2006. The patterns and determinants of price setting in the Belgian industry. European Central Bank Working Paper No. 618. Frankfurt am Main: European Central Bank.

Dixon, R. 1983. Industry structure and the speed of price-adjustment. *Journal of Industrial Economics* 31: 25–37.

Domberger, Simon. 1979. Price adjustment and market structure. *The Economic Journal* 89: 96–108.

Eichner, Alfred S. 1973. A theory of the markup under oligopoly. *The Economic Journal* 83: 1184–1200.

Encaoua, David, and Paul A. Geroski. 1986. Price dynamics and competition in five OECD countries. *OECD Economic Studies* 6: 47–76.

Fabiani, Silvia, Martine Druant, Ignacio Hernando, Claudia Kwapil, Bettina Landau, Claire Loupias, Fernando Martins, Thomas Mathä, Roberto Sabbatini, and Ad Stokman. 2005. The pricing behaviour of firms in the Euro Area: New survey evidence. European Central Bank Working Paper No. 535. Frankfurt am Main: European Central Bank.

Geroski, Paul. 1992. Price dynamics in UK manufacturing: A microeconomic view. *Economica* 59: 403–419.

Ginsburgh, Victor, and Philippe Michel. 1988. Adjustment costs, concentration, and price behavior. *Journal of Industrial Economics* 36: 477–481.

Hall, Simon, Mark Walsh, and Anthony Yates. 2000. How do UK companies set prices? *Oxford Economic Papers* 52: 425–446.

Hoeberichts, Marco, and Ad Stokman. 2006. Pricing behaviour of Dutch companies: Main results from a survey. European Central Bank Working Paper No. 607. Frankfurt am Main: European Central Bank.

Lünnemann, Patrick, and Thomas Mathä. 2005. Consumer price behaviour in Luxembourg: Evidence from micro CPI data. European Central Bank Working Paper No. 541. Frankfurt am Main: European Central Bank.

Martin, Cristopher. 1993. Price adjustment and market structure. *Economics Letters* 41: 139–143.

Means, Gardiner C. 1935. Notes on inflexible prices. *American Economic Review* 26: 23–35.

Mills, Frederick C. 1927. *The Behavior of Prices*. New York. National Bureau of Economic Research.

Nicoletti, Giuseppe, Stefano Scarpetta, and Olivier Boylaud. 1999. Summary indicators of product market regulation with an extension to employment protection legislation. OECD Economics Department Working Papers No. 226. Paris: Organisation for Economic Co-operation and Development.

Nicoletti, Giuseppe, and Frederic L. Pryor. 2006. Subjective and objective measures of governmental regulations in OECD nations. *Journal of Economic Behavior and Organization* 59: 433–449.

Papke, Leslie E., and Jeffrey M. Woolridge. 1996. Econometric methods for fractional response with an application to 401(K) plan participation rates. *Journal of Applied Econometrics* 11: 619–632.

Pryor, Frederic L. 2002. Quantitative notes on the extent of governmental regulations in various OECD nations. *International Journal of Industrial Organization* 20: 693–715.

Silberston, Aubrey. 1970. Surveys of applied economics: Price behaviour of firms. *The Economic Journal* 80: 511–582.

Stigler, George S. 1964. A theory of oligopoly. *Journal of Political Economy* 72: 44–61.

Stiglitz, Joseph E. 1984. Price rigidities and market structure. *American Economic Review* 74: 350–355.

Weiss, Christoph R. 1995. Determinants of price flexibility in oligopolistic markets: Evidence from Austrian manufacturing firms. *Journal of Economics and Business* 47: 423–439.

14

What Quantitative Micro Data Reveal about Price Setting Behavior

Roberto Sabbatini, Luis J. Álvarez, Emmanuel Dhyne,
Marco Hoeberichts, Hervé Le Bihan, Patrick Lünnemann,
Fernando Martins, Fabio Rumler, Harald Stahl,
Philip Vermeulen, Giovanni Veronese, & Jouko Vilmunen

This chapter summarizes the results of studies on price setting based on micro consumer and producer price data, conducted by most national central banks of the euro area in the context of the Inflation Persistence Network. These analyses of individual quantitative price data underlying official consumer (CPI) and producer (PPI) price indices allow us to capture features of price behavior that cannot be fully analyzed with surveys, as well as providing important complementary evidence on the frequency and size of price changes. This evidence is an important input for building macroeconomic models of inflation with adequate microeconomic foundations.

Due to the scarcity of available statistical information, research in this field generally has focused on very specific products or markets.[1] The first studies that exploited large-scale datasets of individual prices regularly collected to compute consumer price indices were those by Bils and Klenow (2004) for the United States, and Baharad and Eden (2004) for Israel.

This chapter focuses on the key features of price setting as identified by Taylor (1999), in particular on the frequency and size of price changes. The evidence collected here is based on studies on consumer prices available for all countries except Greece and Ireland (table 14.1), summarized in Dhyne et al. (2005, 2006), and on studies on producer prices carried out in Belgium, Germany, France, Italy, Portugal, and Spain (table 14.2), summarized in Vermeulen et al. (2006).

The chapter is organized as follows. The first section describes the databases used in the different studies and the main characteristics of the harmonized methodology followed in the empirical analysis to make country results comparable. The second section presents the stylized facts describing firms' price setting. The third section summarizes the main results in the national studies concerning the determinants of the frequency of price changes. Finally, the fourth section offers our conclusions.

DATABASES AND METHODS OF ANALYSIS

The typical quantitative information contained in the databases analyzed here is the price trajectory associated with one particular product sold by a particular outlet (in the case of CPI) or by a specific manufacturing firm (in the case of PPI). Examples of such price trajectories are given in figure 14.1.

The results on consumer prices reported in this chapter refer to all euro area member states (except Greece and Ireland), which together represent around 97% of euro area GDP. Within the euro area, national statistical agencies collect consumer prices on the basis of harmonized methodologies (Eurostat 2001). However, since the coverage of the original national datasets was quite heterogeneous across countries (table 14.1), Dhyne et al. (2006) made a further harmonization effort in terms of product and time period coverage.[2] Specifically, they chose a subsample of 50 product categories, representative of the whole CPI basket, for the period from

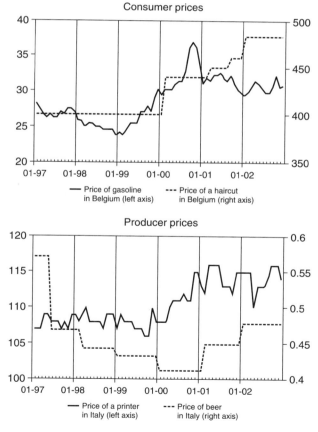

Figure 14.1 Examples of individual price trajectories. Consumer prices are in Belgian francs; producer prices are in euros. *Source:* Álvarez et al. (2006).

Table 14.1 The national studies

Country	Study that reports the results	Percentage of CPI basket covered in the original database and/or number of products	Period covered in the original databases
Austria	Baumgartner et al. 2005	90% (80% considered)	Jan. 1996–Dec. 2003
Belgium	Aucremanne and Dhyne 2004	68%	Jan. 1989–Dec. 2001
Finland	Vilmunen and Laakkonen 2005	100%	Jan. 1997–Dec. 2003
France	Baudry et al. 2004	65%	Jul. 1994–Feb. 2003
Germany	Hoffmann and Kurz-Kim 2006	20% (52 products)	Jan. 1998–Jan. 2004
Italy	Veronese et al. 2004	20% (50 products)	Jan. 1996–Dec. 2003
Luxembourg	Lünnemann and Mathä 2005	100%	Jan. 1999–Dec. 2004
The Netherlands	Jonker et al. 2004	8% (49 products)	Nov. 1998–Apr. 2003
Portugal	Dias et al. 2004	100% (95% considered)	Jan. 1992–Jan. 2001
Spain	Álvarez and Hernando 2004	70%	Jan. 1993–Dec. 2001

Source: National papers.

January 1996 to December 2001, that is, before the euro cash changeover, since this event could bias frequencies of price adjustment.

The results on producer prices refer to Belgium, France, Germany, Italy, Portugal, and Spain, representing around 85% of euro area GDP. The national studies were carried out using nearly the complete set of micro data underlying the computation of the national PPI, with the exception of Italy, where only a subset of price records related to 60 products could be used (a detailed description of each national database is provided in country analyses reported in table 14.2).

In European countries the collection of monthly price records on individual products at the establishment level is harmonized; in particular, the methodological manual from Eurostat (Eurostat 2002) states the following rules: (1) the appropriate price is the ex-factory price, including all duties and taxes except value added tax (VAT); (2) prices are actual transaction prices, and not list prices; (3) prices collected in period *t* refer to orders booked during period *t* (moment of order), not the time when goods leave the factory gate.

In the case of consumer prices, all the methodological aspects followed by national statistical agencies are monitored by Eurostat in the context of the harmonization process conducted at the EU level, but for producer prices it

Table 14.2 Coverage of the national PPI databases

Country	Study that reports the results	Percentage of PPI basket covered in the original database	Period covered in the original databases
Germany	Stahl 2006	100	Jan. 1997–Feb. 2003
France	Gautier 2006	92	Jan. 1994–Jun. 2005
Italy	Sabbatini et al. 2005	44[a]	Jan. 1997–Dec. 2002
Spain	Álvarez et al. 2005a	99	Nov. 1991–Feb. 1999
Belgium	Cornille and Dossche 2006	83	Jan. 2001–Jan. 2005
Portugal	Dias et al 2004	Almost 100	Jan. 1995–Aug. 2002

[a]Estimated on the basis of three-digit weights.

is more difficult to assess precisely to what degree the statistical offices are able to follow strictly the common guidelines for all products. This implies that in the case of PPI data, part of the differences across countries in the statistics reported in this chapter could arise from methodological rather than economic causes. However, as shown below, the fact that summary statistics across countries are remarkably similar is reassuring and allows us to derive stylized facts that can be considered valid for the euro area as a whole.

Unconditional measures of price stickiness with micro data can be obtained following two methodological approaches: the first measures directly the number of months in which a price remains unchanged (duration approach); the second computes the proportion of all price quotes that change in a given period (frequency approach) and then derives an indirect measure of price duration.[3] The national studies summarized here adopt the frequency approach, following Bils and Klenow (2004). As described in Dhyne et al. (2005), this method uses the full information and does not require a long span of data. Moreover, if some months are deemed to be exceptional due to specific events (such as a VAT change), they can be easily dropped in computing the average frequency of price changes.

The frequency of price changes for a given product j (F_j) is computed as the number of price changes (denoted by CHG_{jt}, for the j-th product at time t, where $t = 2, \ldots T$) over the total number of price quotes for that product (TOT_{jt}), that is

$$F_j = \left(\sum_{t=2}^{T} CHG_{jt} \Big/ \sum_{t=2}^{T} TOT_{jt} \right) \qquad (1)$$

Similarly, the frequency of price increases (decreases) for each product can be computed by replacing CHG_{jt} in the numerator with $CHGUP_{jt}$ ($CHGDW_{jt}$), where the latter indicates the number of positive (negative) price changes in each period t.

Under certain assumptions in the process determining price spells, both cross-sectionally and over time (see Lancaster 1990), the average duration of price spells for product j can be computed as the inverse of the frequency of price changes (implied average spell duration):

$$\overline{T}_j = \frac{1}{F_j} \tag{2}$$

Equation 1, and consequently equation 2, are appropriate when retailers or firms change their price only at discrete intervals. Assuming, as in Bils and Klenow (2004), that prices are changed in continuous time, and under a constant hazard model, the implied average duration can be computed as

$$\overline{T}_j = -\frac{1}{\ln(1-F_j)} \tag{3}$$

From an economic point of view, the frequency of price changes of a particular product or group of products provides condensed information on the outcome of price setting, though it should in principle be interpreted simultaneously with the driving factors of price adjustment. If a particular product has a much higher frequency of price changes than another it could be that the price is set more flexibly (that is, it reacts more to shocks) or that it has more reasons to change. Thus, the general conclusions that a higher frequency of price changes automatically reflects stronger price flexibility is not always appropriate.

STYLIZED FACTS ON PRICE SETTING

This section presents a set of facts that emerge consistently in the euro area countries, for both consumer and producer prices.

Fact 1. Prices in the euro area change infrequently. Table 14.3 shows that the share of prices that are changed each month is, on average, equal to 15% for consumer prices and 21% for producer prices.[4] The implied average duration of a consumer price spell is just above one year.[5] Consumer prices are adjusted substantially more often in the United States, where the monthly frequency of price changes is around 25%, implying an average price duration slightly above half a year.[6] Differences between the euro area and the United States are not due to any particular product category but hold for almost all items. These results are also broadly consistent with the evidence based on survey data (see chapters 2 and 12).

There exist sizeable cross-country differences in the frequency of consumer price changes. In the period 1996–2001, the average frequency of price change ranges from 10% in Italy to 23% in Luxembourg. These differences can be attributed to various factors. First, they can be partly explained by consumption structure; indeed, they narrow when the average euro area consumption structure is used to aggregate over products. Specifically, assuming that consumption patterns are equal in all countries to those of the

Table 14.3 Measures of price stickiness in the euro area and in the United States

Source of data	Statistics	Euro Area	United States
CPI	Frequency (percentage per month)	15	25
	Average duration (months)	13	7
	Median duration (months)	11	5
PPI	Frequency (percentage per month)	22	—
Surveys	Frequency (percentage per month)	16	21
	Average duration (months)	11	8
New Keynesian Phillips Curve	Average duration (months)	13–19	7–8

Source: Álvarez et al. (2006).

euro area as a whole, the frequency of price change ranges from 12% in Italy to 20% in France. On the contrary, consumption structure does not help explain the difference between the euro area and the United States, as euro area consumption is characterized by a larger share of food products, where prices change very frequently, and a smaller share of services, with infrequent price changes.

Second, their origin can be "structural," in particular due to the different outlet composition; for instance, some countries, such as Italy, may have stickier prices due to a larger market share of small traditional outlets, which typically change their prices less frequently than supermarkets (see for instance Baudry et al. 2004). Outlet composition also helps explain differences with the United States, since traditional shops have a higher market share in euro area countries (Pilat 1997). More generally, differences in the degree of competition, in particular in the services sector, may be an important reason underlying the lower frequency of price changes in the euro area compared to the United States, which is indeed particularly pronounced in the case of services.[7] Third, for non-energy industrial goods, different treatment by National Statistical Institutes of price cuts during sales periods may be a primary factor in explaining the observed differences in the frequency of price adjustment: in France, which records sales prices, 18% of these prices are found to change every month, as opposed to only around 6% in Belgium, Germany, Italy, and Spain.[8] Finally, a higher variability of wages and other input prices in the United States may help explain more frequent price changes than in the euro area.

As opposed to this, cross-country comparison reveals a more homogeneous behavior for producer prices. The frequency of price changes for Belgium, France, Germany, Spain, and Portugal lies in a narrow interval between 21% and 25%. The lowest frequency is found in Italy (15%); however, energy products for this country, which usually have the highest frequency of price changes, are excluded from the analysis. Comparisons

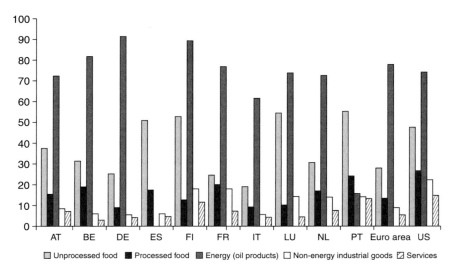

Figure 14.2 Frequency of consumer price changes (percentages). *Source:* Dhyne et al. (2006).

with the United States cannot be made, as there is no study available for the complete set of PPI products.

Fact 2. There is a substantial heterogeneity in price adjustment across sectors. Concerning consumer prices, changes are very frequent for energy and unprocessed food (78 and 28%, respectively, every month), but they are relatively infrequent for non-energy industrial goods and, in particular, for services (9 and 6%, respectively; see figure 14.2); processed food products show an intermediate degree of price flexibility. It is worth remarking that the above ranking of product categories is robust across all euro area countries, and a similar ranking is also found for the United States.

Producer prices exhibit a similar pattern: energy and food products are characterized by more frequent price changes, whereas capital goods and durables are the stickiest components (figure 14.3). This suggests that the frequency of price changes decreases with the degree of sophistication of the product, in the sense that prices of those products that have not undergone a series of transformations change more frequently, as their costs are closely linked to raw material prices, which are typically rather volatile.

The above results confirm survey evidence that points out that prices in the services sector (excluding trade) are stickier than those for manufacturing goods and trade (see chapter 2).

Fact 3. The share of price decreases is surprisingly large, with the exception of services. Around 40% of CPI and 45% of PPI monthly price changes are decreases. This somewhat surprising fact is found for all countries and is also in line with the evidence obtained by Klenow and Kryvstov (2005) for the United States.[9]

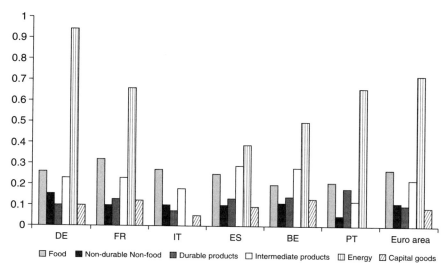

Figure 14.3 Frequency of producer price changes (percentages). *Source:* Vermeulen et al. (2006).

Looking at the breakdown by economic sector, interesting patterns emerge. Concerning consumer prices, food and energy prices exhibit almost symmetric increases and decreases. On the contrary, in the services sector only one price change out of five is a reduction (Dhyne et al. 2006). This result may be partly related to the much higher sectoral average inflation and the relatively higher labor share in services, with wage stickiness translating into prices (see below). As far as producer prices are concerned, all components tend to exhibit quite symmetric price changes, with only slightly higher frequency of price increases than decreases.

Fact 4. When they occur, price increases and decreases are sizeable compared to the average inflation rate. Looking at the magnitude of consumer price changes, reductions are only slightly larger than increases (10% compared to 8%; table 14.4); all in all, their size is high relative to the inflation rate. A similar result is found for the United States. The average size of PPI increases and decreases is much smaller than that found for the CPI.

There is also sectoral heterogeneity in the size of consumer price changes. Unprocessed food price changes are large; price increases and decreases tend to offset each other, since their frequency and size are almost identical. This suggests that prices in this sector are driven largely by supply-side factors related to the seasonal nature of many unprocessed food items. Energy prices also change very often but by a smaller amount. This is consistent with the variability of marginal costs (oil prices in international markets), which is partly attenuated by the large incidence of indirect taxation.

Fact 5. Synchronization of price changes across price setters does not seem to be high at the product level, even within the same country. Using

Table 14.4 Frequency and size of price changes
in the euro area (percentages)

	CPI	PPI
Total		
Frequency	15	22
Average size	9	4
Price increases		
Frequency	8	12
Average size	8	4
Price decreases		
Frequency	6	10
Average size	10	4

Source: Dhyne et al. (2006) and Vermeulen et al. (2006).

the measure proposed by Fisher and Konieczny (2000), the degree of synchronization is rather low, except for energy prices (for details see Dhyne et al. 2006). The median synchronization ratio across the 50 products in the common sample ranges from 0.13 in Germany to 0.48 in Luxembourg, where the number of shops in which prices are collected is relatively small. Note that in the Italian case the low synchronization of price changes at the product level is perfectly compatible with higher synchronization rates computed within a given city (Veronese et al. 2005).

THE DETERMINANTS OF THE FREQUENCY OF PRICE CHANGES

This section focuses on the evidence, reported in the national studies, on the determinants of the frequency of consumer and producer price changes, summarized in Dyhne et al. (2006) and Vermeulen et al. (2006). For both consumer and producer prices, national studies adopted a wide variety of methodological approaches; in spite of these differences, most results are very similar and consistent across countries.

Concerning the determinants of the frequency of consumer price changes, there is some evidence of time dependence in price setting as a clear seasonal pattern emerges. In particular, most price adjustments occur at the beginning of the year (January) and after the summer period (especially in September; table 14.5).[10] There are, however, also indications of state-dependent price behavior: the frequency of price changes is affected by aggregate and sectoral inflation and firms appear to respond quickly to shocks such as indirect tax rate changes. In addition, some national studies show that firms temporarily increased their frequency of price changes around the euro cash changeover period. This coexistence of firms with

Table 14.5 Factors affecting the frequency of consumer price changes[a]

	AT	BE	FI	FR	GE	IT	LU	NL	PT	ES
Seasonality	Yes	Yes	Yes	Yes	Yes	Yes	Yes	Yes	Yes	Yes
Aggregate inflation	—	Yes	No	Yes	Yes	Yes	Yes	No	Yes	Yes
Sectoral or product specific inflation	Yes	Yes	Yes	Yes	Yes	Yes	Yes	—	Yes	Yes
VAT rate changes	—	Yes	Yes	Yes	Yes	Yes	—	Yes	Yes	Yes
Type of outlet	—	—	—	Yes	Yes	Yes	—	Yes[b]	Yes	—
Attractive prices	Yes	Yes	Yes	—	Yes	Yes	Yes	—	—	Yes
Euro cash changeover	Yes	Yes	Yes	Yes	Yes	Yes	Yes	Yes	—	—

Source: Dhyne et al. (2005).
[a]At the time this chapter was completed no results were available for Finland.
[b]Type of outlet proxied by the number of employed persons.

time- and state-dependent pricing strategies is in line with the survey results reported in chapter 2.[11] Among the other explanatory factors, there is evidence indicating that the frequency of price changes is significantly higher in super and hyper markets than in traditional corner shops. This may reflect either differences in the degree of market competition (see chapter 13) or the relative importance of menu costs in those particular types of stores. Some studies have also analyzed the impact of specific commercial practices on the frequency of price changes, in particular the use of psychological pricing thresholds. The latter could be a source of rigidity, as outlets may (temporarily) decide not to reset prices in response to a shock because the optimal response would result in a nonattractive price. Indeed, prices that are set at an attractive level are found to change less frequently than ordinary prices.

As for producer prices, survey evidence suggests that cross-sectoral differences observed in the frequency of price adjustment may be associated with a number of factors at the industry level, in particular, the cost structure, the degree of competition faced by firms, and the demand outlook (see chapters 2 and 13). The analysis carried out at the national level on quantitative data supports the above findings. Indeed, differences in the cost structure across sectors help explain differences in the degree of producer price flexibility; this result is robust across different national studies (table 14.6). Specifically, labor intensity negatively affects the frequency of price adjustments—given that wages are typically changed once a year—whereas the share of costs of intermediate goods in variable costs affects it positively. Moreover, for a few countries there is also some evidence of a positive relationship between market competition and the frequency of price changes (for instance, for Spain see Álvarez et al. 2005a).

Table 14.6 Factors affecting the frequency of producer price changes

	BE	GE	IT	PT	ES
Seasonality	Yes	Yes	Yes	Yes	Yes
Aggregate inflation	—	Yes	—	Yes	Yes
Share of labor on total costs	Yes	Yes	Yes	—	Yes
Share of other inputs on total costs					
energy inputs	Yes	Yes	Yes	Yes	Yes
non-energy inputs	Yes	Yes	Yes	Yes	Yes
Competition	Yes	—	—	Yes	Yes

Source: Authors' calculations on national studies.

CONCLUSIONS

The research summarized in this chapter provides information on the characteristics and determinants of price setting in the euro area based on micro quantitative data and strengthens in several aspects the results obtained from the surveys. First, prices change less frequently in the euro area than in the United States. Second, there is no apparent general downward price rigidity, since quite a large percentage of price changes are negative; however, it is worth stressing that there exist important cross-sectoral differences, with energy and food prices showing more frequent and symmetric variations. Third, the analysis of the determinants of price changes confirms the presence of elements of both time and state dependence. Moreover, in line with the survey information, the cost structure, the degree of market competition faced by firms, and the demand outlook are important determinants of the frequency of price changes.

Acknowledgments This chapter is partly based on a paper published in the Journal of the European Economic Association (Álvarez et al. 2006). We thank JEEA for having allowed us to reproduce this material. We are also grateful to all coauthors of the national papers. Specifically, for consumer prices, L. Aucremanne, L. Baudry, J. Baumgartner, H. Blijenberg, D. Dias, M. Dias, S. Fabiani, C. Folkertsma, A. Gattulli, E. Glatzer, I. Hernando, J. Hoffmann, J.-R. Kurz-Kim, H. Laakkonen, T. Mathä, P. Neves, P. Sevestre, A. Stiglbauer, and S. Tarrieu. For producer prices, P. Burriel, D. Cornille, M. Dossche, E. Gautier, and I. Hernando.

NOTES

1. Relevant contributions to the literature on micro consumer prices are Cecchetti (1986) on newsstand prices of magazines; Lach and Tsiddon (1992) and Eden (2001) on food prices; Kashyap (1995) on catalog prices; Levy et al. (1997) on supermarket prices; and Genesove (2003) on apartment rents. Stigler and Kindhal (1970) and

Carlton (1986), analyzing transaction prices of intermediate products used in manufacturing, are among the few existing micro studies on producer prices.

2. As extensively documented in Dhyne et al. (2006), it was not possible to fully control for some national specificities in the collection of price reports. One of the main cross-country differences that could not be avoided was related to the treatment of sales. Some national statistical institutes collect sales prices, while others do not. As price changes can be less frequent and smaller in countries where sales prices are not reported, this methodological difference has to be kept in mind when comparing results across countries. Dhyne et al. (2005) provide a quantitative estimate of this bias by analyzing the impact of sales in countries that could observe and identify sales prices, such as France and Austria.

3. A *price spell* is an uninterrupted sequence of unchanged price quotes associated with the elementary product; a *price trajectory* is a sequence of successive price spells for the product.

4. Dhyne et al (2005) also compute a euro area aggregate by using not just the 50 common products sample but the full CPI data available. The resulting average frequency of price changes is practically the same, so the use of the 50 product subsample does not seem to have an impact on results.

5. As explained in the technical appendix of Dhyne et al. (2005), this estimate of average implied duration (13 months)—computed by averaging the implied durations at product level—is much larger than the one obtained directly by inverting the average frequency (6.6 months). This gap essentially reflects Jensen's inequality, together with cross-product heterogeneity.

6. These results are also in line with implied durations derived from New Keynesian Phillips Curves for the euro area and the United States by Galí et al. (2001, 2003).

7. On the role of competition in affecting the frequency of price changes, see chapter 13.

8. Using the French and Austrian databases, this factor is found to account only for, at most, three percentage points in the overall frequency of price change. Indeed, for Austria the overall frequency of price change decreases from 15.4 to 12.9% when removing sales, and for France it decreases from 20.9 to 18.4%.

9. It is worth remarking that this stylized fact is not a mere reflection of sales and temporary promotions. In some countries statistical institutes do not report sales prices. Moreover, robustness tests (see for instance Baudry et al. 2004) indicate that excluding sales has a limited impact on the frequency of price decreases. Klenow and Kryvtsov (2006) report a similar finding for the United States.

10. This pattern is confirmed by the shape of the hazard function of price changes, which in most euro area countries is characterized by mass points every 12 months (Álvarez et al. 2005b).

11. These findings are supported by the econometric analysis of the 50 products reported in Dhyne et al. (2006).

REFERENCES

Álvarez, Luis J., and Ignacio Hernando. 2004. Price setting behaviour in Spain. Stylised facts using consumer price micro data. European Central Bank Working Paper No. 416. Frankfurt am Main: European Central Bank.

Álvarez, Luis J., Pablo Burriel, and Ignacio Hernando. 2005a. Price-setting behaviour in Spain: evidence from micro PPI data. European Central Bank Working Paper No. 522. Frankfurt am Main: European Central Bank.

Álvarez, Luis J., Pablo Burriel, and Ignacio Hernando. 2005b. Do decreasing hazard functions of price durations make any sense? Banco de España Working Paper No. 0508. Madrid: Banco de España.

Álvarez, Luis J., Emmanuel Dhyne, Marco Hoeberichts, Claudia Kwapil, Hervé Le Bihan, Patrick Lünnemann, Fernando Martins, Roberto Sabbatini, Harald Stahl, Philip Vermeulen, and Jouko Vilmunen. 2006. Sticky prices in the euro area: A summary of new micro-evidence. *Journal of the European Economic Association* 4: 575–584.

Aucremanne, Luc, and Emmanuel Dhyne. 2004. How frequently do prices change? Evidence based on the micro data underlying the Belgian CPI. European Central Bank Working Paper No. 331. Frankfurt am Main: European Central Bank.

Baharad, Eyal, and Benjamin Eden. 2004. Price rigidity and price dispersion: Evidence from micro data. *Review of Economic Dynamics* 7: 613–641.

Baudry, Laurent, Hervé Le Bihan, Patrick Sevestre, and Sylvie Tarrieu. 2004. Price rigidity: Evidence from French CPI micro-data. European Central Bank Working Paper No. 384. Frankfurt am Main: European Central Bank.

Baumgartner, Josef, Ernst Glatzer, Fabio Rumler, and Alfred Stiglbauer. 2005. How frequently do consumer price change in Austria? Evidence from micro CPI data. European Central Bank Working Paper Series No. 523. Frankfurt am Main: European Central Bank.

Bils, Mark, and Peter J. Klenow. 2004. Some evidence on the importance of sticky prices. *Journal of Political Economy* 112: 947–985.

Carlton, Dennis. 1986. The rigidity of prices. *American Economic Review* 76: 637–658.

Cecchetti, Stephen G. 1986. The frequency of price adjustment: A study of the newsstand prices of magazines. *Journal of Econometrics* 31: 255–274.

Cornille, David, and Maarten Dossche. 2006. The patterns and determinants of price setting in the Belgian industry. National Bank of Belgium Working Paper Series No 82. Brussels: National Bank of Belgium.

Dhyne, Emmanuel, Luis J. Álvarez, Hervé Le Bihan, Giovanni Veronese, Daniel Dias, Johannes Hoffmann, Nicole Jonker, Patrick Lünnemann, Fabio Rumler, and Jouko Vilmunen. 2005. Price setting in the euro area: some stylised facts from individual consumer price data. European Central Bank Working Paper No. 524. Frankfurt am Main: European Central Bank.

Dhyne, Emmanuel, Luis J. Álvarez, Hervé Le Bihan, Giovanni Veronese, Daniel Dias, Johannes Hoffmann, Nicole Jonker, Patrick Lünnemann, Fabio Rumler, and Jouko Vilmunen. 2006. Price changes in the euro area and the United States: Some facts from individual consumer price data. *Journal of Economic Perspectives* 20: 171–192.

Dias, Mònica, Daniel Dias, and Pedro Neves. 2004. Stylised features of price setting behaviour in Portugal: 1999–2001. European Central Bank Working Paper No. 332. Frankfurt am Main: European Central Bank.

Eden, Benjamin. 2001. Inflation and price adjustment: An analysis of microdata. *Review of Economic Dynamics* 4: 607–636.

Eurostat. 2002. *Methodology of Short-term Business Statistics: Interpretation and Guidelines.* Luxembourg: Office for Official Publications of the European Communities.

Fisher, Timothy, and Jerzy D. Konieczny. 2000. Synchronization of price changes by multiproduct firms: Evidence from Canadian newspaper prices. *Economics Letters* 68: 271–277.

Galí, Jordi, Mark Gertler, and David López-Salido. 2001. European inflation dynamics. *European Economic Review* 45: 1237–1270.

Galí, Jodi, Mark Gertler, and David López-Salido. 2003. Erratum to European inflation dynamics [*European Economic Review* 45 (2001), 1237–1270]. *European Economic Review* 47: 759–760.

Genesove, David. 2003. The nominal rigidity of apartment rents. *Review of Economics and Statistics* 85: 844–853

Gautier, Erwan. 2006. The behaviour of producer prices: Some evidence from the French PPI data. Mimeo. Paris: Banque de France.

Hoffmann, Johannes, and Jeong-Reyel Kurz-Kim. 2006. Consumer price adjustment under the microscope: Germany in a period of low inflation. Mimeo. Frankfurt am Main: Deutsche Bundesbank.

Jonker, Nicole, Harry Blijenberg, and Carsten Folkertsma. 2004. Empirical analysis of price setting behaviour in the Netherlands in the period 1998–2003 using micro data. European Central Bank Working Paper No. 413. Frankfurt am Main: European Central Bank.

Kashyap, Anil K. 1995. Sticky prices: New evidence from retail catalogs. *Quarterly Journal of Economics* 110: 245–274.

Klenow, Peter, and Oleksiy Kryvtsov. 2005. State-dependent or time-dependent pricing: Does it matter for recent U.S. inflation? National Bureau of Economic Research Working Paper No. 11043. Cambridge, MA: National Bureau of Economic Research.

Lach, Saul, and Daniel Tsiddon. 1992. The behaviour of prices and inflation: An empirical analysis of disaggregated price data. *Journal of Political Economy* 100: 349–389.

Lancaster, Tony. 1990. *The Econometric Analysis of Transition Data*. Cambridge: Cambridge University Press.

Levy, Daniel, Mark Bergen, Shantanu Dutta, and Robert Venadle. 1997. The magnitude of menu costs: Direct evidence from large US supermarket chains. *Quarterly Journal of Economics* 112: 791–825.

Lünnemann, Patrick, and Thomas Mathä. 2005. Consumer price behaviour in Luxembourg: Evidence from micro CPI data. European Central Bank Working Paper No. 541. Frankfurt am Main: European Central Bank.

Pilat, Dirk. 1997. Regulation and performance in the distribution sector. OECD Economics Department Working Paper No. 180. Paris: Organization for Economic Co-operation and Development.

Sabbatini, Roberto, Silvia Fabiani, Angela Gattulli, and Giovanni Veronese. 2005. Producer price behaviour in Italy: Evidence from micro PPI data. Mimeo. Rome: Banca d'Italia.

Stahl, Harald. 2006. Producer price adjustment at the micro level: Evidence from individual price records underlying the German PPI. Deutsche Bundesbank. Mimeo. Frankfurt am Main: Deutsche Bundesbank.

Stigler, George J., and James K. Kindahl. 1970. *The Behavior of Industrial Prices*. NBER General Series No. 90. New York: Columbia University Press.

Taylor, John B. 1999. Staggered price and wage setting in macroeconomics. In *Handbook of Macroeconomics*, ed. John B. Taylor and Michael Woodford. Amsterdam: North-Holland.

Vermeulen, Philip, Daniel Dias, Maarten Dossche, Ignacio Hernando, Roberto Sabbatini, Patrick Sevestre, and Harald Stahl. 2006. Price setting in the euro area: Some stylised facts from individual producer price data. European Central Bank. Mimeo. Frankfurt am Main: European Central Bank.

Veronese, Giovanni, Silvia Fabiani, Angela Gattulli, and Roberto Sabbatini. 2004. Consumer price behaviour in Italy: Evidence from micro CPI data. European Central Bank Working Paper No. 449.Frankfurt am Main: European Central Bank.

Vilmunen, Jouko, and Helina Laakkonen. 2005. How often do prices change in Finland? Evidence from micro CPI data. Mimeo. Helsinki: Suomen Pankki.

Part IV

Concluding Remarks and Implications

15

Policy Lessons and Directions for Ongoing Research

Vítor Gaspar, Andrew Levin,
Fernando Martins, & Frank Smets

Understanding the determinants of individual price setting behavior is crucial for the formulation of monetary policy, especially in an economy experiencing ongoing structural change. These behavioral mechanisms play a fundamental role in influencing the characteristics of aggregate inflation and in determining how monetary policy affects inflation and real economic activity. Thus, this line of research can strengthen the conceptual foundations of general equilibrium models with sticky prices, enabling these models to provide monetary policymakers with an increasingly useful framework for interpreting and forecasting the evolution of the macroeconomy.

These considerations provided a strong impetus for the Inflation Persistence Network (IPN), a collaborative research effort of the national central banks of the Eurosystem together with the European Central Bank (ECB). The preceding chapters of this book provide a comprehensive report on the surveys of price setting managers that were conducted in nine euro area countries, covering a total of roughly 11,000 firms. In addition, as described in chapter 14, the IPN analyzed a number of huge panel datasets of individual price records used in constructing producer as well as consumer price indices. Clearly, these two sources provide complementary types of information: the micro price data provides a means of quantifying individual price setting behavior, and the survey data facilitates the development of coherent explanations for those findings. Taken together, these two data sources represent a unique opportunity to document and interpret the characteristics of individual price setting behavior in the euro area. Furthermore, as already noted in previous chapters, the breadth and scope of this evidence is unprecedented by international standards, with coverage that goes well beyond the data available for the United States or any other industrial economy.[1] The main results on price setting coming from the analysis of these data sources are summarized in the introduction of this book.

In this chapter, we introduce the Walrasian model as a benchmark for comparison, and we discuss the extent to which recent micro evidence provides significant support for some basic elements of the New Keynesian perspective. We then proceed to analyze the implications of the micro evidence in distinguishing between competing theories of price stickiness. Finally, we conclude with some brief reflections about the lessons for monetary policy and potentially fruitful directions for further research.

THE WALRASIAN BENCHMARK

The Walrasian model provides an invaluable benchmark for understanding resource allocation and price determination in general equilibrium.[2] This model provides us with a precisely formulated set of conditions under which the equilibrium allocation of goods and services emerges as the outcome of a decentralized price mechanism—the "invisible hand" of Adam Smith. For example, the Walrasian model assumes that all markets are perfectly competitive and that every agent has the same information about the economy; furthermore, all prices adjust freely and continuously without any cost to ensure the equilibration of supply and demand of every product at every moment in time.

In general terms, the Walrasian model demonstrates that the price mechanism is capable, at least in principle, of yielding a resource allocation that satisfies some basic normative criteria. In particular, the first fundamental theorem of welfare economics indicates that every competitive equilibrium is Pareto-optimal; that is, no individual's welfare can be strictly improved without a decline in someone else's welfare. Indeed, with some additional regularity conditions, it can also be shown that *all* Pareto-optimal resource allocations can be decentralized as competitive equilibria.

Of course, the assumptions underlying the Walrasian model are highly stylized and hence open to debate. For example, Fisher (1972) emphasized that the Walrasian framework "describes nobody's actual behavior in most markets." Okun (1981) argued that "models that focus on price-takers and auctioneers and that assume continuous clearing of the market generate inaccurate microeconomics as well as misleading macroeconomics." And Kreps (1990) stressed that the Walrasian model provides no description of "who sets prices, or what gets exchanged for what, when and where."

Thus, it is essential to determine the extent to which the Walrasian framework provides a useful description of the actual economy. Perhaps it is not surprising that some specific assumptions can be relaxed without causing the resource allocation to deviate substantially from the benchmark of Pareto optimality.[3]

SUPPORT FOR THE "NEW NEOCLASSICAL SYNTHESIS" AND "NEW KEYNESIAN" PERSPECTIVES

Stimulated by Lucas' (1976) critique of the existing crop of structural macroeconomic models, the subsequent research agenda of "New Neoclassical Synthesis" or "New Keynesian" economics have sought to provide more rigorous microeconomic foundations for the existence of nominal rigidities. These foundations explicitly consider the decision-making problems of firms and consumers in the context of specific departures from the Walrasian benchmark. The recent micro evidence provides significant support for two fundamental elements of such an approach, namely, the infrequent adjustment of prices and the role of imperfectly competitive markets.

The Prices of Many Goods and Services Are Adjusted Relatively Infrequently

The micro evidence for the euro area indicates that retail and producer prices are only adjusted about twice a year on average. Of course, the prices of some items—such as automobile fuel, fresh fruits, and unprocessed meat—do change on a daily or weekly basis. In contrast, the prices of all other retail goods (excluding food and energy) have an average duration of about ten months, and the prices of consumer services typically remain unchanged for a year or longer. Indeed, as described in preceding chapters, surveys of price setting behavior (in the euro area as well as other industrial economies) have consistently found that a majority of firms tend to adjust the price of their main product no more than once a year.

The relatively infrequent adjustment of retail and producer prices is particularly striking in contrast to the evolution of the macroeconomy, which exhibits continually changing levels of aggregate spending, employment, raw materials prices, asset prices, and so forth. Thus, in contrast to the Walrasian framework, it would seem evident that the adjustment of individual prices must be hindered by some sort of costs or constraints; otherwise, even the slightest change in an individual firm's environment would cause a corresponding change in the prices of its products. Furthermore, the fact that price changes tend to be quite large—with a median adjustment exceeding 10% for many categories of the consumer price index—suggests that a firm's decision to change its price is typically driven by sectoral or firm-specific considerations rather than the state of the macroeconomy.

Monopolistic Competition Is a Characteristic of Most Product Markets

Imperfect competition plays a crucial role in providing a rationale for sticky prices. Under perfect competition, each good is produced by many identical firms, all of which must charge exactly the same price (determined by the marginal cost of production) at every moment in time; any firm charging a lower price would operate at a loss, and any firm charging a higher price would have no sales at all. In such a market, all firms earn zero profits in equilibrium, and the price of the item adjusts continuously in response to even the slightest change in its marginal cost, whether due to a fluctuation in the cost of raw materials, the price of electricity, wages, interest rates, or other cause. In contrast, in an environment of monopolistic competition, each individual firm's products are distinct from those of its competitors. In this case, the firm can earn positive profits by charging a price for each item that incorporates a positive markup; that is, the price of the item exceeds its marginal cost of production. The widespread incidence of markup pricing was originally highlighted by the survey of Hall and Hitch (1939), who found that "an overwhelming majority of the entrepreneurs thought that a price based on full average cost (including a conventional allowance for profit) was the 'right' price, the one which 'ought' to be charged." Along similar lines, Okun (1981) indicated that "the setting of prices by marking up costs is a good first approximation to actually observed behavior in most areas of industry, trade, and transportation."

Of course, because the profit maximizing level of the markup depends on the elasticity of demand and on the relative prices of its competitors, the firm's optimal price will vary over time in response to these factors, as well as in response to movements in marginal cost. However, a crucial insight of the New Keynesian approach is that a monopolistic competition framework combined with unsynchronized price setting implies that the firm does not have to adjust its price instantaneously in response to changes in marginal cost or the prices of its competitors: the firm still has substantial sales even if its price is a bit too high, and still earns positive profits even if its price is a bit too low.

The survey evidence provides strong support for the view that imperfect competition characterizes most product markets in the euro area. First, only about one-fourth of the firms report that their prices are primarily set to match the prices of their competitors—as one might expect in the case of a perfectly competitive market—and roughly the same proportion of firms indicate that a price reduction by at least one competitor would be considered "highly important" in determining whether the firm should cut its own price. In contrast, roughly half of the firms describe their prices as being determined by a markup over unit variable cost—consistent with the stylized assumption of a monopolistically competitive market with a constant elasticity of demand—whereas the remainder indicate that their prices are determined by a different approach that is still suggestive of imperfect competition, perhaps with a more complex elasticity of demand.

Second, roughly two-thirds of the firms in these surveys indicated that long-term customers accounted for the bulk of their sales. The predominance of long-term relationships is entirely consistent with product differentiation and specialization, but would be virtually inconceivable in a perfectly competitive market (such as that observed for commodities such as gold) where the match between an individual buyer and an individual seller is random and transitory.

Third, it should be noted that only about 20% of the firms in these surveys report that the price of their main product is the same for all customers, as one would expect in a perfectly competitive market. The remaining 80% indicate that the actual price of their main product varies across customers, either on a case-by-case basis or as a function of the quantity sold. It should be noted that this pattern of price discrimination does not fit neatly into the stylized framework of monopolistic competition, which implies that all customers pay the same price for a given item at a given point in time (just as in the case of perfect competition). Nevertheless, this survey evidence is certainly consistent with the notion that most product markets comprise highly differentiated goods and services and hence exhibit relatively complex forms of imperfect competition.

Finally, as reported in chapter 13, the perceived degree of market competition is statistically significant in explaining cross-sectional variations in the use of markup pricing strategies and in the frequency of price reviews and changes; this evidence highlights the thorough implications of interactions between imperfect competition and nominal price rigidity (for instance, due to the existence of implicit and explicit contracts, menu costs, informational problems, unsynchronized price setting, or interaction between price and wage setting).

EVIDENCE ON COMPETING THEORIES OF
PRICE SETTING BEHAVIOR

The recent micro evidence is also invaluable for performing an empirical assessment of various theories of price setting behavior, especially because many of these theories are difficult to distinguish based on macroeconomic data alone.

Downward Nominal Price Rigidity

This theory reflects the notion that firms may be reluctant to reduce the nominal prices of their products, perhaps because a cut in the nominal price would send an adverse signal to customers regarding a decline in the quality of the product. This form of nominal inertia might be inconsequential in an economy with high aggregate inflation, because a firm seeking to reduce its relative price could do so without actually cutting its nominal price. In contrast, in an economy with low aggregate inflation, one might observe an asymmetric pattern of price increases for those firms seeking to raise their relative price, and unchanged prices for the remaining firms that are constrained by the downward nominal rigidity. Nevertheless, this mechanism is generally inconsistent with the micro evidence. In the euro area, price reductions comprise roughly 40% of all changes in consumer prices and roughly 45% of all changes in producer prices, and the average magnitude of price cuts is nearly identical to the magnitude of price hikes; similar patterns are also evident in retail price data for the United States.[4] And even these modest asymmetries may simply reflect the influence of a non-zero aggregate inflation rate. Furthermore, surveys in the euro area obtained little support for the notion that firms are reluctant to cut their prices due to fears that customers will make judgments about product quality based on price; indeed, this hypothesis was dismissed out of hand by the respondents in the survey conducted for the United States.

Finally, it should be noted that asymmetry in price setting is somewhat more evident in the service sector, where price decreases only account for about 20% of all price changes. This outcome might simply reflect upward trends in the price of services relative to consumer goods (corresponding to underlying sectoral differences in productivity growth), as well as lower volatility of shocks to the service sector. Alternatively, because labor costs constitute a high share of total cost in many service industries, the apparent asymmetry in the adjustment of service prices might result from downward nominal wage rigidity; thus, further research is evidently needed to investigate these hypotheses.

Smoothing Models of Price Adjustment

Suppose that the typical firm incurs convex adjustment costs whenever it changes the nominal price of its product; that is, these adjustment costs rise at an increasing rate as a function of the absolute magnitude of the price change. Given these adjustment costs, the firm's optimal price setting behavior involves smooth and gradual adjustments, implying a persistent series of small consecutive adjustments rather than sudden large movements in either direction.[5] As shown by Rotemberg (1982), convex adjustment costs provide elegant microeconomic foundations for the New Keynesian Phillips Curve; thus, this approach has subsequently been used in numerous analytical and empirical studies. Despite its elegance and tractability, its implications are clearly inconsistent with the micro evidence. First, as noted above, both retail and producer prices tend to be adjusted relatively infrequently (apart from the unprocessed food and energy sectors). Furthermore, as emphasized in chapter 14, the average magnitude of individual price adjustments is quite large: about 8% for consumer price increases, and roughly 10% for consumer price reductions.

Sticky Information

Mankiw and Reis (2002) have proposed an alternative framework in which information collection and processing is subjective to substantial fixed costs, whereas the actual adjustment of prices is completely costless. With sticky information and costless price adjustment, the firm's optimal strategy— apart from certain extraordinary circumstances—is to perform a relatively infrequent updating of its information set and then reoptimize the intended trajectory for its nominal price. This optimal trajectory typically involves some price adjustment in every period, but the trajectory itself remains settled until the next time that the firm updates its information set. As shown by Mankiw and Reis (2002), sticky information yields implications for aggregate inflation dynamics that differ from those of the benchmark New Keynesian Phillips Curve in several important respects.[6]

However, micro evidence is generally inconsistent with this form of price adjustment. As previously noted, most retail and producer prices are adjusted relatively infrequently, rather than changing every period as in the sticky information model. Furthermore, firm-level surveys in the euro area and several other industrial economies have consistently found that the respondents do not perceive that costly information plays a significant role in their price setting decisions. Indeed, the euro area surveys indicate that the frequency of price review generally exceeds the frequency of price changes; that is, many price reviews do not result in a price change.

Of course, as with each of the other mechanisms considered in this section, the sticky information hypothesis almost certainly contains some important grains of truth that should be incorporated into a more nuanced price setting framework. For example, the euro area surveys find that forward-looking considerations play little or no role in the price reviews of a substantial proportion of respondents, perhaps due to difficulties in constructing or updating forecasts on a regular basis. In addition, it could well be the case that some of these price reviews are mainly oriented toward product-specific news and place insufficient emphasis on changes in the macroeconomic outlook. These issues deserve further investigation, perhaps even involving a new set of firm-level surveys.

Staggered Nominal Contracts

Much of the New Keynesian literature has proceeded under the assumption that the price of each product is specified by an explicit or implicit multi-period contract with the firm's customers, who can purchase any desired quantity of the product at the specified price throughout the duration of the contract. Following the seminal work of Taylor (1999) and Calvo (1983), the timing of new contracts is assumed to be evenly staggered across firms and to be invariant to changes in the aggregate economy; thus, a constant fraction of all price contracts are reset at each point in time.[7] Furthermore, the staggered contract structure implies that an aggregate demand shock (such as shift in the stance of monetary policy) will have effects on real economic activity that last longer than the duration of the typical contract.

The micro evidence is broadly consistent with some aspects of the staggered contracts framework. First, as we have already discussed, many retail and producer prices are adjusted only once or twice a year, and these adjustments tend to be staggered fairly evenly throughout the year (although some seasonality is observed in certain sectors). Second, most surveys of price setting managers indicate that nominal contracts play a key role in explaining why prices are not adjusted more frequently; indeed, implicit and explicit contracts were ranked as the two most important explanations by the respondents of the euro area surveys reported in this book. Finally, the evidence from disaggregated price records suggests that the overall frequency of price adjustment is reasonably stable, at least in environments of low and stable aggregate inflation.[8] Nevertheless, the micro evidence directly contradicts the notion that price setting behavior can be generally characterized by staggered contracts with a fixed duration, as in the analysis of Taylor (1999).[9]

The basic problem here is not the observed degree of sectoral heterogeneity in the frequency of price adjustment: although Taylor's original formulation assumed an identical duration for all contracts, that formulation has subsequently been generalized to allow the contract duration to vary across different groups of firms.[10] Rather, the fixed duration approach is clearly inconsistent with the findings of Aucremanne and Dhyne (2005), namely, relatively large variation in the duration of price spells for individual items in almost every product category in the consumer price index; that is, the interval between price changes tends to vary quite widely over time, even for a single item sold by an individual firm. Of course, it should be emphasized that fixed duration contracts may still provide a useful framework for modeling the determination of wages, especially in economies where labor unions represent a large fraction of the labor force. The micro evidence appears somewhat more consistent with the assumption that price contracts have a random duration that is invariant to the state of the aggregate economy, as in Calvo (1983) and numerous subsequent studies. In the special case where every firm faces the same probability in every period of being able to reset its price contract (regardless of how long its current contract has already lasted), this approach provides elegant and tractable foundations for the New Keynesian Phillips Curve.[11]

To capture the sectoral heterogeneity noted above, the random duration contracting framework can be readily extended to permit the adjustment probability to vary across broad groups of firms.[12] Furthermore, in contrast to the counterfactual predictions of the fixed duration framework, Aucremanne and Dhyne (2005) have found that Calvo style contracts yield roughly accurate predictions regarding the relationship between the mean duration and the coefficient of variation of individual price spells for most of the narrow categories of items in the consumer price index (apart from food and energy).

However, the recent evidence also highlights the extent to which the random duration contracting framework does not provide sufficiently deep microeconomic foundations for the analysis of price setting behavior. First, this framework starts from the premise that the contract adjustment probability is a fixed parameter, without providing any interpretation for the extent to which the average duration of price spells varies markedly across different sectors of the economy and even across narrow product categories within each sector.[13] Nor does this framework provide any means of understanding the apparent differences in the frequency of price adjustment across major industrial economies, e.g. the euro area compared with the United States. Furthermore, surveys indicate that the timing of price adjustments typically reflects the incidence of substantial changes in production costs or the level of demand.[14] Finally, the rapid response of prices to specific macroeconomic events (such as indirect tax increases or the euro cash changeover) or shifts in monetary policy regime (such as a decline in aggregate inflation) demonstrates that the frequency of price adjustment is not invariant to the state of the aggregate economy. Clearly, accounting for this evidence requires a framework with elements of state-dependent pricing and some combination of idiosyncratic and aggregate shocks.

Menu Costs and State-Dependent Pricing

Now suppose that the typical firm incurs a fixed cost (menu cost) whenever it changes the nominal price of its product; that is, the adjustment cost is invariant to the absolute magnitude of the price change, as well as to its sign (positive or negative). Given this fixed cost of adjustment, the firm will generally choose to leave its price unchanged until a single large firm-specific or sector-specific shock (or perhaps a sequence of smaller shocks) causes its optimal price to deviate sufficiently far from its actual price, at which point the firm resets its actual price to match the optimal one.[15]

The micro evidence is broadly consistent with several key predictions of the menu cost framework: most prices tend to remain constant for an extended period and then change by a relatively large magnitude, and these characteristics are essentially symmetric for both positive and negative price adjustments. Indeed, Danziger (1999) and Golosov and Lucas (2003) have shown that the underlying parameters of the model can be calibrated to yield empirically reasonable values for the frequency and magnitude of price adjustments; Gertler and Leahy (2005) modify some of the auxiliary assumptions and then proceed to demonstrate that this framework can provide a satisfactory accounting for aggregate inflation dynamics and the persistent real effects of monetary disturbances.

It should be noted, however, that the micro evidence also highlights several dimensions for refinement and further development of the menu cost framework. First, although the average magnitude of price changes is quite large, it is nonetheless apparent that small price adjustments are also very common; this characteristic was initially noted by Carlton (1986) and Kashyap (1995) for specific retail items, but the recent micro evidence reveals the same pattern for virtually every item in the consumer price index. Specific assumptions about the idiosyncratic shock process might account for these small price adjustments, but it also seems plausible that the menu cost itself may exhibit cross sectional variation—related to firms' size and other characteristics—and perhaps also seasonal or business cycle variations.

Furthermore, the notion of literal "menu costs" is clearly inconsistent with the micro evidence. For example, Kashyap (1995) documented that the prices of many individual items remain unchanged across multiple editions of a retailer's catalog—an outcome that is evidently unrelated to typesetting or printing costs—and many barbershops and other small retailers have no printed pricelist at all. Furthermore, the incidence of temporary sales and promotions (after which the price returns to its previous level) cannot be easily explained in terms of a fixed cost of posting new prices. Finally, firm-level surveys in the euro area and other industrial economies have consistently found that "physical costs of adjustment" do not play a significant role in price-setting decisions. Thus, further research is needed to identify other sources of friction with implications broadly similar to those of fixed menu costs.

IMPLICATIONS FOR MONETARY POLICY

When considering the policy implications of analytical or empirical research, it is advisable to draw lessons that are robust to a variety of modeling approaches and econometric methods, rather than relying on any particular formalization of the economy.[16] Thus, rather than trying to formulate any precise guidance for policymakers, we now focus on several broad lessons that can be inferred from the micro evidence.

The Monetary Transmission Mechanism

In the idealized Walrasian framework with competitive markets and flexible prices, the central bank may define the unit of account but its actions have no substantive effect on real economic activity; that is, monetary policy is completely "neutral" in such an environment. In contrast, as discussed above, the recent micro evidence makes it plausible to argue in favor of the New Keynesian view that monetary policy exhibits short-run non-neutrality due to the influence of imperfect competition and sticky prices, and hence that the conduct of monetary policy can have significant consequences for the evolution of the real economy. The intuition for this implication is quite straightforward: when prices are sticky, the central bank can implement a change in the policy rate and thereby affect real interest rates and hence the level of real aggregate expenditures.[17]

In addition, recent analysis has highlighted the extent to which the frequency of price adjustment can play a key role in determining the short-run response of inflation to a shift in real economic activity. Indeed, in a comparison of the macroeconomic dynamics of the euro area vis-à-vis the United States, Altissimo et al. (2006) have found that the persistence of the inflation response to a cost push shock is quite similar for both economies, and the higher persistence of the euro area output gap response can be largely explained by the lower frequency of adjustment of prices in the euro area.[18]

The Case for Price Stability

The recent evidence also highlights the benefits of maintaining price stability over the medium run—an aspect of the New Keynesian approach that was largely missing from the "old Keynesian" analysis that reached a heyday in the 1950s and 1960s. In particular, the earlier analysis placed relatively little emphasis on the social costs of inflation (especially compared with the social costs of unemployment) and typically assumed a long-run downward sloping Phillips Curve, implying that the optimal monetary policy might involve a higher average level of inflation in exchange for a permanent reduction in the unemployment rate.

In contrast, the New Keynesian framework not only incorporates the long-run neutrality of money—whereby a permanent rise in the stock of money eventually generates a corresponding rise in the price level, and hence has no long-run real effects—but also emphasizes the degree to which price stickiness reflects underlying costs, thus implying that a permanent rise in the growth rate of money has adverse long-run effects on the real economy by distorting relative prices and wasting resources through excessively frequent price adjustments.[19]

The Role of Expectations

Finally, the micro evidence provides substantial support for the view that establishing credible policies and managing private sector expectations are crucial aspects of modern central banking.[20] In particular, in an environment with infrequent price changes, each firm has a strong incentive to assess not only current factors but also the future outlook whenever it resets its price. Euro area surveys largely reinforce this view: about half of the firms report that forward-looking considerations play an important role in their price setting behavior, whereas about one-third of them indicate that their assessments are mainly backward looking.

Along these lines, it should be emphasized that the credibility of a monetary policy regime oriented toward price stability is also helpful for stabilizing the economy in response to economic disturbances and hence improves the tradeoff between the variability of inflation and the volatility of other important macroeconomic variables such as output and employment. However, imperfect credibility may be associated with shocks to inflation—caused by "inflation scares" or revised beliefs about the central bank's inflation objective—that may be quite costly to reverse in terms of foregone real economic activity. Moreover, the higher the degree of nominal rigidity, the higher this sacrifice ratio.

DIRECTIONS FOR FURTHER RESEARCH

Recent research reveals a negative relation between the frequency of price changes and the importance of wages as a fraction of costs. In particular, the IPN found that those sectors with a higher labor share, such as services, are typically characterized by a lower frequency of price changes. This suggests that it is essential to look at wage setting in order to understand price dynamics. Given the crucial importance that labor market behavior assumes in explaining business cycle dynamics and the pervasiveness of elements of structural rigidity in labor markets in the euro area, further research is warranted. Empirical research is needed to establish the relevant facts about wage setting. Theoretical research is necessary to incorporate a structural representation of labor markets into stochastic general equilibrium models of growth and business cycles. A new Eurosystem research network on wage dynamics has recently been initiated to shed further light on these issues.

In more general terms, the findings from the surveys constitute a challenge to researchers. The availability of high-quality micro datasets holds the promise of stimulating researchers to further develop theories able to account for both micro and macro facts in a general equilibrium framework.

NOTES

1. For example, Blinder et al. (1998) only obtained responses from about 200 United States firms.

2. See Debreu (1959) and Arrow and Hahn (1970).

3. See Foley (1994).

4. See Bils and Klenow (2004).

5. Convex adjustment costs were first considered in the context of physical capital accumulation as a means of analyzing Tobin's q theory of investment.

6. Kiley (2006) compares the empirical implications of sticky prices versus sticky information by using United States macroeconomic data.

7. See Ball and Romer (1989) for analysis of staggering versus synchronization of price setting behavior.

8. See Klenow and Kryvstov (2005).

9. See King and Wolman (2004) and the analysis and references in Woodford (2003).

10. See Taylor (1993), Guerrieri (2002), and Coenen and Levin (2004).

11. See Yun (1996), Rotemberg and Woodford (1997), and Clarida et al. (1999), as well as the extensive bibliography of Woodford (2003).

12. See Álvarez et al. (2005).

13. For example, chapter 11 shows that price flexibility is positively associated with the cost share of raw materials and negatively associated with the cost share of wages.

14. One revealing example is given by Stahl (2005), who finds that the incidence of price increases by German industrial firms exhibits significant peaks that coincide with hikes in negotiated wage rates.

15. Theoretical analysis of menu costs and price setting behavior includes Barro (1972), Sheshinski and Weiss (1977), Dixit (1991), and Hansen (1999). An important finding is that even "small" menu costs may give rise to considerable nominal stickiness at the macro level; see, for example, Akerlof and Yellen (1985), Mankiw (1985), and Blanchard and Kyotaki (1987).

16. See Issing et al. (2005).

17. See Bernanke and Blinder (1988) and Kashyap and Stein (1994). Christiano and Gust (1999) have formulated an alternative framework in which the non-neutrality of money arises from financial market imperfections rather than sticky prices; however, the subsequent analysis of Christiano et al. (2005) found that nominal rigidities play a crucial role in explaining the real effects of money in a dynamic general equilibrium model. Finally, it should be noted that some models of price stickiness lead to results very close to monetary neutrality. For example, expanding on the earlier work of Caplin and Spulber (1987), the analysis of Golosov and Lucas (2003) demonstrates that monetary policy may have very small real effects in an economy with menu costs and idiosyncratic shocks, because a change in the money stock simply shifts the distribution of firms that choose to adjust their prices in a given period. As shown by Gertler and Leahy (2005), the introduction of real rigidities is crucial for explaining the real effects of monetary policy for an empirically reasonable degree of nominal rigidity.

18. These results are obtained under the assumption that monetary policy responds optimally to the cost push shock; that is, the central bank minimizes a standard objective function that reflects the goals of inflation stabilization and output gap stabilization, as well as a smooth path for the short-term nominal interest rate.

19. See, for example, Goodfriend and King (1997, 2001), Clarida et al. (1999) and Woodford (2003) for analysis in the case of sticky prices, and Ball et al. (2003) for corresponding analysis in the case of sticky information.

20. See Goodfriend and King (1997, 2001), Clarida et al. (1999), and Woodford (2003).

REFERENCES

Akerlof, George, and Janet Yellen. 1985. A near-rational model of the business cycle, with wage and price inertia. *The Quarterly Journal of Economics* 100: 823–838.

Álvarez, Luis J., Pablo Buriel, and Ignacio Hernando. 2005. Price setting behaviour in Spain: Evidence from micro PPI data. European Central Bank Working Paper No. 522. Frankfurt am Main: European Central Bank.

Altissimo, Filippo, Michael Ehrmann, and Frank Smets. 2006. Inflation persistence and price setting behavior in the euro area: A summary of the IPN evidence. European Central Bank Occasional Paper No. 46. Frankfurt am Main: European Central Bank.

Arrow, Kenneth, and Frank Hahn. 1970. *General Competitive Analysis*. San Francisco: Holden-Day.

Aucremanne, Luc, and Emmanuel Dhyne. 2005. Time-dependent vs. state-dependent pricing: A panel data approach to the determinants of Belgian CPI. European Central Bank Working Paper No. 462. Frankfurt am Main: European Central Bank.

Ball, Laurence, and David Romer. 1989. Are prices too sticky? *The Quarterly Journal of Economics* 104: 507–524.

Ball, Laurence, N. Gregory Mankiw, and Ricardo Reis. 2003. Monetary policy for inattentive economies. NBER Working Paper No. 9491. Cambridge MA: National Bureau of Economic Research.

Barro, Robert. 1972. A theory of monopolistic price adjustment. *Review of Economic Studies* 39: 17–26.

Blanchard, Olivier, and Nobuhiro Kiyotaki. 1987. Monopolistic competition and the effects of aggregate demand. *American Economic Review* 77: 647–666.

Bernanke, Ben, and Alan Blinder. 1988. Credit, money, and aggregate demand. *American Economic Review Papers and Proceedings* 78: 435–438.

Bils, Mark, and Peter Klenow. 2004. Some evidence on the importance of sticky prices. *Journal of Political Economy* 112: 947–985.

Blinder, Alan S., Elie R. D. Canetti, David E. Lebow, and Jeremy B. Rudd. 1998. *Asking about Prices: A New Approach to Understanding Price Stickiness*. New York: Russell Sage Foundation.

Calvo, Guillermo. 1983. Staggered prices in a utility maximizing framework. *Journal of Monetary Economics* 12: 383–398.

Caplin, Andrew, and Daniel Spulber. 1987. Menu costs and the neutrality of money. *Quarterly Journal of Economics* 102: 703–725.

Christiano, Lawrence, and Christopher Gust. 1999. Taylor rules in a limited participation model. NBER Working Paper No. 7017. Cambridge MA: National Bureau of Economic Research.

Christiano, Lawrence, Martin Eichenbaum, and Charles Evans. 2005. Nominal rigidities and the dynamic effects of a shock to monetary policy. *Journal of Political Economy* 113: 1–45.

Clarida, Richard, Jordi Galí, and Mark Gertler. 1999. The science of monetary policy: A New Keynesian perspective. *Journal of Economic Literature* 37: 1661–1707.

Coenen, Günter, and Andrew Levin. 2004. Identifying the influences of nominal and real rigidities in aggregate price-setting behaviour. European Central Bank Working Paper No. 418. Frankfurt am Main: European Central Bank.

Danziger, Leif. 1999. A dynamic economy with costly price adjustment. *American Economic Review* 89: 878–901.

Debreu, Gerard. 1959. *Theory of Value*. New Haven: Cowles Foundation.

Dixit, Avinash. 1991. Analytical approximations in models of hysteresis. *Review of Economic Studies* 58: 141–151.

Fisher, Franklin. 1972. On price adjustment without an auctioneer. *Review of Economic Studies* 39: 1–15.

Foley, Duncan. 1994. A statistical equilibrium theory of markets. *Journal of Economic Theory* 62: 321–345.

Gertler, Mark, and John Leahy. 2006. A Philips curve with Ss Foundation. NBER Working Paper No. 11971. Cambridge MA: National Bureau of Economic Research.

Golosov, Mikhail, and Robert Lucas. 2003. Menu costs and Phillips curves. NBER Working Paper No. 10187. Cambridge MA: National Bureau of Economic Research.

Goodfriend, Marvin, and Robert G. King. 1997. The new neoclassical synthesis and the role of monetary policy. *NBER Macroeconomics Annual* 12: 231–283.

Goodfriend, Marvin, and Robert G. King. 2001. The case for price stability. In *Why Price Stability?*, ed. Alícia Garcia-Herrero, Vítor Gaspar, Lex Hoogduin, Julian Morgan, and Bernhard Winkler. Frankfurt am Main: European Central Bank.

Guerrieri, Luca. 2002. Persistent issues in inflation persistence. *Review on Economic Cycles* 5, December.

Hall, Robert L., and Charles J. Hitch. 1939. Price theory and business behavior. *Oxford Economic Papers* 2: 12–45.

Hansen, Per. 1999. Frequent price changes under menu costs. *Journal of Economic Dynamics and Control* 23: 1065–1076.

Issing, Otmar, Vítor Gaspar, Oreste Tristani, and David Vestin. 2005. *Imperfect knowledge and monetary policy*. Cambridge: Cambridge University Press.

Kagel, John, and Alvin Roth. 1995. *Handbook of Experimental Economics*. Princeton: Princeton University Press.

Kashyap, Anil K. 1995. Sticky prices: New evidence from retail catalogs. *Quarterly Journal of Economics* 110: 245–274.

Kashyap, Anil, and Jeremy Stein. 1994. Monetary policy and bank lending. In *Monetary Policy*, ed. N. Gregory Mankiw. Chicago: University of Chicago Press.

Kiley, Michael. 2006. A quantitative comparison of sticky-price and sticky-information models of price setting. Federal Reserve System Finance and Discussion Series No. 45. Washington DC: Federal Reserve.

King, Robert G., and Alenxander L. Wolman. 2004. Monetary discretion, pricing complementarity and dynamic multiple equilibria. *Quarterly Journal of Economics* 119: 1513–1553.

Klenow, Peter, and Oleksiy Kryvtsov. 2005. State-dependent or time-dependent pricing: Does it matter for recent U.S. inflation? Bank of Canada Working Paper No. 2005–4. Ottawa: Bank of Canada.

Kreps, David. 1990. *A Course in Microeconomic Theory*. Princeton: Princeton University Press.

Lucas, Robert. 1976. Econometric Policy Evaluation: A Critique. *Carnegie-Rochester Conference Series on Public Policy* 1: 19–46.

Mankiw, N. Gregory. 1985. Small menu costs and large business cycles: A macroeconomic model of monopoly. *Quarterly Journal of Economics* 100: 529–537.

Mankiw, N. Gregory, and Ricardo Reis. 2002. Sticky information versus sticky prices: A proposal to replace the New Keynesian Phillips Curve. *Quarterly Journal of Economics* 117: 1295–1328.

Okun, Arthur. 1981. *Prices and Quantities: A Macroeconomic Analysis.* Washington, DC: The Brookings Institution.

Rotemberg, Julio J. 1982. Monopolistic price adjustment and aggregate output. *Review of Economic Studies* 49: 517–531.

Rotemberg, Julio J., and Michael Woodford. 1997. An optimization-based econometric framework for the evaluation of monetary policy. In *NBER Macroeconomics Annual*, ed. Ben Bernanke and Julio Rotemberg. Cambridge MA: MIT Press.

Sheshinski, Eytan, and Yoram Weiss. 1977. Inflation and the cost of price adjustment. *Review of Economic Studies* 44: 287–303.

Stahl, Harald. 2005. Time-dependent or state-dependent price setting? Micro-evidence from German Metal Working Industries. European Central Bank Working Paper No. 534. Frankfurt am Main: European Central Bank.

Taylor, John. 1993. *Macroeconomic Policy in the World Economy: From Econometric Design to Practical Operation.* New York: W.W. Norton.

Taylor, John B. 1999. Staggered price and wage setting in macroeconomics. In *Handbook of Macroeconomics*, ed. John B. Taylor and Michael Woodford. Amsterdam: North-Holland.

Woodford, Michael. 2003. *Interest and Prices: Foundations of a Theory of Monetary Policy.* Princeton: Princeton University Press.

Yun, Tack. 1996. Nominal price rigidity, money supply endogeneity, and business cycles. *Journal of Monetary Economics* 37: 345–370.

Appendix: The National Questionnaires

AUSTRIA

Part 1: Manufacturing

General Indications

- This questionnaire is intended to inform us about your pricing policy. When answering the following questions, please reflect on the product that best represents your company. (You can, for example, choose the best-selling product of the year 2003.) This product will be referred to as "main product."

- Please relate all your data to the year 2003.

PART A – INFORMATION ABOUT THE MARKET IN WHICH YOU SELL YOUR PRODUCT

A1. What is your main product? .... |_____|

A2. What percentage of sales does your main product account for? ....…..……….......... ....|__|__|__|%

A3. What share of the turnover of your main product is generated in the following regions?
- in Austria....................................... |__|__|__|%
- in the euro area (except Austria)........... |__|__|__|%
- in other EU countries / in EU acceding countries[1] .... |__|__|__|%
- in other countries............................. |__|__|__|%

Total |1|0|0|%

[1]Great Britain, Sweden, Denmark, Czech Republic, Slovakia, Hungary, Slovenia, Poland, Estonia, Latvia, Lithuania, Cyprus, Malta

NOTE: *When answering the following questions, please reflect on the market which is most important for your main product. Thus, refer all your answers to the market with the highest percentage share in question A3.*

A4. What percentage of sales do you generate by selling your main product....
- to wholesalers?... |__|__|__|%
- to retailers?.. |__|__|__|%
- within the corporate group?....................... |__|__|__|%
- to other companies?................................... |__|__|__|%
- to the government?.................................... |__|__|__|%
- to consumers (directly or via catalogues or the Internet)?............................. |__|__|__|%
- via other channels........................... |__|__|__|%
  Which? |_____|

Total |1|0|0|%

A5. What is the market share of your main product on its most important market?
- 1% - 5% .... ☐
- 6% - 10% .... ☐
- 11% - 20% .... ☐
- 21% - 30% .... ☐
- 31% - 50% .... ☐
- more than 50% .... ☐

A6. How many (national and international) competitors do you have for your main product on its most important market?

Please count only those companies you directly compete with. If, for example, you run a restaurant, please consider only the restaurants in your vicinity (district or town).
- none.. ☐
- fewer than 5 .... ☐
- between 5 and 20............................ ☐
- more than 20............................... ☐

A7. How many customers do you have with regard to your main product on its most important market?

Number of customers........| | | | | | |

A8. What percentage of sales do you achieve through regular customers (customers you have been doing business with for more than one year) and through occasional customers?

- Regular customers............................ | | | |%
- Occasional customers......................... | | |%

Total |1|0|0|%

Part B – PRICING IN YOUR COMPANY

B1. Do you determine the price of your main product within the company or is it set by somebody outside the company?

- We determine the price ……………............. ☐
- The parent company determines the price... ☐
- Our main customers determine the price.... ☐
- Public agencies determine the price......... ☐
- Others………………………………………… ☐
  Please specify _____

B2a. Do you make arrangements with your customers in which you guarantee to offer your main product at a specific price for a certain period of time?

No.....☐   Yes. Transaction under such arrangements account for

0% - 25%....... ☐
26% - 50%....... ☐
51% - 75%....... ☐
76% - 100%....... ☐
of the sales of our main product.

B2b. If you have such arrangements in place, for how long do you usually guarantee the price?

Number of months.......... | | |

B3. Do you allow a discount on the price of your main product?

You may check several boxes.

No....... ☐   Yes. Please specify below.

- Large quantity discounts................ ☐
- Discounts for regular customers..... ☐
- Cash discounts........................ ☐
- Discounts depending on the market situation ☐
- Seasonal discounts (e.g. sales)...... ☐
- Others:_____ ☐

NOTE : The word "price" refers to the actual selling price of your main product. Please refer your answers to the price you actually charge including discounts.

Production costs can be divided into fixed costs and variable costs. Fixed costs remain constant, no matter how much you produce (e.g. rental fee, acquisition costs of machines). Variable costs change with the production level (e.g. raw materials, labor costs).

B4a. How do you determine the price of your main product?
Please indicate the degree to which every statement applies to your company

	describes us very well	applicable	inapplicable	completely inapplicable	don't know
We add a constant mark-up to the variable production costs per unit (mark-up pricing).					
Basically, we apply mark-up pricing. However, when we step up production, the variable costs increase to such a large extent that we cannot raise the price accordingly. As a consequence, we have to reduce the mark-up.					
Basically, we apply mark-up pricing. However, when we step up production, the variable costs decrease so that we can increase the mark-up.					
We set the price at the market level.					
We set the price (slightly) above the market level.					
We set the price (slightly) below the market level.					
We choose the price of our main product in a different way.	Please tell us how:				

| B4b. | Do you base your pricing decisions on data from previous years or on forecasts? | • On data from previous years.............. ❑
• On forecasts.. ❑
• An average of past data and forecasts... ❑ |

| B5. | Suppose you produce at the normal production level and you would like to slightly increase production (within the given capacity limits). How would the variable production costs per unit change for the additional units produced?

Please check only one box. | • They increase strongly........................ ❑
• They increase slightly.......................... ❑
• They remain constant........................... ❑
• They decrease slightly.......................... ❑
• They decrease strongly........................ ❑
• Don't know.............................. ❑ |

B6a. We assume that companies <u>check their prices</u> from time to time, but that they <u>do not necessarily change them.</u>
Do you check the price of your main product...

- regularly?... ❑→ *Continue with question B6b.*
- on specific occasions (e.g. when costs change considerably)?. ❑ → *Continue with question B7.*
- in general regularly and also on specific occasions (e.g. significant changes in costs or demand)?.................................. ❑ → *Continue with question B6b.*
- for other reasons?... ❑ → *Continue with question B7.*
  e.g. _____
- We never check prices without changing them..................... ❑ → *Continue with question B7.*

| B6b. | You check the price of your main product regularly. At which intervals do you check the price? | • daily.................................…................ ❑
• weekly….. ❑
• monthly…................................….......... ❑
• quarterly…....................................…..... ❑
• twice a year…................................ ❑
• yearly…................................…........... ❑
• less frequently than yearly.................... ❑ |

B7. *This question does not deal with checking the prices but with actually changing them.*

How often do you <u>change the price</u> of your main product on average in a given year?　|___| times

B8a. If there are reasons to <u>raise the price of your main product</u>, which of the following factors might <u>prevent</u> an immediate price increase?

	describes us very well	applicable	inapplicable	completely inapplicable	don't know
The concern that our competitors will not raise prices and that we will be the first to raise prices. We will wait until the competitors raise prices and will follow.					
We have arrangements with our customers, in which we guarantee to offer our main product at a specific price.					
The price we used up to now was a psychological price (e.g. 9.90); we would change this price only if the new price were also a psychological price.					
The concern that subsequently we will have to readjust the price in the opposite direction.					
Raising prices entails costs; we have to print new price lists (or catalogues), for example, or we have to modify our website.					
We will raise prices only if costs rise, but as a rule, we wait a bit before raising prices.					
We will do without price increases and will change other product parameters – e.g. extend delivery times.					

B8b. If there are reasons to <u>reduce the price of your main product</u>, which of the following factors might <u>prevent</u> an immediate price reduction?

	describes us very well	applicable	inapplicable	completely inapplicable	don't know
Concerns that our price reduction might trigger a price war with our competitors.					
We have arrangements with our customers, in which we guarantee to offer our main product at a specific price.					

	describes us very well	applicable	inapplicable	completely inapplicable	don't know
Concerns that our customers could interpret the price reduction as a reduction in quality.					
The price we used up to now was a psychological price (e.g. 9.90); we would change this price only if the new price were also a psychological price.					
The concern that subsequently we will have to readjust the price in the opposite direction.					
Reducing prices entails costs; we have to print new price lists (or catalogues), for example, or we have to modify our website.					
We will reduce prices only if costs decrease, but as a rule, we wait a bit before reducing prices.					
We will do without price reductions and will change other product parameters – e.g. shorten delivery times.					
B9a. It could also be that you wish to keep the price of your main product constant because you stand to lose many customers if you raise prices, but do not stand to gain many new customers by reducing prices. *Please indicate the degree to which this statement applies to your company.*	describes us very well	applicable	inapplicable	completely inapplicable	don't know
B9b. Some customers consider price increases resulting from higher demand less fair than those resulting from higher costs. Do you keep prices constant despite demand fluctuations because you do not want to jeopardize your customer relationships. *Please indicate the degree to which this statement applies to your company.*	describes us very well	applicable	inapplicable	completely inapplicable	don't know
B9c. Another reason for not adjusting prices (at least not immediately) is that gathering information relevant for pricing decisions is costly in terms of time and/or money. *Please indicate the degree to which this statement applies to your company.*	describes us very well	applicable	inapplicable	completely inapplicable	don't know

B10a. If <u>demand</u> for your main product <u>rises slightly</u>, how much time passes before you change prices?

Number of months............... |_|_|
We do not change prices............... ❑
Don't know............... ❑

B10b. If <u>demand</u> for your main product <u>rises markedly</u>, how much time passes before you change prices?

Number of months............... |_|_|
We do not change prices............... ❑
Don't know............... ❑

B10c. If <u>demand</u> for your main product <u>drops slightly</u>, how much time passes before you change prices?

Number of months............... |_|_|
We do not change prices............... ❑
Don't know............... ❑

B10d. If <u>demand</u> for your main product <u>drops markedly</u>, how much time passes before you change prices?

Number of months............... |_|_|
We do not change prices............... ❑
Don't know............... ❑

B10e. If the <u>cost</u> for producing your main product <u>rises slightly</u>, how much time passes before you change prices?

Number of months............... |_|_|
We do not change prices............... ❑
Don't know............... ❑

B10f. If the <u>cost</u> for producing your main product <u>rises markedly</u>, how much time passes before you change prices?

Number of months............... |_|_|
We do not change prices............... ❑
Don't know............... ❑

B10g. If the <u>cost</u> for producing your main product <u>drops slightly</u>, how much time passes before you change prices?

Number of months............... |_|_|
We do not change prices............... ❑
Don't know............... ❑

B10h. If the <u>cost</u> for producing your main product <u>drops markedly</u>, how much time passes before you change prices?

Number of months...............
We do not change prices............... ☐
Don't know............... ☐

⊔⊔

B11a. Please reflect on the <u>price increases</u> of your main product in recent years.
In recent years we have not raised the price of our main product. ☐ → *Continue with question B11b.*
Which of the factors below were relevant for the price increases?

	describes us very well	applicable	inapplicable	completely inapplicable	don't know
Wage costs rose.					
Capital costs (loan interest) rose.					
Purchased goods and services or raw materials became more expensive.					
Taxes were raised.					
We improved the quality of our main product.					
The competitors raised their prices.					
We raise prices at regular intervals.					
Demand for our main product rose.					
A public agency (e.g. price regulator) authorized a higher price.					
We link our price to the general price level (indexation).					
Forecasts on inflation and/or business activity for the upcoming years changed.					

B11b. Please reflect on the <u>price reductions</u> of your main product in recent years.
In recent years we have not raised the price of our main product. ☐ → *Continue with question B12a.*
Which of the factors below were relevant for the price increases?

	describes us very well	applicable	inapplicable	completely inapplicable	don't know
Wage costs fell.					
Capital costs (loan interest) fell.					
Purchased goods and services or raw materials became less expensive.					
Taxes were cut.					
We managed to produce the main product at less costs owing to our improved production process.					
The competitors lowered their prices.					
We reduce prices at regular intervals.					
Demand for our main product fell.					
A public agency (e.g. price regulator) called for a lower price.					
We link our price to the general price level (indexation).					
Forecasts on inflation and/or business activity for the upcoming years changed.					

B12a. Did the introduction of euro banknotes and coins (at the beginning of 2002) have any effect on prices of purchased goods and services (e.g. intermediate inputs) in your industry?

No..... ☐   Yes.
Prices increased........ ☐
Prices decreased....... ☐

B12b. Did the introduction of euro banknotes and coins (at the beginning of 2002) have any effect on prices of the products in your industry?

No..... ☐   Yes.
Prices increased........ ☐
Prices decreased....... ☐

B13a. If the demand for your main product <u>decreased temporarily</u>, what would your first reaction be?

You may check several boxes.

- We reduce prices.. ☐
- We cut overtime and/or lay off people....... ☐
- We reduce investment and/or close down facilities ☐
- We build up inventory rather than reducing output ... ☐
- We increase the funds for marketing........
  products... ☐
- Other measures..................................... ... ☐
  such as _____
- We wait and see............................... ☐

B13b.	If that the demand for your main product <u>decreased</u> <u>permanently</u>, what would your reaction be? *You may check several boxes.*	• We reduce prices................................. ❏ • We cut overtime and/or lay off people....... ❏ • We reduce investment and/or close down facilities .. ❏ • We build up inventory rather than reducing output ❏ • We increase the funds for marketing........ ❏ • We offer new products....................... ❏ • Other measures.. ❏ such as _____ • We wait and see............................. ❏
B13c.	If the demand for your main product <u>increased</u> <u>temporarily</u>, what would your first reaction be? *You may check several boxes.*	• We raise prices................................. ❏ • We do more overtime and/or hire more people ❏ • We increase investment and/or buy new facilities ❏ • We reduce inventory rather than raising output ❏ • Other measures.................................... ❏ such as _____ • We wait and see............................. ❏
B13d.	If the demand for your main product <u>increased</u> <u>permanently</u>, what would your reaction be? *You may check several boxes.*	• We raise prices................................. ❏ • We do more overtime and/or hire more people ❏ • We increase investment and/or buy new facilities ❏ • We reduce inventory rather than raising output ❏ • Other measures.................................... ❏ such as _____ • We wait and see............................. ❏

Thank you for taking the time to complete this questionnaire!

Part 2: Services

The same questionnaire was sent to service firms with three main changes:

1. "service" in place of "product"

2. General indications: This questionnaire is intended to inform us about your pricing policy. Please describe one of your services that is typical of your company. (You can, for example, choose the best-selling service of the year 2003.) If you are, for example, the owner of a hairdresser's shop, your "product" for this questionnaire could for example be "shampoo, cut and dry." If you offer specially customized services rather than "standardized products," please indicate the price you charge per working hour or day.

3. Question A4.

A4. How much percentage of sales do you generate by selling your service...	
• within the corporate group?......................	⎵⎵⎵%
• to other companies?..................................	⎵⎵⎵%
• to the government?...................................	⎵⎵⎵%
• to private customers?...............................	⎵⎵⎵%
• to other customers/clients?....................	⎵⎵⎵%
Which? ⎣_____⎦	
Total	1 0 0 %

4. Note before question B8a.

NOTE: If the price of your service is set by a public agency or a chamber (question B1), please continue with question B10a.

BELGIUM

Contact person for the questionnaire: +32(0)2 221 42 70

Please return the questionnaire by 3 March 2004 at the latest.
You can use the enclosed self-addressed envelope or our free of charge fax number 0800 95 969 (only in Belgium) or 32 2 221 31 07 (only from foreign countries)

Preliminary remarks: By "price" we mean the sales price actually charged, even in cases where it deviates from the list price. If you have different prices for different types of customers, please state the most common type of customer in your answer.

Turnover of your company during the last available fiscal year (excluding VAT):..euro
Which percentage of this turnover is generated: - in Belgium .... |_|_|_|%
                                                            - in other euro area countries....................................... |_|_|_|%
                                                            - outside the euro area .... |_|_|_|%
                                                                                                                             |1|0|0|%

Number of employees in your company, according to your latest declaration to the national social security office:
....persons

PART A – INFORMATION ON YOUR MAIN PRODUCT AND ON THE MARKET IN WHICH IT IS SOLD

A1. What is your main product, in other words, the product that generates the highest turnover?   ....

A2. How much percentage of the turnover does your main product account for?   .....%

A3. What is, in terms of turnover, the main market for your main product?   • the Belgian market |_|₁
(tick only one answer please)   • another euro area country |_|₂
                                                                                 • a non-euro area country |_|₃

From now on, your answers should refer to the main market for your main product. In other words, when answering the questions, please always try to bear in mind the main product (A1) and the main market (A3).

A4. How many competitors do you have on your main market for your main product?   • none |_|₁
 (tick only one answer please)   • less than 5 |_|₂
                                                                                      • between 5 and 20 |_|₃
                                                                                      • more than 20 |_|₄
                                                                                      • I don't know |_|₅

A5. How much percentage of your turnover do you generate by selling your main product to:
       • companies and divisions within your own group |_|_|_|%
       • companies outside your own group with a long-term relationship |_|_|_|%
       • companies outside your own group without a long-term relationship |_|_|_|%
       • directly to consumers |_|_|_|%
       • government |_|_|_|%
                                                                      Total |1|0|0|%

A6. If you decided to increase the price of your main product by 10%, all other factors remaining unchanged (including competitors' prices), by what percentage would the turnover of your main product fall?

              by ......% |_| I don't know

A7. Different factors can determine your competitiveness. What is the importance in your company of the factors listed below?
Please quote the relevant importance for each answer, by selecting one of the options:
|1| = *unimportant* |2| = *of minor importance* |3| = *important* |4| = *very important* |?| = *I don't know*

 |_| the price of our product
 |_| the quality of our product
 |_| the degree to which our product can be distinguished from that of our competitors
 |_| delivery period
 |_| long-term relationship with customers
 |_| the after-sales service
 |_| other factors; please specify..

A8. Does your firm have the possibility to set the price of the main product itself, or is it set by somebody else? (tick only one answer please)

- we set our price ourselves $\Box_1 \rightarrow$ continue to A9.
- our price is set by the government $\Box_2$
- our price is set by the parent company/group $\Box_3 \Big\} \rightarrow$ continue to B5.
- others set the price; $\Box_4$
  please specify who ....

A9. There are various ways of setting the price of your main product. How well do the following methods apply to the situation in your company?   *Please quote the relevant importance for each answer, by selecting one of the options:*
$\boxed{1}$ = *unimportant* $\boxed{2}$ = *of minor importance* $\boxed{3}$ = *important* $\boxed{4}$ = *very important* $\boxed{?}$ = *I don't know*

- ☐ we set our price fully according to our costs and a completely self-determined profit margin
- ☐ we set our price according to the price of our main competitor(s), meaning that we do not determine our profit margin ourselves

PART B – PRICE ADJUSTMENTS

B1a. When do you review the price you want to charge for your main product (this does not necessarily mean that the price actually changes)? (tick only one answer please)

- at specific time intervals $\Box_1$
- mainly at specific time intervals, but also in reaction to specific $\Big\} \rightarrow$ continue to A9.
  events (e.g. a considerable change in our costs) $\Box_2$
- in reaction to specific events (e.g. a considerable change in our costs) $\Box_3 \Big\} \rightarrow$ continue to B5.
- I don't know $\Box_4$

B1b. If you review your prices at specific time intervals, how often does this occur (this does not necessarily mean that the price actually changes)? (tick only one answer please)

- more than once a year   how many times a year?   ....
- once a year   in which month?   ....
- less than once a year   once in how many years?   ....

B2a. How did you review the price of your main product the last time? (tick only one answer please)

- we have applied a rule of thumb (e.g. a fixed amount/percentage
  change, indexation based on the consumer price index, ...) $\Box_1 \rightarrow$ continue to B3.
- we have considered a wide range of information (demand, costs,
  competitors' price ...) relevant for profit maximization within our
  company $\Box_2 \rightarrow$ continue to B2b.

B2b. If you considered a wide range of information the last time you reviewed the price, what was it related to? (tick only one answer please)

- this range of information was only related to the present context in which our company operates $\Box_1$
- this range of information was related both to the present and to the expected future context in which our
  company operates $\Box_2$

B3. Which factors cause you to raise/lower the price of your main product?
Please quote the relevant importance for each answer, by selecting one of the options:
$\boxed{1}$ = *unimportant* $\boxed{2}$ = *of minor importance* $\boxed{3}$ = *important* $\boxed{4}$ = *very important* $\boxed{?}$ = *I don't know*
           The importance of each factor may be different from one column to the other.

Factors causing a price increase	Factors causing a price decrease
☐ an increase in our labor costs	☐ a decrease in our labor costs
☐ an increase in our financial costs	☐ a decrease in our financial costs
☐ an increase in our other costs	☐ a decrease in our other costs
☐ a decrease in our productivity	☐ an increase in our productivity
☐ an increase in demand	☐ a fall in demand
☐ an increase in our competitors' price	☐ a decrease in our competitors' price
☐ other factors	☐ other factors
please specify..	please specify..

B4. There can be various reasons as to why a price is not (or only very slightly) changed during a certain period. Please indicate their importance in your company. *Please quote the relevant importance for each answer, by selecting one of the options:*
$\boxed{1}$ = unimportant $\boxed{2}$ = of minor importance $\boxed{3}$ = important $\boxed{4}$ = very important $\boxed{?}$ = I don't know

☐ We have a written contract with our customers specifying that the price can only be adjusted when the contract is renegotiated

☐ Price changes entail "physical" costs (e.g. printing new catalogues, changing price tags, adjusting the website, ...)

☐ It is costly in terms of time and/or money to collect relevant information for pricing decisions

☐ Our customers prefer a stable price and a change could damage customer relations, even if our competitors also change their price

☐ There is a risk that competing companies might not adjust their prices and that we might be first. So we wait for our competitors to act, and then follow suit.

☐ In a recession, when cashflow is low, our price may need to be kept up in order to have sufficient liquidities at one's disposal. A substantial part of our costs is indeed fixed, whereas it takes some time before a price decrease results in a higher turnover.

☐ Our variable costs do not change much over the business cycle, which contributes to the price of our product remaining roughly the same

☐ When our customers buy a lot, they have more interest in comparing prices than when they don't buy a lot. They are more sensitive to price changes in booms than in recessions.

☐ During economic booms the costs incurred by the company to reach customers decline. This contributes to keeping our price down.

☐ During an economic recession, it is more difficult to obtain external financing (e.g. bank loans). This contributes to keeping our price up.

☐ Our customer mix changes over the business cycle, during a recession we lose our least loyal customers, while more loyal customers remain. As the latter are less price-sensitive, our price can be left unchanged during a recession.

☐ Our price is set at an attractive threshold (e.g. 4.99 euro or 25.00 euro) and is only changed when it is convenient to move to a new attractive threshold

☐ There is a risk that we subsequently have to readjust our price in the opposite direction

☐ We are afraid that customers will interpret a price reduction as a reduction in quality

☐ An increase in demand for our product is met by elements other than a price increase, e.g. an extension of the delivery period

---

B5. How often does the price of your main product actually change, including reductions, but excluding sales or sell-off? (tick only one answer please)

- more than once a year   ☐$_1$ how many times a year? ....
- once a year   ☐$_2$
- less than once a year   ☐$_3$ once in how many years? ....

PART C – PRICE BEHAVIOR ON OTHER MARKETS THAN THE MAIN MARKET

(only to be filled out by companies for which the market mentioned in A3 is not the only market)

C1. You may have different prices according to the market on which you operate. Which of the following statements best describes your main product? (tick only one answer please)

- the price denominated in euro is the same for all countries   ☐$_1$ → continue to C3.
- the price denominated in euro is the same for all euro area countries, but not for non-euro area countries   ☐$_2$ → continue to C2.
- the price denominated in euro is different, both for euro area countries and for non-euro area countries   ☐$_3$ → continue to C2.

C2. What is the importance of the following factors in a differentiated price setting behavior between markets?
Please quote the relevant importance for each answer, by selecting one of the options:
$\boxed{1}$ = unimportant $\boxed{2}$ = of minor importance $\boxed{3}$ = important $\boxed{4}$ = very important $\boxed{?}$ = I don't know

☐ exchange rate movement of the currency used for payment

☐ tax system on the market (e.g. VAT-rate)

☐ structural market conditions on the market (e.g. taste, standard of living,....)

☐ cyclical fluctuations in demand on the market

☐ the price of the competitor(s) on the market
☐ rules on the market
☐ other factors; please specify...

C3. Is competition for your main product stronger on the foreign market than on the Belgian market? (tick only one answer please)	• yes	☐₁
	• no	☐₂
	• our company does not operate on the Belgian market	☐₃
	• I don't know	☐₄

Name and phone number of the person who filled out this questionnaire:

NAME: ....
Phone: ....

Thank you for taking part in the survey.

FRANCE

|_|_|_|_|_____
Branch number and name

BANQUE DE FRANCE

EUROSYSTÈME

COMPANY NAME |_____

FUNCTION OF RESPONDENT |_____

TURN OVER OUT OF TAX (thousands of euros) |_|_|_|_|_|_|_|_|_|,0

SHARE OF EXPORTS IN TURNOVER (in %) |_|_|_|,0 %

SIREN   If possible
IDENTIFICATION NO. |_|_|_|_|_|_|_|_|_| ESTABLISHMENT NO. |_|_|_|_|_| APE CODE |_|_|_|_|

1993 Nomenclature (NAF)

MAIN PRODUCT (in full) |_____

This questionnaire has been answered by: ❑ phone   ❑ face to face interview   ❑ other

1. What percentage of your turnover out of tax is accounted for by your main product?............................... ... . |_|_|_|,0%	
	• *I do not know /I do not wish to answer* ...... ❑ (9)
2. What percentage of your turnover out of tax is generated?	• In France (incl. French overseas departments and territories) |_|_|_|%
	• In the euro area (excl. France) .... |_|_|_|%
	• Outside the euro area .... |_|_|_|%
	Total |1|0|0|%
	• *I do not know /I do not wish to answer* ...... ❑ (9)
3. On the <u>French</u> market and for your <u>main product</u>, with how many companies are you in competition? (*tick only one answer*)	• none.. ❑ (1)
	• 1 to 2.. ❑ (2)
	• 3 to 4.. ❑ (3)
	• 5 to 10.. ❑ (4)
	• 11 to 20.. ❑ (5)
	• More than 20.. ❑ (6)
	• *I do not know /I do not wish to answer* .... ❑ (9)
4. On the <u>French</u> market and for your <u>main product</u>, what percentage of your turnover is accounted for by:	• Firms that subcontract work................. |_|_|_|%
	• Other firms.................................. |_|_|_|%
	• Consumers (via your own distribution network, retailers ...)....................... |_|_|_|%
	• General government, local authorities ..... |_|_|_|%
	• Others (Specify)........... |_|_|_|%
	Total |1|0|0|%
	• *I do not know /I do not wish to answer* ...... ❑ (9)
4a. If your firm works as a subcontractor on the <u>French</u> market for your <u>main product</u>, on whose behalf is it? (*tick only one answer*)	• *One firm.......................................* ❑ (1)
	• *Between 2 and 4 firms....................* ❑ (2)
	• *Between 5 and 10 firms....................* ❑ (3)
	• *More than 10 firms.........................* ❑ (4)
	• *I do not know /I do not wish to answer* ...... ❑ (9)

5. What percentage of your turnover out of tax generated by your main product on the French market is derived from a <u>long-term business relationship</u> (e.g. existence of a written contract)?

Long-term relationship with firms	Long-term relationship with households
• Share of turnover............ ⊔⊔⊔‚0%	• Share of turnover........................ ⊔⊔⊔‚0%
• Inapplicable to our firm...... ❏ (1)	• Inapplicable to our firm................. ❏ (1)
• *I do not know /I do not wish to answer.* ❏ (9)	• *I do not know /I do not wish to answer...* ❏ (9)
(tick only one answer)	*(tick only one answer)*

---

6. In general, the purchase price (the price actually charged) of your main product is

(maximum two answers)

- The same for all customers................. ❏ (1)
- Differentiated according to the quantity which is sold .... ❏ (2)
- Decided case by case .... ❏ (3)
- *I do not know /I do not wish to answer* .... ❏ (9)

---

7. On the French market and for your main product, what is the share, in percentage of your <u>total cost</u> of

(tick only one answer)

- Labor cost.. ⊔⊔⊔‚0%
- Intermediate consumption cost............. ⊔⊔⊔‚0%
- Fixed cost .... ⊔⊔⊔‚0%
  Total |1|0|0|%
- *I do not know /I do not wish to answer ...* ❏ (9)

---

8. How do your unit variable costs (costs of labor and of other inputs by unit of production) change when there is an increase in the level of production?

(tick only one answer)

- Increase... ❏ (1)
- Unchanged...................................... ❏ (2)
- Decrease .... ❏ (3)
- *I do not know /I do not wish to answer ...* ❏ (9)

---

9. How do you usually <u>set the price of your main product</u> on the French market?

If several situations arise, answer for the most significant.

(tick only one answer)

- A mark-up is applied to unit variable production costs (your price is different from the price of your competitors)............ ❏ (1)
- The market is very competitive and your price is the same as the one of your competitors...................................... ❏ (2)
- The price is regulated (e.g. medicines...)... ❏ (3)
- Other (please specify) _____ ❏ (4)
- *I do not know /I do not wish to answer ......* ❏ (9)

---

10. In general, how often do you <u>review the price of your main product</u> (without necessarily changing it)?

The exam must be complete enough to possibly lead to a modification of price.

(tick only one answer)

- Daily... ❏ (1)
- Weekly.. ❏ (2)
- Monthly.. ❏ (3)
- Quarterly .... ❏ (4)
- Yearly... ❏ (5)
- Over one year .... ❏ (6)
- Other (specify)................................. ❏ (7)
- No usual frequency........................... ❏ (8)
- *I do not know /I do not wish to answer ......* ❏ (9)

---

11. In general, when you change your price, do you take into account the fact that the next price adjustment can only occur after a certain period of time?

- Yes........... .... ❏ (1)
- No.... .... ❏ (2)
- *I do not know /I do not wish to answer ...* ❏ (9)

(tick only one answer)

---

12. On the French market, do <u>customers sometimes benefit from discount prices</u> on your main product?
(several possible answers for yes)

Firms

Households

- Yes, depending on the quantity bought ☐ (1)
- Yes, depending on the market situation ☐ (2)
- Yes, at certain times of the year ☐ (3)
- Yes, other (please specify) ☐ (4)
- No ☐ (5)
- *I do not know /I do not wish to answer ...* ☐ (9)

- Yes, depending on the quantity bought ☐ (1)
- Yes, depending on the market situation ☐ (2)
- Yes, at certain times of the year ☐ (3)
- Yes, other (please specify) ☐ (4)
- No ☐ (5)
- *I do not know /I do not wish to answer ......* ☐ (9)

13. Which factors, among the ones listed below, would cause you to raise/lower the price of your main product on the French market? For each factor, quote the relevant importance: *(1) = unimportant; (2) = of minor importance; (3) = important; (4) = very important; (5) = this situation has not arisen during the last two years; (9) = I do not know /I do not wish to answer.*

The quotation for each factor might be different from one column to the other.

Reasons to raise the price of your main product

- An increase in labor costs ☐
- An increase in intermediate commodity prices ☐
- A decrease in productivity ☐
- An increase in demand ☐
- A stock decrease or an increase in delivery delay ☐
- An increase in the price offered by your competitor(s) ☐
- A decrease in the number of your competitors ☐
- Other (please specify) ☐

Reasons to lower the price of your main product

- A decrease in labor costs ☐
- A decrease in intermediate commodity prices ☐
- An increase in productivity ☐
- A decrease in demand ☐
- A stock increase or a decrease in delivery delay ☐
- A decrease in the price offered by your competitor(s) ☐
- An increase in the number of your competitors ☐
- Other (please specify) ☐

14. Which factors, among the ones listed below, might deter you from adjusting the price of your main product on the French market? For each factor, quote the relevant importance: *(1) = unimportant; (2) = of minor importance; (3) = important; (4) = very important; (5) = this situation has not arisen during the last two years; (9) = I do not know /I do not wish to answer.*

The quotation for each factor might be different from one column to the other.

Reasons to decide not to raise the price of your main product

- The risk that your competitors will not adjust their price ☐
- The risk that you will subsequently have to readjust your price in the opposite direction ☐
- The existence of a written contract specifying that price can only be adjusted when the contract is renegotiated ☐
- The existence of an implicit contract (regular contact with a customer without any written contract) ☐
- A preference for maintaining price at a psychological threshold (e.g. 499 € instead of 502 €) ☐
- The costs generated by price adjustments (menu costs, IT costs,...) ☐
- Other (specify) ☐

Reasons to decide not to lower the price of your main product

- The risk that your competitors will not adjust their price ☐
- The risk that you will subsequently have to readjust your price in the opposite direction ☐
- The existence of a written contract specifying that price can only be adjusted when the contract is renegotiated ☐
- The existence of an implicit contract (regular contact with a customer without any written contract) ☐
- A preference for maintaining price at a psychological threshold (e.g. 499 € instead of 494 €) ☐
- The costs generated by price adjustments (menu costs, IT costs,...) ☐
- Other (specify) ☐

15. Usually, in the event of a major and lasting change in <u>your environment</u> (change in demand, competitive environment, etc...), do you modify the price of your main product?

<u>Increased demand and/or lower competition</u>   <u>Lower demand and/or increased competition</u>

• Yes, with a delay shorter than 1 month ☐ (1)	• Yes, with a delay shorter than 1 month ☐ (1)
• Yes, with a delay between 1 and 3 months ☐ (2)	• Yes, with a delay between 1 and 3 months ☐ (2)
• Yes, with a delay longer than 3 months ☐ (3)	• Yes, with a delay longer than 3 months ☐ (3)
• With difficulty ☐ (4)	• With difficulty ☐ (4)
• No ☐ (5)	• No ☐ (5)
• This situation has not arisen during the last two years ☐ (6)	• This situation has not arisen during the last two years ☐ (6)
• *I do not know /I do not wish to answer* ☐ (9)	• *I do not know /I do not wish to answer* ☐ (9)
(tick only one answer)	*(tick only one answer)*

16. Usually, in the event of a major and lasting change in <u>your unit variable production costs</u> (costs of labor and of other inputs) on the French market, do you modify the price of your main product?

<u>Lower unit production costs</u>   <u>Higher unit production costs</u>

• Yes, with a delay shorter than 1 month ☐ (1)	• Yes, with a delay shorter than 1 month ☐ (1)
• Yes, with a delay between 1 and 3 months ☐ (2)	• Yes, with a delay between 1 and 3 months ☐ (2)
• Yes, with a delay longer than 3 months ☐ (3)	• Yes, with a delay longer than 3 months ☐ (3)
• With difficulty ☐ (4)	• With difficulty ☐ (4)
• No ☐ (5)	• No ☐ (5)
• This situation has not arisen during the last two years ☐ (6)	• This situation has not arisen during the last two years ☐ (6)
• *I do not know /I do not wish to answer* ☐ (9)	• *I do not know /I do not wish to answer* ☐ (9)
(tick only one answer)	*(tick only one answer)*

17. In <u>2003</u>, how many times did you change the price of your main product? |_|_|_| times

Take as reference the price actually charged for a representative transaction

• *I do not know /I do not wish to answer ....*   ☐ (9)

17a. <u>Between January 2003 and December 2003</u>, what has been (will be) the variation, in percent, of the price of your main |_|_|_|.|_|%
product on the French market?

Take as reference the price actually charged for a representative transaction

• *I do not know /I do not wish to answer ....*   ☐ (9)

GERMANY

ifo Institut / Deutsche Bundesbank
für Wirtschaftsforschung Frankfurt am Main

Forschungsbereich Unternehmensbefragungen
Postfach 86 04 60 81631 München

e-mail: umfragen@ifo.de
internet: http://www.ifo.de

Phone: (089) 9224-0
Contact person: Herr Stahl 069 9566-8239
Telefax: (089) 9224-1463   e-mail: Harald.Stahl@bundesbank.de
                98 53 69

Product (XY):

Special survey on the formation of producer prices

The questions concern the product mentioned below (in the sequel denoted by XY). Please mark the relevant box.

Your answers are analyzed strictly confidential. The respective laws are warranted.

Identification no.

Please refer your answers to the above mentioned product!

GENERAL INFORMATION

1) The share of XY with respect to total sales amounts to..|__|__|__|

2) Our customers for XY are from (share of sales)
   - Germany.. |__|__|__|
   - other Euro-area countries .... |__|__|__|
   - other countries.............................. |__|__|__|%

   |1|0|0|%|

3) Our price setting in the remaining Euro-area / other countries differs from our domestic market with respect to

	other Euro-area countries	other countries
• to the timing	❏	❏
• the amount	❏	❏
• the reasons	❏	❏
• it is not different	❏	❏

Please refer your answers from now on to the domestic market, respectively to the whole Euro-area if the price setting there is not different from the domestic market!

4) The breakdown of our sales with XY with respect to customers is
   - our own group ❏
   - other industrial enterprises ❏
   - wholesale ❏
   - retail, department stores, hypermarkets, mail order houses ❏
   - private costumers ❏
   - government ❏
   - others ❏

5) Our sales share of XY with customers, who regularly ask for prices, amounts to...|__|__|__|

6) The number of our most important competitors for XY on the domestic market amounts to
   - less than 5 ❏
   - between 5 and 20 ❏
   - more than 20 ❏
   - We do not have any significant competitor ❏

	INFORMATION REGARDING PRICE FORMATION

7) Our prices are <u>revised</u> (without being necessarily changed)
- Regularly ☐
  - daily ☐
  - weekly ☐
  - monthly ☐
  - quarterly ☐
  - semi-annual ☐
  - yearly ☐
- On certain events (e.g. if costs changes are large) ☐
- within the scope of an ex post calculation ☐

8) We have a certain margin for setting our price and determine it
- by applying a constant mark-up on calculated unit costs ☐
- taking calculated unit costs as reference and varying the mark-up taking into account market and competition conditions ☐
- by taking the price of our main competitor as a reference ☐
- by tying it to another price (e.g. wage) ☐
- in a different manner ☐

9) We have almost no margin for price setting ☐

10) We warrant our price on average for a period of |__|__| months.

11) Our sales share of XY under written contracts that set prices for a stated period amounts to |__|__|
These prices are tied by contract to the development of other variables (e.g. collectively negotiated wages) |__|__|
Prices are fixed for 9 months on average

12) Our per unit profit is lower during a downturn ☐

13) Our price is constantly reduced during the life-cycle ☐

Please mark according to significance. (1)= minor importance to (4)= great importance

14) The calculations underlying our price setting are based on

	(1)	(2)	(3)	(4)
extrapolating past values (e.g. average price, increase of intermediate inputs during the preceding year, past cost development)	☐	☐	☐	☐
the actual development	☐	☐	☐	☐
expectations, that are not based on extrapolating past values (e.g. future cost increases)	☐	☐	☐	☐

Please take into account from now on only those price changes that belong to transactions and not to pure list price changes.

15) Our price for XY
- is the same for all customers ☐
- depends on the amount bought ☐
- is decided upon case by case ☐

16) Starting from a satisfying business situation, we change our prices if there is a

	minor importance		greater importance	
Price increase	(1)	(2)	(3)	(4)
permanent increase in labor costs (e.g. negotiated wage increase)	☐	☐	☐	☐
transitory increase in labor costs (e.g. overtime hours, bonuses)	☐	☐	☐	☐
increase in financing costs	☐	☐	☐	☐
increase in costs of materials	☐	☐	☐	☐

- product improvement ❏ ❏ ❏ ❏
- demand increase ❏ ❏ ❏ ❏
- demand reduction ❏ ❏ ❏ ❏
- price increase by a competitor ❏ ❏ ❏ ❏
- other reasons ❏ ❏ ❏ ❏

Price reduction

- decrease in labor costs (e.g. bonuses, layoffs) ❏ ❏ ❏ ❏
- decrease in financing costs ❏ ❏ ❏ ❏
- decrease in costs of materials ❏ ❏ ❏ ❏
- increase of productivity ❏ ❏ ❏ ❏
- demand increase ❏ ❏ ❏ ❏
- demand reduction ❏ ❏ ❏ ❏
- price reduction by a competitor ❏ ❏ ❏ ❏
- other reasons ❏ ❏ ❏ ❏

17)
- We change our prices at a regular date if possible (e.g. beginning of the year) ❏ ❏ ❏ ❏
- We change our prices according to a regular time interval if possible (e.g. after 12 months) ❏ ❏ ❏ ❏
- We make a foreseeable price change in advance if possible ❏ ❏ ❏ ❏

We postpone a price change because
- a fixed term contract explicitly prohibits a price change ❏ ❏ ❏ ❏
- a price change entails high costs (e.g. printing of price lists) ❏ ❏ ❏ ❏
- our variable costs hardly vary during the business cycle ❏ ❏ ❏ ❏

We postpone a price increase for fear that
- competitors do not rise their prices too ❏ ❏ ❏ ❏
- after a short while a price reduction would be necessary ❏ ❏ ❏ ❏
- the hoped for additional revenues due to a higher unit price do not compensate for the feared losses due to a lower number of units sold ❏ ❏ ❏ ❏
- other reasons ❏ ❏ ❏ ❏

We postpone a price decrease for fear that
- competitors decrease their prices too ❏ ❏ ❏ ❏
- after a short while a price increase would be necessary ❏ ❏ ❏ ❏
- the hoped for additional revenues due to a higher number of units sold do not compensate for the feared losses due to a lower unit price ❏ ❏ ❏ ❏
- other reasons ❏ ❏ ❏ ❏

Thank you very much for your cooperation!

ITALY

Preliminary remarks

- The answers must refer to year 2002

- If your firm produces (or sells) more goods or services, the answers, where explicitly stated, must refer to the "main product (or service)." For instance, if the firm produces (or sells) several types of hats and shoes, by "product" we mean "hats" and "shoes" (irrespective of the specific type), whereas by "main product" we mean the one which in 2002 generated the highest turnover.

SECTION A - GENERAL INFORMATION ON THE MARKET IN WHICH THE FIRM OPERATES

A1. How many products does your firm produce (or sell)?...|_|_|_|

A2. What is your "main product"?....................................._____

A3. What is the percentage of turnover due to your "main product"?.. |_|_|_|%

A4. What is the most important market (in terms of turnover) for your "main product"?
 (please tick only one answer)
	• Italian market:
	       "Local" market .... ❑
	       "National" market .... ❑
	• Other euro area countries .... ❑
	• Countries outside the euro area................... ❑

A5. If you sell your "main product" abroad, what is the percentage of your turnover due to exports?	• .... |_|_|_|% • I do not know, I do not want to answer .... ❑
A6. With reference to your "main product" and the Italian market, your firm is, in terms of market share (if you sell your "main product" only on the "local" market, please refer the answer to it): *(please tick only one answer)*	• The first firm... ❑ • One of the first 4 firms .... ❑ • One of the first 10 firms .... ❑ • Not among the first 10 firms...................... ❑ • I do not know, I do not want to answer .... ❑
A7. With reference to your "main product" and the Italian market, could you indicate the number of your competitors (if you sell your main product only on the "local" market, please refer the answer to it)? *(please tick only one answer)*	• None... ❑ • < 5 .... ❑ • Between 5 and 20 .... ❑ • > 20... ❑ • I do not know, I do not want to answer .... ❑
A8. In what percentage the turnover generated by your "main product" is due to sales to:	• Other firms .... |_|_|_|% • Consumers, through large retailers.............. |_|_|_|% • Consumers, through your own distribution network or through a network under your control |_|_|_|% • Consumers, through small retailers............... |_|_|_|% • Consumers through other channels (e.g. catalogues, Internet, etc.) .... |_|_|_|% • Public Administration... .... |_|_|_|% Total |1|0|0|%
A9. With reference to your "main product," are the relationships with your customers mostly of a long-term nature (i.e. longer than 1 year) or occasional? *(please tick only 1 answer for each type of customer)*	• Other firms (including those belonging to the retail sector): i) Long-term .... ❑ ii) Occasional.................................... ❑ • Consumers (only for firms which sell their products directly to the public): iii) Long-term .... ❑ iv) Occasional .... ❑
A10. With reference to your "main product" and moving from a normal level of production, how do your unit variable costs (costs of labor and of other inputs) change when there is an increase in the level of production? *(please tick only 1 answer)*	• Large increase...................................... ❑ • Moderate increase.................................. ❑ • Unchanged.... .... ❑ • Moderate decrease................................. ❑ • Large decrease .... ❑

SECTION B - THE DETERMINANTS OF THE PRICE LEVEL

B1. The actual price of your "main product" is: *(please tick at most 2 answers)*	• The same for all customers......................... ❏ • Differentiated according to the quantity which is sold ❏ • Decided case by case .... ❏ • I do not know, I do not want to answer .... ❏
B2. How do you normally set the price of your "main product"?	• A mark-up is applied to unit variable costs (cost of labor and cost of the other inputs) .... ❏ • The price is determined by our competitors........ ❏ • The price is set by the customers of our main product or service .... ❏ • The price is regulated...... .... ❏ • Other (please specify) _____ ❏ • I do not know, I do not want to answer .... ❏
B3. How different would the price of your "main product" be if you did not have any competitor on your market?	• Unchanged.. ❏ • Slightly different................................... ❏ • Fairly different...................................... ❏ • Very different .... ❏
B4. If you decided to increase the price of your "main product" by 10%, *ceteris paribus* (in particular assuming that the prices set by your competitors remain unchanged) by what percentage would the demand for your "main product" fall?	⌊⌊⌊⌋% ❏ I do not know

SECTION C - PRICE ADJUSTMENTS

C.1.1 Under normal condition how do you re-evaluate the price you want to charge for your main product (this does not necessarily mean that the price actually changes)? *(tick only 1 answer please)*

- At pre-determined time intervals (for instance every 3 months, once a year, etc.)   ❏
- Mainly at specific time intervals, but also in reaction to specific events (such as a considerable increase in production costs, a VAT increase, etc.)   ❏
- In reaction to specific events (an increase in production costs, in demand, etc.)   ❏

C.1.2 If you do it at pre-determined time intervals, this takes place:	• Daily... ❏ • Weekly... ❏ • Monthly.. ❏ • Quarterly.. ❏ • Yearly.. ❏

C.2. The information set you typically consider in order to re-evaluate the price of your main product or service is related *(tick only 1 answer please)*

- Only to the past context in which your company operated   ❏
- To the present and to the expected future context relevant for your firm   ❏

C.3 Once you have decided that it is necessary to change the price of your "main product," which of the factors listed below might lead to a delay in the actual price change?

(please attribute the degree of importance to each answer by choosing one of the following four options:
1 = unimportant;   2 = of minor importance;   3 = important;   4 = very important)

C3.1 The fear that competing firms will not adjust their price.......... ☐

C3.2 The fear that subsequently you will need to modify the price in the opposite direction................................... ☐

C3.3 The presence of a contract which states conditions (including price) that can be changed only when the contract is re-negotiated .... ☐

C3.4 The price is set at "attractive" thresholds (e.g. 4.99 euro instead of 5.00) and it is changed only when it is convenient to move to a new attractive threshold... ☐

C3.5 The presence of high costs of changing prices (printing new catalogues, physical costs of adjusting price tags) .... ☐

C3.6 Bureaucratic rigidities (e.g., the need to inform trade associations of the new price) .... ☐

C3.7 Other (please specify if possible) .... ☐

C.4 Once you have decided that it is necessary to change the price of your "main product," might the fear of losing the most loyal customers lead to a delay in the actual price change? *(please attribute the degree of importance to each answer by choosing one of the following four options: 1 = unimportant; 2 = of minor importance; 3 = important; 4 = very important)* ☐

C.5 Is it possible that the price of your "main product" is below your unit variable costs?

Yes.... ☐
No...   ☐

C.6 If the answer to the previous question is "yes," for <u>how many months</u> would you be willing to accept a price level below unit variable costs? |_|_|

C.7 In <u>2001</u> how many times did you actually change the price of your "main product"? |__| times

I do not know ☐

C.8 And in <u>2002</u>? |__| times

I do not know ☐

SECTION D – THE ASYMMETRIES

D.1 Which factors would be likely to cause an <u>increase</u> in the price of your "main product"?

(please attribute the degree of importance to each answer by choosing one of the following four options:
1 = unimportant;   2 = of minor importance;
3 = important;   4 = very important)

- An increase in the cost of labor .... ☐
- An increase in the cost of raw materials......... ☐
- An increase in financial costs .... ☐
- A rise in demand................................... ☐
- Price increase by one or more competitors....... ☐
- Other (please specify)_____ ☐

D.2 If demand for your "main product" increased, before you had raised the price level, would you first consider:

- An extension in delivery time   Yes.... ☐
                                         No...   ☐

- Changing the level of stocks   Yes.... ☐
                                         No...   ☐

D.3 Which factors would be likely to cause a <u>decrease</u> in the price of your "main product"?

(please attribute the degree of importance to each answer by choosing one of the following four options:
1 = unimportant;   2 = of minor importance;
3 = important;   4 = very important)

- A decrease in the cost of labor .... ☐
- A decrease in the cost of raw materials......... ☐
- A decrease in financial costs .... ☐
- A decrease in demand.............................. ☐
- Price decrease by one or more competitors....... ☐
- Other (please specify) _____ ☐

D.4 If you were about to decrease the price of your "main product," would you fear that customers might assume that you had reduced its quality? *(please tick only 1 answer)*

Yes....   ☐
No...   ☐
I do not know... ☐

LUXEMBOURG

You may use the enclosed free of charge self-addressed envelope or our fax number +352 47744920.

> Remark: The notion "price" refers to the price actually charged, even if this price deviates from the pricing list. If different prices are charged for different types of customers, please refer to the most common customer type in your subsequent answers.

Name of Company: ....

Name and position of person completing the survey: ....

Phone number: .... E-mail: ....

GENERAL INFORMATION

1. Total turnover of your company in the last fiscal year (excl. VAT): .... € |_____|

2. What share of the total turnover is generated in the following regions:

   2.1 Luxembourg .... |__|__|%
   2.2 In the euro area (except Luxembourg) .... |__|__|%
   2.3 Outside the euro area .... |__|__|%

                                                Total |1|0|0|%

3. Number of employees in your company   .... |_____|

4. What is your main product, i.e. the product that generates the highest turnover? For companies in the services sector, the main product is to mean the main activity. |_____|

5. What percentage share of the turnover does your main product account for? .... |_____| %

6. Which country reflects in terms of the turnover of your main product the most important market? *(Please tick one answer only)*

   6.1 Luxembourg ....
   6.2 A different country in the euro area .... ❑
   6.3 A country outside the euro area .... ❑

In the following, your answers should exclusively refer to the relevant <u>Luxembourg market</u> of your <u>main product</u> (Q4). For companies in the services sector, the main product is to mean the main activity

If your company is not present on the Luxembourg market, you have already answered all relevant questions. Please use the self-addressed envelope to return the questionnaire. Thank you very much for your cooperation!

7. How many competitors (national and international) do you encounter for your main product on the Luxembourg market? *(Please tick one answer only)*

   7.1 None ....
   7.2 Less than 5.. ❑
   7.3 Between 5 and 10 .... ❑
   7.4 More than 10 .... ❑
   7.5 I don't know .... ❑

8. How large is the market share of your main product on the Luxembourg market? *(Please tick one answer only)*

   8.1 Less or equal 5% ....
   8.2 Between 6% and 25% .... ❑
   8.3 Between 26% and 50% .... ❑
   8.4 Between 51% and 75% .... ❑
   8.5 Between 76% and 99% .... ❑
   8.6 100% .... ❑

9. Do you generate the largest share of your turnover with long-term or short-term customers? *(Please tick one answer only)*

   9.1 Long-term customers (Relationship with customers lasting >1 year) .... ❑
   9.2 Short-term customers (Relationship with customers lasting 1 year or less) .... ❑

10. What percentage share of your turnover, that you generate with your main product on the Luxembourg market, is generated by sales:

10.1 Within own group .... |⎵|⎵|⎵|%
10.2 To wholesalers .... |⎵|⎵|⎵|%
10.3 To retailers .... |⎵|⎵|⎵|%
10.4 To consumers / Final users .... |⎵|⎵|⎵|%
10.5 To public administration (government, municipalities, etc..) .... |⎵|⎵|⎵|%
10.6 Via other channels, namely: _____ |⎵|⎵|⎵|%

                                                                                Total |1|0|0|%

---

11. The competitiveness of your company can depend on several factors. Please indicate the relevance of the factors listed below for the competitiveness of your company

[1] = unimportant   [2] = minor importance   [3] = important   [4] = very important   [9] = don't know

	1	2	3	4	9
11.1 The price of our product	❏	❏	❏	❏	❏
11.2 The quality of our product..	❏	❏	❏	❏	❏
11.3 The degree to which our product is different from our competitors' products	❏	❏	❏	❏	❏
11.4 The delivery period	❏	❏	❏	❏	❏
11.5 The long-term relationship to our customers	❏	❏	❏	❏	❏
11.6 The customer service	❏	❏	❏	❏	❏
11.7 Other factors, namely: _____	❏	❏	❏	❏	❏

GENERAL INFORMATION ON THE PRICING BEHAVIOR OF YOUR COMPANY

---

12. The price of your main product (Please tick one answer only)

12.1 Is identical for all customers ....   ❏
12.2 Depends on the quantity sold, but according to a uniform price list ....   ❏
12.3 Varies case by case ....   ❏

---

13. Suppose you raised the price of your main product by 10%. Given that all other factors remained unchanged (including the prices of your competitors), by what percentage share would the turnover of your main product drop? (Please tick one answer only)

13.1 Substantially more than 10%...   ❏
13.2 Roughly 10 %..   ❏
13.3 Between 0% and 10% ....   ❏
13.4 I don't know ....   ❏

---

14. Do you set the price of your main product yourself or is the price determined elsewhere? (Please tick one answer only)

14.1 We determine the price ourselves ....   ⇨ Proceed with question |15| ❏
14.2 The price is determined by a governmental institution ....   ⇨ Proceed with question |23| ❏
14.3 The price is determined by our mother company or other units of our group..   ⇨ Proceed with question |23| ❏
14.4 The price is determined by someone else, namely:..............................   ⇨ Proceed with question |23| ❏

---

15. Suppose you did not have any direct competitors. What would be the effect for the price of your main product? (Please tick one answer only)

15.1 The price would be much higher (more than 10%) ....   ❏
15.2 The price would be higher (between 5% and 10 %) ....   ❏
15.3 The price would be slightly higher (between 0% and 5%) ....   ❏
15.4 The price would not change ....   ❏
15.5 I don't know ....   ❏

---

16. Companies often review prices without necessarily changing them. Do you review the actually charged sales price of your main product (Please tick one answer only)

16.1 In regular intervals ....   ⇨ Proceed with question |17| ❏
16.2 Generally in regular intervals, but also in response to specific events (e.g. as reaction to a substantial change in costs) ....   ⇨ Proceed with question |17| ❏
16.3 In response to specific events (e.g. as reaction to a substantial change in costs)   ⇨ Proceed with question |18| ❏
16.4 I don't know ....   ⇨ Proceed with question |18| ❏

17. You review prices without necessarily changing them (this does not presuppose that prices change). How often do you normally review the price? *(Please tick one answer only)*

17.1 More than once a year, namely:

daily	weekly	monthly	quarterly	half-yearly
❏	❏	❏	❏	❏

17.2 Once a year ⇨ Typically in which month?

Jan.	Feb.	March	April	May	June	July	August	Sept.	Oct.	Nov.	Dec.
❏	❏	❏	❏	❏	❏	❏	❏	❏	❏	❏	❏

17.3 Fewer than once a year ⇨ At which interval? Every |_____| years

18. How did you proceed with the last price review of your main product? *(Please tick one answer only)*

18.1 We used a pre-defined rule (e.g. change by a fixed amount or a fixed percentage, in accordance with the economy-wide price level [indexation], etc...) .... ❏

18.2 In the review, we took into consideration a lot of information (demand, costs, prices of competitors, etc...). This information exclusively referred to the past and present development of the company's business conditions ...... ❏

18.3 In the review, we took into consideration a lot of information (demand, costs, prices of competitors, etc...). This information exclusively referred to the present and future development of the company's business conditions ...... ❏

19. Prices react different strongly to changes in costs and demand. Please choose one of the following options for each of the next questions:

1 = less than 1 week	2 = between 1 week and 1 month	3 = between 1 month and 3 months
4 = between 3 and 6 months	5 = between 6 months and 1 year	6 = the price remains unchanged

	1	2	3	4	5	6
19.1 If the demand for your main product increased substantially, how much time would evolve until you increased the price?	❏	❏	❏	❏	❏	❏
19.2 The quality of our product...	❏	❏	❏	❏	❏	❏
19.3 If the production costs for your main product increased substantially, how much time would evolve until you increased the price?	❏	❏	❏	❏	❏	❏
19.4 If the demand for your main product decreased substantially, how much time would evolve until you decreased the price?	❏	❏	❏	❏	❏	❏
19.5 If the production costs for your main product decreased substantially, how much time would evolve until you decreased the price	❏	❏	❏	❏	❏	❏

20. There may be numerous reasons why prices are not or only slightly changed during a certain time interval. Please indicate to what extent each of the potential reasons listed below is relevant for your company.

1 = unimportant 2 = minor importance 3 = important 4 = very important 9 = don't know

	1	2	3	4	9
20.1 We have a written contract with our customers specifying that the price can only be adjusted when the contract is renegotiated	❏	❏	❏	❏	❏
20.2 Price changes entail (physical) costs. For example, pricing lists (or catalogues) have to be printed, price labels have to be changed or Internet pages have to be modified	❏	❏	❏	❏	❏
20.3 The gathering and the treatment of the information necessary for making pricing decisions is costly and time consuming.	❏	❏	❏	❏	❏
20.4 Our customers prefer stable prices. Price changes could damage customer relations, even if the competitors were to change prices.	❏	❏	❏	❏	❏
20.5 There is the risk that competing companies do not adjust their prices and that we would be the first to do so. So, we wait for our competitors to act and then follow suit.....................	❏	❏	❏	❏	❏
20.6 In a recession, when cash flow is low, our price needs to be kept high in order to guarantee sufficient liquidity. A large fraction of our costs are fixed and a price reduction would increase our turnover after a time lag only..	❏	❏	❏	❏	❏
20.7 Our variable costs do not change by much during the economic cycle. This is why the price of our main product remains relatively stable.	❏	❏	❏	❏	❏
20.8 When our customers buy a lot, they have a higher interest to compare prices than when they buy little. Our customers therefore react more sensitively to price changes during a boom than during a recession.	❏	❏	❏	❏	❏
20.9 During a boom, the company's costs to reach customers declines. This keeps the price at a relatively low level..	❏	❏	❏	❏	❏
20.10 During a recession, it is more difficult to obtain external financing (e.g. bank loans). This contributes to keeping our price high	❏	❏	❏	❏	❏
20.11 The customer mix varies with the economic cycle. In a recession, we lose our least loyal customers, while the more loyal customers remain. As the latter are less price sensitive our					

price is left unchanged during a recession. .... ❏ ❏ ❏ ❏ ❏

20.12 Our price is set at an attractive threshold (e.g. 4.99 Euro or 25.00 Euro), and is only changed
when it is convenient to move to a new attractive threshold. .... ❏ ❏ ❏ ❏ ❏

20.13 We fear that we subsequently have to readjust our price in the opposite direction. .... ❏ ❏ ❏ ❏ ❏

20.14 We fear that our customers mistake a price reduction as a reduction in quality. .... ❏ ❏ ❏ ❏ ❏

20.15 An increase in demand is at first met by adjustments other than price changes, for example an
extended delivery period. .... ❏ ❏ ❏ ❏ ❏

---

21. Please indicate to what extent the factors listed below are of relevance for price increases of your main product. Please choose one of the following options for each of the factors:

$\boxed{1}$ = unimportant $\boxed{2}$ = minor importance $\quad\boxed{3}$ = important $\quad\boxed{4}$ = very important $\quad\quad\boxed{9}$ = don't know

	1	2	3	4	9
21.1 Increase in our labor costs	❏	❏	❏	❏	❏
21.2 Increase in our financial costs	❏	❏	❏	❏	❏
21.3 Increase of our other costs.	❏	❏	❏	❏	❏
21.4 Reduction of our productivity.	❏	❏	❏	❏	❏
21.5 Increase in demand for our main product.	❏	❏	❏	❏	❏
21.6 Price increase by competitors.	❏	❏	❏	❏	❏
21.7 Price indexation	❏	❏	❏	❏	❏
21.8 Other factors, namely: _____	❏	❏	❏	❏	❏

---

22. Please indicate to what extent the factors listed below are of relevance for price reductions of your main product. Please choose one of the following options for each of the factors:

$\boxed{1}$ = unimportant $\boxed{2}$ = minor importance $\quad\boxed{3}$ = important $\quad\boxed{4}$ = very important $\quad\quad\boxed{9}$ = don't know

	1	2	3	4	9
22.1 Reduction in our labor costs	❏	❏	❏	❏	❏
22.2 Reduction in our financial costs	❏	❏	❏	❏	❏
22.3 Reduction of our other costs.	❏	❏	❏	❏	❏
22.4 Increase of our productivity.	❏	❏	❏	❏	❏
22.5 Reduction in demand for our main product.	❏	❏	❏	❏	❏
22.6 Price reduction by competitors.	❏	❏	❏	❏	❏
22.7 Other factors, namely: _____	❏	❏	❏	❏	❏

---

23. At which interval do you change the price of your main product (please also consider possible discounts, but not end-of season sales or similar) *(Please tick one answer only)*

23.1 More than once a year, namely: daily   weekly   monthly   quarterly   half-yearly
                         ❏   ❏   ❏   ❏   ❏

23.2 Once a year   ⇨ Typically in which month?

Jan.	Feb.	March	April	May	June	July	August	Sept.	Oct.	Nov.	Dec.
❏	❏	❏	❏	❏	❏	❏	❏	❏	❏	❏	❏

23.3 Fewer than once a year   ⇨ At which interval?   Every |_____| years

---

PRICING BEHAVIOR OUTSIDE THE LUXEMBOURG MARKET
To be completed by companies only that are present on foreign markets (see question 2)

---

24. Companies may charge different prices on different markets: Which of the following statements is true for your company? *(Please tick one answer only)*

24.1 The price – expressed in euro - is identical in all countries ....   ⇨ Proceed with question $\boxed{26}$ ❏

24.2 The price – expressed in euro - is identical in all countries of the euro area but not
identical for countries outside the euro area ....   ⇨ Proceed with question $\boxed{25}$ ❏

24.3 The price – expressed in euro - varies both within and outside the euro area.   ⇨ Proceed with question $\boxed{25}$ ❏

---

25. Please indicate to what extent the following factors are relevant for the pricing behavior of a product. Please choose one of the following options for each of the factors:

$\boxed{1}$ = unimportant $\boxed{2}$ = minor importance $\quad\boxed{3}$ = important $\quad\boxed{4}$ = very important $\quad\quad\boxed{9}$ = don't know

		1	2	3	4	9
25.1	Variations in the exchange rate	❑	❑	❑	❑	❑
25.2	Tax system (e.g. VAT)	❑	❑	❑	❑	❑
25.3	Transport costs.	❑	❑	❑	❑	❑
25.4	Structural conditions on the respective market (e.g. preferences, living standard,...).	❑	❑	❑	❑	❑
25.5	Cyclical changes in demand.	❑	❑	❑	❑	❑
25.6	Price of competitor (s)	❑	❑	❑	❑	❑
25.7	Level of regulation	❑	❑	❑	❑	❑
25.8	Other factors, namely: _____	❑	❑	❑	❑	❑

26. With regard to your main product, is competition on the foreign market fiercer than on the Luxembourg market? *(Please tick one answer only)*

26.1	Yes	❑
26.2	No	❑
26.3	I don't know	❑

Thank you very much for your cooperation!

THE NETHERLANDS

The European Central Bank (ECB) and the national central banks in EMU have launched a joint research project on price setting by European companies. Together, they are responsible for price stability in the euro area. Information about pricing behavior is vital to the preparation and conduct of monetary policy. The Nederlandsche Bank (DNB) is involved in surveying Dutch companies on this topic. The information you provide will only be used for research purposes. TNS-NIPO does not deliver company specific information like respondent or branch names. DNB guarantees strict confidentiality of your answers. Answering the questionnaire will take you about 10 minutes. We are very grateful for your cooperation.

0 AVAILABLE BACKGROUND INFORMATION		
0.1 Position of respondent in the company ....____		
0.2 Sector	• Manufacturing	❑
	• Business services	❑
	• Wholesale	❑
	• Retail (food/ non-food/catering)	❑
	• Transportation	❑
	• Other	❑
0.3 Number of employees including owner	• 1 person	❑
	• 2–4 persons	❑
	• 5–9 persons	❑
	• 10–19 persons	❑
	• 20–49 persons	❑
	• 50–99 persons	❑
	• 100 or more persons	❑
1 GENERAL INFORMATION		
1.1 Are you in a position to provide information on the price setting within your company?	• Yes	❑
	• No (end of interview)	❑
1.2 Does your company adopt one pricing policy for all of your products?	• Yes, is basically the same for all our products .	❑
	• Yes, for the greater part of our assortment	❑
	• No, depends on the type of product	❑
	• Don't know/ no answer	❑
Please answer the following questions for the main product or one typical product sold by your company, in the questionnaire referred to as product X.		
1.3 What product (X) do you have in mind?...............................____		
1.4 What percentage of your turnover is accounted for by product X. A rough estimate suffices...................................... | | | |%		
1.5 In what markets do you sell your main products? (more answers allowed)	• Local market	❑
	• Regional market	❑
	• National market	❑
	• Foreign markets	❑
1.6 What is your main market for product X? Please tick only one answer	• Local market	❑
	• Regional market	❑
	• National market	❑
	• Foreign markets	❑
1.7 If you sell your main product abroad, what percentage of your turnover is due to exports?	•	| | |%
	• Don't know / no answer	❑
1.8 Could you roughly indicate the number of competitors for you main product on the Dutch market? Please tick only one answer	• None	❑
	• 1	❑
	• 2 to 5	❑
	• 5 to 20	❑

	• 20 or more .... ❑ • Don't know / no answer .... ❑
1.9 To what extent do you experience competition for product X?	• Severe competition .... ❑ • Strong competition .... ❑ • Weak competition .... ❑ • No competition . ... ❑ • Don't know / no answer .... ❑
1.10 Did you raise or lower the selling price of product X last year?	• Raised it .... ❑ • Lowered it .... ❑ • Left it unchanged .... ❑ • Don't know / no answer .... ❑
1.11 With what percentage has your selling price been changed in 2003 compared to 2002?	• .... ⎣⎣⎣⎦% • Don't know / no answer .... ❑
2 PRICE SETTING BEHAVIOR: TIMING AND DETERMINANTS	
2.1 Do you decide on the price of prod X independently or are prices prescribed by head-office or government rules?	• Determine prices myself .... ❑ • Partially dependent on suggested prices/prices of head-office .... ❑ • Fully dependent on suggested prices/prices of head-office .... ❑ • Price is to a large extent regulated by government ❑ • Other .... ❑ • Don't know / no answer .... ❑
2.2 Do you decide on the price of prod X independently or are prices prescribed by head-office or government rules?	• Yes, daily .... ❑ • Yes, periodically (e.g. once a week, month, year) ... ❑ • Generally periodic, but occasionally in response to specific events (large shocks for example) .... ❑ • No, depends fully on specific events .... ❑
2.3 On average, how many times a year you adjust your selling price of product X?	• Occasionally (less than once a year) .... ❑ • once a year .... ❑ • 2-4 times per year .... ❑ • 5-11 times per year .... ❑ • 12 times per year (monthly) .... ❑ • More often .... ❑ • Don't know / no answer .... ❑
2.4 On average, how often do you check or review the adequacy of the price of product X?	• Daily .... ❑ • Weekly .... ❑ • Monthly .... ❑ • Quarterly .... ❑ • Once a year .... ❑ • Other frequency) .... ❑ • Occasionally .... ❑ • Don't know / no answer .... ❑
2.5 Do you tune the timing of your own price changes to those of your supplier(s)?	• No .... ❑ • Sometimes (e.g. in case of major price change by supplier) .... ❑ • Often .... ❑ • Always .... ❑ • Don't know / no answer .... ❑

2.5 Do customers tune the timing of their price changes to yours?	• No .... ❏ • Sometimes (e.g. in case of major price change by ❏ you) .... ❏ • Often .... ❏ • Always .... ❏ • Don't know / no answer .... ❏

2.7 How do you calculate the price of your "main product"?

- a fixed mark-up is applied to unit variable costs (cost of labor and other inputs) ❏
- a variable mark-up is applied tot unit variable costs, depending on market conditions ❏
- to a large degree on the basis of my competitors' prices ❏
- link it to another price (like wages) ❏
- dictated by our customer(s) ❏
- linked to price index ❏
- fixed by supplier ❏
- differs per customer ❏
- other ❏
- don't know, no answer ❏

2.8 Which factors would likely cause an increase in the price of your "main product"? *Attribute a value of 1 (irrelevant) to 4 (very important)*	• An increase in the cost of labor ❏ • An increase in the cost of raw materials ❏ • An increase in financial costs ❏ • An increase in other production costs ❏ • An increase in demand ❏ • An increase in competitors' prices ❏ • An increase in quality of the product ❏ • A cash-flow or financing problem ❏

2.9 Which factors would likely cause a decrease in the price of your "main product"? *Attribute a value of 1 = irrelevant to 4 = very important to each*	• A decrease in the cost of labor ❏ • A decrease in the cost of raw materials ❏ • A decrease in financial costs ❏ • A decrease in other production costs ❏ • A decrease in demand ❏ • A decrease in competitors' prices ❏ • A decrease in quality of the product ❏ • Liquidity surpluses ❏

2.10 Which of the following factors might delay carrying out price changes for product X?
Attribute a value of 1 = irrelevant to 4 = very important to each

- The presence of a formal contract: prices can only be changed when the contract is re-negotiated ❏
- Our customers expect us to keep prices as stabile as possible ❏
- Lowering prices might mistakenly be interpreted as quality loss ❏
- Fear that competing firms will not adjust their price ❏
- Fear that one may need to revise the price in the opposite direction ❏
- Prices are set at "attractive" thresholds ❏
- Presence of high menu costs of changing prices (e.g. printing new catalogues, costs of adjusting price tags ..) ❏
- Instead of changing prices, prefer to change other conditions like terms-of-payment, service level ❏
- Other (please specify if possible) ❏

2.11 The introduction of the euro enlarges comparability of prices between EMU-member countries.
Has this affected your price setting policy?

- Had no or hardly any effect ❏
- Not yet, but expect this to be the case in the future ❏
- More difficult to differentiate prices across EMU-countries ❏
- Less sensitive to exchange rate movements ❏
- Other ❏
- Don't know / no answer ❏

PORTUGAL

Banco de Portugal

Research Department

Av. Almirante Reis, 71-6°

1150-012 Lisboa

Contact Person: <u>*Fernando Martins*</u>; *Phone: 00351-213130015; E-mail: estudos@bportugal.pt*

The questions concern the main product sold by your company (either a good or a service). You can choose, for instance, the product with the highest turnover in 2003 or any other product that you considered as a reference of your main activity. The answers should refer to this product and, unless otherwise stated, they should also refer to 2003. The Banco de Portugal guarantees the strict confidentiality of your answers, which will be only used for economic research. The Banco de Portugal is very grateful for your collaboration.

Company name: _____

Company economic classification (five-digit code): _____ Fiscal Number: _____

Person that answers the survey: _____

Phone Number: _____ E-mail: _____ Date: _____

GENERAL INFORMATION
1. What is your main product?

2. The percentage that your main product represents in the total turnover is about:
|__|__|__|%

3. What is your main market (*choose only one option*)?

6.1 Portugal .... ☐
6.1 Other euro area countries[1] .... ☐
6.1 United Kingdom .... ☐
6.1 United States .... ☐
6.1 Other countries .... ☐

[1]Germany, Spain, Greece, Italy, Luxembourg, The Netherlands, Belgium, Ireland, Finland, France and Austria.

4. If you sell your product abroad, what percentage of your turnover is due to exports?

4.1 _____

4.2 I don't wish to answer or I don't have enough information to do so .... |__|__|__|% ☐

5. What is the main destination of your sales (*choose only one option*)?

5.1 Wholesalers... ☐
5.2 Retailers .... ☐
5.3 Companies of your own group .... ☐
5.4 Other companies (private and public) .... ☐
5.5 Public Administration (State, Municipalities,...)................................. ☐
5.6 Directly to consumers (via your own stores or through catalogues or Internet) .... ☐
5.7 Others channels, please specify _____ ☐

6. In the Portuguese market, how many competitors do you have?

6.1 We don't have any main competitor ...... ☐
6.2 Less than 5 .... ☐
6.3 Between 5 and 20 .... ☐
6.4 More than 20 .... ☐

7. What is the market share of your main product in Portugal (*choose only one option*)?

7.1 Less than 5%	❑
7.2 6%–20%	❑
7.3 21%–50%	❑
7.4 51%–99%	❑
7.5 100%	❑

8. The kind of relationship that you have with your customers is essentially (*choose only one option*):

8.1 Long-term (more than 1 year)	❑
8.2 Short-term (less than 1 year)	❑

9. The percentage of your sales that goes to long-term customers is approximately |__|__|__|%

10. What is the importance of the following factors for the competitiveness of your product? *[Use the following options: 1-unimportant; 2-of minor importance; 3-important; 4-very important; 0-I can't evaluate]*

	1	2	3	4	0
10.1 The price	❑	❑	❑	❑	❑
10.2 The quality	❑	❑	❑	❑	❑
10.3 The degree your product is different from your competitors	❑	❑	❑	❑	❑
10.4 The delivery period	❑	❑	❑	❑	❑
10.5 The presence of a long-term relationship	❑	❑	❑	❑	❑
10.6 The after-sales service	❑	❑	❑	❑	❑
10.7 Other factors, please specify _____	❑	❑	❑	❑	❑

GENERAL INFORMATION ON PRICE SETTING

11. The price of your main product (*choose only one option*):

11.1 Is the same for all customers	❑
11.2 Depends on the quantity sold but according to a uniform price list	❑
11.3 Is decided case by case	❑

12. Is there any particular month (or months) where the price of your main product is most likely to change?

12.1 No.	❑
12.2 Yes. Which?	❑

| J | F | M | A | M | J | J | A | S | O | N | D |

13. How many times did the price of your main product change in 2002 and 2003?

	2002	2003
Number of times	☐	☐

14. Taking as a reference, for instance, the last changes in price (increases or reductions), indicate (approximately) the percentage of them that implied a price increase (suggestion: consider for instance the last ten price changes) |__|__|__|%

15. How many times did the price of your main product change in 2002 and 2003?

	Up to 2%	From 2 to 5%	From 5 to 8%	More than 8%
For price increases [choose only one option]	❑	❑	❑	❑
For price reductions [choose only one option]	❑	❑	❑	❑

16. Which of the following situations is a better description of the way your price is normally set (*choose only one option*):

16.1 The price is set by our company	❑
16.2 The price is set by an external entity (Government, regulatory body,)	❑
16.3 The price is set by our main customer(s)	❑
16.4 The price is set by our main competitor(s)	❑
16.5 Others, please specify _____	❑

17. Does your company usually set formal contracts that fix the price for a stated period?

17.1 No	❑
Yes. The percentage that these contracts represent in total sales is	
17.2 Less than 10%	❑
17.3 11–25%	❑
	❑

17.4 26–50% .... ❏
17.5 51–90% .... ❏
17.6 Almost all (>90%) .... ❏

---

18. The price in your company is reviewed, without necessarily being changed (*choose only one option*):

18.1 At a well-defined frequency (annually, quarterly...) (*If yes, go to question 19*) .... ❏
18.2 Generally at a defined frequency, but sometimes also in reaction to market conditions (changes in the price of raw materials or in demand conditions) (*If yes, go to question 19*) .... ❏
18.3 Without any defined frequency, being reviewed in reaction to market conditions (changes in the price of raw materials or in demand conditions) (*If yes, go to question 20*) .... ❏
18.4 None of these cases applies to my company (*If yes, go to question 20*) .... ❏

---

19. [Answer to this question if you chose options 18.1 or 18.2 in the previous question.] At what frequency is the price in your company normally reviewed, without necessarily being changed? (Consider a price revision as an assessment of all information relevant for price determination)

19.1 Daily .... ❏
19.2 Once a week .... ❏
19.3 Once a month .... ❏
19.4 Quarterly .... ❏
19.5 Two times a year .... ❏
19.6 Once a year .... ❏
19.7 Less than once a year .... ❏

---

20. [Answer to this question if you chose options 18.1 or 18.2 in the previous question.] At what frequency is the price in your company normally reviewed, without necessarily being changed? (Consider a price revision as an assessment of all information relevant for price determination)

20.1 Daily .... ❏
20.2 Once a week .... ❏
20.3 Once a month .... ❏
20.4 Quarterly .... ❏
20.5 Two times a year .... ❏
20.6 Once a year .... ❏
20.7 Less than once a year .... ❏

---

21. Which information do you most take into account when calculating the price of your main product (*choose only one option*)?

21.1 Information regarding the current and past behavior of all variables relevant for profit maximization (demand, costs, the price of main competitors...) .... ❏
21.2 Information regarding the recent behavior of all variables relevant for profit maximization as well as their future prospects .... ❏
21.3 We basically apply an indexation rule over one or more variables relevant for profit maximization (e.g. consumer price inflation, wage growth...) .... ❏

---

22. All other things being equal, including the price of your competitors, if you decide to increase the price of your main product for instance by 10% by what percentage do you think the quantities sold by your company would fall?

22.1 More than 20% .... ❏
22.2 Between 10 and 20% .... ❏
22.3 About 10% .... ❏
22.4 Less than 10% .... ❏
22.5 Quantities would remain unchanged . ❏

REASONS FOR CHANGING PRICES

23. What is the importance of the factors listed below in terms of a price increase decision? [*Use the following options: 1-unimportant; 2-of minor importance; 3-important; 4-very important; 0-I can't evaluate*]

	1	2	3	4	0
23.1 An increase in the price of raw materials	❏	❏	❏	❏	❏
23.2 An increase in wage costs (including taxes)	❏	❏	❏	❏	❏
23.3 An increase in demand	❏	❏	❏	❏	❏
23.4 An increase in our competitors' price	❏	❏	❏	❏	❏
23.5 An increase in financing costs	❏	❏	❏	❏	❏
23.6 Other, please specify	❏	❏	❏	❏	❏

---

24. What is the importance of the factors listed below in terms of a price decrease decision? [*Use the following options: 1-unimportant; 2-of minor importance; 3-important; 4-very important; 0-I can't evaluate*]

	1	2	3	4	0
24.1 A decrease in the price of raw materials	❏	❏	❏	❏	❏
24.2 A decrease in wage costs (including taxes)	❏	❏	❏	❏	❏
24.3 A decrease in demand	❏	❏	❏	❏	❏
24.4 A decrease in our competitors' price	❏	❏	❏	❏	❏
24.5 A decrease in financing costs	❏	❏	❏	❏	❏

24.6 Other, please specify .... ❏ ❏ ❏ ❏ ❏

---

25. Companies sometimes differ in the speed their prices respond to changes in demand and costs: [*Use the following options: 1 - Less than 1 week; 2 - From 1 week to 1 month; 3 - From 1 to 3 months; 4 - From 3 to 6 months; 5 - From 6 months to 1 year; 6 - The price remains unchanged*]

		1	2	3	4	5	6
25.1	After a significant increase in demand, how much time on average elapses before you raise your prices?	❏	❏	❏	❏	❏	❏
25.2	After a significant increase in production costs, how much time on average elapses before you raise your prices?	❏	❏	❏	❏	❏	❏
25.3	After a significant fall in demand, how much time on average elapses before you reduce your prices?	❏	❏	❏	❏	❏	❏
25.4	After a significant decline in production costs, how much time on average elapses costs before you reduce your prices?	❏	❏	❏	❏	❏	❏

REASONS TO POSTPONE PRICE CHANGES

26. Companies sometimes decide to postpone price changes or to change their price only slightly. There is often a variety of reasons for this. Some of them are listed below. Please indicate their importance in your company. [*Use the following options: 1-unimportant; 2-of minor importance; 3-important; 4-very important; 0- I can't evaluate*]

		1	2	3	4	0
26.1	The risk that our competitors do not change their prices	❏	❏	❏	❏	❏
26.2	The fact that the next price adjustment can only occur after a certain period of time	❏	❏	❏	❏	❏
26.3	The risk that we subsequently have to readjust our prices in the opposite direction	❏	❏	❏	❏	❏
26.4	The existence of written contracts specifying that prices can only be changed when the contract is renegotiated	❏	❏	❏	❏	❏
26.5	The preference for maintaining prices at a certain psychological threshold (ex. 199 euros)	❏	❏	❏	❏	❏
26.6	The costs implied by price changes (ex. changing price lists)	❏	❏	❏	❏	❏
26.7	The preference of our customers for stable prices. Changing prices frequently could threaten customer relations	❏	❏	❏	❏	❏
26.8	The costs involved in collecting the relevant information for price decisions	❏	❏	❏	❏	❏
26.9	An important part of our costs is fixed hampering price decreases when, for instance, market conditions are less favorable	❏	❏	❏	❏	❏
26.10	There is a risk that customers may interpret a reduction in price as a reduction in quality	❏	❏	❏	❏	❏
26.11	The variable costs in our company do not change by much with market conditions, making our price quite stable	❏	❏	❏	❏	❏
26.12	Our type of customers changes over the business cycle. During a recession we lose the least loyal customers and retain the most loyal ones. As the latter are less sensitive to price changes, the price can be kept basically unchanged during a recession	❏	❏	❏	❏	❏

---

27. Some products are characterized by having a short duration (sometimes less than 1 year). This is the case for instance of those products that change collections seasonally, such as clothing or footwear, or products that change their models regularly, such as house appliances or computers. For some of these products the price may be kept unchanged during the (relatively short) lifetime of each collection or model. Is this situation valid for your main product?

27.1 Yes ❏
27.2 No ❏

INFORMATION REGARDING PRICE BEHAVIOR IN INTERNATIONAL MARKETS
(only to be filled out by companies operating in international markets)

28. What is the importance of the following factors in discriminating your price between markets? [*Use the following options: 1-unimportant; 2-of minor importance; 3-important; 4-very important; 0- I can't evaluate*]

		1	2	3	4	0
28.1	Exchange rate changes	❏	❏	❏	❏	❏
28.2	The country tax system	❏	❏	❏	❏	❏
28.3	Structural market conditions (tastes, standard of living,. . .)	❏	❏	❏	❏	❏
28.4	Cyclical fluctuations in country demand	❏	❏	❏	❏	❏
28.5	Market rules	❏	❏	❏	❏	❏
28.6	Transportation costs	❏	❏	❏	❏	❏
28.7	Other factors, please specify	❏	❏	❏	❏	❏

| 29. If a significant share of your sales (at least 20 percent) goes to one single country outside the euro area, if the euro appreciates by 5 percent vis-à-vis the currency of that country how would you change the price in that market of your main product (choose only one option)? | 29.1 The price would increase more than 5% .. ❑
29.2 The price would increase less than 5% .... ❑
29.3 The price would increase by 5% .... ❑
29.4 The price would remain basically unchanged ❑ |

INFORMATION ON WAGE SETTING

| 30. On average, at what frequency wages are normally changed in your company? | 30.1 More than 2 times a year......................... ❑
30.2 Twice a year .... ❑
30.3 Once a year .... ❑
30.4 Less than once a year .... ❑ |

31. Is there any particular month (or months) where the wages are most likely changed?

31.1 No. .... ❑

31.2 Yes. Which one? ....…..... ❑

| J | F | M | A | M | J | J | A | S | O | N | D |

THANK YOU

SPAIN

A. CHANGES IN THE ADDRESS OF THE COMPANY
(indicate only those items that differ with respect to those in the survey label)

1. |_____| |__ __ __ __ __ __ __|
   Name   I.D. Card No

2. |_____|
   Company address

3. |_____|
   Other identification data

4. |_____| |_____| |_____| |_____|
   Zip Code   Municipality   Province   Web page

B. PERSON IN CHARGE OF ANSWERING THE QUESTIONNAIRE.

1. |_____| 3. |__ __ __ __ __ __ __| 4. |__ __ __ __ __ __ __ __|
   First name and surname   Tel   Fax

2. |_____| 5. |_____|
   Position   E-mail

C. INDICATE THE MAIN ACTIVITY IN WHICH YOUR COMPANY ENGAGES	**D. TOTAL NUMBER OF EMPLOYEES (AVERAGE FOR THE YEAR 2003)**
|__ __ __ __ __ __ __ _____ _____|	|__ __ __ __ __ __ __| Average number of employees

---

INSTRUCTIONS

This survey has been designed to learn about the key features of the pricing process at Spanish companies. Throughout the survey, the term *price* refers to the actual sale price of the product/service, even if it should differ from the list price.

Many of the questions in this survey refer to your main product/service. The main product/service may correspond to a group of products/services provided that these are relatively homogenous in terms of your company's pricing policy.

Should your company set prices differently according to the customer involved, please refer to the price applied to the most usual type of customer.

Should you have any doubts or require further clarification, or if you wish to send the completed survey by fax, the following channels are open:

Tel: 902.888.906
Fax: 902.889.509
e-mail: precios@cuestionet.com

To complete the survey on-line, go to the following website: www.cuestionet.com/bde/precios

and use the following: User: pe4966
Password: preciso

Once at the website, the data identifying your company must be introduced: Clave_Web and Seg_Web. These feature on the survey label.

A. MARKET STRUCTURE

1. What is your company's main product/service? What percentage of turnover do sales of this product/service account for?
_____ |__|__|__|%

2. What percentage of sales of your main product/service is generated in the following areas?

		Don't have	Have	Percentage	
1.	Spain	❏ 6	❏ 1	|__|__|__|%	→ (5)
2.	Euro area* (excluding Spain)	❏ 7	❏ 2	|__|__|__|%	
3.	Other countries	❏ 8	❏ 3	|__|__|__|%	(3)
			Total	|1|0|0|%	

* The euro area Member States are: Belgium, Germany, Greece, Spain, France, Ireland, Italy, Luxembourg, Netherlands, Austria, Portugal and Finland.

3. If your company sells some portion of its products/services outside Spain, it may set different prices according to the market concerned. If so, indicate which of the following statements best describes your main product/service:

A. The price in euro is the same for all countries/markets........	❑ 1 → (5)
B. The price in euro on the domestic market (Spain) differs from that set for the other.	❑ 2
C. The price in euro is the same in all euro	❑ 3 } (4)
E. The price in euro is different for each country/market	❑ 4

4. If the price set in the various markets/countries differs, i.e. if you have ticked the second, third or fourth boxes, indicate how important the following factors are in setting different prices for different markets/countries:

	Unimportant	Of minor importance	Important	Very important
1. Exchange rate movement of the currency used for payment	❑ 11	❑ 12	❑ 13	❑ 14
2. Tax system (e.g. VAT rate)	❑ 21	❑ 22	❑ 23	❑ 24
3. Demand	❑ 31	❑ 32	❑ 33	❑ 34
4. Competitors' prices	❑ 41	❑ 42	❑ 43	❑ 44
5. Other market characteristics (e.g. consumer preferences, income levels)	❑ 51	❑ 52	❑ 53	❑ 54

5. What is your main market? Indicate the country area accounting for the highest percentage of sales of your main product/service:

A.	Local	❑ 61
B.	Regional	❑ 62
C.	National	❑ 63
D.	International	❑ 64

6. Regarding sales of your main product/service in your main market, what is your market share (your company's sales as a proportion of total sales of that product/service in that market)?

A.	Not significant	❑ 71
B.	Less than 5%	❑ 72
C.	5–25%	❑ 73
D.	25–50%	❑ 74
E.	Over 50%	❑ 75

7. How many competitors are there in your main market for your main product/service?

A.	None	❑ 81
B.	Fewer than 5	❑ 82
C.	5–20	❑ 83
D.	More than 20	❑ 84

8. What is the percentage of sales to:

		Don't have	Have	Percentage
1.	Group companies:			
1.1	Wholesalers	❑ 6	❑ 1	|___|___|%
1.2	Retailers	❑ 7	❑ 2	|___|___|%
1.3	Other	❑ 8	❑ 3	|___|___|%
2.	Companies outside the group:			
2.1	Wholesalers	❑ 9	❑ 4	|___|___|%
2.2	Retailers	❑ 6	❑ 1	|___|___|%
2.3	Other	❑ 7	❑ 2	|___|___|%
3.	General government agencies	❑ 8	❑ 3	|___|___|%
4.	Consumers	❑ 9	❑ 4	|___|___|%
			Total	|1|0|0|%

9. Regarding sales of your main product/service on your main market, are most of your customers occasional or regular? Regular customers are understood to be those with whom there is a stable commercial relationship.

A.	Occasional	❑ 6
B.	Regular	❑ 1

10. Indicate whether your company:

	No	Yes
1. Undertakes regular promotional activities	❑ 7	❑ 2
2. Pursues a habitual customer-discount policy	❑ 8	❑ 3

B. PRICING AT YOUR COMPANY

1. The price of your main product/service is set by:

A. Your own company	❑ 11 → (2)
B. The parent company, without involvement of the company itself............................	❑ 12 }

C. The main customers, without involvement of the company itself	❑ 13	(4)
D. Certain general government sectors, without involvement of the company itself	❑ 14	
E. Other (please specify) _____	❑ 15	

---

2. To what extent are the following pricing methods applied in your company?

	Unimportant	Of minor importance	Important	Very important
1. Pricing is on the basis of costs	❑ 21	❑ 22	❑ 23	❑ 24
2. Pricing depends on the prices of our main competitor	❑ 31	❑ 32	❑ 33	❑ 34

---

3. The price of your main product/service:

A. Is the same for all your customers	❑ 41
B. Differs depending on the amount sold..	❑ 42
C. Is decided on a case-by-case basis	❑ 43
D. depending on other criteria (please specify) _____	❑ 44

---

4. How often do you recalculate (this does not necessarily mean change) the price of your main product/service?

A. Periodically (at specific time intervals)...	❑ 51
B. Mainly at specific time intervals, but also in response to specific events (e.g. a considerable change in costs)	❑ 52
C. Essentially in response to specific events (e.g. a considerable change in costs)	❑ 43
D. Other criteria (please specify) _____	❑ 44

(5) } A, B
(6) } C, D

---

5. If your company recalculates its prices at specific intervals, how often does this occur?

A. More than once a year	❑ 61
A.1 If so, how many times a year?	⌞⌞⌟
B. Once a year	❑ 62
B.1 If so, in which month?	⌞⌞⌟
C. Less than once a year..	❑ 63
C.1 If so, once in how many years?	⌞⌞⌟

---

6. How did you recalculate the price of your main product/service on the last occasion?

A. Applying a rule of thumb (e.g. a fixed amount/percentage change, a CPI indexation rule)	❑ 71
B. Using a wide range of indicators (demand, costs, competitors' prices) relevant for profit maximization	
B.1 These indicators relate to the company's current operating environment	❑ 72
B.2 These indicators relate both to the current and expected future environment	❑ 73

---

7. How often do you change the price of your main product/service?

A. More than once a year	❑ 81
A.1 If so, how many times a year?	⌞⌞⌟
B. Once a year	❑ 82
B.1 If so, in which month?	⌞⌞⌟
C. Less than once a year..	❑ 83
C.1 If so, once in how many years?	⌞⌞⌟

---

8. Over 2003 as whole, was there any change (in percentage terms) in the price of your main product/service?

A. No   B. Yes

❑ 7 → (9)   ❑ 2
↓

If any, by how much ⌞⌞⌞⌟ %

---

9. Do you recall a significant recent change in the indirect taxation (VAT/excise duties) on your main product/service? If yes, to what extent was it passed on?

A. No   B. Yes
❑ 8 → (C1)   ❑ 3
                                                                          ↓

                                              A.   In full .... ❑ 11
                                              B.   Partly .... ❑ 12
                                              C.   It was not passed on .... ❑ 13

C. DETERMINANTS OF PRICE CHANGES

1. Indicate the significance of the factors that may cause you to raise/lower the price of your company's main product/service? Give a value of 1 (unimportant) to 4 (very important) for the following factors:

		Factors causing a:	
		Price increase	Price reduction
1.	A change in labor costs	❑	❑
2.	A change in financial costs	❑	❑
3.	A change in the cost of raw materials	❑	❑
4.	A change in energy and fuel prices	❑	❑
5.	A change in other production costs	❑	❑
6.	A change in productivity	❑	❑
7.	A change in demand	❑	❑
8.	A change in competitors' prices	❑	❑
9.	An improvement in design, quality or the product range	❑	❑
10.	The intention of gaining market share	❑	❑
11.	Other factors (please specify) _____	❑	❑

2. Indicate how long it takes your company to make price changes as a result of changes in production costs and/or changes in demand

	Less than 1 month	1 – 3 Months	3 – 6 months	6 months – 1 year	Over 1 year	Price are not changed
1. Significant increase in demand	❑ 41	❑ 42	❑ 43	❑ 44	❑ 45	❑ 46
2. Significant increase in production costs	❑ 51	❑ 52	❑ 53	❑ 54	❑ 55	❑ 56
3. Significant decline in demand	❑ 61	❑ 62	❑ 63	❑ 64	❑ 65	❑ 66
4. significant decline in production costs	❑ 71	❑ 72	❑ 73	❑ 74	❑ 75	❑ 76

D. FACTORS HAMPERING PRICE ADJUSTMENTS

1. Indicate which factors may lead to a delay in the adjustment of the price of your main product/service?

   Give a value of 1 (unimportant) to 4 (very important) for the following factors:

		Reasons for deferring an increase in the price	Reasons for deferring a reduction in the price
1.	Competitors might not adjust their price	❑	❑
2.	In the near future, it might be necessary to readjust the price in the opposite direction	❑	❑
3.	The existence of some type of contract that sets the price	❑	❑
4.	The price is set in commercially attractive terms (e.g. 10 euro or 4.99 euro) and is only changed when it is advisable to move to a new attractive threshold	❑	❑
5.	The existence of costs arising from changing prices (new catalogues, menu costs, changing price tags)	❑	❑
6.	The costs of collecting and processing the information associated with the decision to change prices	❑	❑
7.	The possibility of using some alternative measure to a change in price (change in delivery periods)	❑	❑
8.	The possibility of losing customers (even if competitors also raise their prices) ...	❑	❑
9.	The possibility that customers will interpret a reduction in price as a reduction in quality	❑	❑
10.	Other (please specify) _____	❑	❑

Index

adjustment process, stages of, 7–8, 34, 38, 42, 45, 74, 77, 129, 161, 163
anticipations. *See* expectations
asymmetries in price responses. *See also* price rigidity, factors driving, 13–14, 18, 45–47, 60–65, 83, 102, 117–121, 149–150, 173–174
Austrian Institute of Economic Research (WIFO), 55–56

backward-looking price setting. *See* price setting
Ball, Laurence, 15, 18, 49, 118, 149
Belgium, National Bank of, 70
Bils, Mark, 222
Blanchard, Olivier, 15
Blinder, Alan, 4, 14, 16, 17, 21, 59, 88, 158, 185–198
Bundesbank, the Deutsche, 97
bureaucracy, 116, 117

Caballero, Ricardo, 18
Calvo, Guillermo, 17–18, 241–242
Canada, Bank of, 186
capital costs, 135, 194, 195
capital goods, 65, 84, 85, 166–172, 225
Carlton, Dennis, 16, 126, 243
Central de Balanços, 152
cluster analysis, 97, 103–108
collusion. *See* competition
competition
    imperfect, 6, 8, 16, 34, 39–40, 69, 72, 74, 98, 104, 119–120,
    indicators of, 34, 58, 73, 112, 119, 126–128, 142–143, 155, 167–168, 189, 201–202
    monopolistic, 6, 74, 237–239
    perceived, 33–34, 128, 142–143, 149, 167–168, 170, 201–213, 239
    perfect, 190, 237, 239

and price setting. *See* price setting, and competition
See also coordination failure
competitors' prices
    relevance in price setting, 8, 16, 38–41, 44–46, 74, 98, 101–102, 113, 117–118, 135, 145–146, 149, 173–174, 190, 193, 204, 238
    and perceived competition. *See* competition, perceived
contracts
    explicit, 8, 15, 43–44, 78–81, 99–100, 116, 133–135, 146, 148, 161–162, 175–176, 195–197, 241–242
    implicit, 8, 15, 43–44, 63, 78–81, 116, 133–135, 146, 148, 161–162, 175–176, 195–197, 241–242
    staggered. *See* Taylor, John; Calvo, Guillermo
coordination failure, 8, 16, 44, 79–80, 99–100, 104–107, 116–117, 162, 175–176, 195–196
cost
    fixed (menu costs), 5, 8, 14, 44–45, 50, 61, 78–80, 100, 106, 116–117, 133–134, 146, 148, 162, 175–176, 195–196, 243, 246
    flat (constant) marginal, 78–79, 119–120, 133–134, 196
    pricing based on, 8, 14, 44, 162, 195–197
    search, 120–121
customer
    fear of loss of, 15, 116–117, 122
    relationships with, 22, 33–34, 72–73, 78–80, 113, 119, 126, 155, 161, 167, 175, 189–190, 195, 238
    main, 33, 57, 58, 78, 146, 155, 167, 168, 176, 189, 204